Olive Schreiner

Olive Schreiner
A Biography

Ruth First and Ann Scott

Foreword by Nadine Gordimer

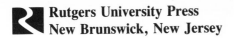 **Rutgers University Press**
New Brunswick, New Jersey

First published by André Deutsch Limited and Schoken Books, 1980

Published in the United Kingdom by Women's Press, 1989
Published in the United States of America by Rutgers University Press, 1990

Library of Congress Cataloging-in-Publication Data

First, Ruth.
   Olive Schreiner : a biography / Ruth First and Ann Scott ;
  foreword by Nadine Gordimer.
     p.   cm.
   Reprint. Originally published: New York : Schocken Books, 1980.
   Includes bibliographical references and index.
   ISBN 0-8135-1621-8 (cloth)   ISBN 0-8135-1622-6 (pbk.)
   1. Schreiner, Olive, 1855–1920—Biography. 2. Authors, South
African—19th century—Biography. 3. Feminists—South Africa—
Biography. I. Scott, Ann, 1950–   . II. Title.
PR9369.2.S37Z64   1990
823'B—dc20
                                        90-36032
                                           CIP

For Tilly and Julius First and Hilda Scott

CONTENTS

	Foreword by Nadine Gordimer	3
	List of Illustrations	9
	Acknowledgements	11
	Introduction	15
1	Early Life on a Mission Station	27
2	Governess and Freethinker	51
3	Two Novels	82
4	England 1881–1889	108
5	South Africa 1890–1894	189
6	The Boer War and Union	215
7	Woman and Labour	265
8	World War One and Old Age	298
9	Broken and Untried?	333
	Notes	341
	Schreiner Family Tree	368
	Chronology	369
	Bibliography of Schreiner's work	371
	Index	377

Who is qualified to write about whom? Subjects very often don't get
the biographers their works and lives demand; they are transformed,
after death, into what they were not. There must be a lot of fuming,
beyond the grave.

Olive Schreiner was one of the worst-served, from her spouse's
version of her life in accordance with what a husband would have
liked his famous writer wife to be, to the different hagiographic
selectivity of two or three other biographers whose books have
appeared since her death in 1920. Then in 1980 the perfectly
qualified candidacy presented itself – a double one. Ruth First and
Ann Scott themselves represent a combination of the two dominant
aspects of Schreiner's character, her feminism and her political
sense, and each writer provides a corrective for the preoccupational
bias of the other.

Schreiner's feminism followed the tug of colonial cultural liens
with a European 'home'. It was conceived in relation to the position
of women in late 19th century Europe; through her feminist tract
Woman and Labour, she was a Founding Mother of women's
liberation in Britain, and Ann Scott is a young English feminist.
Schreiner's political awareness was specific, through her understanding of the relation of capitalist imperialism to racialism in South
Africa, and Ruth First was a South African radical activist, thinker
and fine writer who went into exile in Britain in 1964 and later taught
– close to her own and Schreiner's home, again – at the Eduardo
Mondlane University in Moçambique. She was tragically assassinated by South African agents in 1982.

First and Scott make a superb combination and one is curious
about how they did it: overcame the tremendous differences in their
ideological approach. Take the statement: 'We have tried to create a
psychologically believable woman of the late 19th Century largely on
the basis of the psychoanalytic language of the 20th.' Was Ruth First
able to work on this basic approach because of the new attitude to
psychoanalysis that has been penetrating Marxist thinking through

the work of Lacan and others since the failure of the 1968 student uprising in Paris? The book is a paradigm of disinterested collaboration and scholarship, in which the incredibly difficult and disciplined virtue of reconciling someone else's viewpoints with one's own brings great rewards for the reader.

This biography establishes a level of inquiry no previous biographer was perhaps him or herself at a level of consciousness to attempt. So far ahead of her times, Schreiner was obscured by intervening ones in the kind of critical assessment they could produce. Now First and Scott can write: 'We see Olive Schreiner's life and writing as a product of a specific social history. We are not only looking at what she experienced but at how she, and others, perceived that experience; at the concept with which her contemporaries understood their world, and, again, at the consciousness that was possible for her time – after Darwin, before Freud, and during the period when Marx's *Capital* was written.'

Olive Schreiner was born in South Africa of missionary parents and as a 21-year-old governess in 1886 wrote *The Story of an African Farm*, a novel which brought her immediate and enduring world fame. In her work and life (she had the missionary sense of their oneness), it becomes clear from this study, she was hampered crucially by the necessity to fight the concepts that imprisoned her and others, equipped only with the modes available within those concepts. She invented a mode to carry her advanced perceptions only once – a literary one, for *Story of an African Farm*. Her short novel about the conquest of Rhodesia, *Trooper Peter Halket*, showed as true an interpretation of historical realities, when I re-read it during the week of Zimbabwe's independence celebrations, as she claimed when she wrote it during Rhodes' conquest of Mashonaland; but it has the preachy, nasal sing-song of a boring sermon. When she wanted to find a way to express her political vision, she took up the form of allegory typical of the Victorian hypocritical high-mindedness she had rejected along with religious beliefs.

About sex, she lied to herself continually – protesting to her men friends she wanted 'love and friendship without any sex element' in letters whose very syntax paces out yearning sexual desire. She recognized the sexual demands of women in a period when they were trained that their role was merely to 'endure' male sexual demands, but she used Victorian subterfuges (on a par with the 'vapours'), disguised as feminism, to hide a sense of shame at the idea of her own sexual appetite. The spectacle of the rebel dashing herself against the cold panes of convention is that of a creature doubly trapped: by a specific social history, and by the consciousness that was possible for her time.

First and Scott suggest further that her reputation as an imaginative writer has suffered by the 'persistent view that her social comment is obtrusive and damaging to her work': the novel – *The Story of an African Farm* – on which that reputation rests has been acclaimed, sometimes by people who would not share even her liberal views, let alone the radical element in them, as having its genius in 'transcending politics', and by extension, her political fervours. A reverse trend has lately appeared in South African criticism; Schreiner is no longer praised for soaring above politics, but attacked for turning out to be nothing but the broken-winged albatross of white liberal thinking. C.I. Hofmeyer,* a white university lecturer, has argued that 'Although Schreiner was cognisant of the power of the speculator and capitalist to triumph because of their access to power, she nonetheless continued to harbour a tenuous optimism that justice, equality and rightness of the liberal democracy would come to triumph via the operation of the "enlightened" liberal remnant of the English community. Of course, it did not, and the bourgeois democracy that Schreiner had hope for soon developed into the repressive colonial state. This development is significant insofar as it shows the weaknesses in the thinking of Schreiner and her class.' If Schreiner was a 'genius', the lecturer continued, this was 'a critical category that obscures the extent to which she was rooted in 19th century assumptions.'

Whether or not one can swallow this (old) view of genius as a class-determined concept rather than an innate, congenital attribute, and whether Schreiner had it or not, the tension of her relationship to these 19th century assumptions, so brilliantly conveyed in First and Scott's book, was the source of her achievements and her failures.

Olive Schreiner, like other South African writers (Plomer, Campbell, van der Post) up till after the Second World War, looked to

*C.I. Hofmeyer, 'S.A. Liberalism & the Novel', *The AUETSA Papers*, published by the Association of University Teachers of Southern Africa, University of Durban-Westville, 1979.

Europe, went to Europe after the initial success of work born specifically of their South African consciousness. Some went ostensibly because they were reviled for their exposure of the 'traditional' South African way of life for what it is (Plomer; *Turbott Wolfe*). But the general motivation was a deep sense of deprivation of the world of ideas, living in South Africa. Underlying that incontestable fact (particularly for Schreiner, in her time) was a reason some had a restless inkling of, as the *real* source of their alienation at home, but – each more or less imprisoned by the consciousness of their times – all could express only negatively: by the act of taking the Union Castle mailship to what was the only cultural 'home' they could conceive of, much as they all repudiated jingoism – indeed, it was part of the philistinism they wanted to put at an ocean's distance. Even Sol Plaatje, one of the first black writers, had this instinct, since he was using western modes – journalism, the diary, the novel – to express black consciousness.

They went because the culture in which their writings could take root was not being created: one in which the base would be the indigenous black cultures of the country, acting in interpenetration with imported European cultural forms, of which literature was one. They left because the works they had written, or wanted to write, would have found it imperative to attempt, if they were to express the life around them, would be lone contradictions of the way in which that life was being conceptualized, politically, socially, morally.

Olive Schreiner felt (her asthma is a perfect metaphor) stifled by the lack of a questioning exchange of ideas in the frontier society in which she lived. I suppose one must allow that she had a right to concern herself with a generic, universal predicament, that of the female sex. During her restless, self-searching years in England and Europe, her association with Havelock Ellis, Eleanor Marx, Karl Pearson, women's suffrage, English socialism in the 1880s, although she was intense in study of theories on race and evolution, and in participation in general progressive political and social movements, feminism was her strongest motivation. With hindsight, it might appear that she gave too much emphasis to an issue of human freedom that was certainly not the principal one in South Africa – which was the voteless, powerless state of blacks, irrespective of their sex. The biographers point out that she resigned, when living again in South Africa, from the Women's Enfranchisement League when its definition of the franchise qualification was changed to exclude black women. What about the men? Even at that period, decades before blacks were finally excluded from the franchise by apartheid, few blacks had the vote, and it was heavily qualified and confined to the Cape Colony. Her wronged sense of self, as a woman, *her* liberation, may have led her, ironically, into the most persistent characteristic of her fellow colonials: inability to recognize the real entities of the life around her. But then again she may have anticipated (as she did much else) the realization, now, by South Africans of all colours in the liberation movements, that feminism South African style is an essential component in the struggle to free our country from all forms of oppression, political and economic, racist and sexist. In this amazing woman's tortured, neurotic, heightened sense of being, all the inherent contradictions of her sex and time existed.

For myself, I am led to take up the question of Olive Schreiner's achievement exclusively as an imaginative writer in relation to the conceptual determinants within which she lived, even while warring against them. First and Scott quote the viewpoint – and I think they see her wronged by it – that after *African Farm* her creativity disappeared 'into the sands of liberal pamphleteering'. The observation was mine in an early essay on South African literature. Their book confirms, for me, that she dissipated her imaginative creativity, whatever ever else she may have achieved, in writing tracts and pamphlets rather than fiction. This is *not* to discount her social and political mission in the claims of formalist symmetries and aesthetic hoverings. Neither is it to attempt to nail her to the apartheid *Tendenzroman*. It is to assert that by abandoning the search for adequate modes to write fiction containing South African experience after her abortive experiments with 'distancing' allegory, her tragedy as a writer was that in the end she was unable to put the best she had – the power of her creative imagination – to the service of her original thought, fiercely profound convictions, and political and human insight. It is true that, as First and Scott claim, 'Almost alone she perceived the race conflicts during South Africa's industrial revolution in terms of a world-wide struggle between capital and labour'. But she wrote *about* these insights instead of transforming them through living beings into an expression of the lives they shaped and distorted. This could have achieved the only real synthesis of life and work, ideology and praxis, for her, raising the consciousness of the oppressed from out of the colonial nightmare and the oppressor from out of the colonial dream, and telling the world what she, uniquely, knew about the quality of human life deformed by those experiences.

'It is only literature, which contains history, that is able to confer a more than statistical reality on a country.' That quote from a conservative iconoclast, Anthony Burgess, is a perception Olive Schreiner, brave and brilliant iconoclast of the Left as she was, would not, or could not act upon. Was the definitive reason her historical situation or the limitation of her talents?

ILLUSTRATIONS

Wittebergen mission station, birthplace of Olive Schreiner (*Albany Museum, Grahamstown*)

Rebecca Schreiner (*William Plomer Collection, University Library, Durham*)

The Great Karoo in the area of Cradock

New Rush, *c.* 1872 (*Kimberley Mine Museum*)

Gottlob Schreiner (*Albany Museum, Grahamstown*)

Erilda Cawood (*Cradock Municipal Council*)

Julius Gau (*South African Who's Who, 1908*)

Dr John and Mrs Mary Brown (*William Plomer Collection*)

The Cawoods' farm at Ganna Hoek, Cradock (*The Africana Museum, Johannesburg*)

Schreiner family group at Eastbourne, April 1881 (*Findlay Family Papers, University of the Witwatersrand Library, Johannesburg*)

Havelock Ellis

Eleanor Marx (*Institute of Marxism-Leninism, Berlin*)

Edward Carpenter (*Carpenter Collection, Sheffield City Libraries*)

Elizabeth Cobb (*Papers and correspondence of Karl Pearson, University College, London*)

Karl Pearson (*Pearson family collection*)

Bryan Donkin (*British Medical Association*)

A Men and Women's Club picnic (*Papers and correspondence of Karl Pearson*)

Cecil Rhodes

Betty Molteno and Alice Greene (*J. W. Jagger Library, University of Cape Town Libraries*)

Olive and Cronwright Schreiner at Krantz Plaats, *c.* 1894 (*Albany Museum, Grahamstown*)

Olive Schreiner with a young African servant (*William Plomer Collection*)

Olive Schreiner's medicine case (*Cradock Municipal Council*)

Olive Schreiner in 1915, five years before her death (*Albany Museum, Grahamstown*)

MAPS AND LINE-DRAWINGS

Map of the Cape as it was during Olive Schreiner's youth, based on T. Baines, 'Cape Colony', London 1876 (*British Library*)   36

Map of Cradock and Environs, based on M. J. Brink, 'Divisional Map of Cradock', Cape Town, Surveyor General's Office, 1901 (*British Library*)   71

Title-page of *The Story of an African Farm*   120

Front cover of *Dreams*   186

Women's Enfranchisement League leaflet   263

ACKNOWLEDGEMENTS

The idea for this book originated with a BBC radio broadcast about Olive Schreiner by Ruth First in 1970. For although Schreiner had never been forgotten by individual South Africans or feminists, it was only with the emergence in the Sixties of a women's liberation movement in Britain and the USA that her life had been at all widely studied, her books reprinted, and her political stances evaluated; in short, that a context for reconstructing her had arisen. In 1973 a full-length biography was commissioned by André Deutsch Ltd; the following year Ann Scott, then with *Spare Rib* magazine, heard of Ruth First's work and interviewed her about it. The book, still at research stage, now turned into a collaboration as we became aware of the complementary perspectives each could bring to the subject – one that of a South African woman who had known of Olive Schreiner since childhood and been involved in radical and underground politics in South Africa until the early Sixties; the other that of an English woman formed by feminism with its stress on a language of personal life. Throughout our five years' work together we have tried hard neither to restrict each other's special interests nor to allow these to distort the main themes we set ourselves to explore; we owe a special debt, therefore, to our editor Faith Evans, who always retained a sense of the manuscript as a whole and edited relentlessly.

Several individuals contributed at the research stage. Nancy Dick transcribed several thousand microfilmed letters onto cards, and assiduously did library research into the persons Olive Schreiner met and the books she read. Cecil Williams, who died some months before this book appeared, read and selected letters from the Olive Schreiner–Edward Carpenter correspondence in the Central Library, Sheffield, which Keith Nield referred us to. Ruth Vaughan researched and made notes from the London Missionary Society archives held on deposit at the School of Oriental and African Studies, London. Betty Fradkin sent us her article 'Olive Schreiner and Karl Pearson' from the *Quarterly Bulletin of the South African Library* and referred us to material in the Albany Museum, Grahamstown. Dr Ridley Beeton of the Department of English, University of South Africa, sent a manuscript copy of his *In Texas, In*

Search of Olive Schreiner, a description of some of the manuscript
material in the Humanities Research Center, University of Texas at
Austin. The late George Findlay, a great-nephew of Olive Schreiner's in
Pretoria, sent a selection of unpublished family letters in his possession.
Kurt Ninck and Paul Jenkins, librarians at the Basler Mission, Basel,
supplied photocopies of Gottlob Schreiner's letters from the field; Miss
Preiswerk transcribed them from the old German script; and Eric Laufer
then translated them into English. As a young doctor, Petronella van
Heerden knew and looked after Olive Schreiner during World War One
in London, and wrote from Claremont, Cape Town, shortly before she
herself died, with reminiscences of her. We are also indebted to Richard
Rive, who, in the course of work for his thesis 'Olive Schreiner, 1855–
1920. A Critical Biography' (Oxford University, Department of Education
Studies), wrote a three-part article (*Cape Argus*, 2, 9 and 16 June 1973) in
which he generously cited new sources he had traced. Miss M. F. Cart-
wright, one of Olive Schreiner's great-great-nieces and Senior Librarian
in the Department of Manuscripts, South African Library, Cape Town,
traced the bibliographic history of some of Schreiner's essays, correspondence about her *Trooper Peter Halket of Mashonaland* in the J. H.
Hofmeyr Papers, and material about the South African Women's
Enfranchisement League. Martin Legassick, Stanley Trapido and Denis
Bransky helped with South African sources generally.

Staff at the following libraries have been of particular help: Manu-
scripts and Rare Books Room, D. M. S. Watson Library, University
College, London, for Karl Pearson's archive; the British Library,
Reference Division and Newspaper Library; Schlesinger Institute,
Radcliffe College, Cambridge, Mass., for material on female pacifism in
the USA; Tavistock Joint Library and Wellcome Institute for the
History of Medicine, London, for material on asthma; Library of the
Royal Society of Medicine, London, for permission to consult the *Index
Medicus*; Mary Evans Picture Library, Blackheath.

Many friends and colleagues discussed our work with us, invariably
offering source material, specialist advice or criticism of particular
sections of it. We owe thanks to Sally Alexander, Joyce Berkman, Vincent
Brome, Beatrix Campbell, Karl Figlio, the late Hilary Flegg-Mitchell,
Adrian Forty, Dr John Gabbay, Jane Graves, Phyllis Grosskurth, Cathy
Haw, Dr Colin James, Peter Klein, Ros de Lanerolle, Julius Lewin,
Marion Miliband, Jill Nicholls, Rozsika Parker, Egon and Sarah

Pearson, Jean Radford, Olga Reckitt, Alastair Reid, Michele Roberts, Shawn, Gillian and Robyn Slovo, Jenny Stein, John Stokes, Diana Surman, Jenny Taylor, Will Vaughan, Martha Vicinus, Hilary Wainwright, Michelene Wandor and Bob Young. In addition, Marion Friedmann, John Goode, Shula Marks, Sheila Rowbotham and Jeffrey Weeks read and commented on the whole MS in first draft.

Jocelyn Cornwell, Ruthie Petrie, Janie Prince, Joanna Ryan, Margot Waddell and Joe Slovo, Ruth First's husband, were particularly supportive; Louise Richey, Ruth Vaughan, and Nancy White re-typed large parts of the manuscript at very short notice; Jennifer Kane produced the index.

For permission to consult and quote from copyright sources we would like to thank the Basel Mission Archives for extracts from Gottlob Schreiner's Personal File; Church Missionary Society Archives; the Council for World Mission for LMS Archives; Mrs Ina Ellis, Assistant Archivist, The Methodist Church Overseas Division (Methodist Missionary Society); the Department of Historical Papers, University of the Witwatersrand Library, Johannesburg (A1199), where the late George Findlay's papers are now deposited; Syfrets Trust and Executor Company, Grahamstown, for the estate of Olive Schreiner; Humanities Research Center, University of Texas at Austin, for the Olive Schreiner-Havelock Ellis correspondence; The Society of Authors on behalf of the estate of Havelock Ellis; Sheffield City Libraries Archives Divisions for the Carpenter MSS; Miss Sarah Pearson and Mrs Judith Walker for the Papers and Correspondence of Karl Pearson, University College, including the typescript compilation made by Mrs Helga Pearson Hacker; Dr Muriel Radford, for a letter from Olive Schreiner to Dollie Radford in June 1898; the Department of Manuscripts, British Library, for quotations from the Gladstone Papers, the Rhys and Dirks Collection, and the Bentley Manuscripts; Albany Museum, 1820 Settlers Division, Grahamstown; J. W. Jagger Library, University of Cape Town Libraries, for extracts from the Olive Schreiner Collection in their possession; The National English Documentation Centre in Grahamstown in co-operation with The Public Library, Cradock, and the Cory Library for Historical Research, Rhodes University, Grahamstown; South African Library (formerly South African Public Library), Cape Town; Central Archives Depot, Pretoria, for extracts from Accession No. A1, General J. C. Smuts Collection (1886–1910); Neville Spearman

Ltd for a series of quotations from Havelock Ellis' *My Life*. Our apologies to other copyright holders who may have been inadvertently omitted.

Ruth First, Maputo
Ann Scott, London
July 1979

INTRODUCTION

The life of Olive Schreiner offers a striking example of the dilemmas women writers have always faced, however unconsciously, in working and living. By her own account, Schreiner decided as a 'little child' that a woman owed it to herself to be financially independent, and much of her writing, inspired by a freethinking radicalism, was explicitly feminist in theme. Each of her three novels, though one was unfinished at the time of her death, dealt with the oppression of women in childhood, adolescence and marriage as she had observed or experienced it in her own life. She began *The Story of an African Farm*, the best and most famous, as a twenty-one-year-old governess in the Cape Colony in 1876; but, remarkably, she had had no contact with a feminist movement of the kind then active in England and pressing for women's access to higher education and the professions.

Although the 'pessimistic' dénouement of that novel can be related specifically to the conditions of ostracism and alienation in which Olive Schreiner's childhood and adolescence were passed, *African Farm* has also spoken to successive generations of women. It is a work to which the adjective 'timeless' has often been applied, as though the fragmentary reality of Lyndall, its strong-minded rebel and obvious heroine, has somehow assumed eternal life. But though the last few years, in this country and the USA, have seen the emergence of a body of theory debating the existence of a discrete female or feminist literary tradition,[1] we have been unable confidently to place Olive Schreiner within it. This most successful novel of hers, for one thing, springs from a culture sustained primarily by the Bible; moreover she herself had little time for novels, had read almost none at the time when she wrote *African Farm*, and was, as we argue, then directing her thoughts chiefly to such general questions as guilt, self, and the crisis of faith.

With the publication of *Woman and Labour* in 1911, Olive Schreiner returned to the themes of her fiction in a studious but polemical essay which became a central text of the women's movement during the first decades of the century. Though the work made its appearance during the campaign for female suffrage, it was not preoccupied with that issue

alone but with women's disinheritance from labour and their conse-
quently unequal relationship with men in production and in society at
large. Schreiner's was one of the few attempts, after Engels' *Origin of the
Family*, Bebel's *Woman*, and Eleanor Marx and Edward Aveling's *The
Woman Question*, to produce a materialist exposition of women's subordination, yet in its scope it fell far short of her understanding of her own
life. Only in letters to close friends, among them two white South African
women who had lived together for seventeen years and for whose intimacy
she had great respect, did she allow herself to explore issues of female
sensibility, sexual morality, and relations with men; most importantly, of
her own failed attempts to assert her needs and her autonomy as a woman.

Twenty-eight years elapse between the publication of *African Farm*
and *Woman and Labour*. This period, between 1883 and 1911, sees the
emergence, especially in women's writing of the 1890s, of a concern with
fantasy and utopia.[2] In novels it takes the form of intricacies of plot
involving cross-dressing and role reversal; in allegory with the visionary
portrayal of the real world of the future. In this new world the divisions
between men and women are overcome by recourse to idealization and
retreat – this to a 'far-away' place, perhaps uninhabited, perhaps a colony
of 'new' men and women. What we know historically, of course, is that
women had begun to take a more active part in the public life of the time;
it seems that a public discussion of 'private' life – at least as it is reflected
in the idealizing allegory of the period – remained elliptical, even fey.
It was at this time that Olive Schreiner's imaginative writing was also at
its most obscure, though its subject matter was real enough: the allegorical
writing to which she turned in the late 1880s rehearsed over and over
again the theme of sexual love, self-esteem, and the struggle for 'love'.

Between the writing of the early novels and her later feminist testament, she published only these allegories and a series of political essays.
This was the long, unproductive period when she was unable to sustain
her work beyond the length of a brief sketch or the urgency of journalism.
She worked and reworked old manuscripts, carrying the unfinished
sheets with her wherever she moved. Her writing was changing and
experimental; she was now making a self-conscious attempt to find an
appropriate literary form, but in her eyes, and those of others, she failed.
After a spell in Britain in the 1880s she returned to South Africa as a
literary celebrity, and she used her influence and her reputation to
espouse minority radical causes. In her experience Victorian society

secluded and silenced women, colonial society even more so; but she moved from themes of women's subjection and powerlessness to those of national oppression and the struggles of subject races and classes. She was an advocate first of the Boer cause against British imperialism, and then of the African people of South Africa subordinated in the interests of both Boer and Briton. Almost alone of her contemporaries she perceived the race conflicts during South Africa's industrial revolution in terms of a worldwide struggle between capital and labour. She was an outspoken critic and mentor of politicians in public life, but she cut a lonely, isolated figure, issuing prophetic warnings about the future of the country and retreating into a shy personal life.

The range and seeming incompatibility of her imaginative work and her political writing have placed her at continuing risk of being fragmented by admirers and detractors alike. In general, those interested in her novels have not been attentive to her politics. Her concerns in both South Africa and Britain have not been easily reconciled, for while her place in English socialism of the 1880s is acknowledged within the Havelock Ellis, Edward Carpenter and Eleanor Marx circles, her relations in South Africa with figures like Jan Smuts, John X. Merriman and Gandhi are less well understood. Within her South African context she has always been dismembered. Her famous novel is seen as transcending politics, while her social comment is obtrusive and damaging to her reputation as a writer of fiction: thus for some her creativity was to disappear after *African Farm* into the 'sands of liberal pamphleteering'.[3] Since her death she has been seen as a novelist who never mastered the form; as a poet rather than a novelist; as a visionary rather than a cogent political thinker. In her lifetime she was similarly contained. A leading Cape politician thought *African Farm* a work of genius; he dismissed her allegories about women as 'rhapsodic', since 'God almighty has made the sexes separate.'[4] By some Olive Schreiner is revered because she surmounted the female condition; to others her achievements were due to her special qualities as a woman; to others still her feminism is irrelevant to her radicalism.

For all its inconsistencies, her life is significant because many of the issues that confront our own period – how to connect not only social radicalism and feminism but also personal liberation – are refracted through her consciousness and writing. Whether she is an explicit feminist or not, however, a woman writer does seem to us to present special problems as subject for a biography, and some of these have been luminously expressed by E. P. Thompson in his comments on Mary Wollstonecraft's life and the inequitable treatment she has received at the hands of historians and critics.[5] By some Wollstonecraft has been seen less as a significant intellectual or courageous moralist, Thompson argues, than as an 'Extraordinary Woman'. 'And the moral confusions or personal crises of a woman are always somehow more interesting than those of a man: they engross all other aspects of the subject. As indeed, from the inexorable facts of the woman's "situation" they often do.' Thompson's point is that none of her biographies has wholly satisfied, for she presents not one subject but two. From one aspect Wollstonecraft was one of five or six ultra-radical intellectuals of the late eighteenth century, requiring no manner of condescension because she also happened to be a woman. It had been her notion that 'mind has no sex'. 'But from another aspect, Wollstonecraft was reminded by every fact of nature and of society that she was a woman. She was *not* a mind which has no sex, but a human being exceptionally exposed within a feminine predicament.'

The feminine predicament is the persistent theme of Olive Schreiner's life. Like Mary Wollstonecraft she aimed to reconcile her needs and her sense of self as a woman with her work as a writer. In her resolution of the predicament she sacrificed one half of her need: she wanted to find men who would regard her not merely as a woman, but as a co-worker, with whom she could have 'love and friendship without any sex element'. Throughout her life, her writing explored the contradictory expectations of the self-affirming woman. But even more than in her writing, the emotional conflicts of her life were expressed in physical restlessness. She moved from one place to another, failed to finish a piece of work, explored relationships with friends and lovers, and cried out her despair in letters. These struggles with self-realization sometimes inspired her to write, but at other times prevented her from doing so: her creativity and her failure were expressions of the same struggle. She herself made no separation of her life and work, and to Havelock Ellis, her lifelong friend and correspondent, she wrote: 'I would like to have your critical judgement of my mind, or rather of my work, which is really me.' And again: 'I don't seem to have any self; I am all lost in my work.'

Sexually, however, she was unable to reconcile her theory and her experience. She was rare among feminists of her period in her recognition of the sexual needs of women, refusing to concede that their sex drive was weaker than men's, and even advocating the need, in a 'highly complex' society, for sexual experiment. Not that she ever suggested what form this experiment might take; for the most part she was a relentless advocate of a monogamous but passionate heterosexuality. At the same time, her relationship to her own sexuality, at source to her individuality, was extremely problematic. She withdrew, wounded, when she was suspected, or when she suspected herself, of asserting sexual demands. As biographers we are aware that this is the most difficult of areas to interpret: we have tried to create a psychologically believable woman of the late nineteenth century largely on the basis of the psychoanalytic language of the twentieth. We have been attentive on the one hand to certain turns of phrase in Olive's own letters – or to their absence – and to the historical feel of the discussions in which she participated, while bringing an individual focus to bear on her chronic illness as an adult on the other. We suspect that her asthmatic condition, which developed in late adolescence after her first and very stressful relationship with a man, may have been continually reinforced by guilt at both her rejection of the sexual mores of her time and her failure to achieve the idealized model of a relationship which she imposed on herself. There were times, moreover, when she appeared to recognize the relationship between her illness and her situation: 'My chest is getting worse . . . now my legs are bad. Oh, it isn't my chest, it isn't my legs, it's I, myself, my life.' For the tensions of her life were difficult to resolve. She sought solitude to work, and yet could not stand the strain of isolation. She had an ideal of a perfect marriage, even proclaimed that hers fulfilled it, but lived apart from her husband for years on end. She was admired and fêted, yet died feeling a failure. Seen impressionistically, then, her illness 'is' the theme of her life. It was through illness, with its periods of utter collapse, that she negotiated these contradictions, and indeed the whole split between her public and private personae. The split is perhaps exemplified in the fact of her celebrity: lionized in England as a sexual radical – sales of the 'notorious' *African Farm*, with Lyndall's child born out of wedlock, reached 100,000 by the turn of the century – she was in many ways the most fragile of women.

The biographies of her that do exist, whether by women or men, demonstrate the general reluctance to confront failure and contradiction as well as success as an expression of the feminine predicament. The first, and most influential, was written by her farmer politician husband, Samuel Cron Cronwright-Schreiner, and appeared in 1924, four years after her death.[6] *The Times* reviewed it as 'a pious memorial, as pious as

any husband could erect to his wife', and suggested that he had written it
to anticipate any unauthorized biography.[7] In many respects, Cronwright
had barely understood his wife, but his presentation of her personality and
behaviour created the Olive Schreiner of most subsequent biographies
and commentary. For Cronwright was not only concerned to build a
monument to her as a writer, but also, by destroying much of the material
to which he had access, to perpetuate a view of Olive acceptable to
himself. Anxious to come to a proper definition of genius, he constructed
a picture of a woman endowed with and then hampered by her 'Creative
Faculty'; in doing so he produced the wholly conventional notion of
genius as having no social context, a state apart and above. Most
significantly, he made her into an almost amoral innocent, for it was only
as such that he could reconcile the demanding, eccentric adult and the
frightened child with a 'shy, nervous look like a wild creature when she
met strangers'. Indeed, outside all social convention and prey to 'nerve
storms' occasioned by trifles, she came near to being, in his eyes, the
hysterical personality of the 1880s;[8] a child still, but wayward in its loss
of control. 'Olive seems almost without moral judgement as concerns her
own *acts*,' he wrote to Havelock Ellis, whose help he enlisted. 'Her
thought was sacred to her; her *mental* ideas seem to have been unswerving
and splendid; her *acts* often seem to have no relation whatever to her
mental code of morality.'[9]

Some of Olive's close women friends refused to cooperate in its
preparation and when it appeared felt justified in their opposition; in their
circles it was described as 'Cronwright's autobiography of his wife'. For
though he had Olive's childhood notebooks and her diaries as a governess,
he used them sparingly and only fragments survive; there is no trace of
the diary she wrote in the later years of her life, especially during her
marriage. But whatever its omissions, of course, Cronwright-Schreiner's
Life remains indispensable as a biographical source. In that it does
provide unequalled access to original material we have drawn on it,
though relying on Cronwright as husband rather than biographer, and
using it most extensively for her own account of her childhood, and his
of their marriage. We have relied more on his edited collection of her
Letters,[10] though these too were carefully selected.*

---

* Evidence of Olive's relationship with eugenicist and social statistician Karl
Pearson has been virtually eliminated. A certain Rev. Lloyd claimed that he had
received a thousand letters from her; three are reproduced in the *Letters*.

In 1934 Ellis and Cronwright-Schreiner learned of a young woman who proposed to write a new biography, but of whom Ellis did not expect much. 'Neither do I,' Cronwright wrote to him, 'unless from you or me, and I don't mean to write another. You and I (in strictest truth) could set the Thames on fire, if we would or *could*, and that is outside human thought!'[11] In the event no new biography appears to have been published in the Thirties.* But over the next twenty years two books by women did appear, one timed to coincide with the centenary of Olive's birth.[12] Both were in the tradition of commemorative writings. Vera Buchanan-Gould and Daisy Hobman saw Olive Schreiner as an unquestionably exceptional woman, by whose example womanhood itself was elevated; her work, like that of George Eliot, George Sand and Emily Brontë, ample proof of women's ability. Their search for equivalents, however, took Olive herself out of her time and judged her by an abstract criterion of value. Nor should her novels be seen 'simply' as the expression of her personality, however intense,† and reference to them in an attempt to verify or reiterate the content of her life can be misleading. Vera Buchanan-Gould, for example, used *Undine*, the first, as straightforward documentary material when she tried to sum up the psychological consequences of Olive's first involvement with a man; in doing so she ignored the fact that the text itself contains anomalies, remains inconclusive, and resolves the actual difficulties of Olive's experience through fantasy.

If an exclusive focus on personality makes for an ahistorical reading of a writer's work, Johannes Meintjes' biography, published in 1965,[13] makes Olive Schreiner a complete paradox: representative of all women but unique. Instead of looking at the real constraints and options for women in nineteenth-century South Africa, Meintjes' generalizations across time incline him to moral judgement, sometimes denigration. The 'morbidity' of Olive's jottings as a governess, for example, 'must not be taken too seriously. There is the inclination to self-dramatisation common to most young diarists'; and of course Olive only remembered her journal when she was 'in a particular state of depression or illness'. Unlike the

* The intending biographer could have been Winifred Horrabin, the feminist and socialist writer, whose notebooks, preserved in Hull University Library, include several on Olive Schreiner.

† cf. Jan Smuts' preface to Buchanan-Gould's biography: 'I love her [Olive Schreiner] as I love Emily Brontë . . . In both cases their creations were simply the expression of the intense personality of the writers.'

editors of a recent collection of nineteenth- and twentieth-century women's diaries,[14] Meintjes fails to comprehend that the diary form has always offered invaluable source material for women's experience precisely because of the peculiarly fragmented nature of their daily lives. Olive Schreiner was no exception; the pity of it is that so little of her diary remains.

Of all the biographical or critical studies, Marion Friedmann's psycho-analytic *Olive Schreiner: A Study in Latent Meanings*, published in 1955,[15] is the most coherent. Its stated concern is the relationship between Olive's personality and her material: in that she felt 'compelled' to go on writing, what was she trying to express? Friedmann's is an argument about punishment, self-punishment, and motherlessness as the insistent themes of the fiction, and she is obviously right to describe Olive as neurotic: as she puts it,

> From the time we have any description at length of it, her behaviour was neurotic: she did not seem able to deal appropriately with her environment, and her behaviour did not seem to result in satisfaction of her needs.[16]

Still, there are problems with this type of psychoanalytic approach. It tends to be reductionist, collapsing adolescent or adult behaviour solely into a defence against infantile hurts. It discounts the family's structural or cultural relationship to the society in which it is placed. It interprets political activism as the expression of a purely personal difficulty, and although we do not deny the patterns within the political and personal choices Olive made, we feel that Friedmann's perspective ignores important areas of her experience.*

The real strength of a psychoanalytic approach, however, is that it provides us with a way into the illness: symptoms are neither arbitrary nor 'external' to the individual's life, but carry meaning and history. They are expressive of conflicts and failure in the most important relationships, initially within the family, later with lovers and friends. But in bio-graphical work there must always be the caveat that we are not in an analytic relationship with a living patient. Psychoanalysis is a therapeutic endeavour, the investigation of a two-person relationship that proceeds

---

* For example, Friedmann suggests that Olive resigned from the South African Women's Enfranchisement League 'because she couldn't get on with fellow committee members'; it was, in fact, primarily because the definition of the franchise qualification was changed to exclude black women.

under strictly controlled conditions.[17] We are not psychoanalysing Olive Schreiner, but applying a Freudian theory of the mind and its constructs to that part of our source material which concerns Olive's inner world and the course of her personal life. At the same time we are primarily historians, and have tried to relate psychoanalytic insight to a growing body of information on the medical control of sexuality at the turn of the century.[18] Meintjes sees sexuality solely as the practice of sex; we see Olive as someone struggling to come to terms with her identity as a whole, trying 'to fulfil both parts of her nature, to work and live like a man, but like a woman as well'.[19] We have tried to understand her illness and unhappiness as an expression of the split between her sense of her own needs and the reality of what was possible for women in the cultures in which she lived.

We see Olive Schreiner's life and writing as a product of a specific social history. We are not only looking at what she experienced but at how she, and others, perceived that experience: at the concepts with which her contemporaries understood their world, and, again, at the consciousness that was possible for her time – after Darwin, before Freud, and during the period when Marx's *Capital* was written. Unlike Vera Buchanan-Gould we do not see her as having grown 'untrammelled in a wild free land'. We have written at length about the missionary life and politics of which her parents were a part precisely because it *was* part of a European culture, and we see the missionary presence in the colonial society as part of the imperial presence of the time. Race and cultural prejudice were all-pervasive: English-speaking South Africans were contemptuous of Afrikaners; all Whites despised all Blacks.* This was a colonial culture almost bare of serious books, and one in which the struggle between good and evil was conveyed through religious texts. Farming communities in the interior operated restrictive and punitive moral codes; girls were raised for household duties and marriage, and little beyond. Somehow, alone of the large family of Schreiner children,

* The term 'kafir' was common usage at the time when Olive was growing up and she seems to have used it uncritically, though there has been no more pejorative word for the African people. In *Undine*, written by the age of twenty, she used the word 'nigger' equally uncritically. By the 1900s, when she had come to see race questions as part of the labour question, she tended in the main to write of 'natives', though the odd 'nigger' still appears. Howard Thurman, a black American who introduced an anthology of Olive's writings in 1973, and who had been reading her since the Twenties, found his enthusiasm for her diminished by it; he would never forget his 'shock and anger' at her use of the word. *A Track to the Water's Edge* (New York 1973), p. xxix.

Olive was filled with religious doubt from an early age. She endured censorious parents and then, in early adolescence, a break from family life. She had virtually no formal schooling, but as a governess she schooled others. The introspective but spirited child grew into an independent but tormented woman, drawing from books what she could not experience, and writing her own in search of an alternative way of life.

Her growth and her achievement must be read against the constraints of that colonial society, and simultaneously within the context of the intellectual history of the time. This involves an awareness of the two main currents to which she was exposed in England during the 1880s: the social evolutionism on which she had already read fairly extensively; and the proliferation of radical groups debating socialism, relations between the sexes, and the 'new spirit'. Her participation in these debates was formative for her; more so still was the experience of trying to live in English intellectual circles as a free and equal woman. Back in South Africa, radicalism was not easily transplanted to colonial conditions. How well she managed the transfer must be gauged from a scrutiny of her writing on South African affairs, measured against the political thinking and practice of the time. For in South Africa she was as much partisan as commentator. Today she is cited for her political foresight; then she was an adherent of unpopular causes. This threw her back into the isolation which had nurtured her early talent, but had also crippled it.

This biography tries to explain how significant she was in her time. How important is she to ours? If *Woman and Labour* was a central text in the feminist movement of the early twentieth century, does it enrich feminist theory in ours? How is it that Lyndall in *African Farm* is still so real? In her South African context, were Olive Schreiner's politics little in advance of those of Cape liberal politicians, or did she anticipate the class and national liberation politics of this century? And how convincingly can it be demonstrated from her life and her writing that religious doubt, her experience as a woman, and her social vision cannot be dissociated?

Is it, indeed, possible and legitimate to make connections between her experience as a woman and her view of the world? Margaret Walters, in a recent and brilliant essay on Wollstonecraft, Harriet Martineau and Simone de Beauvoir,[20] finds it significant that Wollstonecraft wrote not only the *Rights of Woman*, but was working at the time of her death on a novel called *The Wrongs of Woman, or Maria*. Her point here was partly that the oppression of women is personally experienced, that their protest springs out of a deep sense of injustice and wrong. Like her heroine Maria, Wollstonecraft was wrestling with the way in which conventional feminine stereotypes confined and imprisoned women, and she demanded her rights as a human being. But, in Walters' words, both author and character found that 'woman's problems go deeper than that, that sexual feelings and affections somehow escape rational understanding, and that there is a gap between the demand for her rights and her overwhelming sense of her wrongs. There's an odd sense that even if she got her rights, a sense of wrong would persist.'[21] Something of the same dynamic holds true for Olive Schreiner, and underpins the split between public and private to which we have already referred. So it is in this sense that we have tried to relate her work to her politics, her politics to her personal life, and her personality to her career as a writer. Ours is a concern with her failures as well as her achievements; the reputation she achieved during her lifetime and afterwards; and, centrally, her own view of herself.

CHAPTER ONE

Early Life on a Mission Station

Until the middle of the nineteenth century, white settlement in South Africa was thin and patchy, and autonomous African societies were still able to offer considerable resistance to threats against their land and independence. Britain had occupied the Cape Colony in 1806, but no consistent settlement policy was pursued until the end of the Napoleonic wars in 1815, when emigration was seen as a cure for the country's unemployment problems.

The arrival of the 1820 Settlers from Britain doubled the English-speaking population at the Cape. British colonial government had at first been reluctant, largely for reasons of economy, to extend its frontiers from the coastal strip into the interior. When it did so, in spurts of military activity during much of the nineteenth century, it was as part of a scheme to station settlers to guard the boundaries of a colony which had made itself precarious by excluding the indigenous African pastoralists from its territory. Like the Boer trek-farmers of the Cape, the Africans were cattle farmers needing large tracts of land. The abolition of slavery in the British Empire in 1834 meant that slave labour was no longer available in the Cape and cheap and tractable local labour had to be induced to take its place. It was thus in search of both land and labour that the white settlers, equipped with arms and supported by a colonial state, set out to conquer a people far more numerous but lacking the power of arms or a central state authority.

These were the formative years of a South African society in which whites were to be masters and Africans servants. It was the period before the alienation of huge tracts of land by white capitalist farmers; before the discovery of minerals and the foundations of industry, when the Black peasantry was forcibly dragged from the countryside to form an industrial working class; and before the formation of a unified national state in which British colonies and Boer republics, established when Boer trek-farmers moved away from British control, would sink their differences in a combined subjugation of the Black majority. But if the outlines of contemporary South Africa were still forming, they were visible enough as white conquest moved steadily east and northward, and white cattle farmer, itinerant trader, military garrison and missionary formed frontier societies at the furthest reaches of the new colony. Here at the frontier were improvised the legends which sustain white society to this day: of white communities threatened by black hordes; of white womanhood at the mercy of the black rapist; of white civilization struggling for survival; and of white missionaries, some succouring colonial outposts, but others, cranky and credulous, taking the side of the blacks, drawing labour away from the service of the farmer and spoiling it beyond repair with seditious visions of social equality.

The largest and most influential of the mission societies was the London Missionary Society (the LMS), which made its first appearance at the Cape as early as 1799.[1] In time Moravians, Wesleyan Methodists, Scottish Presbyterians, German Lutherans, Anglicans, Roman Catholics and American Board missionaries were all busy in the field with more or less tolerance for one another: Church, like State, was engaged in conquest but with differing interpretations of the divine will for the people of the country. Some, like the ministers of the Dutch Reformed Church, pursued their Christianizing mission only among the colonists, and preached exclusively to whites.[2] Thus the ministers of the Dutch Reformed Church became the ideologues of a theory of segregation which cited Biblical testimony for the lowly place of the sons of Ham. The LMS lacked white congregations but it held an almost continuous line of stations along the northern border, on the mission road to the interior of the continent, inspired by Thomas Powell Buxton's conviction that the blacks were blessed with a peculiar aptitude for the reception of moral and religious instruction.

All evangelical activity impinged on matters of politics, so missionaries became interested parties in the societies among which they worked, but none more effectively than Dr John Philip, a close friend of Buxton and other leading Evangelicals.[3] At the request of the LMS Philip had reluctantly left his Aberdeen congregation in 1819 for a short spell in South

Africa, stayed for thirty years as LMS Superintendent, and was chief representative in South Africa of the Clapham Sect or the Saints. That celebrated group of Evangelical politicians gave an altruistic Christian purpose to Empire, for in their concern to convert the peoples of Africa – and India, and the South Seas – they became a major pressure group for the extension of British rule.

Philip was the Evangelicals' most sophisticated and far-reaching advocate abroad, and it was largely due to his efforts that after 1835 the Cape was included in the list of colonies for parliamentary commissions of inquiry. These inquiries were intended to demonstrate the imperial government's interest in the condition of aboriginal peoples and ultimately played an important part in shaping British colonial policy. Philip provided the framework for a forceful indictment of the South African colonists. His early testimony, which subsequently became *Researches in South Africa*, documented the maladministration of the Khoikhoi (then called the Hottentots), whom 'the *landdrosts* [magistrates] and clerks and farmers . . . consider the absolute property of the colonists and as such made for their use as their cattle and sheep'.⁴ Philip's model was the working man of his home country, 'free' to labour for a wage: industrious, sober and submissive, and fired by the morality preached to the British working class by Philip's counterparts at home in response to the class conflicts and popular protests of early capitalism.

On the stations of the LMS converts were given religious instruction but were also trained as agriculturalists and as artisans in their own right.* The intention was to foster occupations which offered alternatives to tied farm labour in the service of whites. In England Philip's efforts for free labour were hailed as the work of a new Wilberforce; in South Africa they aroused the fury of farmers and frontiersmen. This was a measure of the clash between contesting interests – those of an expanding pastoral economy versus those of British capital and its ascendant classes. Philip, a

* During 1838–40 the Rev. James Backhouse visited every mission station at work in South Africa. There were then twenty-six stations of the London Mission, and thirty-two Wesleyan stations; and a grand total of eighty-five stations in all. At Philipton Backhouse met the aged missionary James Read and wrote: 'It was pleasant to see an air of comfort and independence in the Hottentots, who are truly free. Many of the half naked degraded Hottentots have been raised to a state nearly equal to that of the labouring classes in England, and in some respects superior, certainly above that found in the manufacturing districts . . . They are dressed like decent plain people of that class.' *A Narrative of a Visit to the Mauritius and South Africa* (1844), pp. 185–6. John Joseph Freeman, *A Tour in South Africa* (1851), has a very similar account.

confirmed adherent of Adam Smith's principles of political economy, saw the economic growth machine as needing a continuing supply of labourer-consumers. The problem with 'the abettors of the present system', he wrote, was that they 'seem never to have contemplated the aborigines of the Colony as consumers.' Consumers needed opportunities not only to improve their lot but also to add to the prosperity of the Colony. Where the missionary placed his standard among savage tribes, Philip explained, their prejudice against the colonial government gave way, and their dependence was further increased by 'the creation of artificial wants . . . industry, trade and agriculture spring up.'[5] Philip was an eloquent exponent of Christianity not only as a religious calling, but as a way of labour, and one which required the formation of the kind of society in which the organization of labour would be given a permanent place.

Missionaries had to be modernizers, and Philip has been recognized as the head of a party in that cause.[6] A Christianizing mission was essentially a 'civilizing mission', and while natives were variously seen as vacant, depraved or corrupted, yet they had immortal souls which were not beyond salvation. The gospel of work and training in self-discipline would save their souls as it would those of the nation at home, and since its moral precepts were drawn from a Western industrial society, the acceptance of Christianity implied radical changes in the convert's way of life. Communities were persuaded to settle in villages round the church. The sexual division of labour was reorganized as men were persuaded to cultivate the fields in place of women. Imposed standards of clothing and housing required Africans to earn money and thus to enter into employment. This process of Westernization thus tied the Africans to a cash economy and, as the numbers of converts grew, weakened the political authority of the African principalities under their chiefs.

It was in this way that the modernizing missionaries helped to effect a profound shift within South Africa's autonomous African societies as a whole, and in their relationship to colonial economy and government. Mission work was also instrumental in forming the first of South Africa's black elites, small groups of trained Christians who were the agents of Western culture and thus the medium of communication between Africans and government, even representing, on occasion, the power of the colonial government. Furthermore, when mission stations were established several hundreds of miles inland along the Orange River and then beyond those boundaries of the colony, Philip himself became an advocate of colonial expansion. The mission station was to serve as the natural ally of government in pacifying the extending frontier. He argued the importance of having 'belts of civilized natives' between the colonists and their less civilized neighbours, for the mission stations could be the cheapest and best military posts that wise government could employ to defend its frontier against the predatory incursions of tribes. His diplomacy was thus calculated to advance not only the work of the missions but the outposts of Empire. His effectiveness as politician and diplomat arose not only from his unequalled collection of intelligence from the network of mission stations, but also from his contacts and leverage in the British political system.

Philip visited England in 1836 with fresh testimony, including that of LMS convert John Tzatsoe, son of a Xhosa chief, whom he produced in person before the parliamentary Select Committee on Aborigines. It was during this stay that he recruited a young missionary couple, Gottlob and Rebecca Schreiner, who were to be inducted into the role of frontier missionaries nearly two years later at a time when their mission station lay across the route of the Great Trek, the large-scale exodus of Boer farmers from British colonial control that year.

The details of Gottlob Schreiner's early life are shadowy. He was born in 1814 in the village of Fellbach, near Stuttgart, capital of Württemberg, one of the smaller German states. Until he was eighteen he worked as a shoemaker. He then entered the Basel Mission House, from which he emerged, four years later, not as a trained missionary – apparently he lacked the education for the theological training – but as a scholar of the mission school. In the 1830s, when different mission societies were finding spheres of influence in Southern Africa – the Rhenish societies secured a foothold in Namaqualand, the Berlin Society worked in the Orange Free State, the Paris societies in Basutoland and the American Board among the Zulu – the London and the Church Missionary Societies in London were heavily supplied with recruits from the German and Swiss seminaries.

Gottlob was one of four students sent by the Basel Society to the Church Missionary Society to train at their Islington College. But Gottlob, an evangelical Lutheran, thought the ordination of 'our native church . . . as good as that of the church of England', and in any case he preferred the form of Lutheran ordination. He and a fellow student lodged formal objection in a letter to CMS authorities in which they complained that they could see no reason to spend one or two years in England 'only for taking orders in the church of England'. As for the Islington Institute, its laws were 'unworthy of the Christian liberty and of the English character'; it seemed that their rooms had no fireside and they were not permitted to smoke.[7] The CMS washed its hands of the fractious young men and they were severely censured by the Basel Committee. For a while it seemed that Gottlob's endeavour to work among the pagan might be in ruins. Fulsome pleas were sent to the Basel office: 'We must taste the cup of our aberration to the dregs; our prayers and those of our friends during the last eight days cannot have been in vain; the Lord would not have said "amen" . . . The Lord wished it in order to test us.'[8] Finally the Basel authorities relented, and the young men were ordained on 27 June 1837. They were now free to take up positions with the London Missionary Society, hoping to be able to adapt themselves to its interdenominational structure.

Gottlob told his superior in the Basel Mission how he disliked the sternness of religious meetings in England, the striving for the extra-ordinary, the lengthy speeches and the clapping. 'These meetings', he wrote, 'are of such duration that one leaves them mentally and physically exhausted for the rest of the day.' He had attended a meeting chaired by Lord John Russell and the Duchess of Sutherland, who were applauded 'nine times on coming and going, not counting all the other clapping and foot-stamping, sufficient to break the floor'.[9] The ardent, independent young Lutheran with a talent for disputation found his English experience painful. Yet he managed to make contact with the daughter of a York-shire Nonconformist minister and, in what must have been a constrained yet whirlwind courtship, persuaded Rebecca Lyndall to marry him on 7 November 1837. They embarked to South Africa less than three weeks later.

Gottlob and Rebecca appear to have met in the house facing St John's Church at Hoxton where Rebecca's mother, Catherine Lyndall, widowed the year before, took an interest in foreign missionary students. The marriage was an unconventional union, witnessed unconventionally by a product of the missionary labour which the young couple was setting out to emulate, Philip's convert John Tzatsoe. The ceremony in Hoxton Chapel was conducted according to the rites of Independent Dissenters.

By the time of her marriage at nineteen, Rebecca had been a member of the Moorfields Tabernacle for half her life. She had been subjected to a fervently religious upbringing by a revivalist minister involved in the theological and doctrinal debates of the time and the schisms and separations they induced in the Church. This was the great romantic age of religion, when personal salvation was a dramatic event and sermons were accompanied by the groans and sobs of congregations. The Reverend Samuel Lyndall, born in 1761 in Epworth, Lincolnshire, Wesley's birthplace, had been Wesleyan like his parents before him, and left shoemaking to train for the ministry at Northowram Academy in Yorkshire, later serving as a minister at Bridlington. By the time he moved to London's East End at the end of the century he had become bitter against the Wesleyans and called himself a dissenter, an independent and a Methodist Calvinist.[10] His mentor appears to have been George Whitefield, the field preacher second only to Wesley in his ability to move the unchurched masses, but who broke with Wesley when he accepted Calvin's teaching of predestination. Whitefield had preached to great crowds in Moorfields and after his death his followers built the chapel later to be known as the Tabernacle, to which Rebecca adhered and with which her father had been associated.

It was a time of popular preachers, and people crowded the chapels to hear their favourites, to study their style and memorize their sayings. According to a contemporary handwritten account, Lyndall's congregation was 'so much increased since his settlement here that the place has been enlarged'. One family walked seven miles every Sunday to join the congregation, and divided the whole day between the chapel and Sunday School.[11] But not everyone approved of Lyndall's preaching. He was reputed to be 'staunch for orthodoxy, but withall dogmatical and illiberal, and is too much given to asperse characters in the pulpit . . .' 'Though rigid in his principles', this account concluded – though without adducing evidence – 'his conduct has been thought to be some time not so strict as becomes the Christian Minister.'[12]

The Lyndall family lived in Gloucester Terrace, Hoxton, near Shoreditch, a respectable residential area, and in one of his sermons Lyndall railed against those who broke the Sabbath by music, card-playing and tea gardens, warning that they would be damned. Their neighbours included a merchant, an officer of Her Majesty's Customs, a watchmaker, and a surgeon; several of the households in the street had servants, including the Lyndalls.[13] In an account drawn from her mother's reminiscences, Olive Schreiner described the Hoxton house as a sad place: psalm-learning and catechism, cold meat and sermons; odd-looking little boys being marched up to the top of the house to eat bread and water for having 'laughed on Sunday'. Yet Olive claimed that her mother's memories of Samuel Lyndall were sweet. He had called her Rebecca after his first wife, and for her name's sake he was very gentle to her.

Rebecca had died in 1810, leaving seven children. In 1815 Samuel Lyndall married Catherine James, Olive's maternal grandmother, then an apparently illiterate twenty-year-old from Newcastle who signed the register by making her mark. Of this marriage there were unnumbered 'accomplished daughters' and 'two bright sons'. Rebecca, Olive Schreiner's mother, was one of the accomplished daughters.

In 1817, shortly before Rebecca was born, Lyndall resigned from his Cannon Street congregation. According to the deacon who made the announcement, the events leading to this separation from the church were painful and unexpected, but he added that no attempt would be made to justify or condemn the action. A few years later Lyndall led yet another secession from a small East End church, this time the Jewry Street Chapel in Aldgate, and had his followers acknowledged as a separate church by several ministers. In all probability the differences lay in varying interpretations of the liturgy or prayer book.

Lyndall died in 1836 and was buried in Bunhill Fields. He left a heavy religious imprint on his family. The eldest son was a Sunday School teacher as well as a doctor; Elizabeth, Rebecca's half-sister, married Samuel Rolland, a missionary of the Paris Evangelical Society whom Dr Philip had escorted to South Africa eight years earlier, and moved to Basotho country.

Rebecca once recounted to her friends how she became a missionary. At a revival meeting in London one of the hymns asked: 'Who will go and join the throng?' The young girl sang among the others: '*I* will go and join the throng.'[14] Since she could not carry out a vocation in her own right, she had to do it as her husband's helpmate, as a missionary wife. In Victorian England rescue work – helping the poor, the suffering and the ill – was the only way in which middle-class women could escape from the home. Working abroad among the heathen enabled a young woman to make an independent career, even if as a wife, and to share in the tradition of Christian philanthropy which middle-class evangelists were assuming in the interests of moral change.

For medical reasons Rebecca had some difficulty in obtaining permission to emigrate: it took four doctors to testify that any weakness caused by two attacks of rheumatic fever would only benefit from the South African climate. Rebecca was the protégée of the Reverend John Campbell, a member of the LMS Africa Committee, and he gave her a glowing testimonial. After the marriage ceremony, when the couple went into the vestry to sign their names, Campbell took the wreath out of her bonnet, remarking that these frivolities were not for a missionary's bride.[15]

Rebecca thus began her South African mission with a vigorous training in the religion of the evangelical revival and the middle-class morality it had helped to create. In the words of Hannah More, the Church of England's great evangelical sermonizer, religion was 'not . . . merely an opinion or a sentiment . . . neither merely an act or a performance; but . . . a disposition, a habit, a temper; . . . not merely a name but a nature; it is turning the whole mind to God.' Religion had to be a way of life.[16] Obsessed with the fate awaiting sinful man faced with a wrathful God on the day of judgement, the convert suffered a perpetual sense of accountability for every lapse, and this led to agonizing self-scrutiny and a stern regime of self-deprivation which placed a premium on piety and proper conduct.

Rebecca's model of good behaviour was deeply puritanical and prohibitive. It stressed the primacy of duty, the sinfulness of enjoyment and self-indulgence, the sanctity of home and family and the presence of an ever-watchful God. This religion had been a potent force in Rebecca's family and she was to make it so in her own. But if her family and the mission Sunday School were to be Rebecca's realm in the new country, Gottlob's was far wider. He had to instil not only the practices of Christian worship, but the ethic of the new religion among peoples who were part of different social systems and who observed distinct social practices.

One probable outcome for the missionary was that in his incapacity to confront these differences he would preach an impoverished version of his own religion, with the stress on the purely external symbols of conversion, like baptism and marriage by Christian rite, abstention from drink and observance of the Sabbath. Gottlob's correspondence, for example, is replete with these concerns. For the next thirty years virtually

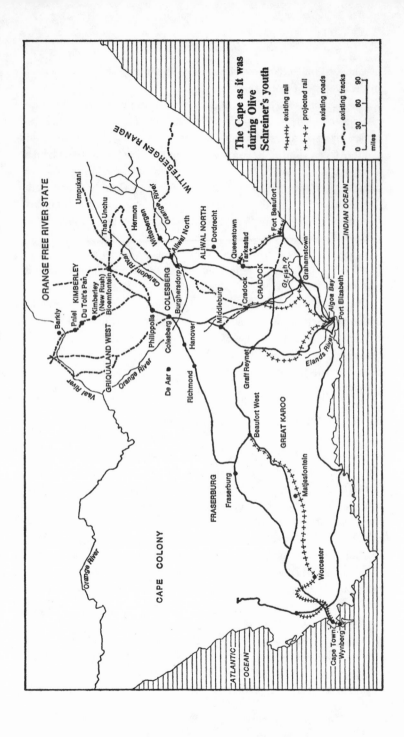

The Cape as it was
during Olive
Schreiner's youth

++++++ existing rail
++++++ projected rail
-·-·-· existing roads
------- existing tracks

miles
0   30   60   90

ORANGE FREE RIVER STATE

WITTEBERGEN RANGE

Umpukani
Thab Unchu
Hermon
Witteberge
Orange River
Aliwal North
Dordrecht
Barkly
Pniel   KIMBERLEY
Du Toit's Pan
Kimberley
(New Rush)
Bloemfontein
Caledon River
COLESBERG
Burghersdorp
ALIWAL NORTH
Queenstown
Tarkastad
Fort Beaufort
Philippolis
Colesberg
Hanover
Middleburg
Cradock
CRADOCK
Gt. Fish R.
Grahamstown
Algoa Bay
Port Elizabeth
INDIAN OCEAN
Elands River
De Aar
Richmond
Graff Reynet
GRIQUALAND WEST
Orange River
Vaal River

CAPE COLONY

Orange River

FRASERBURG
Fraserburg
Beaufort West
GREAT KAROO
Matjesfontein
Worcester
Cape Town
Wynberg
ATLANTIC
OCEAN

the only record of the lives of Gottlob and Rebecca is provided by his reports to his missionary superiors. They are stiff and formal, awkward in their English expression and in their pietistic assertions of his 'joy to labour in this part of the Lord's Vineyard'.[17]

Gottlob was not easily placed in the field and, quoting Elijah's laments, he reported to LMS headquarters in London his distress at being moved from one temporary appointment to another. There is a hint, but no more than an occasional sentence or two, at the ordeals experienced by Rebecca. Transplanted from a suburban London home into an unknown land, not to one of its coastal towns where settler drawing-rooms tried to mimic the social rituals she had known, but to an interior still poorly mapped and wholly lacking in social and health amenities, she must have been appallingly unprepared for the rigours of her new life. In these conditions she gave birth to twelve children over the next twenty-four years, five of whom died in infancy. Gottlob had to officiate at the delivery of their first child, Catherine, and wrote, even at this early stage, that Rebecca was 'almost a giant' compared with what she had been twelve months earlier. He thanked God for this.

In December 1838, just under a year after their arrival in the country, Gottlob was posted to Philippolis in the Orange Free State on the main route into the interior and found himself drawn, despite himself, into missionary frontier politics. Philippolis was an LMS station in the heart of Griqua country. Here descendants of early Afrikaner frontiersmen, of freed and escaped slaves, and of Africans detached from their tribes, tried to live as an independent settled agricultural community as an escape from the oppressive labour demands of the Cape Colonists. The missionaries whom Dr Philip controlled lived as permanent residents among the Griquas, becoming embroiled not only in the contest between Griquas and Boer trek-farmers, to whom the Griqua were leasing land in the long process of land alienation that was to lead to their total subjection, but also in the internal factional politics and succession crises between various members of the Griqua captaincy.[18]

When the Schreiners lived in the district the town of Philippolis came to life only intermittently; most of the Griquas lived on farms away from the centre of government. The missionary settlement comprised some thousands, largely Griqua who spoke Dutch, but also Basotho and Tswana refugees who had fled from areas dislocated by intertribal wars.

There were separate mission congregations of Griqua and Sechuana-speaking converts and it was among the latter that Gottlob concentrated his labours. Rebecca instructed the children in the mission school.

Gottlob was appointed assistant to the senior missionary, Mr Atkinson, but within a year the two men had to be separated. The issues that were in dispute vary according to the informant; Atkinson's version is that Schreiner was not only determined to act without regard to the advice and feelings of his colleagues, but he was a 'foreigner' and therefore 'unsuitable for a place like this'. On at least one occasion the missionaries appear to have identified with different parties in a Griqua dispute. After some attempts at arbitration Philip concluded that they could not be made to work together; and since Rebecca's state of health made it important that they live as close as possible to such medical advice as was available, the Atkinsons were moved on and the Schreiners stayed in Philippolis.[19]

Gottlob's reports concentrate on the tally of communicants, baptisms and marriages and the progress of his abstinence campaign, with little social commentary except where the condition of the people impinged directly upon his congregation. This was the case in the early 1840s, when congregation and school attendance dropped heavily as the people left for months at a time to do seasonal work for farmers in the region or to hunt or trade to the north. By this time Boer farmers were settling in considerable numbers, having 'seen the goodness of the land', and advice to the Griquas not to sell was in vain. They hired out their farms to the Trekboers on long leases, 'after which the farmers grasp with both hands and would fain have the whole land'. And it grieved Gottlob especially that most of the immigrant farmers were dealers in spirits: he feared that at their hands his flock was destined to 'furnish another melancholy proof of the black man withering before the white'.[20]

The station at Philippolis was considered one of the most difficult in South Africa, and Gottlob's tenure, even as he began to get a feel of the situation, proved disastrous. In 1842 he was the subject of an LMS commission of inquiry, conducted by Dr Philip, which confronted him with eight formal charges. They included hiring a man to sell goods and fire-arms, taking part in land speculation, undertaking to collect debts for a trader from his congregation, and failing to appear before the Chief and Council to answer charges. Schreiner's defence was that the witnesses against him had been pressured; 'how well it was plotted', he wrote.[21]

Dr Philip's report to LMS headquarters in London concluded that it was much to be regretted that Mr Schreiner ever took charge of the station.[22] This was a crushing admonition, but it was mitigated by a request that the report not be made public, out of sympathy for Mr Schreiner and his wife and her family. Respect for Rebecca's connections may have prompted Dr Philip's decision to give the man another trial. It was finally suggested that he work in Basotho country, near the Rollands, 'where it would be a great comfort and advantage to his wife to be near her sister.' Gottlob was relieved to leave Philippolis, which was a station for political affairs, for as a minister of the gospel he was determined 'to have as little as possible to do with such matters'. He felt that this had weighed heavily with Dr Philip's decision to remove him: 'being a German, not acquainted with the niceties of the English language might make me unfit to do much for the people in political affairs'.[23] He was replaced at Philippolis by the Reverend Peter Wright, Philip's closest aide in ecclesiastical politics, whose son Samuel was to marry Gottlob's daughter Olive some fifty years later.

Gottlob liked the idea of erecting a new station rather than entering upon 'another man's labours'. In search of a suitable site in Basotho country, where the Wesleyans and the Paris Evangelical Mission were by then well established, he sought an audience with Moshesh, the renowned Chief of the Basotho, who used missionaries as diplomats and advisers in his attempts to counter encroachments on his territory. Gottlob took him a present of a double-barrelled gun and concluded that Moshesh was 'a man of singular penetration and intelligence and well-disposed towards the cause of God'.[24]

Sanction for the new station did not arrive, however, either because the LMS had grown cautious of Gottlob after the Philippolis inquiry or because they were uncertain about the venture at a time when Moshesh was embroiled in disputes with immigrant white farmers and a treaty contemplated with the colonial government was still being negotiated. Floods washed out the Schreiners' home on one occasion and the family had to go and live in their wagon, where Rebecca suffered from what Gottlob described as inflammation of the brain.

With Gottlob in virtual disgrace with the LMS and unplaced in the missionary field, there followed several wretched years for the Schreiners, especially Rebecca. By this time there were two children, Catherine (known as Kate) and Frederick; a third child, Albert, lived only a few months: medicines fetched from the nearest large town were of no use.

In the next two years two more children were born, Theophilus and Alice.

At this time, apparently without instruction from the LMS but reporting to his original training school in Switzerland, Gottlob founded a new mission station which he called Basel. He preached in the Sotho language, using a Bible translated by French missionaries. He built a house and a church with great effort, making bricks, quarrying stone, and cutting reeds for thatching with the help of labourers whom he described as 'not at all like those at home in Württemberg': they demanded coffee, bread and meat and worked as little as possible.[25] But the Basel station had to be relinquished. The LMS, under whose auspices he was still working, considered it a waste of strength while important localities were still 'destitute of Christian endeavour'.[26]

Towards the end of 1846 Gottlob turned to the Wesleyans, ostensibly on a matter of doctrine. He was resolved to dissolve his previous church connection, he wrote, because 'examining my view again in the sight of God, I found that I had been all along a Wesleyan in doctrine and principle as far as I know it'. He had read and considered the sermons of John Wesley and his notes on the New Testament, and had found them 'in consonance with my own ideas of the truth as revealed in the Scripture'.[27] It was not unusual for missionaries in the field to cross from one denomination to another; in her later years Rebecca entered a Catholic convent. In Gottlob's case this espousal of the Wesleyans might also have been for reasons of expediency, like the three years he had spent learning Sesuto, which the lack of an LMS station in Basutoland would have wasted. The Wesleyan Mission Society accepted Gottlob as a catechist and he began to prepare for written and oral examinations; meanwhile he functioned as assistant missionary at Umpukani and Lishuani, high up the Caledon River, adjoining Basutoland.

In 1850 false reports reached Gottlob in Cape Town of the death of his wife and family. The Umpukani station had been almost totally destroyed during an onslaught by armed Africans, during which many converts had fled to the mission house as a place of safety. The incident was part of the tumult in the region caused by the espousal by the Cape government of the claims of minor chiefs as a check on the growing power of the Basotho, and by white commando raids against the corn-lands of the Bataung people who were dependents of Moshesh. In fact the Schreiners had had twenty minutes' warning of the attack from a messenger on horseback who had ridden from a neighbouring station, and they managed to escape even though a flying bullet had sailed over twelve-year-old Kate's head.[28] Rebecca had only just returned to the Umpukani station with Henrietta, an infant of three weeks, and the family had no wagon or oxen. They set out on foot for the nearest station, hiding from marauding groups along the route as they went. It was a twenty-four-mile journey.

There followed another period in the wilderness as Gottlob, his station at Umpukani ruined, ministered temporarily at small stations in the region and then, from 1853, for some two years in Bloemfontein, where having to preach in English was a new burden to him. By then, he wrote to the Basel Society, he had spent fourteen years among 'Natives' without seeing or speaking to whites. But the few years at Bloemfontein must have been a haven for Rebecca after the ghastly Umpukani experience and a decade of raising children in permanently arduous conditions. The town of Bloemfontein consisted at the time of only one distinguishable street of one-storey houses, but there was a store, a butcher's shop, a boarding house and the beginnings of an English church.

For Rebecca and the children there was also the companionship of the Murrays: the Reverend Andrew Murray Jnr, who was the Dutch Reformed Church minister there, and his wife Emma Rutherford, whose vivid letters are virtually the only social record of the period.[29] The Murrays read the *Illustrated London News*, *News of the Churches* and the *Commercial Advertiser*, South Africa's first newspaper. Emma was inundated with visitors who would talk on Sundays about worldly things – 'farms and people' – whereas she and her husband would have liked to confine their thoughts to religious matters. She ran a schoolroom for Coloured children with classes several times a week; but it was not popular with the Dutch or the English, and for her charity she was called a 'little Philippian and a little Philanthropist'. She also wanted to interest the women in something more than gossip, cooking and mending, and she thought of a magic lantern to show pictures; her husband said they would have to be of religious subjects. Though Bloemfontein was much better served than most of the places where the Schreiners had lived, Emma had to make her husband's clothes, as there was no tailor in the town. The doctor who attended her confinements was not fully qualified, having come to the country as a missionary with only a little medical knowledge. There were no trained nurses anywhere, and Emma's mother told her to put trust in God.

It was during her stay in Bloemfontein that Rebecca fell desperately ill and was thought to be dying. (For the most part relatives and friends diagnosed illness as well as they could, and sent for remedies to the nearest apothecary, often in another remote town. Gottlob's references to family illnesses tend to be vague but alarming; they give little clue to their real character.) Rebecca had no sooner recovered than Gottlob and Kate fell ill, and six-year-old Oliver, born at Umpukani, died. Rebecca described herself as sorrowful and very poorly; she longed to visit Oliver's grave but shrank from it. Kate, then aged thirteen, developed religious doubts, and became aware of 'clouds and darkness about the Throne of God'. From her English grandmother, Catherine Lyndall, living in Stoke Newington, she received cold comfort. In one letter she wrote to Kate:

> How infinitely preferable, my dear child, is your life of hallowed usefulness to the clumsy, listless half-awake manner in which so many young ladies drag through the best part of their earthly existence, or the frivolous and the giddy who are ever in the chase after pleasure and never finding it. There is a bright, very bright side in your lot in that far-off scene of your labour.[30]

The children were expected to share in the sense of mission, and also in the work: Kate had already taken her place beside Rebecca teaching the children of the mission schools.

The life of isolation and toil were resumed in 1855, when the Schreiners were posted to the Wesleyan station of Wittebergen on the edge of Basutoland. The nearest post office was a hundred miles away, but here at least Gottlob did not have to build his house. The Wittebergen mission house and chapel stood on a broad level promontory of rock which ended abruptly in a deep crag. Beyond it stretched a grass plain and, beyond that, the range of white sandstone mountains which gave the mountain chain its name.

The mission house was ninety feet long and sixteen feet wide, with thick mud-baked exterior walls only eight and a half feet high but nearly two feet thick. The outside walls were covered with white rough-cast; on the inside they were simply whitewashed. The roof was thatched, keeping the house cool in the summer and warm in the winter. The chapel, according to a careful account by Gottlob's immediate successor, was of the same construction, though the walls were at least half as high again.

It seated two hundred and fifty people on seats of plastered brick. The pulpit was made of packing case deal and the communion rail of bamboo.

The Wittebergen area had been closed to white settlement and designated a native reserve. Among those living within it, under British law, were fairly prosperous peasant families who had accumulated small flocks, and even some whose freehold plots had registered title deeds.* A government officer was posted in the reserve, and under him chiefs and headmen settled disputes and collected an annual hut tax. Some of the Africans had abandoned the beehive hut and built cottages of wattle and daub, or even of brick and stone with thatched roofs which, in the eyes of one of the missionaries, resembled English cottages. By the same account the Sabbath was the missionary's dream come true: round the station were innumerable roads and footpaths along which there converged on Sundays 'companies of decently clad natives cheerfully wending their way to the chapel'.

By the time the Schreiners arrived at Wittebergen in 1854 there were six children: Kate, Fred, Theo, Alice, Henrietta and Emile. Albert had died in infancy and Oliver at the age of six; Emile died on arriving at Wittebergen after the long wagon journey. Olive was born shortly afterwards.

Outside the larger towns the population was too scattered to support schools, and mission stations were in any case expected to be self-reliant. But boys had to be educated and Gottlob made strenuous efforts to send first Fred and then Theo to England to Taunton College, a school for the sons of Wesleyan ministers. His children's allowance from the Wesleyans was only six guineas a year, half the amount paid to ministers who had been ordained in England. Perhaps his most pointed letters were written in the interests of his sons' education, as he pleaded for an advance or a loan to pay for it.

* The Wittebergen Native Reserve later became the magisterial district of Herschel, Ciskei, the north-eastern corner of the Cape that bordered on Lesotho. This area has been extensively studied, notably by Colin Bundy, 'Peasants in Herschel', in S. Marks and A. Atmore (eds), *Economy and Society in Pre-industrial South Africa* (1979). The period in which the Schreiners lived in Wittebergen saw the emergence of a relatively prosperous African peasantry later followed, as a result of labour demands placed on the area, by falling productivity, overcrowding and the underdevelopment characteristic of those areas. The Wittebergen Mission Station is described by Gottlob Schreiner's successor, Rev. Arthur Brigg, in a letter to the Wesleyan Mission Society, 13 August 1868. This and other records of the later period are available in the archives of the Methodist Church Overseas Division.

He and Rebecca had thought much about schools in South Africa, but they were more expensive than English ones and 'as far as I have been informed, considerably inferior to most schools at home in various ways'. But Gottlob conceded he had no direct experience of them, having crossed the Orange River nineteen years earlier after a single night in Cape Town and one in Grahamstown. He and Rebecca had decided that 'it would be very much better to get [the children] altogether beyond the reach of native influence, and then if the Lord saw fit to call them for mission work, they would come with a freshness to it'.[31]

It is clear that the only relationship Gottlob could conceive of whites having with Africans was as their mentors. At the same time missionaries saw themselves as a special breed, needing to set an example: they had to keep their distance from the 'natives' but also from white colonial society. The conflict is evident in Rebecca's instructions to Kate when she was living away from the mission home with a white family. She should not, Rebecca advised, 'judge harshly concerning . . . ladies who think servants should be treated as servants, and not as they often are by missionaries, as being of a superior order'. The children of missionaries, she went on, often grew up with very false notions of this matter of how to treat servants and other matters referring to the 'natives'. Missionaries found 'everything they say and do interesting' and they 'placed them in quite a different light from a European, viewed with a kind of romance'. Rebecca had clearly grown cynical of this sentimental patronage, but her calling demanded that like other missionaries she 'desire their welfare, regard them with benevolence', and so she admonished Kate to do, though not 'for their sakes to call good evil and evil good'.[32]

This is one of the rare instances we have of an attempt by Rebecca to contemplate the dilemmas raised by life in an alien society. She appears for the most part to have endured without reflection the transfer from suburban London life to these lonely South African outposts. This, of course, was an essential component of the saintly purpose with which missionaries were imbued. Their sense of a civilizing mission, with its self-denial and self-sacrifice, among 'natives' whose childishness was taken for granted, became a substitute for a sense of identity. If anything, the rigours of their encounters with strange indigenous cultures served to reinforce their conviction that they represented not only a different but an infinitely superior culture.

Not that Gottlob and Rebecca responded in the same way. Gottlob went about his religious work with an almost mindless fervour; the Biblical literalisms of his fundamentalist religious practice were the only ways he knew to convey the new way of life. Yet he continued all his life to feel alien, not as a white missionary in Africa but as a German attached to an English mission society. Reproved many years after he had been identified with the British societies for his failure to submit regular field reports, he pleaded his difficulty in 'writing letters to persons with whom I am personally unacquainted and whom I must address in a strange language'. But he also had an additional difficulty in meeting the requirements of the Society, for he had never been able fully to 'overcome a certain bashfulness from my childhood to address strangers if not first addressed by them, except that they be below me'.[33] He remained an awkward outsider, ingenuous and artless, with a naïve and saintly view of the world, and a record of muddle and incompetence. He was tender and trusting, but a failure as a missionary and head of a household, if not as a loving father: when Rebecca was away he would talk to his children and 'be with them like a child'. His two great passions were his wife and Christ.

About Rebecca we have far less evidence: by Olive's account, she did not reciprocate her husband's affection. She was certainly far better educated than he – she was said to have a great love of literature, and was critical of the 'credulity and unreason' that he revealed in his sermons. To Olive her mother was cold and distant, and several of her brothers and sisters seemed to share these memories of her. She had steeled herself to survive the stern life, and it is conceivable that she was purposefully preparing her children for the harshness of their circumstances.

It was impossible for the Schreiner girls to have regular schooling and Rebecca taught them all they knew. From an early age they were indispensable for household duties at home, and from time to time they also participated in an exchange system with other white families – an informal network which supplied governesses for the education and care of younger children. Children were expected to share in the parents' sense of mission and Rebecca was a stern teacher and moralist. At the age of ten Kate was left in charge of three younger children when Rebecca went to a nearby mission station to give birth to Oliver; Kate was later sent to the family in return for the hospitality they had shown to her mother. Writing to her young daughter about missing the family during her absence, Rebecca enjoined self-restraint: 'Oh it is a great mercy, nay the greatest, to have our wills subdued.' Kate was already expected to know 'the pleasure of giving as superior to that of receiving'. Treated as a little woman, permitted to knit and work her worsted only when her duties allowed, she suffered from headaches, and when she was away from home she had letters from her mother advising her to 'take her pills'. The letters from all the Schreiner children sound prematurely old and care-worn: at the age of twelve Theo wrote of his mother starting to ride out on horseback, 'which I think does her good'.

The Victorian obsession with proper conduct was taken to extremes in the Schreiner family and the girls were 'kept close', even when grown up, as young John Findlay discovered when he began his courtship of Kate, then aged twenty-two. Alarmed, Rebecca persuaded herself that Kate had encouraged his attentions; her idea of feminine propriety had, she confessed, always restrained her from showing kindness to young men: 'A husband-catching mother is a character abhorrent to my every feeling.' The Schreiners refused to prohibit the marriage but made it plain to Kate that they wanted her to abandon it. Kate postponed the marriage for three months to prove herself a dutiful child. This was an agonizing period for her, 'continually reminded of my position, my intended husband talked against, the children forbidden any intercourse with me since they would be polluted'. In the Schreiner household love and marriage were judged unfit for discussion in the presence of the children; John Findlay was only allowed to call on Sundays and he had to undertake to 'behave in the presence of the little ones as if there was nothing between us'.

Rebecca went to some lengths to explain her attitude. 'You likely do not know how difficult it is, living as we do among gross sensual heathen, to preserve that delicacy of thought and feeling so indispensable to a right development of the female character. You will, I trust, not enhance the difficulties.' But Findlay offended even more seriously, for he and Kate were seen exchanging winks in church. This prompted a severe, eloquent letter from Rebecca. 'A place of worship,' she wrote, 'is no place for the exchange of looks which, passed in such a place, are little less than sacrilegious . . . Chaste love is shy and reserved and shrinks from observation.' The Schreiners were unable to reconcile themselves to the marriage even after it had taken place and refused to meet Findlay's parents. John's attempt to protect Kate from her parents' criticism prompted extreme action from Gottlob: he announced that he had 'excommunicated' Kate from taking sacrament in his church. Only the death of another Schreiner baby helped to effect a reconciliation.

Kate's brothers Theo and Fred, by then both in England for their education, felt free to come down on her side of the dispute. After she had left home Theo wrote to her of his sense of relief that he could now express himself freely, 'for I need not be afraid of my letters to you being read by those for whom they were not intended'. How happy Kate must be, he wrote, 'to have escaped from the thraldom and miserable position' she had been placed in at home. He had received reports from their parents about their opposition to the marriage, 'but I am sorry to say that I can't believe a word I was told, for I remember olden times when truth was not the prevailing principle in statements I have heard so solemnly made by lips which ought ever to have given me example as well as precept.'

It was a strong indictment of parents who indoctrinated their children in the standards of a punctilious moral discipline. Was this an indictment of one or both? Theo's letter was silent on the subject of Gottlob but said that he had never understood Rebecca's conduct towards Kate, so 'unnatural and unmotherly, and I am so happy that it is over, and that you will never more be subjected to such tyranny as you have experienced in your lifetime'. Theo had felt at odds with his mother since the age of twelve, and the letter was an expression of personal discontent rather than a rejection of the parental role itself. It was only some six years later that Theo was to head Olive's substitute family in a fashion that Olive described as persecuting, intolerant and dogmatic.[34]

Years later, trying to reconstruct memories of her childhood for Havelock Ellis, Olive said that her father was 'infinitely tenderer to us as children and had a much greater heart than my mother. A woman loves her own little babies with a selfish animal instinct, but, as children grow up, it is continually the father who gives the widest, most sympathetic love.'

Olive, five years old when Kate married and left home, was born on the Wittebergen mission station on 24 March 1855. Rebecca was melancholy that year, and suffered fainting fits which gave her a premonition of death but also a reminder of the glories of the afterlife. She confided to Kate that she had been 'threatened with strange attacks, one of which will, I think, be appointed to dismiss my, I humbly trust, ransomed spirit from this body of sin and death. Oh this feverish dream of being; when, ah when, shall we awake, and how shall we awake? I trust as the redeemed of the Lord with songs of everlasting gladness!' Even so, she had been able on one occasion – after a confinement – to express resentment that she was 'once again inspanned, sometimes much disliking the presence of the yoke'.

Olive was Rebecca's ninth child, though she had already lost three, and of the three children subsequently born only one survived. In a sad but maudlin touch the baby was named Olive Emilie Albertina after her three dead brothers. But Olive was not yet three years old when Rebecca described her as 'still rather self-willed and impetuous, needing much patient firmness. It is however very pleasing to see the effort the dear little thing makes to conquer herself.' The child seems already to have acquired a diffuse sense of guilt, for Rebecca added: 'She often asks "Mama have I been a little better today?" '

Rebecca gave her children a strict English upbringing. It was a mark of gentility to speak English – and Dutch, or Afrikaans, was a forbidden language in the Schreiner household. Olive was later to recall two great whippings in her childhood which she considered did her immense harm 'and made me hate everything in the heavens above and in the earth beneath'. One beating was administered on the occasion when she was swinging on a doorhandle of the Wittebergen house and said, '*Ach*, how nice it is outside.' Because 'Ach' was Dutch she was taken down the little passage into the bedroom where she was born, laid out on her mother's knee, and given about fifty strokes with a bunch of quince rods tied together. 'The bitter wild fierce agony in my heart was against God and man.'

In 1861 the Schreiners were on the move again, this time to Healdtown in the eastern Cape, 250 miles nearer the coast; Gottlob was to run the Wesleyan training institute there which gave industrial training and groomed African candidates for the ministry. Although his letters suggest that the eight years at Wittebergen had been a period of economic hardship, he had in fact managed to amass cattle and sheep, as well as wagons and domestic furniture, all of which now had to be sold.

From all accounts the family were sad to leave Wittebergen. They arrived in the eastern Cape during a severe measles epidemic which the children fortunately survived. Rebecca complained of being overworked, and wrote to Kate: 'Olive and I will have plenty to do.' Olive was then six years old. Her sixteen-year-old sister Alice was in charge of her and her younger brother William's education, together with that of other children in the mission station classroom. Rebecca was keeping house for a family of fifty, of whom forty-four were Africans, while Gottlob struggled to perform his missionary duties and to run the training institute. He failed in both, and four years later was forced to leave the ministry in disgrace for having infringed the strict regulations against trading. After twenty-seven years as a missionary he was thrown onto his own resources, and tried a business venture; within a year he was insolvent; some said his credulity was his undoing. The family lived in considerable poverty for the next few years. Gottlob tried to make ends meet by trading in the district on horseback, selling or bartering skins and packets of sugar and coffee. Rebecca lived in an outhouse in a village, cared for by neighbours.

Gottlob's bankruptcy led to the scattering of the children and marked the end of the family home. Theo, who had returned to South Africa from his English education, taught in Grahamstown from 1866, and the following year became headmaster of a school in Cradock. He then took in the three youngest children, Ettie, now seventeen, Olive, barely twelve, and Will, the youngest at ten.

Most of the accounts of Olive's childhood were compiled by her husband Cronwright for the biography he published shortly after her death, and when those who had known her in her earliest years were still alive. In Wittebergen she was observed as a 'lively and intelligent child, physically powerful and healthy, unusually bright, very shy and sensitive and absorbed almost uncannily in her own thoughts'. An unusually acute observer, the Reverend Zadoc Robinson, visited the Schreiners at Healdtown when Olive was six and described how she addressed him, without any preliminaries, as he was saying goodbye. Olive: 'But you can't go away.' Robinson: 'Why can't I go away?' 'You haven't got your hat and you can't go without a hat.' 'But I can get it.' 'But you can't get it.' 'Why can't I get it?' 'Because I've hidden it.' 'Well, I can find it.' 'But you don't know where it is.' 'I can get the others to find it for me.' To this the child replied: 'But they don't know where it is, and if I forget my personal identity, *I* shan't know where it is, and shan't be able to tell them, and you won't be able to find your hat.'[35]

Olive was to spend much of her life and energy trying to rediscover and reinforce her sense of self. She returned continually to her childhood, to its context of parental, certainly maternal severity; to the brooding presence of a wrathful God watching over children raised with a sense of original sin; to the superior civilizing mission that inspired these Victorian colonizing evangelizers; to the assertion of England's dominance over not only the black heathen but the lesser white breed who spoke Afrikaans. Olive's recall of her early years was extremely self-conscious, even strained. She was to try to recreate the conditions of her own formation in her novels and to struggle to transcend them.

CHAPTER TWO

Governess and Freethinker

At the age of twelve Olive wrote that she wanted above all 'to be clever, to be wise'. In a small book into which she copied poems and other things that interested her, each of the children wrote down what they most wished for: 'Theo, something to do; Ettie – to be at rest . . . Will – to be a soldier'. But when she looked in the glass she saw a 'wicked, keen bright little face' looking back at her 'as though it were someone else'.[1] She was already questioning the authority of received opinion, and wisdom and wickedness, because of this, were becoming blurred for her. Her domestic environment was punitive; she struggled to explain it to herself and to free herself from it.

Most of what we know about her subjective world in childhood comes from her adult writings on other topics. In 'The Dawn of Civilisation', for instance, printed in the *Nation and Athenaeum* in 1921, she describes the origins of her conviction that societies were susceptible to change. She was out on the veld, 'not yet nine years old', puzzled and heartbroken at the life around her.

> Why did everyone press on everyone and try to make them do what they wanted? Why did the strong always crush the weak? Why did we hate and kill and torture? Why was it all as it was? Why had the world ever been made? Why, oh why, had I ever been born?

As she sat looking at a little island ahead of her, the sun began to rise.

> It shot its light across the long, grassy slopes of the mountains and struck the little mound of earth in the water. All the leaves and flowers and grasses on it turned bright gold, and the dewdrops hanging from them were like diamonds; and the water in the stream glinted as it ran.

And, as I looked at that almost intolerable beauty, a curious feeling came over me. It was not what I *thought* put into exact words, but I seemed to *see* a world in which creatures no more hated and crushed [one another], in which the strong helped the weak, and men forgave each other and did not try to crush others but to help. I did not think of it as something to be in a distant future; it was there, about me, and I was in it, a part of it. And there came to me, as I sat there, a joy such as never besides have I experienced, except perhaps once, a joy without limit.[2]

She found inspiration in the Sermon on the Mount as well: it made sense of her experience of punishment, but also gave her a way of dealing with it. 'Love your enemies,' Jesus told his disciples, 'bless them that curse you, do good to them that hate you, and pray for them which despitefully use you, and persecute you.' She ran to her mother with the Bible; she felt her own creed formulated. 'Blessed are the poor in spirit,' the Sermon continued, 'for theirs is the kingdom of heaven. Blessed are they that mourn; for they shall be comforted . . . Blessed are they which do hunger and thirst after righteousness: for they shall be filled. Blessed are the pure in heart for they shall see God.' But her mother rebuffed her, apparently very coldly, and the incident made a lasting impression on her.

It was a particularly important one in that it brought together issues of the state of Christianity at the time, Olive's relationship with her mother, and, most significantly, its consequences for her relationship with herself. Olive later told Arthur Symons, the critic and poet, that her strongest desire as a child was that her mother should understand her;[3] it seems clear from Rebecca's response to Olive's feeling about the sermon that Olive felt deeply misunderstood. In itself the coldness reflects something of the paradox of nineteenth-century Wesleyanism: the fervent devotion to the figure of Jesus without the anger and compassion of the very movement he inspired: the vision of a world where there was no longer the impulse to dominate or oppress, a vision very similar to Olive's on the veld which she described in 'The Dawn of Civilisation'. Of necessity, then, her feeling for Jesus became intensely private.*

In her role as mother, Rebecca was a powerful authority figure in the

---

* She later told Karl Pearson that the dream of her life, and a 'fixed intention' until a few years previously, had been to write a life of Jesus, although she does not indicate what made her abandon the idea. To Karl Pearson, 12 June 1886, *Pearson*.

home. Olive claimed that the beatings she received made her hate 'God and man'; Marion Friedmann, following a basically psychoanalytic model of personality development, thinks it more likely that Olive's resentment was caused by a powerful conflict of feeling. A child beaten by its mother hates the mother, she argues, and not abstractions like 'God' and 'man'. The child is in an intolerable situation in which the hated mother is also the loved mother of infancy, the source of all gratifications. However dreadful the rejection of God must have been to a small child brought up in a religious home, it was the lesser of what were literally two evils. Her aggression towards Rebecca was redirected towards an object easily identifiable with her.[4] Suggestive as this is, it cannot be a definitive account of Olive's childhood, for this kind of explanation, by its very nature, is speculative. It has coherence, however, in the context of Olive's later statement 'My mother has never been a mother to me',[5] her persistent feeling of loneliness and isolation combined with an overwhelming sense of guilt, and her inability to acknowledge feelings of aggression.[6]

Her mother's failure to respond to her excitement over the humanity of the New Testament forced her to take her religious feelings outside the family, outside the domestic structure of authority,* and to affirm the relationship between 'great truths' and solitude for herself. 'To the days when Martin Luther wept and prayed in the convent cells and cloisters of Aubse down to this nineteenth century,' she wrote in her first notebook, in 1865, 'all great truths have first seen the light, [and] the foundation of all great works have been laid, in solitude and silence; whether it were in the heart of great cities or the solitude of everlasting mountains.' She appears to have found her one source of peace – and made her own definition of God – in her feeling for nature, substituting a kind of pantheism for the restricted formulae of Christianity: free will, eternal torment and retributive justice. She had never been able to conceive of God and man and the material universe as distinct from one another, she wrote in 1892 to a Presbyterian minister at Port Elizabeth:

The laws of my mind do not allow it. When I was a little child of five

---

* cf. Terry Eagleton's discussion of the rift between 'imagination' and 'society' in relation to the Brontës, and the way in which her relationship with Heathcliff in *Wuthering Heights* takes Catherine 'outside the family and society into an opposing realm which can be adequately imaged only as "Nature" '; in this way 'both become the "outside" of the domestic structure'. *Myths of Power* (1975), pp. 12, 103.

and sat alone among the tall weeds at the back of our house, this perception of the unity of all things, and that they were alive, and that I was part of them, was as clear and overpowering to me as it is today. It is the one thing I am never able to doubt.

On matters of life and death and immortality, she had confronted these issues in a search for comfort when her baby sister Ellie died at the age of two:

> You ask me, do I believe in Immortality? I cannot conceive of either birth or death, or anything but simple changes in the endless existence: how can I then believe or disbelieve in Immortality in the ordinary sense. *There is Nothing but God!* If you ask me what is the practical effect of this feeling, it is to make all life very precious to me, and also to rob death of all its horrors.
>
> I think I first had this feeling with regard to death clearly when my favourite little sister died when I was nine years old. I slept with her little body until it was buried, and after that I used to sit for hours by her grave, and it was impossible for me then, as it is impossible for me now, to accept the ordinary doctrine that she was living somewhere without a body. I felt then, and have always felt since when I have been brought face to face with death, that it is [in] a larger doctrine than that, [that] joy and beauty must be sought. I used to love the birds and animals and inanimate nature better after she was dead; the whole of existence seemed to me more beautiful because it had brought forth and taken back to itself such a beautiful thing as she was to me. Can you understand the feeling?[7]

Olive always maintained that it was Ellie's death that made her a free-thinker,[8] for at about that time she rejected the organized Christian faith; but hers was a freethought informed by mysticism, an alternative in the awe of a rather undefined 'nature' to her experience of Christianity.

Though she rejected the Church, the Bible always remained significant. She told Havelock Ellis, when they discussed her childhood, that it had been her only education; and Karl Pearson, a colleague in the 1880s, that it was given to her before she could read and was her companion all through childhood: she pressed flowers in it and hid it in a hollow tree in the bush. She then gave it to Pearson, complete with annotations, explaining the significance it had had for her. 'All those marks mean some particular crisis in my life. I never marked, but when it was very important.'* Her underlinings bear witness, particularly in the Psalms, to the depth of her sense of sin, and there is a consistent similarity between the New Testament passages that she marked and the moral position she came to assume and then maintained throughout her life. She was struck over and over again by the importance of loving one's neighbour and giving to others, 'since laying up treasure for self is not rich towards God'; she was impressed by the virtue of charity, which 'suffereth long, and is kind', 'is not easily provoked, thinketh no evil', and – this last became particularly important when she worked, very unhappily, as a governess – 'beareth all things, hopeth all things . . . endureth all things'.[9]

When Olive moved to Cradock after Gottlob's bankruptcy it was to live in a substitute home headed by Theo, then twenty-three, who was helped with the housekeeping by Ettie, by then seventeen and five years Olive's senior. Since Theo ran a school Olive could now get formal tuition for the first time, and she recorded her timetable under the date in her journal, 'Cradock, January 1869':

> 6 to 8 French and German. 9 to 10 Music. 10 to 11 Latin. 11 to 12 Mathematics. 1 to 2 Drawing. 2 to 3 Painting. 3 to 4 Latin. 4 to 5 Mathematics. 6 to 7 Study with Theo. 7 to 9 Read. 10 to 1 Write, etc.

It was an ambitious, probably impossible timetable. It was reading and writing that she worked hardest at, and here she could rely on a private world of thought and imagination; she is remembered walking up and down the lane in front of their house, talking to herself, and as having a 'far, far far away look in her eyes'.

Her three years in Cradock, a small country town, were in fact very unhappy. Cradock had been developed as one of a line of garrison towns on the northern frontier, but declined in military importance as the frontier moved east. Although by the middle of the century the town was being referred to as the Cheltenham of the colony on account of its

---

* The Bible is preserved with Pearson's papers at University College, London. The quotes about it are from the note she sent him with it, 14 December 1886. She practised her handwriting on the inside covers and wrote a note to herself which she explained to Pearson: 'That writing . . . that is on the first page, was written when I was 13, to remind me when I got rich and strong to be tender to everything that was weak and lonely as I was then.' The Bible, which cost tenpence and was distributed by the British and Foreign Bible Society in 1860, still contains Olive's pressed flowers.

nearby spring water, it was still very isolated.[10] Ettie, no real companion for Olive, was content to lead an orthodox life – keeping house for the other children, corresponding with Kate about the family's affairs, and calling on the minister of the Coloured Congregational Church.[11] However, it was through her sister that Olive made her first significant attachment outside the family – with Erilda Cawood, then farming with her husband Richard at Ganna Hoek, twelve miles south of Cradock. Mrs Cawood was a good deal older than Olive, and called her 'my shy little friend with the wondrous eyes'. Within the family, Olive felt defenceless in her lack of belief, for Theo and Ettie were quite as fervently religious as Rebecca, even if Theo had expressed such grave reservations about their mother's treatment of Kate's marriage, and Olive was easily singled out as different. Her relationship with Ettie, a Sabbatarian literalist, became very tense – indeed persecutory, by Olive's account – and her departure from Cradock was followed by great fits of remorse on Ettie's part.

The manner of Olive's movement from Christianity to unbelief would not have been unusual, had she lived in England.[12] It followed the typical pattern for someone from a Wesleyan background with a primarily moral or intuitive critique of the Bible. In attributing her loss of faith to her baby sister's death, Olive expressed the same doubts about the morality of Christian eschatology as did many members of the secular and freethought movement in the middle of the century. Further, her sense of herself was of someone 'outside' her society, marginal to it; she felt both rejecting of it and rejected by it. What was extraordinary was the fact that this crisis of faith had occurred in a particularly closed culture, in which a system of theology co-terminous with family authority had not yet been challenged. Still, her age and sex would have put her at some disadvantage, even in England. There people tended to become freethinkers in their thirties or forties, few women – aside from very public individuals like Harriet Martineau and George Eliot – were involved in the secular movement, and the doubts of adults and the well-educated tended to be taken more seriously than those of children or the poor. Olive would have been triply stigmatized: she was adolescent, she was a girl, and she had had almost no formal education.

But however painful the individual's crisis of faith, in a country like England it could proceed with some sense of reference-point. Olive was entirely alone in the relatively advanced conclusions to which she had come. There was at least a secular movement in England, as important a part of the response to industrialization as evangelicalism. The more radical secularists, particularly in the latter half of the century, emphasized the creation of an alternative culture, and it was within this grouping that socialist pioneer Edward Carpenter, later to be one of Olive's closest friends, was able to find the roots of a sympathetic political tradition. There was at least discussion of the impact of evolutionary theory on man's conception of the Creation and, from the 1870s, a discussion of the assumptive status of the concept of immortality in journals and learned societies. In South Africa there was nothing of this. Only Bishop J. W. Colenso, who had trained as a Cambridge mathematician before he began mission work in Natal, and became bishop of that province, wrote a critical examination of the Pentateuch, and was as a result excommunicated from his church.[13] As late as 1889 the curator of the Albany Museum in Grahamstown lamented the absence of a first-class microscope anywhere in the country and the fact that only two other institutions were cultivating natural science 'from a scientific point of view'.[14]

When Olive was fifteen in October 1870, Theo, taking Will with him, left for the diamond fields in Griqualand West, hoping to make money on the quick for their parents as well as for themselves, and Olive was sent to her first position as governess to the Orpen family at Barkly East, some thirty miles north-east of Cradock. She left Cradock in an extremely agitated state of mind; the extent of her distress can be measured in a series of letters from Ettie who, once Olive had left, reproached herself for the 'hard wrong sinning things' she had thought against her sister. She 'burst out sobbing and crying' at a letter Olive sent her and knew how 'hard and sore and dreadful' her sister must feel. Ettie wished she could prove her love of Jesus 'by having you once more and acting differently', but she resigned herself. 'He knows best, and if it is His will that I may never make up for the past, I would be content.'

While Ettie found solace in religious resignation Olive, pilloried first by her mother and then by her brother and sister, was less easily comforted. On her way to her post at Barkly East she spent a few weeks with her twenty-five-year-old sister Alice, married to Robert Hemming, the resident magistrate at Burgersdorp. Here she was heard by Alice 'walking up and down her room nearly all night, talking to herself, often crying, then suddenly laughing'. When Alice went in to her room very early in the morning to see if she wanted anything, she found Olive fully dressed and looking rather weary, clearly not having slept at all. When Olive emerged from her room, a visitor to the home described her as 'elegantly dressed in the style of the time; wearing a neat little hat from which a thick veil fell down and hid her face from my view, which probably enough was keen'. She was already known as an unusual, even eccentric young woman.

Even at this age she made a strong impression on the people she met. Physically she was small and slight with smooth skin, good colour, thick brown hair and large, dark eyes that were remarked on throughout her life. She is described as being of a retiring disposition but animated in speech, talking brilliantly, and dominating social gatherings without effort. Children loved her and she would improvise stories for them that went on for days on end. Always sought out, she could excite strong feelings of envy as well as admiration, a facet of her effect on people that she tended, perhaps slightly unconvincingly, to deny or ignore. Her feelings of guilt, despair, self-hatred and an obsession with death were expressed only in her diary. Unable to share her inner conflicts she maintained a precarious balance between health and breakdown even as a teenager: travelling from place to place, in contact with family and family friends, exciting general interest wherever she was, but anxious and self-doubting all the while.

When she moved on to the Orpens' house at Barkly East Olive was still in an overwrought condition, and the idea that she should help the children with their lessons was soon abandoned. Instead she spent a few weeks at Hermon, another twenty miles north, where her uncle and aunt, the Rollands, ran the mission station. Here she met her first avowed freethinker. Willie Bertram, then employed in the Native Affairs Department of the Cape Colony, was touring the magistracy. 'Don't get spooney on him,' Olive was urged in a note from the husband of the Rollands' daughter Emmie; 'he's very intellectual they say.'

'There was no house within fifty miles,' Olive told Ellis thirteen years later, 'so he slept there; the next morning he talked with me for a little while and after that I saw him twice for half an hour, and then I never saw him again.' He had with him a copy of Herbert Spencer's *First Principles*, the text which was to assuage much of her religious anguish. She had only three days in which to read the book, but many years later he could still recall the sensation of lying before the fire with it. 'I always think that when Christianity burst on the dark Roman world it was what that book was to me, I was in such complete blank atheism. I did not believe in my own nature, in any right or wrong, or certainty.' Bertram was the model for Waldo's Stranger in *The Story of an African Farm*; just after Olive wrote that part of the novel, six years later, she heard he had committed suicide, at the age of thirty-five. She understood that life must have been 'too sore for him', as she told Ellis, but he had helped her, and 'I cannot bear to think of all he suffered before he did it'.

First Principles had been published in England nine years before; Spencer intended its doctrine of the Unknowable as the final resolution of the struggle between science and religion which had developed thirty years previously and was then at its height. The work appeared only three years after *The Origin of Species* and two years after *Essays and Reviews*, in which liberal clergymen suggested how Christian teaching would need to be revised in the light of both German Biblical criticism and the findings of evolutionary science. Olive, of course, had no background in this debate, which was conducted largely in the periodicals of the Victorian intelligentsia; she encountered a style of argument which was completely new to her. In acknowledging the irrationality and absurdities associated with the defence of existing religious creeds, Spencer validated her doubts, but he also provided her with an alternative to nihilism. He introduced the possibility that religion expressed 'some eternal fact', that 'positive knowledge' could never fill 'the whole region of possible thought': one always asked what lay beyond.[15] Thus there would always be a place, in his words, for something of the nature of religion, for its subject matter passed the sphere of the intellect. As for the chronic antagonism between religion and science, their only reconciliation lay in a belief in an Absolute transcending not just human knowledge, but human conception.[16]

Olive expressed what she learned from Spencer in characteristically Spencerian terms. 'He helped me believe in a unity underlying all nature,' she told Ellis: it was her formal introduction to scientific naturalism. Until then the Bible had been the only explanation available to her; now she learned that 'all matter is alive', that the social order reflected a deeper biological order, and that progress was not an accident but a necessity – indeed a law underlying the whole of organic creation. And just as Spencer's evolutionism referred to the cosmic scheme of things in so abstract a way as to be entirely ahistorical, so Olive's sense of

social disengagement could be translated into a belief in the unim-
portance of an individual life. But at the same time as Spencer insisted on
the universality of religious belief, he opposed all dogma and strict
definitions of good and evil: suddenly creeds were not priestly inventions
or supernaturally devised, but expressed a basic human need. All religions
became valid. Olive's receptiveness to his ideas led her to a religious
tolerance that was both eclectic and unacceptable within the parochial
communities in which she lived.

After the brief but crucial meeting with Bertram at Hermon, Olive
moved to two other homes in quick succession, first to Aliwal North with
a cousin and then to Dordrecht, to the home of the Reverend Zadoc
Robinson. Since Gottlob and Rebecca were now virtually destitute and
could not support her, she had to be passed between the homes of family
members, relatives and friends until she was of an age to be hired
formally as a governess. Rebecca was very conscious that others were
'offering her a home when I [have] none for myself and so none to offer
my child',[17] though it is not clear whether she realized the psychological
effect of these constant moves between different families on a young
girl at a formative period of her life. Nor do we know how Rebecca
responded to Olive's loss of faith. She appears never to have referred
to it.

Olive stayed at Dordrecht for about a year. Family letters indicate that
for the most part she was relatively happy: the Robinsons were kind to
her and the house was comfortable.[18] It was here that she began the reading in contemporary European theology, science and anthropology that
sustained her until she went to England ten years later; in the absence of
a sympathetic culture from which to draw support, books and chance
meetings acquired a special importance. She read avidly: after Herbert
Spencer, John Stuart Mill, Buckle's *History of Civilisation in England*,
four volumes of *The Spanish Conquest of America*, Liddle's *Student's
Rome* and Carl Vogt's very influential *Lectures on Man*. Books could be
sent round the district from the little Cradock library, for which she felt
a special affection after borrowing from it Darwin's *Variation of Plants
and Animals*.[19] She tended to describe her allegiances in moral and
emotional terms; Mill, for instance, was 'the only man to whose moral
teaching I am conscious of owing a profound and unending debt'.[20] She
was finding her way to a morality independent of an organized religion in
which she had never had confidence, and to scientific rationalism through

books like Vogt's *Lectures on Man*. Though progressive in their stress on the data of physical anthropology, the *Lectures* were convinced of the mental inferiority of the Negro and reproduced the racist view of civilization that had sent her parents to Africa a generation before.*

Robinson was struck by how widely and variously she read: 'She spoke to me of Herbert Spencer's works which surprised me, as at that time they were rarely found in the Colony.' It was apparent that 'she had *read* and she had *thought*', though he was also struck by 'the reserved territories she had in her mentality'. By this he meant not that she was reticent but that she did not reveal all her thinking; she had apparently already experienced the limits of intellectual tolerance in these colonial communities. She was, however, outspoken to him on the relation of the Church and its Ministry to Marriage, affirming – at the age of sixteen – that she did not believe the Church added anything of sanctity and permanence to the ceremony.

Although there was almost no chance for her to discuss her reading in the small towns and on the farms where she lived, in Dordrecht she was one of a group of young people who met at Robinson's Wesleyan manse in the evenings, for 'conversation of the freest kind, with music and coffee at the close'. According to Robinson she became very intimate with two of them, a Mr and Miss Gau from Hesse. Julius Gau had arrived in Johannesburg in 1860 to represent a Swiss insurance company[21] and, as was often the case, was accompanied by his sister, about whom little is known except that Olive nursed her through typhoid fever.

Olive's relationship with Julius Gau had a highly destructive effect on her. On this all her biographers – except Cronwright-Schreiner, who fails to mention Gau at all – are agreed, though the factual basis of the accounts is thin. Olive left the Robinson household for a while to nurse Miss Gau through her fever, and after her recovery left Dordrecht for Hertzog to spend some time with her parents. The journey was one of over a hundred miles, and Robinson described it as 'very toilsome'. Julius Gau travelled with her – although at this time it was unusual and most improper for an

* Vogt's *Lectures on Man: His Place in Creation, and in the History of the Earth* (1864) were introduced by James Hunt, President of the Anthropological Society of London, whose view of a causal relationship between race and civilization was not disputed during this period, though his formulation was extreme. See Gay Webber, 'Science and Society in Nineteenth Century Anthropology', *Hist. Sci* xii (1974), p. 270.

unmarried woman to travel unchaperoned with a man. When she wrote
to Kate after her arrival at Hertzog she made almost no reference to the
journey, a particularly striking omission in a family correspondence that
was normally full of safe arrivals and dangers on the road.[22] There
followed an obliquely understated letter to her sister on 18 August:
'Mama said she would write you all the news by this post, but being at
Balfour she may forget to do so. So I had better tell you what little there
is myself. I am engaged to be married to a Mr Julius Gau of Dordrecht.'
Olive couldn't say when they would marry. 'It may be very soon. That is in
four or five months; or it may not be for a year at least to come. I will be
able to tell you more definitely next week.' But she remained defiantly
nonchalant: if they were not married in January, they would not be for
another year, 'and before that there is no knowing what may not have
taken place'. And asking Kate not to mention her engagement to anyone
in writing, she continued: 'As a rule I think it great nonsense to wish such
a thing not to be spoken of, but circumstances alter cases, you know,'
concluding, almost irritably, that people take 'such an interest in other
people's affairs that when one person knows the whole country knows in a
few weeks'.[23]

The next letter to Kate, nine days later, mentions Kate's children and
a journey of their father's, but nothing of her possible marriage; it
appears that at some stage the engagement, if such it was, was broken off.
By the end of September Olive was in despair, as her journal entries
reveal: everything was 'all dark, dark, no hope, none, wish for nothing;
the only bright spot is my foolish dream . . . the waking in the morning
is hell'. The next day she made some 'horrid verses':

> I gaze across the dark abyss
> From the golden brink of heaven
> To the gulf below
> From deathless woe.

Olive's withdrawal – and her isolation – are evident from a series of
anxious family letters. 'Poor dear Olive is passing through great trials and
I can do so little to comfort her,' Rebecca wrote to Kate at the beginning
of October. But she made an abstraction out of it straight away, remarking
stiffly how difficult it was 'to write about things one would find it quite a
relief to talk of'.[24]

In the Buchanan-Gould biography (in which Julius Gau is wrongly named Zaar) the secrecy over the professed engagement to Olive is explained by the suggestion that 'he was a man of far greater sophistication than Olive, who was indulging in an old trick to enable him to make love to the girl without binding himself too irrevocably. Had he been sincere in his love, he would surely have wished the news to be broadcast.'[25] Meintjes' biography is emphatic that Olive 'allowed him to seduce her. She missed a period, and she became terrified that she was pregnant. Julius Gau promised that if it was really so, he would stand by her and marry her. They thus became engaged, but he did not really want to marry her, and neither did Olive want to marry him for she soon found him to be quite different from the man she had imagined.'[26] This is pure supposition, based only upon Olive's uncertainty about the announcement of the engagement, her mention of 'next week', and the wry comment about 'circumstances altering cases'.

Whatever the nature of Olive's relationship with Gau, she clearly could not confide in parents who had treated Kate's winking in church during her courtship by Findlay as blasphemy. The restrained letter of 18 August to Kate was as far as she dared go, and its references remain elliptical and obscure. If she had been guilty not of any sexual transgression but merely of the suspicion of unchaste behaviour, that too would have brought on her extremely harsh parental sanction. Rebecca in fact emerges from this episode sympathetic to Olive's distress, which suggests that she drew no drastic conclusions about Olive's conduct. 'You must not be vexed with me,' she wrote to Kate, 'that I do not throw more light on Olive's affair. I can't. We are in the dark too.'[27] It is quite possible that it was nothing more than a broken tryst, but one which Olive had invested with great emotion. She was already very private, even secretive, about her personal affairs and the habit of preserving her own confidences was soon ingrained. Her independence was vital to her, it is true, but although she rejected social condemnation in a thoroughly conformist society, she could not easily expose herself to it, particularly at the age of seventeen.

Soon after the Gau episode, because she was sleeping badly and had so little appetite, she was invited to join Theo and Ettie, still at the diamond fields.[28] Theo and his friend John Pursglove had acquired a claim of their own at Du Toit's Pan, the first of the dry diamond diggings. In 1870, when they made their first, unsuccessful visit to the Fields, there were said to be a thousand diggers on all the Vaal river sites;* eighteen months later New Rush alone, the richest of the dry diggings, had an estimated population of ten thousand Africans and four to five thousand whites. Within two weeks of its discovery in July 1871, claims at this 'new rush' were selling for between £20 and £100, within three months for £2,000 to £4,000; it was estimated that people who bought a half- or quarter-claim were getting their purchase money back in a week or two. One Englishman at the Fields advised 'any young, active, strong, "smart", and above all, *steady*, young man with a few hundreds to spare' to go out there; his list of expenses for two men working together for six months indicates how casual the move could be – first-class fares to South Africa, a tent, bedding, cooking utensils, a couple of sieves, a pick, a couple of shovels, a crowbar, several buckets, and 'four Kafirs at 30s per month'.

Whites took it for granted that Kafirs – the word is derived from the Arabic for infidel – were there to work for them; the New Rush correspondent of the *Natal Mercury* merely noted that the blacks might 'regard with astonishment the sudden rise of so large a town by the white people'. Indeed Europeans ascribed the same civilizing function to the Fields as they had to the missions: the Fields were a 'School in which the Natives are taught the Theory of Modern Civilization'. Here they learned lessons in reconciling 'the rights and duties of labour and capital, of muscular force and of intellectual power'. For Europeans, on the other hand, the pleasure of camp life was said to lie in the freedom from landlords, rates and taxes, and a chance to 'sit under an awning and sort' while Kafirs engaged in 'the more active operations' of picking, shovelling, hauling, breaking or sifting.

Theo, Ettie and Olive were at the New Rush when claims were still worked by individuals. None of the administering authorities in the territory had been prepared for the rush, and housing, hospitals, water supplies and sanitation had to be improvised. Diggers and their wives, sisters and children lived in tents; fresh vegetables were very expensive, and most had to settle for bread and meat. Fever, diarrhoea and dysentery, scurvy and colic were especially common in the summer months, and the death rate in Kimberley – as New Rush was renamed in 1873 – only began to go down after the township became a municipality in 1878 and sanitary regulations were introduced.

* The term 'digger' refers to the Europeans who went to the Fields to stake diamond claims, although they hired Africans to do the manual work of the claim.

Nor was the work automatically profitable. Working by hand it took months to dig out a claim thirty-foot square to a depth of thirty or forty feet. And although Du Toit's Pan yielded large stones, often more than a hundred carats, diggers were warned against expecting daily or even weekly finds. Other ways of making money had to be found: the wives of the poorer diggers made bread, cakes, baskets and trays which their children carried round the claims; diggers could also sell water if their claim included a well. It was an arduous existence, and the concern with diamond prices and the anxiety that Theo should find a 'very large one' that come through in Olive's letters to Kate are probably typical of life for the majority of Europeans at the Fields.[29]

The 'constant nervous excitement' of the digger's work and its equally frequent frustrations were felt to be responsible for all the gambling and drinking that went on at the Fields: John Matthews, one of the few qualified doctors there, estimated that seventy per cent of illness among the whites could be traced to the effects of alcohol. Laws against gambling were passed in 1873, though Matthews commented scornfully that there was little difference between the 'precarious business of digging for diamonds and gambling at a faro table'. The *Digger's Song*, to banjo accompaniment, summed up the need for both drink and resilience:

> Now straying cattle and wayward 'boys',
> And diamonds never handy,
> Have brought me down, and all my joys
> Are centred in Cape Brandy;
>
> . . .
>
> Bad luck, however, cannot last,
> A turn must come some day,
> A ninety-carat would change the past
> And make the future gay.

However unsteady or spectacular the digger's life, however, it was only made possible by a racial division of labour codified in a government proclamation of 10 August 1872. Regulations of the earlier, ad hoc, Diamond Diggers' Protection Society stipulated that no licence to dig should be granted to a native, and that no one could buy diamonds from any servant, 'black or white, without a certificate from such servant's master or mistress'. The rules lost all semblance of legal validity after

Britain annexed Griqualand West in 1871;* there were riots in New Rush and an outraged letter to *The Times* the following year when Africans and Coloured started to work their own claims. Hence the significance of the 1872 proclamation which regulated the fields. Licences could now be held by Africans and Coloured, but prospective claim-holders had to be certified of good character by a magistrate or justice of the peace. Servants had to produce a certificate of registration on demand and have it endorsed on taking their discharge; to leave the diggings lawfully, a servant had to produce the endorsed certificate and take out a pass under a system of labour control used first by farmers and later extended into the industrial era. All the digger memoirs indicate this preoccupation with social control and a generalized suspicion of the African.

In that Olive was living the life of a white at the Fields, she performed the conventional role of a white woman – she tidied up the tent with their 'boy' or servant, made trips to the river with her brother and sister, picked flowers, taught in the New Rush school every evening – but she also read (Mill, Darwin and Buckle) and wrote.† It was at this point in her life that she first started to write seriously – stories, now, not merely diary entries. She wrote part of a story entitled 'The Ghost' and worked on 'The Story of a Diamond', which she called 'very poor'. By June 1873, seven months after her arrival at the Fields, she had written the first chapter of *Undine*, and had 'thought out' and started *Other Men's Sins*, possibly the original of *From Man to Man*, her unfinished novel about prostitution. The titles she used in her diary record of her writing changed frequently, and it is difficult to know which of the early drafts survived unchanged, but during her time on the diamond fields Olive

---

* Up to this time the Orange Free State was claiming the administration of the diggings; however, the ownership of the diamond fields was still in dispute. The Griqua leader appealed to Britain for protection, since Britain had acknowledged Griqua claims to the territory by treaty in 1836 and 1846, and an arbitration court awarded the territory to the Griquas. Britain annexed it in 1871 under the title of Griqualand West, and a payment of £90,000 was made to the Orange Free State for the loss of the title. See H. J. and R. E. Simons, *Class and Colour in South Africa, 1850–1950* (1969), pp. 34–7.

† European women usually appear in the digger memoirs as washerwomen and seamstresses on the one hand, or as fashionably dressed 'sirens' at the roulette table on the other. These women were 'of a speculative turn, but without family ties . . . attracted to the new Eldorado, as much as the men had been, to seek their fortunes'. See J. W. Matthews, *Incwadi Yami, or Twenty Years' Personal Experience of South Africa* (1867), p. 41.

worked on characters and themes later recognizable in all three of her novels: *Undine*, *From Man to Man*, and *The Story of an African Farm*.

This period also marked the onset of a chest condition that remained with her for the rest of her life. As a child she had been robust to the point that her mother made her an exception when it came to wrapping up the children against the weather: 'Oh, it doesn't matter about Olive.' Later, Olive was to offer several different explanations of her changed state of health. She told Fan Schreiner, Will's wife, that her illness started when she was sixteen and still living at Dordrecht with the Robinson family, and was caused by her sitting in a Cape cart during a four-day journey to or from Queenstown with the rainwater dripping down her neck.[30] In 1884 she gave a somewhat fuller account to Havelock Ellis:

> Did I ever tell you how my chest first got bad? I was four days quite without food, and travelling all the time; I had nothing but a little cold water all that time. I had no money to buy food. When I ate the first mouthful at the end of the time I got this horrible agony in my chest, and had to rush out, and for weeks I never [lay] down night or day. I suffocated even if I leaned back. Ever since that if I get to a place that is close and damp and hot, it comes back. I have been to many doctors. Some say it is an affection of the heart, some say it is asthma of a very peculiar kind; they all say they have never seen a case just like it, and I don't like to tell them how it began. Somehow one can't go back into the past without blaming those that are dearest to one.[31]

On another occasion Olive told Ellis that she arrived home from Kimberley in 1873 – presumably from this same journey – 'and was received very coldly. When she began eating, the agony was intense. She rushed outside and lay on the ground. They then were kinder to her.'

In spite of her confusion it is unquestionably the case that her ill-health developed after the Gau episode, at a time when she was also without a stable home or family, and was needing to work and rework her sense of herself in relation to her parents and other adults. She was especially sensitive on issues of coldness and kindness: if you love, how do you show it? Her illness provided only the most neurotic of solutions, but it may have been necessary given the culture she had to negotiate.

Only in the light of her dissatisfaction with the mothering she received and her subsequent guilts about love and attachment can we infer a relationship between her illness and the affair with Julius Gau. We know from the markings in her Bible that she had been particularly struck by one passage in Romans 8: 'to be carnally minded *is* death; but to be spiritually minded *is* life and peace', and by the necessity of suffering implied in another: 'For as much then as Christ hath suffered for us in the flesh, arm yourself likewise with the same mind: for he that hath suffered in the flesh hath ceased from sin.'[32] Her symptoms – which were frequent and acute – might then be interpreted as an unconscious attempt to free herself from the sinfulness of her sexuality.*

From the early 1870s onwards there are increasing references in family letters to her physical condition. Ettie felt that a change would do her good but for a while she could not be prevailed upon to take one: Theo was not finding many diamonds, and there was always anxiety about money. This did not prevent her from dreaming about travelling to far places, and she wrote to Kate that Theo had promised to send her to America, if he got a very large diamond, to study 'at one of the large colleges that they have there for ladies'. It was the great wish of her life, she continued, but she was determinedly – and rather formally – subdued: 'I hope that it is destined to be realised one of these days, and not like so many of our hopes to come to nothing.'[33] Her journal entries about her writing are interspersed with feelings of hopelessness: she didn't believe she would ever do anything in the world, didn't know what to make of herself, was a 'queer mixture of good and bad'.

Olive left Kimberley in November 1873 to stay with her sister, Alice Hemming, in Fraserburg, 300 miles away in the heart of the Karoo, the semi-desert area of the Cape whose scenery she evoked so memorably in *The Story of an African Farm*. Will, then sixteen and still with Theo and Ettie, had somehow got hold of £5 and gave it to her, but she could not afford to buy food. It was a demanding journey, probably the one that ended with a cold reception. Olive, in any case, felt that Alice's nature was a suspicious, somewhat difficult one,[34] and she may not have been looking forward to the visit, though she enjoyed Alice's children very much.

Soon after her arrival Alice introduced her to Dr John Brown and his

---

* Perhaps this gives an overly 'psychogenic' bias to Olive's asthma; unfortunately we have no information at all about the state of her respiratory system in childhood.

wife Mary, a niece of the Cape liberal politician Saul Solomon.* Olive was very taken with them: they were like 'two stars that shone in my sky when all the rest was dark'. Preoccupied with her own depression, even with thoughts of suicide, she was reassured by the strength of feeling the Browns had for one another: Olive found it 'so wonderful' that Mary should cry such '*bitter* tears' at the prospect of a brief separation from the man to whom she had already been married for five years.

Mary Brown later wrote a rather self-effacing memoir of Olive. From the time they met, she says, when Olive was eighteen and she twenty-six with young children, Olive held her 'with a sort of subtle power', though 'I did not know that I had made any sort of impression upon her':

> The arrival of a young girl like Olive Schreiner to stay amongst us for a time was a novelty, and I, for one, looked forward to her coming with curiosity. Her sister had told me that she was very pretty and clever but very peculiar, and 'had no religion' . . . When I went to call on the newcomer I entered the house by a side door and so saw her without her seeing me. I stood and looked at her, for she seemed like one walking in her sleep. Backwards and forwards on the long front *stoep* [verandah] she walked rapidly with her small hands clenched behind her back, her long hair fell like a mantle over her shoulders, and her soft white muslin dress clung closely to her girlish figure. She was talking to herself and, though she looked before her, she was quite oblivious of her surroundings.
> . . . I asked Mrs H [Alice Hemming] what she was doing, and she replied: 'She is like that sometimes. Even when she was a child she would walk about, talking to herself.'[35]

Mary Brown wanted to record a friendship, a 'constancy of . . . affection', and seems to have felt that her husband, then thirty years old, better understood Olive's 'heresies' and 'unorthodox views'. This may have been true; the reminiscences of his practice that he wrote forty years later indicate an observant and thorough doctor, concerned that childbirth

---

* John Brown was born in Cape Town, left for England with his family at the age of five, and returned to the Cape as a doctor at the age of twenty-two. He was appointed district surgeon of Fraserburg in 1865, speaking no Dutch and with his nearest colleague ninety miles away. See E. H. Burrows, *A History of Medicine in South Africa* (Cape Town and Amsterdam 1958), pp. 325–6. Saul Solomon was one of the opponents of the 1856 Masters and Servants Act, designed to enforce discipline on ex-slaves, pastoralists, peasants and a rural proletariat. Simons and Simons, *Class and Colour*, p. 24.

should be made safer and less humiliating for women, and interested in the culture around him. He recalls his second confinement at Fraserburg, at which an old African woman was present as midwife; the husband, a merchant, told him a couple of days later that it was

> something quite new and unheard of for them to have a man attending to their wives, and they will always wish to be present; nor would their wives wish to have it otherwise; very many of these peopl? have never consulted a doctor in their lives before; that is just what your predecessor forgot.
>
> . . . Those 'ignorant' Boers, as they are often called, had a natural delicacy and refinement that led them to see in its true light the anomaly of what, even in these days of women doctors, we must still call the usual custom of men attending women in their confinements.[36]

Olive spent much of her time in Fraserburg talking to Dr Brown. One of the subjects of their discussions was a decision that she had recently taken to study medicine. She had read John Russell's *History and Heroes of the Art of Medicine* at the Diamond Fields, and Dr Brown 'entered into her hopes and plans'. He kept himself informed of medical developments in England and Scotland – he subscribed to *The Lancet* and was the first doctor in South Africa to try out Lister's carbolic acid method of anti-sepsis[37] – and was able to advise her about training possibilities. He told her, for instance, that if she wanted to become a doctor she would have to go to England or America. Olive saw herself as following a traditional family interest in doctoring, and she had no inclination to nurse, although nursing was just beginning to be systematized in the Colony. The trained nurses that there were tended to be organized through religious orders and, in any case, were not paid.[38]

Whatever her own ambitions, the family's poverty made it imperative that she find work. She visited Gottlob and Rebecca in Hertzog in April 1874, found Gottlob wearing Will's cast-off clothes, and decided to answer an advertisement for a governess straight away.[39] Governesses were in some demand because qualified teachers – often men – aimed to open their own schools in the towns, and even the better-off rural families found it hard to attract teachers to live on their farms. But governesses were always much less well-paid, and had no redress against their employer's demands to help out in whatever way he asked.

For the next seven years, from 1874 to 1881, Olive worked as a governess. While the earlier, informal teaching arrangements had been more like expressions of hospitality towards her, she was now definitely placed at an ambiguous point in the social structure: she became a 'higher servant', socially subservient but culturally superior.[40] Within the contradictions of her position she experienced the extremes of a 'delicious' independence – 'It took me years to save the £60 that brought me to England, but it was so delicious'[41] – and deep loneliness. It was also during these years that she completed two novels and worked on a third, exploring and asserting a series of positions on women, personal freedom, religion and love. It may be that this was what she meant when she described herself as having 'uncurled' for the first time since the age of nine;[42] the novels which she wrote during these years in teaching became, in a way, her experience of herself.

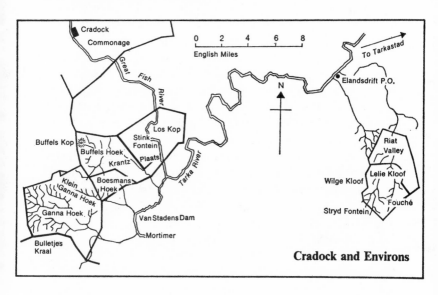

Cradock and Environs

Olive's departure from Hertzog upset Rebecca, who would have liked her to stay on in spite of the financial pressures. But Olive disliked Hertzog, she told Kate, was 'determined to do something for herself', and was 'not one who yields to advice'.[43] Her first position as governess, with George Weakly and his family in Colesberg, over fifty miles away, lasted for most of 1874. Weakly was an agent and auctioneer; he had a shop and edited and owned the local paper, and Olive described the work in a letter to her mother. She started before breakfast and was in school with the children till one o'clock. After dinner she worked in the shop with Mrs Weakly till sunset. 'This is the hard part of my day's work and I like it less and less every day.' By the time supper was over 'and the little ones put to bed Mrs W and I get to needlework which we keep on till half past ten'. There was no machine, she told Rebecca, so she had a good deal to do.

But the work got harder still. Olive had to correct proofs for the newspaper – at this time journalism was very much a one-man business – and said that she used to sleep in her clothes from weariness. There is also the possibility of some kind of sexual advance from Weakly. (He was thirty-three, Olive nineteen.) Later she told Ellis that he tyrannized her and tried to kiss her, but exerted a fascination over her: finally he 'did something which made her leave' but told her that until now she had stayed 'from her own desire'.[44] In addition, it was proving hard to keep her writing going; she had been with the Weaklys a good two months before she was able to do any work on her novel.

She found another post at Klein Ganna Hoek, near Cradock, with the Stoffel Fouchés, who were friends of the Cawoods and had a neighbouring farm. Fouché only paid her £30 a year, she wrote to Kate, 'but after the first quarter I am to have Mrs Cawood's children and several others to teach, and hope at least £40'. Although her chest was badly affected by heavy rains a month after her arrival, she soon became much calmer. She was enormously relieved to be away from Colesberg, 'that most miserable of all the stony holes on the face of the earth', and she enjoyed the quietness of the tiny Dutch community 'buried among the mountains'.[45] She was also able to read what she wanted. There had been a public library in Cradock since 1858, its collection enlarged by the books of an English doctor who had come to the area as a district surgeon.* Rebecca sent Olive twenty-one shillings for her subscription; she was reading Shelley, and Spencer again. She was happy to be near the Cawoods, and used to visit them regularly, walking over from the Fouchés 'swinging her hat in her hand backwards and forwards'.

It was at Klein Ganna Hoek – where she felt a 'vague restlessness', a

---

* Rural libraries tended to become established through individual bequests, and it was only in the larger towns that parliamentary grants were given for their development. See Alan F. Hattersley, *An Illustrated Social History of South Africa* (Cape Town 1969), p. 244. The Cradock library is described in Alan F. Hattersley, *A Victorian Lady at the Cape 1849–1851* (Cape Town 1951), pp. 1, 50.

'sense of joy to come'[46] – that Olive wrote most of her first novel, *Undine*, about an irreligious and much-maligned young woman. There was no railway within a hundred miles, and Cradock was twenty-five miles by road. The houses of the adjoining Fouché and Cawood farms were on the southern slopes of a mountain, and Olive's room looked straight up it. Building materials were scarce in the district and floors were made of mud; Olive's room was not in the main part of the house but a flat-roofed lean-to, and it leaked badly. It contained a primitive bedstead and a box for her books; when the rain was heavy she used to put an umbrella over herself.

After a while, however, she succumbed to a sense of claustrophobic isolation and a state of ill health that were mutually reinforcing. She only went into Cradock once in the first eight months of her stay and she longed for the day when she would live in a little room all by herself and be 'free, freer, freest'. On the other hand she was very 'ill and low-spirited' and ached for someone to look after her, for some mothering: 'Everyone loves me here but I want to be loved down upon, not loved up to.' Only her writing was going well, but 'that dreadful writing out' of *Undine* was still to come – she planned to finish the first draft in July, and the rewriting in August. The writing, of course, went more slowly than she anticipated, and she made a series of rather discontinuous, absent-minded entries in her journal. In August she was reading Mill's *Logic* with the aid of candles, but hadn't written a line for three weeks: 'If only I could live for ever.' A week later she was being driven 'half mad' in the schoolroom, and in September she was berating herself for her slowness: 'I don't get on very fast but mean to do better in future, always do.' Now she gave up the idea of going to America that she and Theo had discussed at the Diamond Fields; it was impossible to save enough. She turned down her brother-in-law John Findlay's offer of help with the fare, and insisted on sending Rebecca some of what money she did have for matting and blinds. All her family's attempts at supporting her materially were rejected, as though they would compromise the choices she was making about her life: 'I made up my mind when I was quite a little child' Olive told Kate, 'that as soon as I was able I would support myself for I see no reason why a woman should be dependent on her friends any more than a man should.'[47]

It is clear that Olive found her work as a governess very trying; at the same time she was a capable teacher and urged on her employers the

importance of educating girls as well as boys. The work was done solely
from her desire for independence, but she liked it when her charges made
progress or showed signs of thought, and she enjoyed teaching them to
recite poetry. But the salary was always an issue. She needed more money
than she could earn with the Fouché family and she began thinking of
moving at the end of the year. In the end the children's provocation gave
her a good reason for handing in her notice. Her description of the
event reveals both the pettiness and the powerlessness of a governess's
situation. 'Yesterday in school,' she wrote in her diary, 'Annie had
twenty-two words and Andrew twenty-four. She began to beat and stamp
him and when school went out she seized the slate. I told her to put it
down; she struck me.' Olive advertised in the *Cradock Advertiser* for a
position, though all the old longing to become a doctor had surfaced
again. A reply came from a Mr Martin, an ex-minister in the Dutch
Reformed Church who was now farming at Ratel Hoek in the Cradock
hinterland. Olive let him know that she could not teach religion since she
was a freethinker; he told her she ought therefore to be satisfied with a
lower salary; Olive had to accept.

The farm lay on the Tarka River, twenty-five miles from Tarkastad,
and the house itself was 150 yards from the river, on level arable ground.
Gottlob wrote to Kate that the 'poor child' was 'not at all well'.[48] But,
despite this, Olive was pleased with her situation. Mrs Martin was 'one
of the sweetest-tempered women' she had ever met and Mr Martin a very
intelligent man. She had plenty of school books and a nice piano, so
teaching was easy work; the only drawback, she wrote to Kate, was that
she seemed so far away from people she knew.

While she was with the Martins, however, news came that Gottlob had
died; he had collapsed suddenly at the end of August 1876. The letter
was sent to her employer, and Olive described the event in a peculiarly
detached journal entry.

On Thursday evening I got the news that he was gone. I was walking
up and down in the moonlight and the children were picking oranges.
At last I went in and Mimmie came to my window and said that he
had come. I went in to the dining room and caught the letter out of
Willie's hand. There was one with black all round. 'This is mine,' I
said, but it was addressed to Mr Martin. There were some samples of
things and a bottle of oil for me so I went into my room. Esther came

in and said that her papa would not tell her from whom the black letter came. At supper Mr and Mrs Martin looked strange and after supper Mr M called me as I was going into my room. I went into the parlour and he told me . . . I sent a letter to Theo and Mamma by a Caffir. I wonder what we shall do.[49]

A week later she was busy making her mourning and teaching, and felt as though she could not keep on any longer; her journal is listless. She was waiting to hear whether the family would decide that she should come and live with Rebecca; two months later Rebecca went to stay with friends but was anxious that Olive should look after her. Olive kept seeing her father's eyes 'with tears in them and that is very maddening . . . but what does it matter. Soon I shall have rest like he has'.[50] The most despairing note in her diary dates from this period: 'I am 21 today; I suppose about half of my life has run out . . . I hope I shall not die soon though my chest is so bad as to almost make life a burden to me.' Montaigne and Goethe provided only a temporary release; she felt utterly alone.

As at Klein Ganna Hoek, only her writing really helped her. She worked on *From Man to Man* and planned a critique of Shelley. But she never sustained her confidence in herself and she was sure that *Undine* was a 'tissue of faults' and her story *Thorn Kloof*, which later became *The Story of an African Farm*, 'bald'. Her own explanation for this lack of progress was that she doubted her ability. But Gottlob's death had provided an additional stress and made communication with her family even more difficult: Theo's letter about it was kind but made her feel 'so cold'. She was weak and ill after a short stay at Cradock with Ettie and Theo and felt that life was 'all one big delusion'. Then the following year she made an unsuccessful visit to her mother and confided to Kate that she could see 'no way in which we can manage to be together'.[51]

Olive felt she had only herself to rely on for the 'friendship and love' that she wanted, and she conjured up an impossible solution. She would try fewer hours of sleep and exercise in order to make time for study, for 'only in self-forgetfulness and absorption in that can happiness ever be found'. For a while it seemed to work, and she described herself as living 'in the present and a world of visions'. But her happiness was precarious: she would be unable to write on the days a family letter arrived because it 'always distracts and unhinges me'. There followed several uncertain months: a frontier war, which had started after a border incident between the Xhosas and Fingoes, meant that isolated farms were considered unsafe, and in October 1877 the Martins moved from Ratel Hoek to Kat Kop, a farm nearer Cradock. Olive merely noted that she had done 'absolutely nothing' since the first war news had reached them twelve days before, but she worried on Rebecca's account that the excitement would do her harm.[52]

For herself she began to wonder if she should not start a school in Tarkastad, about ten miles north-east of Cradock. The Martins would send their daughters as boarders and a great many other country people could be relied upon to do the same. She rehearsed the pros and cons in a letter to Mrs Cawood, her Cradock friend with whom she continued to correspond. Olive was confident that all the 'big guns' would support her, and it would pay splendidly; however, 'there are some poor girls who have a school here, and my coming would knock it on the head at once. I can't face that'.[53] Running a school would have enabled her to save enough to go to England and study, but eventually she decided against the project, even though she had had to accept a reduction in her salary during a bout of illness at Ratel Hoek.

Her next move was back to Ganna Hoek, this time to teach the Cawood children, whom she already knew well. She was not sure whether she should come, she wrote to Mrs Cawood in a letter that indicates how much she needed the older woman's affection and approval. She was living so much in her books and her scribbling that she wasn't a bit a 'bright, pleasant person to have in a house. I can't bear to think of your being disappointed in me in any way'. Her letters to Mrs Cawood before the move also show a real pessimism about relationships for someone of only twenty-three, and one that could only be the product of a very basic feeling of failure. Mrs Cawood referred to Olive's brother Will's engagement, expressing the wish that it were Olive's. The reply was cool and quiet: 'You will never hear of that. The power of loving has burnt itself out in me; not in the widest sense, for I don't think I ever cared for so many people as I do now. But no one will ever absorb me and make me lose myself utterly, and unless someone did I should never marry.'[54] Only her writing gave her any peace; for the rest, she was bewildered: sometimes she got so tired that she wished it were all over, she wrote to Mrs Cawood, 'yet at others there is such a clinging to life'. Issues of loving had come to the surface in a particularly acute way:

I am getting to be such a selfish miserable creature. I wish I were as good as you. Perhaps if I saw you I would get like you. I would like to be so good that everything that I loved and that loved me was better and nobler and stronger for that love, but now it isn't so. I am so selfish. I'm not content to love. I want to be loved back again. We talk so much of intellect and of knowledge, but what are they! . . . One would barter all one's knowledge for one kiss and all one's intellect for one tender touch.[55]

Olive had come to rely on Mrs Cawood as someone in whom she could confide, as far as she ever did during this period, about personal matters. Mrs Cawood and her six children provided a warm, supportive family environment for Olive, who reciprocated by making clothes for the babies and going over to sit up with Mrs Cawood when her children were ill. The two were remembered as talking of 'everything under the sun', and Olive would read her manuscripts out to her, teasing her about putting her in a book, and giving Mrs Cawood the impression that she had 'laid at rest many of the problems that troubled her poor little brain.'

Olive arrived at Ganna Hoek in March 1879. In her journal there is only the suggestion of an explanation of the 'fever and madness' that she felt she'd come out of by leaving Ratel Hoek. The impression given is one of attraction to a man, possibly Mr Martin, her Ratel Hoek employer, possibly mutual. 'I was too tired to feel much on the ride and one little thought made me happy – three words,' she wrote two weeks after her arrival at the Cawoods. But she had not heard a word from the Martins since she left, she continued. 'I thought *he* would have written to me but it does not matter.' Ten days later, however, she was feeling 'a kind of quiet pleasure that I did not expect to have. Those last [letters] were as good as anything that I deserved to get; what was my love but selfishness, not quite selfish either though.'[56] Olive needed both to give and to get attention but did neither easily; she tried to understand her responses from a belief in the superiority of self-denial that could only make her more distressed.

Only three months were spent at Ganna Hoek in all, but they were very productive. The writing of the book that was to become *The Story of an African Farm* had to be done in fits and starts, teaching permitting. In the Cawood home, though there were frequent interruptions as people came in to her room to talk to her or to invite her to walk with them, the manuscript was almost finished. It was also a light-hearted time, and Olive, who had always liked going about naked, felt quite daring.

Olive had a favourite spot – a nice, large flat rock at the back of Ganna Hoek where she loved to sunbathe . . . 'Supposing someone sees you,' said [Mrs Cawood]. 'Oh, everybody knows I shall be naked on the rock at that time,' said Olive, 'and if anyone wants to spy, that is all right.'[57]

The Fouché family, now farming at Lelie Kloof, had offered to pay her £55 a year to teach two children and promised to build a new school-room and bedroom for her as well. She left the Cawoods at the end of June, apparently on good terms, although one of the daughters felt that Mrs Cawood, while being very 'liberal and broad-minded, was afraid of her religious views'. Would she otherwise have stayed longer? Or had they never discussed religion openly? Several weeks passed, during which four letters to Mrs Cawood went unanswered. Olive, referring jokingly to herself as an 'ill-used individual', still asked for a reply; she appears to have had no suspicion of the letter she was about to receive.

My dear Olive,

I have the less reluctance to write as I now do; because I think, from what you know of me, you are quite prepared for what I have to say. I no longer love you, and cannot act hypocritically. If you needed friends, I could not have allowed my heart to turn against you. You are rich in intellectual, influential friends. And I am quite sure you only valued my acquaintance because you thought I loved you. And I have *loved* you, at times with an almost idolatrous love. I have sometimes felt it in my heart to say, Olive Schreiner, I love you so, that for your sake I could become anything. That is why God in His goodness and wisdom used you as a means to show me what an awful soul-destroying thing freethinking is. You know, I have often told you I can only learn through my affections.

I must tell you I am not alone in what I now feel. Richard and I have both, while pointing out to the children that they owe you gratitude, told them that you are God's enemy and that they cannot love God and you at the same time. I tell you this, so that you shall be spared the pain and humiliation of expecting more from them, than they have been taught to give.

You know, Olive, if I were a freethinker I should be a much prouder one than you are. I would never be able to accept hospitality and kindness from Christians, knowing, that if they knew me as I really was, they would fly from me, affrighted. You will say, why did I accept help and friendship and kindness from you, then? The reason is I really did not know what freethinking was till you taught me.

Yours truly,

Erilda Cawood.

It was a deeply wounding letter in its absolute rejection of Olive by a woman whom she had loved and needed, charging her as it did not only with the unforgivable sin of freethinking, but of having exploited her friendship with her and her husband.

Olive had long seen herself as being very different from other women; at times she even despised them, though this was sometimes a judgement of individual women, sometimes of the social limitations of the female condition. Ironically, some of her hostility had been undermined by her friendship with Erilda Cawood. 'She is such a dear noble-hearted woman,' she had written to Will, 'she is quite converting my woman hatred into woman love. A sex that can contain such women as she and Ettie cannot be quite an invention of the Devil, though I still think he must have been very active about the time it came into existence.'[58] Now Mrs Cawood, who had been the exception among the women she knew, excluded her from her affection and that of her family, not because Olive had changed in herself, but because her lack of religious belief was so threatening in a church-bound community.

Mrs Cawood's letter also shows a real discrepancy between Olive's basic perception of herself as weak and inadequate – in relation to her work, and her ability to control herself – and other people's perception of her as almost uncannily powerful. Mrs Cawood writes about goodness and wisdom but the letter demonstrates her anger and resentment at Olive's capacity to elicit such strong feeling in others. On Olive's side the letter must have deepened the sense of isolation and of the inevitability of loss that she already had. But for her moral system to remain valid, it was essential that she be forgiving, even that she accept the rejection. After a delay of some weeks she wrote an unnaturally restrained reply. She did not at all blame Mrs Cawood for not loving her any more, she wrote:

We cannot help love's going, any more than we can help its coming;

and when it is gone, it is better to say so. For myself, I have always liked you not for anything you were to me, but what you were in yourself, and I feel to you as I have felt from the beginning. Therefore, believe me to remain, if not your friend, one who loves you.*

Early the following year, in 1880, she sent the manuscript of *The Story of an African Farm* to Dr and Mrs Brown, who had returned to England to live in Burnley, Lancashire, asking them if they could try and find a publisher for it. Mrs Brown later recalled:

> The bulky parcel was sewn up in a piece of coarse cotton cloth to keep its pages together, and then in brown paper. When I opened it in those wintry surroundings – with the noise and stir of a manufacturing town about me – a flood of emotion came over me, for I was met with the strange, pungent smell of the smoke of wood fires, familiar to those who know a Karoo farm . . .
>
> The manuscript was very indifferently written; many blots, many erasions were on almost every page, and here and there a grease mark as though the tallow candle, by which she probably wrote, had dropped a tear.[59]

The Browns consulted a relative living in Edinburgh who had contact with a publisher there, David Douglass. Douglass gave his response to the manuscript a few months later. It showed a good deal of talent, he felt, but was too long and would require to be cut down considerably. He was hopeful, however, and had found her letter very interesting and touching; he could sympathize 'very sincerely' with her lonely position and apparent friendlessness. The manuscript was returned to her at Lelie Kloof, presumably with suggestions for changes.[60]

With the Browns back in England, 'the English plan' that they had apparently formed during the Fraserburg days, to help Olive leave South Africa to study, seemed slowly to mature over the next year. Olive's suspense grew as, in between coping with a bad-tempered Mrs Fouché, about whom she stormed in her diary: 'How glorious [it would be] to be in the power of no woman', she revised the manuscript, rising each morning at dawn, finding a reworked chapter 'delightful' one day, wanting to burn it the next, and feeling heartsore at all she had to leave out.

By Christmas 1880 she was completely exhausted. 'Brain and body

* We don't know on whose initiative or at what time exactly, but within a few years the friendship between Olive and Mrs Cawood was restored. Apparently Olive never raised the topic of religion again.

must have rest. I *must* give up writing at night, or else give up getting up so early.' Then on New Year's Eve she had 'that weary worn feeling . . . Even any kind of love I want. Death is so near and I have loved so little and been loved so little'.[61] It was a period of enormous fluctuations in her mood, and though her letters to family members were calm, even mundane, her diary recorded that she was 'profoundly dissatisfied with myself. Hate myself'. When she pictured meeting Mrs Brown she was stronger – 'but perhaps she won't love me', she thought, as the date of her departure approached.

Olive had asked the Browns to send her the application form for training as a nurse at the Royal Infirmary in Edinburgh. She was just old enough to qualify – single women or widows between twenty-five and thirty-five were eligible for the year's course – and she sent the completed form back to the Browns at the end of that year. She gave her religion as 'Freethinker – Father Lutheran'; weight? 'There are no scales here'; where educated? 'At home'. She described her health as 'delicate at one time but have wholly recovered'.[62] For she had decided not to become a doctor after all: 'That costs money of which I have none,' she told Kate, 'but can become a nurse without paying anything and after all, if they cannot be of so much use as the doctors, they can still relieve a great deal of suffering'.[63] If the climate in England suited her, she would never return. Soon she heard from Mrs Brown that she would 'very likely get on' at the Royal Infirmary. Rebecca, who had converted to Catholicism after Gottlob's death and was living in a convent in Grahamstown, was finally persuaded to let her go.

The last letter she had from Theo before she left enclosed a banknote for £10. They had been in only sporadic contact once Olive left the Diamond Fields, but he couldn't help feeling she was doing the right thing. Still, he wished he could believe she was going 'with Jesus Christ as your Saviour and Friend in your heart and life, confessed there as the Son of God who died for you. I sometimes can't help thinking, and that despite your assertions, you believe in Him'. She left Lelie Kloof in an ox wagon and was ill all the way to Grahamstown, where she said goodbye to Rebecca. In her journal she recorded that her mother had been 'very kind'; there were letters from Mrs Brown and Will, and money from Ettie. Once on the boat her journal entries were worried but determined: 'I have not much hope. I shall *never* be well.' But then she added: '. . . but I *will* strive, I *will*.'

CHAPTER THREE

Two Novels

Olive Schreiner could never remember a time when she was not making stories. Family visitors recalled the little girl who walked up and down talking to herself in an imaginative world all her own, reciting from Coleridge and Tennyson. From childhood she kept a journal – though erratically – writing in a large, decorative, rather adult script with much crossing-out. In this manner she acquired the habit of inventing her own world, initially entirely immersing herself in it – as when she talked to her baby sister Ellie's dead body – by late adolescence achieving a measure of detachment from it and using it to do much more ambitious writing. Her intellectual development proceeded without any consistent supports, and she was isolated from any personally sustaining contact (a feature of her youth that she was never to forget and frequently to refer to in adult life), but this prolonged solitude was punctuated by a series of crises or moments which were crucial to her formation as a writer.

Books were always a model and a solace, and by the time she was twelve she was spending something like six hours a day reading and writing. The Sermon on the Mount gave her her first illustration of a moral teaching with which she could identify, and the Bible as a whole a style which moved her beyond words. Willie Bertram, the man who had introduced her to Spencer, spoke to her briefly about art, and recommended Emerson's *Essays*, which helped her through a suicidal patch at the age of nineteen. English political economy and historiography, the life of Christ, and, later, Gibbon's *Decline and Fall* and Goethe's *Wilhelm Meister*, which, she felt, released her from the overwhelming sense of sin she had inherited, provided her with the outlines of a project – to trace the evolution of morality. Her situation as a woman enabled this to be expressed in terms of the relations between the sexes. Modernist critics of the early twentieth century were to see Olive Schreiner's novels as quintessentially Victorian, in their evolutionism, their moralizing, and the passion of their feminism. In her own time, however, *The Story of an African Farm* stood out from other 'theological romances' as a completely new book – a work of serious fiction that was also a disquisition on Christianity and religious guilt, marking an epoch, as Hugh Walpole acknowledged, 'as scarcely any other book can do'.[1]

Aside from the influence of her reading, a number of experiences combined to make Olive Schreiner write fiction. One observer at Dordrecht in 1872 doubted that she had the 'idea of authorship'; by the end of that year – and after the Gau episode – a certain detachment had developed: 'how queer all this will read in ten years' time,' she wrote in her diary. She was beginning to see writing as having a perspective of its own; now she spent whole days on a rough sketch of a story. Her year on the Diamond Fields provided her with material; her admiration of the Browns a model relationship. In Fraserburg in 1873 she gave the impression, to family and friends, of seeing a vision. However long it took her to come to terms with the Gau experience, she was now engaged in creating an internal world of people whom she called her 'children' and whom she wished to keep for herself. 'I love them too much,' she told Mrs Cawood a couple of years later when asked why she didn't publish anything. 'Would you give *your* children to other people?' These children of hers, however, were not under her control. On one occasion, for example, she became extremely agitated when the woman she was writing about wouldn't do what she wanted her to. 'But Olive,' Mrs Cawood said, '*you* can make her.' 'No,' she replied, 'she won't do it.'

The tension between writing as an omnipotent activity and her sense of her characters being utterly real and beyond her control led Olive Schreiner to experiment with three novels, gather material that was later used in her allegories, and work on a number of short stories over the eight years to 1881. She herself felt she was most successful when her characters led her and not the other way round; thus *Undine*, the most closely autobiographical of the three, pleased her least; she was so dissatisfied with *The Story of an African Farm* that she nearly threw it into a dam at Lelie Kloof in 1880; with *From Man to Man* she was convinced she had the makings of a great novel with her 'strong, quiet married love' and her plan of a suicide at the end.

For all that she had access to books through the privately endowed libraries of South Africa, Olive Schreiner's adolescence and young adulthood were marked by great loneliness. She was in correspondence only with her family, the Cawoods, and a few acquaintances. Absence and loss, failure and deterioration were more real to her than presence and belonging. This is reflected in her titles, often of stories that were never finished: 'The Ghost', 'Wrecked', or her sense of having 'the outlines (vague) of a song that was never sung'. She had to create her own linkages in time, and she did this through her imaginative writing. Later, when she went to England, her letters to Havelock Ellis took over some of this overwhelming need for purposive communication, becoming an expressive, almost structureless diary in which her experience could be mirrored by an intimate friend. Before then – and obviously affected by the greater formality of the circles in which she was placed – her letters have an anxious, perturbed, rather distant quality. Perhaps she was never able to make her sexual development very clear – to herself or to others. From the subject matter of her novels, however, we have some idea of her preoccupations: seduction and male hypocrisy, women as gossips and informers, the difficulties of the self-educated. A picture emerges of a social milieu in which Olive Schreiner felt herself to be entirely 'unwomanly'.

Olive began *Undine* in 1873 at the Diamond Fields. During the next two years she worked on the novel and gained experiences that she made use of in her allegories and *The Story of an African Farm*. By Christmas 1875, when she was twenty, *Undine* was nearly finished and *African Farm* begun; by the following summer she had decided not to publish 'poor little' *Undine* and was preoccupied with *From Man to Man*; over the next year she worked on *African Farm* and *From Man to Man* alternately. By summer 1879 *African Farm* was almost finished, and by autumn the following year she had returned to *From Man to Man*; in the last four months before her departure for England in March 1881 she revised *African Farm*. When she left for England, then, she had with her three novels in manuscript, one which she had plans to publish, one which was unfinished, and one she had resolved not to bring out: *Undine*, *A Queer Little Child*.

'I was tired of being called queer and strange and odd.' The novel *Undine*, which opens in this way, is both Undine's and Olive's story. As narrator Olive makes an explicit critique of sexual oppression; as Undine she provides her reader with the development of her subjective world; as narrator, again, she exposes Undine's mistakes. Using themes of love, identity and death the work attempted, not unsuccessfully, to situate different kinds of female experience within a series of confrontations, longings, and power relationships.

The plot is this: Undine, a child with religious doubts on a Boer farm in South Africa, goes to England as an adolescent, rejecting the revivalist Methodism of her grandfather's chapel, though not without a sense of guilt and sin. Soon afterwards her freethinking brother Frank is drowned. Undine moves to her grandmother's, and gets involved in two unsatisfactory relationships: the first with a young narcissist, Albert Blair, which elicits deep self-hatred, and the second with his father, George, whom she marries. She has a baby, which dies; when her husband dies too she goes back to South Africa to find work. Exhausted and demoralized after a long journey, she gets ironing and sewing work at the Diamond Fields, making friends only with a twelve-year-old girl for whom she makes up stories. She finds out that Albert Blair has been living at the Fields but has just died; she spends the night before his funeral with his dead body, unobserved in the cottage where his wife has had him put. Once he is dead she feels able to tell him how much she loved him, and the catharsis over she too is able to die. She becomes delirious, goes out 'alone with the stars', imagines Albert Blair's arms around her, and dies.

Olive's purpose in *Undine* is far from clear, particularly since she later put the material behind her and claimed she could barely remember it. Nevertheless, the novel can still be 'read' and understood for the light it sheds on her transition from the privacy of a diary to the more assured language of *African Farm*. Despite the melodrama involved, the critique of sexual oppression carried a great deal of energy and satire. Olive was able successfully to pinpoint the characteristic strategies of a man in search of a submissive woman.

When Albert Blair asks Undine to explain how she comes to have 'such extraordinary views and manner', for example, Undine replies:

'Why do you not put some other word in the place of "extraordinary" – say, "pernicious", "reprehensible"? That is what you really think' . . .
He never paid her compliments or spoke to her as he would to

another woman, so he answered quietly: 'Those words would be almost too strong; say, unwomanly.'

Undine asks him about his idea of what a woman ought to be, and he continues:

'A woman to be womanly should have nothing striking or peculiar about her; she should shun all extremes in manners and modes of expression; she should have no strong views on any question; especially when they differ from those of her surroundings; she should not be too reserved in her manners, and still less too affable and undignified. There is between all extremes a happy mediate, and there a woman should always be found. Men may turn to one side or the other; woman never must.'

Undine said nothing when he ended. She could not help it; she had been born with strong and determined ideas on every subject, sub- and super-lunar, and not one step of her sixteen years' journey had she walked in the happy mediate road. It was too late to change now.[2]

At the same time, Olive saw that men's experience was characterized by a tangible participation in the world, women's by illness, servitude and dependence, a set of negatives to man's positive that gave them an utterly different relation to life. Having returned to South Africa, Undine asks herself why she shouldn't enjoy a 'wild, free, true life, as a man may . . . forget the old morbid loves and longings'? Her question is answered for her:

If she had been a man she might have thrown off her jacket and set to work instantly, carrying the endless iron buckets and coils of rope and wire with which the wagon beside which she stood was being laden. She might have made enough in half an hour to pay for a bed at one of the lower hotels, might have wandered about the town, seen something of life, and enjoyed herself in a manner. As it was, being only a woman and a fine little lady with the scent not yet out of her hair nor the softness rubbed from her hands, she stood there in the street, feeling very weak, bodily, after her illness, and mentally, after her long life of servitude and dependence – very weak and very heartsick.[3]

In one way the novel is a simple exposé of the impossibility of Undine's fantasy of what 'womanhood' brings – knowledge and love – for the proper female sphere is defined once and for all by her grandmother's generation. Women should be attractive and receptive to men, but without views. especially 'idiotic' religious views like Undine's. In terms of religion and sexuality women therefore have no real access to culture, no active space of their own; indeed, a dialogue about literature within the novel mirrors that division in culture. Her cousin Jonathan asks her if she's reading Elizabeth Barrett Browning, referring to it as 'poetry and effete nonsense'. Undine retorts that she's reading Mill: 'Nothing very sentimental in that.' So non-sense and non-sentiment are polarized, as though symbolizing the meaning of female and male.

Throughout the novel, Undine's perception of herself, however confused, is at odds with others' perceptions of her. Her governess in Africa sees her as stupid and wicked because she would rather go to hell than be good and go to heaven merely because she was afraid of hell; cousin Jonathan in England sees her as having a cold, feelingless shell. She agrees to marry a wealthy middle-aged man on condition that he make over a large amount of money before their marriage – which she intends to give to his son Albert, whom she loves and he has disinherited – and the loathing that Albert Blair, ignorant of her plan, then feels for her makes him take up his father's position that 'all women have their value in coins, though some mount high'. Undine is thus taken as representative of the schemer by the world she has characterized as scheming. At every step she is disconfirmed by an outside world which reads her generosity as manipulation and her relationships as immorality.

One very early moment, however, marks a decisive transition for her sense of herself. It comes when Frank drowns – in circumstances remarkably similar to Shelley's death in Italy in 1822* – and Aunt Margaret has 'gone mad', accusing Undine of being the devil, and hence responsible for his death. Undine's formulation of the event is that her childhood is over and a strange 'deadness' seems to have settled; now she becomes a very self-punishing young woman. When asked what she thinks of Albert Blair – to whom she is tremendously attracted – she refers to Eve and the story of the fall, inferring her own fall from her concern with her gloves and her hair. So when she sees Albert she can't integrate the attraction

---

* This is to the point where Frank is drowned off the coast at Leeford, Shelley at Leghorn. See 'Notes on Poems of 1822, by Mrs Shelley', in Thomas Hutchinson (ed.), *Shelley, Poetical Works* (1904), pp. 761–6, and 'A Sunny Afternoon and a Wild Night', *Undine*, pp. 57–61.

she feels, and loses her identity as an intellectual: she literally drops the book she's been reading, prepared to do anything to gain his approval.

It was through overhearing her grandmother's friends' gossip about the local loose woman that Undine lost what she terms her 'ignorance of evil':

> Much . . . was made clear to me that night, and I was wretched; for alas! is it not the old, old story – that the tree of knowledge is the tree of pain, and that 'In the day wherein thou eatest thou shalt surely die', stands written on every fruit of the wonderful tree?[4]

But Undine also knows that women are abused by men when she compares the 'unenviable fate of both women and pictures' – to be possessed by a man. She splits body and soul, however, when she refers to gold as God of the body and love as God of the soul. At the same time she indentifies with the 'very wicked woman' who has an illegitimate child because her child is a child 'of love', unlike her own, the child 'of loathing'. And she will defend love when it is misrepresented, particularly when it is associated with an affront to conventional morality. To the shabby woman on board ship to South Africa who had been told Shelley was wicked, Undine says it's always right to love:

> 'I used to read poems' [the woman says], 'I used to like Shelley – it was wicked, but I used to wish I could have seen him.'
>
> 'I don't think he was wicked.'
>
> 'I thought he loved another woman.'
>
> 'That's not a reason for not liking him. It's always right to love. It is not wrong to feel warm or to feel strong, and we can as little help loving as feeling either.'
>
> 'But if it hurts other people,' said the woman slowly.
>
> 'Then it must be silent as the dead are, who, they say, live, yet we never hear them.'[5]

Undine's advocacy of love, however, bears little relation to the actual condition of her life, which is one of repeated loss. When one of the men for whom she irons falls ill and she nurses him, the practice of love becomes one of renunciation: Undine uses the money she has saved to pay for his return to England. On the day of his departure he tells her he's sure they'll meet again. The narrator mocks him:

> Meet again! Who ever met again? The child we love goes from us

and comes back to us a man, and all others praise the change; but we, even while we run our fingers through his curls, we hunger for the little child that sat upon our knee.

Only when we come so close that nothing separates us can we meet again, only when what binds us is not my need of you or your need of me nor any chance circumstance, but a deep ingrained likeness of nature that cannot pass away.[6]

This concept of love is abstract – 'not my need of you nor your need of me'; belittles the significance of daily reality in forming bonds between people – 'nor any chance circumstance'; and narcissistic – 'a deep ingrained likeness of nature'. The clear understanding of men's degradation of women which informs the novel is then confused by the proposal of a love whose meaning can be found only in loss and, ultimately, in death.

The sharpness of the novel's critique of religion derived from the support Olive Schreiner's reading provided – an awareness, however theoretical or self-contained, that such issues mattered to others. Her account of women's attraction to men, on the other hand, has a derivative quality, as though she is working from a male model of the female. This sentimentality may have been a product of a patriarchal culture in which female sexuality was diffused into notions of service, and women had no access to their specifically sexual feelings. So Undine's rejection of her social situation as a married woman represents a kind of sexual rebellion, but one that can be concluded only by a de-sexing: her return to Africa and her childhood. The shabby woman on board ship who befriends her had experienced something of the same kind of regression, but hers was into silence. In the context of a basically passive orientation on life, she had loved her man friend because he wanted to have someone care for him; but there was also the paradox that this fantasy lover – for the man was married, and the relationship covert – made all the other people in her life seem like dreams: a double irreality. Love had to be invisible, and sexuality restricted to touch: the woman liked simply to touch his coat and his brushes in the hall. She came to feel she could tolerate her own wickedness in 'seducing' him, but not his in deceiving his wife. As she sewed stockings one day, she realized she must leave him, but she could make it right for him 'if I worked for other people all my life'. She became a nurse, basing her loveless penance on the archaic moral assumption that suffering annuls the bad consequences of an act.[7]

All these confusions about loving are organized around the Biblical image of Eve. The Bible appears in *Undine* both in dialogue within religious meetings, and as part of a literary form; as when Undine has 'taken the first bite at the forbidden tree'. For Undine believes that women corrupt men, and Eve is an explicit personification of evil. Yet both Undine and Olive are also working through a belief in female self-expression, in the validity of women's emotional and – however inexplicitly expressed – sexual feeling. There are bound to be conflicting models of behaviour: on the one hand the bad Eve, who corrupts because she feels desire; on the other the defence of Shelley and the advocacy of love. The contradictions which emerge can only be resolved through death: in Undine's words, 'only that which has no existence lasts for ever.'

The dénouement, in Undine's death, tells of peace, escape, and rescue from struggle. Olive sought to transcend the constraining world she was placed in by an ahistorical displacement of the self: backwards and forwards in death, and backwards and forwards in a Spencerian concept of change. The constant presence of illness and death in her environment – one of high infant and maternal mortality, with little or no diagnostic or 'scientific' medicine – took on a mystical quality of release in her fiction.[8] The distinction between *living* and *dying* is made to seem unimportant and death is always an option. In *Undine* the issue is brought out in an allegory Undine tells Diogenes, her friend at the Diamond Fields, in which a dying woman asks Life to take her child.

Death and Life take it in turns to tell her what they can give: Death, very tall and calm, is presented as a strange and mysterious individual, in no way frightening – 'his eyelids were half closed and in the eyes beneath them lay the shadows of wonderful dreams' – and as an alternative world in which to live. Life is beautiful, 'but when the mother looked at her forehead, knit with thought and pain . . . she feared her also'. Death offers rest and sleep, but the mother eventually offers the child to Life, since 'your best is bitter sweet, but it is sweet'. Even so, death always has the ultimate moral force: when Undine almost dies in childbirth and is then nursed back to health, her riches are made tawdry by their juxtaposition with death: the dressing gown and shawl symbolize recovery, but falsehood as well.

'Medical' reasons for death or recovery are never given, only their moral associations indicated. Concepts of illness are always vague, as when Undine asks the African who comes to order Mrs Blair's mourning what her husband died of: 'he took ill, something wrong inside'; and whereas Albert Blair's wife is unable to deal with his death and has his body put outside the house, Undine has no fear. Their different responses become a statement about their worth as individuals. Albert's death enables Undine to reveal the truth about her feeling for him. She goes to the shed where he has been laid out and takes the sheet from his face:

> In his ear she whispered the wild words of love that to the living she would never utter – wild passionate words, the outpourings of a life's crushed-out love, the breaking forth of a fiercely suppressed passion. And the dead man lies so still; he does not send her from him; he does not silence her; he understands her now; he loves her now.[9]

Here death creates both equality and exclusive possession.

Undine's own fatal illness is equally unexplained, though Albert's death seems to deprive her of life, a sensation that she displaces onto an empty barrel the next morning in a search for water: 'There must be some living thing withholding life from her.' But death is an old attraction, though not that of the Christian deathbed. When Undine leaves her tent that night and looks up in the sky, she remembers the stars who shed their light on the Karoo and looked at the child who read the Testament so long ago. One star in particular describes himself as her brother, a few million years older than she, who has 'seen that the thing which you call death is the father of all life and beauty . . . to make a man a million million forms have been and are not. Without death there is no change, without change no life.' Undine is comforted by the absorption in nature he suggests:

> 'If what you fear in the death that is upon you is not change but a fearful endless silence and annihilation, then take comfort . . . Nature is too poor to lose, too poor to let rest; her work is not yet done; she has other things to make.'[10]

It is a comfort as ideological as was Undine's attempt to live by rationality in her first days at New Rush.

Olive never wanted *Undine* to be published. She told Ellis in 1884 that she had not looked at it since she wrote it, and 'ought to have burnt it long ago', but the autobiographical element in it made her 'soft' to it.[11]

It was published, but posthumously, and then reprinted only once. In some ways, in fact, it is harder to interpret than *The Story of an African Farm*, precisely because it *is* so raw, so unclearly differentiated from its author's experience, so overtly split between a critique of culture and a sentimental endorsement of it. *African Farm*, on the other hand, is a much more articulate and successful novel. It was an attempt at accommodating the polarities of truth and dream, religion and freedom, and male and female that were presenting themselves in Olive Schreiner's own life but which she had been unable to integrate within *Undine*. Now she broke with the exaggerated intricacies of plot that characterized her first novel in favour of a combination of mysticism, allegory and realism that allowed her to explore states of being and consciousness. The famous passage from the preface to the second edition indicates a form that is only apparently formless; Olive was much more positively advocating a method in a way that anticipates Virginia Woolf:

> Human life may be painted according to two methods. There is the stage method. According to that each character is duly marshalled at first, and ticketed; we know with an immutable certainty that at the right crises each one will reappear and act his part, and, when the curtain falls, all will stand before it bowing. There is another method – the method of the life we all lead. Here nothing can be prophesied. There is a strange coming and going of feet. Men appear, act and re-act upon each other, and pass away. When the curtain falls no one is ready. When the footlights are brightest they are blown out; and what the name of the play is no one knows. If there sits a spectator who knows, he sits so high that the players in the gaslight cannot hear his breathing. Life may be painted according to either method; but the methods are different. The canons of criticism that bear upon the one cut cruelly upon the other.[12]

She could almost have been describing her own progression as a writer. Now she was dealing with the uncertainties of her own situation, the landscape of the Karoo. This was a landscape which contained and expressed the passage of time, and the originality of *The Story of an African Farm* lay in its attempt to present time as experience and to give that experience a historical dimension. But in the language of this novel the Karoo was a particularly complex symbol for it held not just the passage of time in the ordinary sense, but, in South African writer Dan

Jacobson's words, the history of a colonial culture robbed of a memory of itself.

> The discontinuities of colonial experience make it almost inevitable that this should be so. A political entity which has been brought into existence by the actions of an external power; a population consisting of the descendants of conquerors, of slaves and indentured labourers, and of dispossessed aboriginals; a language in the courts and schools which has been imported like an item of heavy machinery; a prolonged economic and psychological subservience to a metropolitan centre a great distance away . . . [13]

That seeming absence of an indigenous culture was reflected in *Undine*, with its deference to a fantasy England of constant tea parties, snowfalls and woodland. How difficult it must have been, Jacobson continues, for Olive Schreiner to *see* the material around herself as a source of fiction.

The Karoo was the motif by which Olive asserted the possibility of memory – of a history and a language – and it is this consciousness and acceptance of the Karoo as a fictional device which distinguishes *Undine* and *The Story of an African Farm* as novels. But more than this, for it marks an important moment of transition for Olive Schreiner as a novelist. Having broken with the synonym of colonial and metropolitan, her confidence (and competence) as a writer could develop. 'It has been suggested by a kind critic', her preface continues,

> that he would better have liked the little book if it had been a history of wild adventure; of cattle driven into inaccessible 'kranzes' by Bushmen; 'of encounters with ravening lions, and hair-breadth escapes'. This could not be. Such books are best written in Piccadilly or the Strand: there the gifts of the creative imagination untrammelled by contact with any fact, may spread their wings.
>
> But, should one sit down to paint the scenes among which he has grown, he will find that the facts creep in upon him . . . Sadly he must squeeze the colour from his brush, and dip it into the grey pigments around him. He must paint what lies before him.

That Olive was successful in her project is clear from another South African writer's response to it. Doris Lessing read *African Farm* at the age of fourteen, 'understanding very well the isolation described in it; responding to [Schreiner's] sense of Africa the magnificent – mine, and everyone's who knows Africa . . . I had only to hear the title, or "Olive Schreiner", and my deepest self was touched.' It was the first 'real' book she had read which had Africa as a setting.[14]

The novel deals with the daily lives of a group of people on a Boer farm in South Africa, and it opens with a description of the homestead by night.

> The full African moon poured down its light from the blue sky into the wide, lonely plain. The dry, sandy earth, with its coating of stunted 'karoo' bushes a few inches high, the low hills that skirted the plain, the milk-bushes with their long, finger-like leaves, all were touched by a weird and an almost oppressive beauty as they lay in the white light.
>
> In one spot only was the solemn monotony of the plain broken. Near the centre a small, solitary 'kopje' rose. Alone it lay there, a heap of round iron-stones piled one upon another, as over some giant's grave. Here and there a few tufts of grass or small succulent plants had sprung up among its stones, and on the very summit a clump of prickly-pears lifted their thorny arms, and reflected, as from mirrors, the moonlight on their broad, fleshy leaves. At the foot of the 'kopje' lay the homestead. First, the stone-walled 'sheep-kraals' and Kaffir huts; beyond them the dwelling-house – a square red-brick building with thatched roof. Even on its bare red walls, and the wooden ladder that led up to the loft, the moonlight cast a kind of dreamy beauty.[15]

Twelve-year-old Lyndall, an orphan, lives there with her cousin Emily, Tant Sannie's stepdaughter. Em wants to marry; Lyndall intends to go to school since Em is going to inherit the farm and she will have nothing. There are a gentle German overseer, Old Otto, and his 'heavy, slouching' fourteen-year-old son, Waldo – like Undine, with religious doubts, but, significantly, male. Waldo attempts to make contact with Lyndall; Lyndall is apparently supercilious, though later tender and affirming.

An Irish entrepreneur, Bonaparte Blenkins, comes to the farm and ingratiates himself with Old Otto by making up stories about his past and his connections with the first Napoleon. Lyndall, overhearing while reading, casts doubts on the stories; Old Otto continues credulous, and suggests that Bonaparte stay and teach the girls. Bonaparte begins courting Tant Sannie; Old Otto dies and Tant Sannie and Bonaparte decide between themselves that Bonaparte will become overseer in his place.

There follows a show of gratuitous violence on the part of Bonaparte, designed to enforce his authority over the children: he crushes a sheep-shearing machine that Waldo has spent nine months making; he locks Waldo in the fuel-house for supposedly eating Tant Sannie's peaches; he and Tant Sannie burn a volume of political economy, belonging to Waldo, that they find in the loft.

Em grows into a fat sixteen-year-old; Lyndall goes to school, though it is never clear where or for how long; Bonaparte leaves the farm and Tant Sannie seeks another husband. Waldo, still working on the farm, meets a Stranger on horseback who asks to rest for an hour, staying long enough to tell him an allegory of a hunter in search of the Bird of Truth. A new man comes to the farm, the passive and 'effeminate' Gregory Rose, and becomes engaged to Em. As Em is preparing for her marriage, Lyndall returns to the farm after a four-year absence, telling first Em and then Waldo about her views on men, love, and the bitterness of the female condition. Gregory Rose becomes infatuated with Lyndall, breaks off his engagement to Em, and pleads with Lyndall to let him serve her.

She replies that he could do this by letting her take his name in marriage, but she will give no reason why. She invites an English traveller to stay at the farm, and now it becomes clear that there has been an affair during her absence. He travels a hundred miles to see her, and she explains her decision to marry Rose rather than him: she cannot marry because she cannot be tied, but if he wants he can take her away and take care of her.

Lyndall's departure from the farm marks her last direct appearance in the novel. When Waldo returns to the farm, having spent an unspecified time learning about the world outside, he tells Em that he has had one letter from her, but that over a year before. He begins to write to her about what he had been doing and pondering, but Em tells him there is no point, for Lyndall is dead. When did she die? And in what circumstances? Her death has a devastating effect on Waldo and Em, who are unable to refer to it, and it is up to Gregory Rose to tell the story of her illness.

Rose, still besotted with Lyndall, had found it impossible to stay on the farm once Lyndall had left. Determined to trace her and her lover, he travelled through the Free State, inquiring in all the villages. After a long time he found her very ill in a small country hotel. The landlady told him that a woman had arrived alone six months before. Eight days later she had given birth to a child which lived two hours; the woman herself almost died, but began to recover. Now she was wasting away after taking ill one day when she was out in the rain. Aware that he had found her at last, Rose dressed in women's clothing and returned to the hotel in order to be accepted as a nurse for her. He nursed her gently over an unspecified length of time, discovering how determined she was to bear her pain alone, how when it was clear that she was dying, she refused any religious blessing. Her English lover wrote to her, imploring her to marry him and let him come back to her. She began a letter to him, reiterating the impossibility of marriage but telling him that she would always love him for the sake of the baby. When she got very near death she asked Rose to take her out into the veld.

On the night when Rose tells this story, Waldo dreams of Lyndall, first as a small child gathering shells on the sand, then as a woman. He wakes in great pain, crying for the old faith. But what answers do the various religious positions provide? The true Bible Christian tells him he will see Lyndall again but invokes the lake of fire because she did not repent; the nineteenth-century Christian says the same but emphasizes God as love; the Transcendentalist says he will see her but not in the flesh. Waldo eventually finds peace in contemplation of

> that vast land where there is always peace; that land where the soul, gazing long, loses all consciousness of its little self, and almost feels its hand on the old mystery of Universal Unity that surrounds it. 'No death, no death', he muttered; 'there is that which never dies – which abides. It is but the individual that perishes, the whole remains.'[16]

The placid routine of the farm resumes: Em and Rose marry, Tant Sannie marries and has children, Waldo stays on the farm. He has come to terms with Lyndall's death and with the simplicity of his own life. Now he refuses Em's offer of money to help him go away to study; the world around him seems lovely enough, and he falls asleep in the sun. Or does he die?

> His soul rested. Was it only John, think you, who saw the heavens open? The dreamers see it every day.
> . . . Our fathers had their dreams; we have ours; the generation that follows will have its own. Without dreams and phantoms man cannot exist.[17]

In its exposition of the relationships within this group of children and adults, *The Story of an African Farm* effectively made a statement about the violence of colonialism. It has, however, been criticized for not being the 'race relations novel' that people expect, in that the blacks are merely 'extras'.[18] But that was the point about the colonial condition: Africans were kept so far outside white society that that in itself was a statement about it. The European frontier society insulated itself from the indigenous society but internalized the violence it used against it; hence the violence of Bonaparte and Tant Sannie's behaviour. The blankness of it was the exclusion of those who were not white. Olive was writing, in fact, about what colonialism did to whites, and in her novel the children are both symbol and expression of that system and its consequences. They are the victims of a shallow, bigoted religion with its anti-intellectualism and its easy references to God and authority. Hence the impossibility of a religious rebellion without the rejection of the adult world as well.

The children's experience of adult violence has created a solidarity between them. When Waldo is locked in after supposedly eating Tant Sannie's peaches, Lyndall comforts him by telling him that 'we will have the power some day'. She finds it 'glorious' that Napoleon could have instilled terror in so many minds – but the fantasy of terrorizing is no stronger than the one of support: 'When I'm strong, I'll hate everything that has power, and help everything that is weak.' In that one of the narrative perspectives of the novel is that of the child, the sense of mutuality between the children is set against the manipulative individualism of the adult, with Bonaparte as its symbol. He has come to Africa because 'they want capital, a struggling country'; he bought £8000 worth of machinery, but the ship which was bringing it got lost. His wife wanted to borrow money, but he refused. 'While this frame has power to endure, NO. Never shall it be said that Bonaparte Blenkins asked of any man.' Old Otto characterizes his position as one of 'noble independence', but it is precisely the entrepreneurial ideology of an emergent capitalism to which Bonaparte adheres, the belief in 'work and labour as the secret of all happiness'.

And it is in this setting that human labour acquires its monetary value. When Bonaparte comes upon Waldo's sheep-shearing machine, which had so comforted the boy after his father's death, Bonaparte merely admires it and suggests it be patented. Similarly, the 'pure' emotion of the child in its relation to the natural world is counterposed to the mercenary emotion of the adult marriage. After Otto's death Bonaparte searches for his money; finds only a plain gold wedding ring, and imagines marrying Tant Sannie.

> 'Thy fair body, oh, my girl,
> Shall Bonaparte possess;
> His fingers in thy money-bags,
> He therein, too, shall mess.'[19]

Love is wealth and hoarding and woman another possession.

The violence done to children is sometimes justified in the name of parental authority – Bonaparte tells Waldo he is going to act as a father to him before beating him – but is equally often arbitrary and gratuitous. When Waldo finds a volume of political economy in the loft, and delights in finding thoughts that 'were his', the authoritarian adult world takes what's his away from him, doing violence to his desire to read. Tant Sannie, proud of never having read any other book than the Bible, can't understand English but knows 'from the very sound' how ungodly it is. 'Take your Polity-gollity-gominy, your devil's book!' So the very term political economy, which means so much to the boy, is turned into non-sense by the adult. The child, knowing the adult world makes decisions about individual behaviour, responds by walking away, aware of its impotence.

Two sections of the novel pursue this theme of religion, rejection and isolation. Both stand outside the narrative, and both are centred on the character of Waldo. The central section of the book, 'Times and Seasons', is an account of the seasons of the soul; it is, in a way, self-contained, a work within a work. It describes Olive's religious development but mediated directly through Waldo, now fifteen. A mystical exploration of the nature of self, it traces the hostility to God, the sense of personal wickedness, the hostility to church finery and the identification, first with the person of Jesus, and then with a Spencerian model of nature. With the imagery of the red sunset, the thunderstorm, the deep blue sky, the great rainbow shaping the infant's recollections, Olive was describing a taken-for-granted, pre-verbal world that was imagined but in no way arbitrary: it was identical, in its religious fervour, to the most popular Bible illustrations of the day – in particular to the dramatization of the Old Testament.[20] This use of illustration was seen as central in the moral education of the child, as imparting a proper sense of awe before the Lord; in Olive's words:

> One day we sit there and look up at the blue sky . . . and suddenly it strikes us, Who are we? This *I*, what is it? . . . Then we get up in great fear and run home as hard as we can.

But having been swayed by this orthodox representation of nature, Waldo refused it. From infancy, Olive says, we were taught to see nature as

> a poor plastic thing, to be toyed with this way or that, as man happens to please his deity or not . . . All these years we have lived beside her, and we have never seen her; now we open our eyes and look at her.[21]

Waldo rejects the mystification of landscape, in which earth is a 'weltering chaos', in favour of a consciousness of fossil footprints on rock, the anatomical structure of birds, and the social relations of the ant. The theme of the search for absolute truth is then developed in the allegory of the Hunter which Waldo's Stranger tells.

This is the story of a man who left his village community in search of a Bird of Truth, whose reflection he had once seen by the shores of a lake. Wisdom told him that 'he who has once seen her never rests again. Till death he desires her'. The Hunter asked him where he could find her; Wisdom told him he had not suffered enough. He must go to the Land of Absolute Negation and Denial; he must climb the mountains of stern reality; and beyond them lay Truth. As he left the valley the villagers stoned him and called him a fool and an atheist. He went into the woods and was tempted by the twins Sensuality, but refused to go with them. He came on the mountain range Wisdom had told him about; the path grew steeper and then disappeared. The rarefied air was hard to breathe: 'Every breath he drew hurt him, and the blood oozed out from the tips of his fingers . . . Years passed over him, yet he worked on; but the wall towered up always above him to heaven.' Even though he was cutting steps in the rock, he laughed at the Echoes of Despair when they told him that the next step would be his last. But finally he knew he was dying, and he said that other men would climb by his stair and find Truth through him. He died holding a feather from the Bird of Truth that had fallen into his hand, never realizing how near Truth he had been.

This allegory, with its classical symbolism of a voyage and a series of temptations, expresses ideas about individual suffering and integrity that Olive was later to formulate more directly, both in her own life and in her identification with the feminist and anti-imperialist causes. The hunt for truth, the inevitability of isolation, the necessity of solitude, though they were to be continually rediscovered in her later allegories, were not always so obscurely written out. In *The Buddhist Priest's Wife*, for instance, written some ten years later, where she dealt more openly with the situation of a woman who travels to the Far East in search of herself, she found her story in the actual difficulties of love. In *The Story of an African Farm* the allegory of the hunter stood for the most extreme abstractions of good and evil, the fight between freedom and death. In so far as the novel attempted to explore that conflict within the context of an individual reality, Lyndall's subsequent pregnancy and death provide the setting.

On her return to the farm from boarding school, Lyndall is introduced as someone who finds all the old familiar objects in place, 'but the old self was gone'. She is still hard, but sophisticated now; telling Em that a man's love blazes one day only to be gone the next; that she is in no hurry to marry since it means only subservience. Only when she is on her own, however, is the reader allowed into her equally powerful sense of weariness and frailty, but this is a frailty that is never really explained. And then through Waldo's questioning she reveals the depths of her bitterness about the female condition in a series of monologues that have been seen as an analysis of the connections between sex-role conditioning, narcissism, parasitism and frustration.[22]

Waldo wants to know what she has learnt in her years away. She emphasizes the spiritual wasting in a girls' boarding school, which she mocks as a 'nicely adapted machine for experimenting on the question, "Into how little space a human soul can be crushed?"' She had been appalled at the prospect of being shut up with 'cackling old women, who are without knowledge of life, without love of the beautiful, without strength'. But she had been imaginative, even so. She managed to get out of the classes where the girls made cushions and footstools, and was somehow able to get hold of books and newspapers. She saw a few places and some different ways of living, she says almost casually. Is Waldo interested in the position of women, she asks? She scorns his negative answer with the comment that no one is unless they want a chance to show off their wit, and says that the women's question is the one thing about which she herself thinks or feels much – and here there is a striking rejection of the classic 'sensibility' of the feminine, when Lyndall adds off-handedly, 'if, indeed, I have any feeling about anything.'

She describes women as being cursed from birth to grave, working through the stages of infancy and childhood and the growth into adulthood, describing the demands made on girl children to cultivate only their appearance, to give up their desires for freedom or for learning. We come into the world as little plastic beings, Lyndall says, and the world tells us what we are to be. 'To you it says – *Work*; and to us it says – *Seem!*' To women it says that strength, knowledge and labour will be of no use, but our bodies can win us love, power and fame.

> 'They begin to shape us to our cursed end . . . when we are tiny things in shoes and socks. We sit with our little feet drawn up under us in the window, and look out at the boys in their happy play. We want to go. Then a loving hand is laid on us: "Little one, you cannot go", they say; "your little face will burn and your nice white dress be spoiled". We feel it must be for our good, it is so lovingly said; but we cannot understand; and we kneel still with one little cheek wistfully pressed against the pane. Afterwards we go and string blue beads, and make a string for our neck; and we go and stand before the glass. We see the complexion we were not to spoil, and the white frock, and we begin to look into our own great eyes. Then the curse begins to act on us. It finishes its work when we are grown women, who no more look out wistfully at a more healthy life; we are contented.'[23]

Lyndall keeps returning to the brokenness of women's lives, the constraints on their aspirations. How differently she and Waldo would be treated, for example, if they both went alone to a farm one night: she would have 'strange questions asked me, strange glances cast on me'. Yes, women do have one advantage over men – they can use weeping, wheedling and self-degradation to secure a proposal of marriage. Yes, some women have power – but since they can't expend it on healing, or making law or money, they expend it on men. They cannot study for a career – so they study men.

In juxtaposing the notions of *working* and *seeming* Lyndall pinpoints that division of roles which becomes internalized as the archetypal distinctions of male and female: between creativity/receptivity, expression/reflection, self-expression/self-reflection. She is elaborating the narcissism which, though forced on women, becomes their choice and their bondage. But as for its solution, she presents only intellectual growth as the way out of the paralysis of the feminine. She longs for a time when each woman will have her own independent labour, for then love will be neither bought nor sold. Waldo asks her why she does nothing to bring that time closer. Lyndall's reply, like her presence in the novel generally, is cryptic, elliptical, uninformative:

> 'I will do nothing good for myself, nothing for the world, till someone wakes me. I am asleep, swathed, shut up in self; till I have been delivered I will deliver no one.'[24]

She presents herself as being able to *see* the good and beautiful and to have no strength to *live* it, a distinction analogous to that between working and seeming. She is capable only of perception of an alternative, not of bringing it about, and thus remains almost caught in the predicament of the female who cannot act on the world, but can only experience it.

In her search for deliverance – albeit from something unnamed, some deep sense of personal inadequacy – Lyndall hardens herself against the involvement of a loving relationship. The attachments in her life, with the exception of that for her childhood friend Waldo, are deliberately vague. Similarly, her conversation with her lover does not elucidate her feelings at all. Referring only to an ill-explained 'sense of conscience' she reveals her ambivalence about him: she loves him when she sees him, but hates him when they are apart. At the moment, she says, the 'madness' of her love stops her from seeing that he is like any other man.

If she is implying the madness of those sexual emotions that escape rational understanding then all she can do in the novel is refer to the hypocrisy of her culture which divides seducer/seduced: she takes herself, in his eyes, to be a woman 'who has put herself into my power, and who has lost the right of meeting me on equal terms'. She mocks his feeling for her as having been aroused by her decision to marry another man, charging him with liking her because she seemed unattainable, because she treated all men with indifference. Yes, he can take her away and take care of her, and when they don't love one another any more they can part. But she is most emphatic that they must go to a part of the country where they cannot be traced; she wants an ephemeral stopping-place.

He felt a strong inclination to stoop down and kiss the little lips that defied him; but he restrained himself. He said quietly, 'And you loved me – ?'

'Because you are strong. You are the first man I ever was afraid of. And' – a dreamy look came into her face – 'because I like to experience, I like to try. You don't understand that.'[25]

Once more, this time when she later visits Otto's grave, Lyndall shows something of her inner experience of herself, an experience markedly at odds with the dispassionate self she presents to her lovers and friends. Here are light and warmth, she says; why is she so alone, so hard, so cold? So weary of herself! She wants to love! She wants something great and pure to lift her to itself! Will no one help her? And then the one comment that says as much as is ever known about the remorse that she can so easily feel: 'One day I will love something utterly, and then I will be better.' But Lyndall is very much alone, very much a product of her thought rather than her interactions; and her reminder to herself, as she prepares to leave the farm, that her eyes will always be her companion, suggests the very aloneness, the imperative to self-reliance that haunts her to the end of her life.[26]

Some of the confusion within that imperative, however, is revealed in the letter to her lover that Lyndall writes shortly before her death. It is full of contradictions. 'I must know, and see, I cannot be bound to one whom I love as I love you.' One day she would find what she had wanted all her life, someone to worship: 'something nobler and stronger than I, before which I can kneel down'.[27] She rejects her lover even though she loves him. She regards herself as a bad person, though not, apparently, because she wants freedom; the feeling of badness runs deeper. The freedom she yearns for and regards as a right does not, in itself, provide a solution or a *way into* the problem of loving. Lyndall writes no more and feels only 'the sudden drowsiness of great weakness'. But marvelling at Gregory's care and attention, she asks out loud: 'What makes you all love me so? . . . Not utterly bad, not quite bad.' During the night she has a vision of 'a poor weak soul striving after good; which finally learnt that holiness was an infinite compassion for others.'[28] Strangely unreal, her vision has the quality of a catechism. She dies, and Olive leaves the reader only with this question:

Had she found what she sought for – something to worship? Had she ceased from being? Who shall tell us?[29]

*   *   *

To Elaine Showalter, who has recently analysed the female literary tradition of the nineteenth and twentieth centuries, Lyndall is the 'first wholly feminist' heroine in the English novel, and Schreiner's writing part of an 'effort to articulate the tense, indirect perceptions of a new womanhood':

> Even her insistent and sometimes nagging narrative voice takes us to the reality of female experience. That voice, soft, heavy, continuous, is a genuine accent of womanhood . . . the fitful, fretful rhythm of women's daily lives.

Showalter is struck by the power of Lyndall's analyses, the authenticity of Schreiner's critique of femininity. At the same time, she finds her novels ultimately depressing and claustrophobic in that, in *African Farm*, for example, Lyndall's 'brief rebellion does not succeed'.

> In the world Schreiner describes, men are redeemed by female suffering, while women perish in teaching the lesson* . . . The heroines are granted only the narrowest of possibilities; the treatment of them is disconcerting and unadventurous, even timid.[30]

It has become almost a commonplace to describe *The Story of an African Farm* as a deeply pessimistic novel. In one sense rightly, for the ending, in which an unmarried mother dies, can be read as punishment for the threat of deviance from the right moral path. Lyndall's illness is unspecified and she is isolated for nameless reasons after going away with a shadowy strong male figure. This ending, a mixture of intense absences and presences, requires the reader to take as read the working out of Lyndall's relationship with her lover. The reader is told that the two of them quarrelled, but not over what; nor why she refuses to see him, except in her struggle to be her own person, to be independent. Her 'illness', like the illnesses in *Undine*, is as much spiritual and 'political' as physical.[31]

---

* Lyndall's death scene was apparently inspired by the death of a sister of Willie Bertram's after childbirth, and Olive herself would presumably not have agreed with this notion of redemption in her fiction. Some years after *The Story of an African Farm* was published, she told an enthusiastic critic that Lyndall's death was emphatically not a retribution. Olive 'meant to show the struggle of helpless human nature against the great forces of the universe – a sheer physical struggle'. Quoted in *Life*, p. 189. Showalter is making a valid observation about the distribution of roles between men and women in the novels, however.

And yet there is the spiritual strength of Lyndall's feminism, an equally forceful counterpoint to the spiritual loneliness of her life and its last representation in the shrinking of her body that so horrified Gregory Rose. This is a feminism which is in no way seduced by the apparent comforts of the female role, its shelter and protection, its sentimentality. Lyndall has a critique of marriage, ladies' education, and men's indifference to the women's question. She endures the moral isolation of a feminist in a world, whether South Africa or England, in which feminism is very problematic indeed. But in her struggle to make herself different as a woman – in mocking the classic wiles of the feminine – she makes herself different as a person. Hence the paradox of her rejection of love and attachment in the context of an apparently freely chosen relationship, seemingly neither mercenary nor opportunist. The price she pays for her commitment to learning and rationality, to the development of her self, is her inability to accept or trust any loving feelings that others might have for her. In her mind they interfere with, distort or crush whatever chance of autonomy she feels she has. In that she is presented as someone whose situation forces her to confront the social options for women – it is Em who will inherit the farm – she must guard her independence or she will have nothing. She is absolutely unable to show her own weakness and vulnerability, to confess to physical pain or her sense of her own 'badness', lest she compromise her freedom. As a social person she makes a great impact on people and in doing so shows nothing but disdain for convention, an intelligent superiority, and a shrewdness about others' motives. In private, on the other hand, she is dominated by a sense of deep personal inadequacy which is never to be assuaged.

These moral dilemmas are more successfully integrated into Lyndall as a personification of rebellion than as a personality, and in the novel she ends up more as a presence than a person. Who is she, where is she going? There is a great elusiveness about her person. Where Undine made a disastrous marriage and involved herself in the vicissitudes of wealth and self-loathing in a petty English society, Lyndall rejects all the shallowness of her own. Her absence from that society is reflected in the almost deliberate vagueness of her whereabouts. Yet precisely because she has put herself outside all conventional social boundaries, she can take risks, almost play with her individuality. The fact that she dies is secondary; she has had the experience of personal freedom.

Sustained by her rejection of marriage and the formality of that bond, she remains, if not 'wholly feminist' – for her rejection of love is always unresolved – wholly free.

Undine shows a single individual pitted unhappily and ceaselessly against a malicious and basically undifferentiated world. In *The Story of an African Farm* Lyndall, Waldo and Em exist in a complex interplay of solidarity, interdependence, and difference. This is borne out in the ambiguity of the ending – is Waldo dead or not? – where the reader is left wondering whether Lyndall's death requires Waldo's, or whether, quite the reverse, it frees him to resume the very life that Lyndall would not have tolerated for herself. So although the novel is set against a similar social conflict – the subordination of women as a sex – its meaning for the individuals concerned is less stark and all-encompassing than that of *Undine*: no longer individual to world, but child to child and woman to man. Lyndall's death stands as a kind of 'truth' for Waldo and allows him to immerse himself in a benevolent world of dreams and the everyday life of the farm.

In that Lyndall and Waldo, though deeply involved with one another, are of different sexes and thus doomed, in Lyndall's eyes, to lead very different lives, Gregory Rose represents the novel's attempt at some kind of androgynous resolution to the problem of sexual difference. In no way conventionally masculine, indeed designated as 'effeminate', Rose is allowed an interior world of feeling and yearning usually denied to men. The device of the disguise enabled Olive to bring male and female together in a fantasy world where sex roles dissolved, and where seemingly eternal oppositions might be brought to an end: as Lyndall says to Waldo,

> 'Men are like the earth, and we are the moon; we turn always one side to them, and they think there is no other, because they don't see it – but there is.'[32]

Gregory Rose's point of entry in the novel is Lyndall's despair at the impossibility of love. His sex disguised, he becomes a caring, gentle mother. At the same time he had always been the object of Lyndall's scorn: a 'man-woman' who would be happy sewing his daughter's clothes. She tolerated his love for her, but had him emphatically under her control. In this way he became less than a man, perhaps not worthy of respect at all.

The novel did not resolve the paradox of the 'woman', however much it understood the spiritual needs of a feminist. In that it presented Rose as one – wanting, almost abjectly, nothing more than to serve Lyndall – it resorted to the conventional view of men degenerating to womanhood if they had any human or 'maternal' qualities at all. Yet there is as much ambiguity in the meaning of Rose's disguise as in Waldo's sleep/death at the very end of the book. Olive Schreiner had apparently come to regard mothering as the highest function in life; one brief reference to it in *The Story of an African Farm* was the first of many that she was to make throughout her life. But she had also worked out her objections to the constraints of femininity, and she was trying to live differently from the women of her time. Perhaps she was forced to use a fantasy mode in *African Farm*; a fantasy designed not just to conceal the real antagonisms between men and women but to anticipate their resolution. In doing so, she created a compelling world of possibility, an imaginative experiment which was both retreat and liberation.

CHAPTER FOUR

England 1881–1889

Olive Schreiner came to England in 1881 and lived there, with some absences abroad, until 1889. It was a time when Britain's unquestioned industrial supremacy was at an end and the outlines of a distinctive socialist tradition were being laid. The era of the Great Depression initiated the imperialist partition of Africa; it also marked the failure of Victorian capitalism to deal with the social and political problems at home.

Until this time the condition of the poor had largely been analysed in terms familiar to Rebecca Lyndall's generation: poverty was a product of drink, improvidence and idleness, and charitable help, including the use of the Poor Law to impress on the fallen the necessity of self-help, was an essentially moralistic effort. But whereas until then the chronically poor were thought to exist in isolated pockets in the lower depths of the industrial cities, the social investigations of the 1880s were beginning to reveal that a substantial proportion of the working class fell into this category. To a researcher like Beatrice Webb, for instance, the facts of poverty promoted 'a new consciousness of sin among men of intellect and property'. But guilt was mixed with apprehension. Though presented as neglected, even to a certain extent exploited, the poor did not emerge as objects of compassion. Was it not rather that 'the discovery of a huge and swelling residuum and the growing uncertainty about the mood of the respectable working class portended the threat of revolution'?[1]

The Democratic Federation, Britain's first avowedly socialist party, was formed in 1881, the year of Olive's arrival in England; in the ensuing years there was a massive growth in trade union membership and a spread of socialist ideas, leading in 1892 to the formation of the Independent

Labour Party. But the socialism of the 1880s had no single coherent ideology, let alone organization. By the middle of the decade the Fabians had retreated from all notions of class struggle and were advocating a state turned socialist by a leadership of intellectuals and scientific administrators. As for the SDF,* a series of dissensions on the aims and tactics of socialist propaganda and against arbitrary leadership prompted the departure in 1884 of William Morris, Eleanor Marx, Edward Aveling and others to form the Socialist League.

The history of the different varieties of socialism in this period, before it was institutionalized in party machines and political programmes, has raised important problems of analysis. For some the intellectual tendencies within British socialism, especially between 1880 and 1900, produced a socialism which had lost the cutting edge of serious theoretical analysis. Marx had introduced theoretical rigour but few had read him, and already in SDF secretary H. M. Hyndman, who had, there was the mechanistic determinism of a vulgar marxism. For the rest there had been an assimilation of marxism into Christian nonconformity, utilitarianism, and the romantic tradition. This, however, can be read as a 'yawning condescension' of the ideas of William Morris, the most significant member of the socialist circles of the 1880s, and, by implication, of others. The critical question in this opposing argument would be the extent to which the new socialist theory constituted a revolutionary break with the prevailing ideology of Victorian capitalism. At the same time it need not follow that this early socialism was in all respects 'mature, coherent and without self-contradiction'.[2] Its consciousness was eclectic, plastic and individualistic, often expressed with great visionary power and within a religious idiom, and many were concerned less with problems of strategy than with an alternative life. Socialism, to trade union militant Tom Maguire, had to be 'inside the self, not an opinion hung around';[3] it was much more than a struggle for material betterment.

Socialism in the 1880s appealed to some among the middle-class intellectuals, the organized proletariat, and the unemployed: trade union militants, self-educated working-class intellectuals, individuals in revolt against Victorian conventionality, secularists and nonconformists, social reformers unhappy about privilege and poverty. It had many of the aspects of a new religion, and conversions to it were often preceded by

* The Democratic Federation became the Social Democratic Federation (SDF) in 1883.

poverty, unresolved guilt, domestic unhappiness, or wealthy unease. During the Sixties and Seventies the secular religion of positivism had secured the legal emancipation of the trade union movement and anticipated the formation of the Labour Party with its advocacy of a distinctive working-class programme. By 1880, however, it had lost its influence on the TUC and its stance of moralizing the capitalists was under attack from socialists. In addition, its insistence on the sacredness of marriage and monogamy was out of touch with the needs of those individuals searching for ways of living free of the cant and callousness of Victorian society.

In some this preoccupation with individual change led to a severance from organized working-class and socialist politics, and socialist movements, for their part, became hostile to personal issues or uninterested in them. At the same time, small groups of socialists were trying to put their ideas into practice in their own lives. A notion of politics that went beyond parliament and elections – or even change in the ownership of the means of production – was developing. Now there was a preoccupation with sexual pleasure, with the issue of love in a loveless world, with a democratic creation of beauty.[4] This 'religion of socialism' had a power to release the energies of its adherents for positive political work, however limited its effects and however untheorized its demands.

Olive lived in the context of this socialist revival but was never fully part of it. She almost invariably declined to join organizations, often giving her ill health as the reason. Her socialist declamations have a markedly Christian-humanist ring to them, and although she became an intimate friend of Eleanor Marx, there is no mention in her writing or papers of any attempt to read *Capital*. But she knew and valued the friendship of several working-class militants and became a determined advocate of the rights of organized labour. More than most she led a lonely, restless and introspective existence; yet even as she grappled with her personal conflicts, she was seeking connections between the personal and the political. Sometimes she seems exclusively preoccupied with subjective experience; at others with external conditions and issues of radical social change. Her attempts to theorize the connection were constrained by the limits of an evolutionist social science, but she never surrendered the attempt. The personal and political elements of her life were constantly interwoven, though in an anarchic, seemingly temperamental belief in a new quality of life in a new society. Her socialism was more felt than enunciated. Her search for a sexual radicalism was more often than not locked in her personal predicament rather than advocated to others. She was alive to the social injustice that shackled women's freedom, but above all to the way in which women's own uncertainties perpetuated this bondage. Though never a leader of women, she pioneered a feminism convinced of the necessity of a new social order.

Understandably, however – and although she had always thought of England as 'home' – Olive continued to live mentally in South Africa for some time after her arrival in England. Her brothers Fred and Will met her boat on arrival and carried her off to Eastbourne, where Fred was running a school for two hundred boys, New College. Fred was fifteen years older than Olive and he undertook her support during most of her years in England, though it went against her decision to be financially independent. She had very little money, however, and came to rely heavily on him. Will was at Cambridge on a law scholarship and Olive, who had not seen him for three years, made a determined if saddened judgement of his political views, describing him as a 'Beaconsfield young man', conservative, strongly imperialistic and anti-native.[5] Will appears to have been hurt by her reserve towards him. However, these were first optimistic days in a new country, and to her sister Kate back home Olive confided that she had never been so happy in her life.

A visit to Dr and Mary Brown in Burnley, where Olive was shown round a cotton mill, was the prelude to her enrolment at the Edinburgh Royal Infirmary as a nurse probationer.* As the Browns had once taken publishing soundings for *The Story of an African Farm*, now they had cleared the way for her application to Edinburgh. In spite of Olive's love for Mrs Brown and her confidence in the couple, she had been apprehensive about their meeting. 'I think of Mrs Brown and am stronger,' she had written in her diary the month before leaving South Africa, 'but perhaps she won't love me.'[6] The fear of self-exposure and rejection which were to block her writing extended to her closest friends and protectors as well, lest she failed to meet the standards she had set for herself.

Mrs Brown found her changed.

She was still beautiful, but much of the girlish grace and spontaneity

* The Browns had moved back to Edinburgh in 1876, Dr Brown to obtain post-graduate qualifications in surgery and public health. They then moved to Lancashire.

had gone. The constant effort of breathing had raised her shoulders, and at times it was evident that she was fighting an invisible foe.[7]

At Burnley they talked about the project mooted seven years before in the Fraserburg surgery. Mrs Brown found Olive's hopes of becoming a doctor were not as high as they had been then, though she was still purposeful. Olive herself wondered whether she would remain at the Infirmary or study medicine, but financial considerations made nursing seem a more likely prospect.

Although after 1876 there were no legal disqualifications to a medical training for women, they still faced severe difficulties: they had to find acceptance at a medical school, and one with facilities for their clinical training: only in 1877, for instance, did London's Royal Free Hospital manage to provide beds for women medical students to examine patients. Although the 1882 Royal Commission on Medical Education concluded that it was only fair for women to be entitled to register as doctors, the British Medical Association stood by its 1878 decision not to admit them. Some of the opposition derived from men's desire not to offend feminine propriety: Sir Henry Acland, for instance, remembering his fellow medical students as 'low men of low habits', was genuinely distressed at the thought of the horrors women would have to undergo. The women pioneers took a different view, Elizabeth Garrett Anderson telling her students they were in a better position than men to understand the conditions of life which underlay much of the chronic disease and disability of their own sex.

Students, generally coming from wealthy clerical or professional families and usually male, often had a classical education behind them, and as part of a move to affirm the scientific status of medical education, training now required students to pass a preliminary examination; in 1881 this included Latin, algebra, geometry, physics, and chemistry. The nurse, however, was at the other end of the social and professional scale. The precursors of trained nurses were domestic servants, and no particular qualifications had been required; hospitals were initially for the poor, and the well-to-do employed nurses in their homes. Only with the hospital reforms of the second half of the century, prompted by the work of Florence Nightingale on her return from the Crimean War, was nursing established as a possible career.

The impetus for its reform came in part from the extension of medical knowledge; in part to meet a social need, the provision of a suitable occupation for women. In nursing, unlike the learned professions, women would not have to compete with men. The nurse's 'special endowments', according to an authority of the time, would give her a 'special advantage', for 'where does the character of the helpmeet come out so strongly as in the sick-room'?[8]

Nurse probationers in Nightingale hospitals were under constant supervision while on ward duty, were obliged to keep a diary, and were reported on weekly. Training was free, with board and lodgings provided, as were tea, sugar, clothing and some washing, and there was a payment of £10 for the one-year course. Supervision was extended to off-duty hours, with living-in considered essential for character training. Intending probationers were warned that the training required 'a very great outlay of health and strength' and was a trial of courage and physical endurance: 'attendance on death beds, operations and other painful scenes requires continuous efforts of self command hardly to be over-estimated'.[9]

Edinburgh was one of Europe's leading medical centres. The University had pioneered clinical training for doctors in the eighteenth century and the Infirmary was one of three British hospitals to initiate nurse training on Nightingale lines in the mid-Seventies. Olive's stay there, however, lasted only three days. She was unhappy and ill and Fred had to go to Scotland to fetch her. He offered to support her while she underwent medical training, so she decided to stay in Eastbourne and study for the preliminary examination. Dr Brown must have intervened to get her out of the Infirmary, for on her return to Eastbourne she wrote to him in Burnley:

> New College
> Eastbourne
> May 5th 1881

My dear Mr Brown,

You see I have followed your advice for the second time. Here I am at Eastbourne and am going to begin my studies as soon as possible.

My brother arrived in Edinburgh on Tuesday evening. I should like to have remained my month out at the Infirmary but he said I was not well, and brought me down with him, goods and all.

. . .

It's awfully good of you to have taken so much trouble about me.

I hope my health will remain good enough for me to justify all expectations, but I have half a fear I shall find myself a great fool when I
come to measure myself mind by mind with other people.

Give my best love to Mrs Brown: tell her I liked the work at the
Infirmary much, I liked Miss Pringle [the nursing Superintendent],
and liked best of all Miss Spencer.

Your sister wrote me a very kind note which I got the evening
before I left. I was very sorry I had not time to go and see her.

I am, yours in haste and with thanks

Olive Schreiner[10]

It was a formal and prim letter, and only the fear of finding herself to
be a fool comes across with any immediacy. But the pretence had to be
kept up. A letter written the following day to one of the Cawoods in
South Africa described Edinburgh as 'the prettiest grandest place in
the world'. Now she was excited at the prospect of studying medicine
instead of nursing. 'My generous old brother Fred has promised to let
me have as much money as I wish, and I hope to begin my studies very
soon. Isn't it jolly to be able to realise an old daydream at last?'[11]

Olive spent the summer months of 1881 in Fred's study trying to
learn algebra and Latin, but there is no record of her ever having sat,
let alone passed, the preliminary examination. Her patchy history of
self-education made it in all likelihood an unrealistic objective. Fred and
Will may have been aware of this, for during that summer they advised
her to 'stick to literature'. But 'I can't quite see it,' she wrote to Mrs
Cawood. 'I am a man with two loves and don't know which to choose.'[12]

Her next attempt at independence was a stay at the Women's Hospital
in Endell Street, adjoining Shorts Gardens. This was one of London's
five lying-in hospitals, set up to provide 'proper nursing, medical attendance and nourishment'[13] for poor women during childbirth. Endell
Street did not have training facilities for midwives or nurses, and the
basis on which Olive went to it is unclear. It was, however, her initiation
into the street life of the London poor. Here was a district where men
and women known as crawlers huddled on workhouse steps, begging
stale bread and half-used tea leaves, 'constantly dozing, yet never really
asleep'.* At night Olive heard the shouts of 'brutal or drunken men',

---

* This is a quote from John Thomson and Adolphe Smith's *Street Life in London*
(1877), a pioneering combination of text and photographs designed to illustrate the
real conditions of the very poor. Shorts Gardens is described on p. 116.

and 'the screams of women frequently rang through the night'.[14] To be a nurse, according to an account of the time, would bring a first opportunity for contact with the working classes: this 'valuable experience', with its 'frequent possibilities for the exercise of Christian charity', required 'forbearance in a mixed community'; everything had to be done 'with ready pleasure as though the Lord, indeed, were at hand'.[15] Olive's stay in the wards was too short for her to test the sources of her support; she was there for only five days before falling ill with inflammation of the lungs.

She was upset at having let Fred down. 'Poor old brother mine is heartsore and tired,' she wrote in her diary. 'I wonder if he will ever come to see me. Where am I blowing to? Where am I going to? I sometimes fear I shall never be well again.' A few days later Fred called and arranged to take her to the Isle of Wight for the winter. 'I am going to write,' she resolved in her diary, but then drifted into: 'My body is weak. It is a rainy morning . . . The Browns have written me such kind letters.'[16] The drifting was as much a part of her life as of her diary. She had failed to stay the course in both nursing and medicine; she was berating herself for disappointing her family and friends; perhaps, also, regretting her lack of material independence.

Olive spent the winter of 1881 at Rose Cottage, Ventnor, reading Herbert Spencer's *Sociology*, G. H. Lewes' *History of Philosophy*, and George Eliot's *The Mill on the Floss*, and taking desultory German lessons to enable her to read Goethe. Cronwright's *Life* is silent about this period but Arthur Calder-Marshall, in his biography of Havelock Ellis, unearths a love affair with 'a man who was a sadist', in which Olive is said to have 'discovered to her horror that she liked being a masochist'.* Olive herself was secretive, even furtive, about her personal life, and her journal entries for the period give no clue to any of this. When she began

---

* Although Calder-Marshall does not reveal his source, this relationship could be derived from the 'Notes' on Olive that Havelock Ellis made in 1885, now in the Humanities Research Center, University of Texas at Austin. '*He* promised to come and stay with her for a week or so during the first holidays . . . But he never came. At Guilford Street [where she lived the following year] she feared to go out of the house, lest *he* should come when she was away.' 'She says still quite calmly, "I would like *him* to tread on me and stamp me fine into powder." ' See Calder-Marshall, *Havelock Ellis* (1959), p. 91. Johannes Meintjes' *Olive Schreiner* appeared a few years after Calder-Marshall and accepts his version, though without throwing further light on it. No names or particulars are given, no sources revealed. We discuss the significance of Ellis' 'Notes' below, p. 132.

to confide in Havelock Ellis three years later, she made occasional allusions to a previous association with a man from whom she recoiled, but the references are veiled and elliptical; was she still haunted by her association with Julius Gau, or had some other relationship renewed her fright?

Whatever else she experienced on the Isle of Wight, that Christmas she was reading through the manuscript of *The Story of an African Farm*; it was the first time she mentioned the book by this name. By the end of the year it had been dispatched to Macmillan. Slowly she began to write again: a short story for *New College Magazine*, and then several allegories; short bursts of writing seemed to be all she could sustain.

Macmillan must have sent their rejection slip in record time, for by March 1882 Olive was in London preparing to do the rounds of the publishing houses. She boarded for twenty-six shillings a week in the house where Will was staying before his return to South Africa. They went out together, to Kensington Gardens and, on the night before he left, to see Madame Ristori in *Macbeth* at the Drury Lane Theatre. She began attending lectures at the London School of Medicine for Women, but gave up after a few days when she got congestion of the lungs. Her diary was flat and dispirited and her letters rueful. 'How does your baby fare?' she asked Mrs Cawood. 'Why have you got so many? I'm sure you don't need them all. And I would give anything for one. I'm going to adopt a child as soon as ever I'm rich enough.'[17]

After Will had left she stayed on in his rented accommodation in Guilford Street, near Russell Square, and then moved to Palace Road, near Crystal Palace. Fred was constantly in the background, supporting her where she was unable to care for herself: nearly a year after her arrival in England she was 'sitting in my bedroom before the fire my Dadda [Fred] telegraphed me to make'.[18] She spent much of her time crying, ate almost nothing, and took large doses of potassium bromide more or less continuously.* Her responses to new people and places were impulsive and erratic. Normally she would hurtle from enthusiasm to despondency, but of the three years between 1881 and 1884 her

---

* Olive was given to self-medication following Robert Farquharson's very successful *Guide to Therapeutics*, of which there were five editions between 1877 and 1891. Farquharson describes bromide of potassium (which was used mainly in convulsive conditions) as lessening the functions of the central nervous system and having a hypnotic effect on the circulation, with an 'undoubted influence over the generative organs, lowering their excitability, and even in large doses suspending their action'. See *Guide* (3rd edn, 1883), pp. 55–6. Ellis' 'Notes' record Olive taking 'much bromide of pot.[assium] for its influence on sexual system till she deadened her nervous system'.

accounts were unusually constant: 'For the first three years I spent in England I cried every night for hours.'[19] She must have been unnerved by the persistence of her illness, and shamed by her failure in the career she had been planning for years. If she was also bewildered by this first experience of a huge city after years of isolation, she did not say so, though her unease may perhaps be deduced from constant references to a sense of pressure when too many people crowded in on her time and attention. Those who met her in company found her vivacious and striking; left to her inner resources she fled back to books, her incomplete manuscripts, and a fright in herself which cannot have been alleviated by her treks around publishing houses:

> I remember when I walked up Regent Street with *Story* in the rain, thinking everyone could know that what was stuck under my cloak was a rejected manuscript. Oh, so heart-sick.[20]

The 1880s saw a steady increase in the number of British publishers, and some houses brought out as many if not more novels written by women than by men. Although this meant that the woman writer had herself outgrown one part of the constraining female role, the Victorians none the less expected women's novels to reflect the feminine values they exalted,[21] and publishers' readers were the guardians of these stereotypes. Bentley and Sons, to whom Olive submitted her manuscript after its rejection by Macmillan, might well have been interested in a novel set in South Africa; they had published Louisa Hutchinson's *In Tents in the Transvaal* in 1879, and Hutchinson's articles on the Zulus and Boers appeared in the firm's magazine *Temple Bar*.* But while loosely political travel experiences were likely to find favour, the tone of novelist Geraldine Jewsbury's reports for Bentley would explain why the firm turned down *The Story of an African Farm*. A novel about a secret marriage in Sicily

---

* This was the period of conflict between Disraeli and Gladstone over imperial policy in South Africa. Disraeli's government annexed the Transvaal in 1877 as part of a move to maintain British influence in South Africa and convince the Boers to federate. The then colonial secretary, Lord Carnarvon, was intent on incorporating the whole of the Transkei in the Cape, extending British protectorates, and destroying Zulu power. There was growing Boer opposition to British sovereignty, and early in 1879 a series of protest rallies was held. Gladstone's election victory of April 1880 checked talk of rebellion for a while, for he had criticized Disraeli's South African policy, but early in 1881 fighting began, with three defeats for the British, notably at Majuba. By the Convention of Pretoria of August 1881 the 'Transvaal state' was made independent, but Boer settlement was prohibited beyond its frontiers. See T. R. H. Davenport, *South Africa, A Modern History* (1977), pp. 129–32.

was clever but 'decidedly unpleasant. There are two [underlined twice] *accouchements* in the first volume . . . [and] the graphic account of the cholera . . . is not *gay* reading.' As an alternative Jewsbury singled out a novel showing that 'a rich loving nature and a pure truthful heart' were far superior to 'learning and dry intellect'.[22]

The house of Chapman and Hall had established itself by publishing Dickens, and had also brought out Elizabeth Gaskell, and Elizabeth Barrett Browning's *Aurora Leigh*. Olive took her manuscript to them in April 1882. 'Saw Merithett,' her diary recorded a few months later. 'Think Chapman will publish all right.' Only after their meeting did she find out that George Meredith, Chapman's reader, was a controversial novelist in his own right. By the time she met him, between the publication of *The Egoist* in 1879 and the serialization of *Diana of the Crossways* in the *Fortnightly Review* in 1884–5, his reputation was established, but he had become a reader for Chapman's to supplement his income. Batches of manuscripts were forwarded to his home, where he wrote 'crisp, sharp, epigrammatic'[23] judgements in a bound and ruled volume; once a week he interviewed authors. An idiosyncratic reader, he turned down Samuel Butler's *Erewhon* and Sergei Stepniak's *Underground Russia*, but encouraged Thomas Hardy and George Gissing. In his own life, however, he was more consistent: a freethinker with agnostic friends, and later a supporter of female suffrage, in sympathy with the militants for their rejection of 'timidity'.[24] His novels engaged in a radical way with the relationship between sexuality and social reality, *The Egoist*, in particular, exposing the connection between male domination and the sanctity of property.[25]

The Story of an African Farm was one of three manuscripts that Meredith read in the same week. Miss E. A. Dilwyn's *A Burglary: or, Unconscious Influence* was 'entirely weak and silly'. *The Flower and the Spirit*, by Frederica Richardson, was 'very sentimental, better than the above, but impossible'. As for Olive's book he was impressed but undecided:

> The African Farm has far more merit than any of the above. I am compelled to retain it, having no further time to do the work justice, and with a view that the publication of it would not pay. The strong interest seems wanting, though the picturing is good.[26]

Chapman promised their final opinion within a week of their meeting

with Olive. She felt very hopeful, though during the second interview
flew into a rage at Frederic Chapman's suggestion that she should add
a few sentences to make Lyndall marry her Stranger in secret, otherwise
'the British public would think it wicked, and Smiths, the railway
booksellers, would not put it on their stalls!'* Olive described the incident
to Havelock Ellis some thirty years later; then, she said, she told Chapman
to

> leave the book alone or I would take it elsewhere. He climbed down
> at once and said it was only out of consideration for me; I was young,
> and people would think I was not respectable if I wrote such a book,
> but of course if I insisted on saying she was not married to him it
> must be so.[27]

Olive was convinced that George Meredith had nothing to do with
this proposal; after all, 'he *was* an artist'. They had met for a few minutes
in the waiting room before she saw Chapman. On the table lay a magazine
containing illustrations of the battle of Majuba in the Transvaal; Olive
was 'at the time feeling very hotly on the matter', and stated her opinion
that the Boers were 'a noble race, and had been most unjustly treated by
us [*sic*]. To my astonishment the gentleman entirely agreed with me.'
Before they parted Meredith gave her a piece of advice: never to make
any agreement with a publisher without putting everything down in black
and white, and 'always to get some friend who was a competent businessman to make the arrangements'. It was, however, already too late, for
by this time the preliminary business details had been negotiated. Olive
claimed that she was paid £18 2s 11d for the first edition of *African Farm*.

Published in a small edition in two volumes early in 1883, its spine
embossed in a gold ostrich, the front cover incorporating a palm tree
and a desert landscape, *The Story of an African Farm* appeared under
the pseudonym of Ralph Iron, as did the second edition. However, it
quickly became known in London that Olive was the book's author. In
all, three editions appeared in 1883, and over the next forty years there
were twelve more. Olive was at St Leonards-on-Sea nursing her chest

---

* Publishers operated censorship in fear of two of their major customers: W. H.
Smith & Son, who started out as a circulating library and then opened bookstalls on
the principal railway stations from 1858; and Charles Mudie's lending bookshop,
which opened in London's Southampton Row in 1842. Mudie was a strict Nonconformist, and both he and Smith's had a restrictive influence on publishing. See Arthur
Waugh, *A Hundred Years of Publishing* (1930), pp. 100–4.

THE STORY OF

AN AFRICAN FARM

A Novel.

BY
RALPH IRON.

IN TWO VOLUMES.
VOL. I.

LONDON:
CHAPMAN AND HALL, Limited, 11 HENRIETTA ST.,
COVENT GARDEN.
1883.
[All Rights reserved.]

Title-page of the first edition of *African Farm*

when the book was published. Four days afterwards she received a letter
from Philip Kent, then critic of the weekly journal *Life*, enclosing his
review. The letter was written under the impression that she was a man
(though several of the other reviewers guessed she was a woman). The
review was 'one of the only two that have ever touched me or been valued
very greatly by me', the other being Canon MacColl's in the *Spectator*
four years later.[28]

Life usually reviewed new fiction under a general heading of 'Current

Literature', but Kent, writing anonymously, thought the book so exceptional that he devoted a long article to it on its own.[29] Putting it in a class with *Père Goriot*, *Jane Eyre* and *Adam Bede*, he was impressed with *African Farm* as being 'as sad as life', and in no way 'a reflection of any other book, but a *new book*'. More than other reviewers he picked up on the compelling quality of appearance and disappearance in the novel, quoting Tennyson in what must have seemed to Olive an uncanny reminder of Willie Bertram's arrival at her house in 1871:

> There strode a stranger to the door
> And it was windy weather.

Olive felt Kent had 'intense mental sympathy' for what she called 'the artist side of the little book', and she would always remember the surprise she felt, she said, as she walked up and down the sea front reading it: 'I'd thought no one would understand!'

Mrs Brown later recalled the impact the book had on working people:

> I asked a Lancashire working woman what she thought of *Story of an African Farm* and a strange expression came over her face as she said 'I read parts of it over and over.' 'What parts?' I asked, and her reply was 'About yon poor lass' (Lyndall), and with a far-off look in her eyes added 'I think there is hundreds of women what feels like that but can't speak it, but *she* could speak what we feel.'[30]

Historian W. E. Lecky, convinced of the existence of an original moral faculty, acclaimed it as one of the best novels in the English language.[31] He would have supported its freethinking feminism: his *History of European Morals* of 1869, especially its closing section expounding a theme of the modern prostitute as guardian of virtue, had been widely denounced.[32] Sir Charles Dilke, the politician and liberal apologist of Empire, compared it with *Pilgrim's Progress*[33] and placed Schreiner first in importance in a discussion of colonial writing in his two-volume *Problems of Greater Britain* of 1890:

> Although literature and art cannot be called into existence by administrative ability, because they are things of the soul and not merely things of skill, it is impossible to believe that . . . the colonies will not fulfil the promise that is given by such a work of genius as *The Story of an African Farm*.[34]

Gladstone, presently engaged in a thirty-year controversy with unbelief, was sufficiently struck by *African Farm* to write a memorandum on the novel on Downing Street notepaper.[35] Open-minded on the issue of sin as a mortal disease, emphatic on man's ignorance of the afterlife beyond his own certainty that the judgement of an utterly just God awaited him, Gladstone opposed all dogmatic theologizing and wrote sympathetically on the crises of faith of his period.[36] From 'Gregory's Womanhood' in *African Farm* he noted the comment that 'holiness is an infinite compassion for the weak and erring', reminding himself of the main train of thought in Waldo's 'Dreams' about Christianity and transcendentalism after Lyndall's death. The novel confirmed that God was love and that there was no death; he appears to have felt, like Olive, that: 'It is but the individual that perishes, the whole remains.'

Of all the reviews of *African Farm*, the only one that approached doctrinal exegesis was Canon MacColl's 'An Agnostic Novel', the second of the two to which Olive was so attached.[37] MacColl, who had been recommended to *African Farm* by Gladstone, thought the book remarkable, but felt the authoress had made a mistake in counterposing the 'ghastly theology' of Calvinism, with its impossibility of moral goodness, and agnosticism, with the result that her heroine landed in 'moral chaos, ending in a wild wail of despair'. No, there were other forms of Christianity; but nor was this, as was thought in some quarters, a blasphemous or immoral book. No bad woman could have written it, for it was penetrated with a longing to solve the 'dark enigmas' and 'riddle' of life. Alert to Lyndall's conflict of desire between independence and self-abnegation, MacColl considered that an equally important mistake had been to assume happiness could ever lie in independence. 'Like climbing plants,' he concluded, 'we need some support outside of ourselves to which we can cling, and thereby raise ourselves.' It was a very fair review, Olive felt, one that had taken the book 'on the ground on which it must either be praised or condemned'.[38]

Among other readers the book gained notoriety for anything but Christian ideals. Laurence Housman, the early twentieth-century playwright and pacifist pamphleteer, recalled student days in the 1880s, when he and his friends appalled their Worcestershire community by ordering it through the local circulating library:

It was not only for its bad morals that it deserved reprobation; it toyed also with unbelief, and thereby endangered the 'simple faith' of our Victorian sisters . . . I had not imagined my native town to contain so many 'sisters' and so few 'brothers'.

But this was not the end of it. He also met a woman who, in a 'tone of vengeful relish', described 'how having read it she took it up in the tongs, and put it upon the fire'.[39] Olive dedicated the second edition to Mary Brown, but the dedication disconcerted some of Mrs Brown's relatives and friends, one of whom urged its withdrawal. The Grahamstown Public Library declined to order the book, along with works by Fielding, Smollett, Swift and Sterne.

African Farm received several inconsequential reviews; inconsequential not because they are unfavourable but because they are shallow in their approval. The *Evening News* thought it fresh and powerful and that it shed light on 'the most complex problems of modern life'.[40] The *Athenaeum* noted that Mr Iron had followed 'no recognised model of romance' but was struck by the vigour of his description and his obvious familiarity with the life of an ostrich farm.[41] *The Englishwoman's Review*, focusing mainly on the position of middle-class women in other countries and the expansion of women's education, handled the novel as reportage, drawing on one of Lyndall's speeches to Waldo thus: 'We have been more especially attracted, however, by some remarks on the narrow education of women, which . . . tend to show that the Colony has quite as necessary lessons to learn as the mother country.'[42] More serious reviewers, preoccupied with the state of fiction at the end of the century, were excited by *African Farm* as a departure from the extravagance and affectation of modern novelists. Henry Norman, writing in the *Fortnightly Review*, made a passionate appeal for fiction to be closely based upon the realities of life, using *African Farm* as an example:

> In spite of the very masculine name on the title-page it is clearly the work of a woman, and almost equally clearly of a young one, which makes it all the more remarkable . . . The modest title gives no clue to the contents. It is the story of the growth of a human mind cut off from all but the most commonplace influences, facing its own doubts . . . The book might well be called the *Romance of the New Ethics*.*[43]

* In a letter to Henry Norman a few months after his review appeared, Olive expressed pleasure at his sympathetic account of the novel. 'I was glad especially that you felt interested in Waldo, because few people are for him so much as for Lyndall, and I am fond of him.' 22 May 1884, HRC.

Equally enthusiastic – he entitled his review 'A Notable Book' – and
writing from a committed socialist standpoint, was Edward Aveling in
Progress, a journal whose writers included Frederick Engels and Eleanor
Marx.[44] Aveling found the book 'cosmopolitan and human'. But most
striking about it was its vagueness: the characters were 'so many minds
rather than bodies' and the reader was confused as to what they were
doing, because 'we are so interested in what they think and say'. But
to Aveling, 'as probably to all readers, Lyndall is the soul of the book',
and it was 'pathetic that this Lyndall of indomitable will, of unflinching
courage . . . also does little or nothing'. Her life was one long struggle
to be free, ending in failure; he took Lyndall's failure as proof of the need
for 'the great socialistic revolution that is rapidly approaching'. But by
posing socialist optimism as a counterpart to personal failure, Aveling
managed to co-opt *African Farm* into a much more coherent political
tradition than that from which it had actually emerged.

While at St Leonards Olive was working on *From Man to Man*, and
she was moved by letters from people she did not know telling her that
her book had helped and gladdened them. She had become a literary
figure, and she now came to know other writers and to meet some of the
people – Eleanor Marx and Bryan Donkin, her doctor, for instance – who
were to be part of her intimate circle over the next five years.* These
occasional encounters apart, she lived more or less alone with her
incomplete manuscripts until a correspondence with Havelock Ellis
opened a new period in her life.

Olive Schreiner and Havelock Ellis came to know one another during the
first half of 1884. Their relationship opened formally, with an admiring
but critical letter from Ellis about *African Farm*, and a grateful, rather
coy response from Olive conceding that it carried too much moralizing,
though this, she suggested in a bout of special pleading, was a consequence
of a solitary life which made writing the outlet for 'all one's superfluous

---

* The dates and whereabouts of Olive's first meetings with Eleanor and Donkin are
not known, although Havelock Ellis describes Eleanor as Olive's 'chief friend' at the
time when he first met her, in May 1884. See Ellis, *My Life* (1940), p. 183. Eleanor and
Donkin had known each other since 1879, when Donkin attended Eleanor's mother,
and it is likely that Eleanor recommended him to Olive as a doctor. Yvonne Kapp
gives the place and date of Eleanor and Olive's meeting as London, 1882, though
without saying where or through whom. See her *Eleanor Marx, Vol I Family Life,
1855–1883* (1972), p. 217, and *Vol II The Crowded Years, 1884–1898* (1977), p. 22.

feelings'.[45] They began to explore like experiences in their early lives, and an immediate bond was established.

Ellis was born four years after Olive, in 1859. His father was a merchant seaman and spent only three months of each year at home in England; his mother a strict evangelical Christian who was, like Olive's, the dominant parent. Ellis had also experienced an early loss of faith, which had left him enmeshed in an 'empty and mechanical world';[46] in his autobiography, however, he went on to draw an explicit parallel – of a kind Olive either never saw or never expressed – between his adolescent experience of spiritual lifelessness and his sexual guilt and fears for himself. When he was sixteen his father took him on what was to be a round-the-world trip, but he stopped off in Australia, and took a post as tutor to a family in a mountain district west of Sydney. Here he found pleasure in the moonlight, the bird life and the trees, though it coexisted with intervals of unrest, 'even of misery and despair', for there was still the 'trouble of youthful sex and the trouble of youthful religion'.[47] He read a great deal and kept a diary. During a subsequent teaching stint in the bush he was more physically isolated than before, but he had the experience of emotional calm:

> I met no woman there, or man either, who meant anything to me, but I was to find there one who must mean more than any person: I found there myself. This year 1878 was in all exterior relationships the loneliest, the most isolated of my life. But it was also to be for my interior development the most fateful, the most decisive, of all my years.[48]

Here he read James Hinton's *Life in Nature* and underwent a typically Victorian semi-religious conversion. Organized religion was dead to him, and scientific dogma had reduced society to mechanical laws outside human control. Hinton, a doctor at Guy's Hospital who had resolved his own religious doubts by evolving a homespun philosophy based on the mystical and scientific unity of man with his surroundings, offered him new purpose.

Hinton's basic argument was that there was no distinction between the organic and the inorganic, that life was a 'universal character in Nature'.[49] It was an argument that brought life and the machine together, for were they not subject to the same forces and forms? But there was also room for the individual meaning of life: for if Nature was perceived as dead, was this not because 'there is a deadness, unsuspected by himself, in man'? This deadness Hinton called spiritual, and he advocated a moral change to combat it, a change in man's 'being'. From this he improvised the idea of a perfected life and a notion of perfect character in which the individual could achieve a life where nature and passion were at one with 'goodness', for the free expression of passion was rooted in the 'laws' of nature. Using the language of the biological and mechanical sciences he proposed that rigidity be replaced by fluidity: just as Nature was always destroying and rebuilding, so there could be no single, binding morality. Aspects of Hinton's theory and feeling recall Olive's in *Undine* and *African Farm*: the sense of death as change, and as a way to move beyond the merely personal. Hinton's was a philosophy of individual action, implicit in the idea of a perfected life, but one avoiding the isolation of individualism – for since the action of any one man was assumed to change the consciousness of all, it followed that all were united with others, 'even though they might be unconscious of the tie'.

Although Hinton was a very minor figure in late nineteenth-century philosophical and radical thought – indeed, he was considered something of an eccentric – his *Life in Nature* occupied much the same place in Havelock Ellis' formation as Spencer's *First Principles* in Olive's. Both Olive and Ellis had lost religion but found it again; in Olive's case, through a belief in a 'unity underlying all nature'; in Ellis', through a 'sort of home-feeling in the universe'.[50] Both expressed their conversion in religious, though not in theological terms. Ellis' account of his inner transformation is the more developed; he later reconstructed it for his autobiography, begun twenty years after his meeting with Olive.

> The clash in my inner life was due to what had come to seem to me the hopeless discrepancy of two different conceptions of the universe. On the one hand was the divine vision of life and beauty which for me had been associated with a religion I had lost. On the other was the scientific conception of an evolutionary world which might be marvellous in its mechanism but was completely alien to the individual soul, and quite inapt to attract love. The great revelation brought to me by Hinton – a man of science who was also, though he made no definite claim to the name, a mystic – was that these two conflicting attitudes are really but harmonious though different aspects of the same unity.[51]

On this basis religion was a 'natural manifestation, a process that take place spontaneously in the individual soul'. This view of creeds falling into insignificance was, for Olive, derived from Spencer; Ellis' came from Hinton. Both then put their mentors behind them; Olive announced that she had no further need of Spencer; Ellis never re-read *Life in Nature*: 'its work was done, once and for ever, in a moment.'[52]

Now preoccupied with the fact that none of the careers open to someone of his class background – the Church, teaching or the law – attracted him, Ellis read a biography of Hinton and a 'voice from within' made him decide to become a doctor. He aimed to lay bare the truth of human nature, including sexual behaviour, feeling that he could not reach any 'new conception of sex without studying the established conventions of medical science'. He returned to England in the spring of 1880, the year before Olive arrived, enrolled as a medical student at St Thomas's Hospital in London, and entered on seven years of examinations. When he met Olive he was just beginning his training – which allowed her vicariously to indulge her fantasies about herself as a doctor – but he had other interests: he was writing literary criticism for the *Westminster Review*, planning to edit a Contemporary Science series and to write articles on religion, philosophy, travel and politics. He was also pursuing his interest in Hinton, and in the course of working his way through Hinton's unpublished writing came to know his widow and her sister, Caroline Haddon, who helped pay for his medical training. He began to edit Hinton's *The Lawbreaker* for publication.

This was Hinton's attempt to develop the notion of selflessness in the context of an ethical system related to the teachings of Jesus and a sexual philosophy in which women were closer to nature than men. Jesus, as 'lawbreaker', had told men to put away arbitrary laws, but his work had necessitated personal suffering, for the work of seeing the 'better good, the truer right' must always bring grief.[53] And were not Christ's time and our own similar? Hinton drew an analogy with the sickness unto death that had come into the relations of man and woman. Goodness, to him, was not the refusal of pleasure, but his ethic was based, paradoxically, on a rejection of the materiality of the body: 'The individual alone is in the flesh. *Man* is not in the flesh.' His references to women were similarly mystified:

Is not woman in her own nature the lawbreaker? . . . In spite of all her proneness to rigid conventionality and strict adherence to the forms of morals when she is 'good', is not the lawbreaking deepest in her?

To Hinton, the soul of woman was 'intense, tremulous, passion-laden', but he offered no explanation, only an assertion of her greater naturalness.

Out of it came a proposal for a new society ruled by the law of 'service'; for was not 'regarding self' opposed to service? It would consist in doing pleasant things, but pleasure would also reflect the higher morality, so that 'the bodily relation between man and woman would be no more "sensual"; so that there would be no ground for its avoidance, any more than for avoiding fresh air, or flowers'. Nature's path was not against sensuality, he continued: indeed, to degrade pleasure was to degrade woman. But when it came to degradation Hinton made almost no references to lived reality, even though he pictured his system as a way out of the contemporary (though still undefined) sexual problem; his concern was with the 'moral life of the future'.

These ideas were to haunt the relationship between Olive and Ellis, and even, for a time, the discussions of the very select Men and Women's Club which Olive later joined. Hinton had apparently been completely 'unhinged'* by his discovery of female sexuality at the end of his life, and his circle gained a reputation for licentiousness and polygamy that appalled radicals just as much as conservatives. Still, his notion of 'service' was designed to provide an alternative to the stifling institution of monogamous marriage, and perhaps it was because so little was written on sexuality that the unorthodoxy of Hintonism became such a focus; perhaps, too, because his argument was so veiled as to be open to any number of interpretations. It was also the case that the analogy with Jesus drew very powerfully on the distinction between Jesus – the personality – and Christianity – the 'dead', organized religion – made by many late-Victorian rebels. To Ellis, for example, Hinton's treatment of Jesus was 'fascinating'; this was a Jesus

> sensitive to the elemental touch of Nature, struggling, passionate, tempted, only attaining towards the end of his career the statement of that 'new commandment', love one another, which, as Hinton conceived it, superseded all other moral laws.[54]

To its detractors of the right, on the other hand, *The Lawbreaker* sounded suspiciously like a case for free love or polygamy.[55] At source,

* See below, p. 152.

it was a fairly inexplicit validation of sexual pleasure, and one in which the actual conditions of women's lives were lost in the abstraction of woman and nature.

In the three months of 1884 when Olive and Ellis wrote to one another without meeting they exchanged views on writers and books, and then, rather tentatively, explored one another for mutual sensitivities. It was Hinton's work that cleared the way for more intimate exchanges. By coincidence Olive had read Jane Ellice Hopkins' hagiographic *Life and Letters of James Hinton* and, with characteristic literary abandon, wrote that he had a feeling for women like few other men. Yet she had a sense that the 'writer, without meaning to be untrue, is not quite showing the real man'.[56] It proved, for Olive, to be an unusually canny judgement: did she, somehow, detect the mountebank within Hopkins' wholesome tradition of Christian self-sacrifice?[57] She deferred to Ellis' judgement; after all, he knew Hinton's work far better, and though Olive found his ideas vague, he had 'chimed in with the thoughts and feelings that are just now dominant in my life'.[58]

This was the question of women. She was trying to revise *From Man to Man*, the story of a 'simple, childlike woman, that goes down, down'.[59] She wanted to tell Havelock 'what my feeling is about woman' but there was too much to say by letter. Ibsen's *Nora* (later *A Doll's House*) showed that Ibsen did 'see the other side of the question . . . [that] men suffer as much as women from the falseness of the relations. Helmer's life lost as much as Nora's did through the fact that they never really lived together.'[60] But this was a work of art, and she wanted scientific reading: 'my mind needs it just now'. In that she looked to Hinton for it, she was bestowing a doubtful accolade on his work, but that and Edward Carpenter's poem *Towards Democracy*, which Ellis recommended, were virtually the limits of what was then available to her on personal and sexual relations in a wider context. She liked *Towards Democracy* – indeed 'I like it more the more I read it'. Carpenter's delight at inner freedom as the precursor of true democracy expressed 'what is in our hearts, ours of to-day'.[61]

Ellis and Olive also discussed socialism in their letters, Olive glad that their views were identical. Now she gave expression to an almost unbearable sentimentality that also characterized *From Man to Man*:

What we want is more love, and more sympathy. Does it ever strike

you, it often does me, how within the sixteen miles that make London
lie all the materials for heaven on earth, if only something could come
suddenly and touch our hearts one night; there would be nobody
lonely: every aching head with a hand on it, every miserable old maid
let out of her drawing room and her old life-blood flowing; every
wailing little child hushed in somebody's arms and making them warm;
nobody hungry and nobody untaught; the prisons emptied and the
back slums cleared, everybody looking with loving eyes at the world
about them. That would be heaven and it only wants a little change of
heart. I haven't faith in anything that promises to raise us by purely
material means.[62]

Olive and Ellis finally met in May 1884 when she returned to London.
Though she proclaimed herself to have little faith in societies, she agreed
to go with him to a meeting of the Progressive Association. This was the
small group of freethinkers, cooperative pioneers, and ethical socialists
brought together by the editor of the radical monthly *To-day* for the
purpose of lectures and discussion. Ellis as secretary compiled a little
book of secular *Hymns of Progress*, arranged speakers, and booked the
hall on Islington Green for the Sunday evening meetings, but shyly
removed himself from the public proceedings. Through the Progressive
Association he had made contact with Thomas Davidson, then in Europe
lecturing on the utopian communities of New England and yearning
for a community of superior people withdrawn from the world and its
wickedness. In 1882 Davidson had founded an equally small Fellowship
of the New Life in London, its members committing themselves to the
cultivation of the perfect character and a new life. There was a short-
lived attempt at community living in Doughty Street, but the Fellowship's
chief achievement was the publication, from 1889 to 1898, of an up-
market quarterly, *Seed-time*, dedicated to diet reform and other organic
pursuits. George Bernard Shaw, on mischievous form, told a friend that
when Davidson spoke on perfect character, the audience fell into 'bewildered silence'. Ellis attended only casually – though it was here that
his friendship with Edward Carpenter, the writer and socialist, began –
but stayed with the Fellowship when some of its members broke away
in 1884 to form the Fabian Society. Relations continued friendly, however;
the boundaries between political, moral and aesthetic revolt were still
very fluid.[63]

Ellis came to collect Olive from her rooms in South Kensington to take her to the Progressive Association meeting. He was impressed by the

> short sturdy vigorous body in loose shapeless clothes, sitting on the couch, with hands spread on thighs, and above, the beautiful head with the large dark eyes, at once so expressive and so observant.[64]

Olive enjoyed the evening; the following day she wrote to him:

> If you are not too busy and do not feel it would be a waste of time I should be glad if you could sometimes come and see me. It would be a help to me.[65]

It was both a retiring, self-effacing approach to him, and an appeal.

Ellis considers that there was 'an instinctive movement of approach on both sides'.[66] They were soon seeing each other frequently and writing even more often. At the outset it was ostensibly an intellectual exchange, but subjects like Hinton as a sexual theorist persisted precisely because they opened an area of intimacy which both of them needed. Olive was suspicious of Hinton's sexual ethic: did he apply the same measures to man and to woman, she asked?[67] Its importance to Ellis was that it discouraged 'our artificially morbid modest horror of the human body' and encouraged freedom in relations between the sexes. But he was unsure and needed Olive's perceptions, 'that is, if you can trust me enough to tell me sincerely', because there were so few women whose opinions were worth knowing that one could ask.* That Ellis referred to a 'decisive moment of complete trust' as early as June 1884 indicates the significance the relationship had come to assume for Olive:

> She suddenly confided to me the exact cause of the great emotional crisis from which at that time she was slowly recovering, I without doubt being a main factor in that recovery.†[68]

* This account of the relationship is based on a collection of roughly 400 letters, the Olive Schreiner-Havelock Ellis correspondence, held at the Humanities Research Center, University of Texas at Austin. They date for the most part from 1884; in 1917 Ellis destroyed Olive's letters back to 1885. Individual letters are dated only with the day of the week, and taken as a whole the correspondence provides a picture of the early period of the relationship rather than a chronology of it. Of Olive's letters quoted between pp. 131–44, we have made a reference only to those that are reproduced, in part or in full, in Cronwright-Schreiner's *Letters*; all of Ellis' are in HRC.

† There is no way of knowing whether she was referring to her general sense of emotional crisis, or to any particular relationship; perhaps the encounter during the Isle of Wight stay in the winter of 1881-2 was still on her mind.

From the start Olive and Ellis developed an ambiguous relationship. It led to an absorption in their shared experiences that grew into a delight at a sense of shared self. It led to a closeness, as they probed one another's emotions, with overtones of a love affair. He began as confidant but also as diagnostician, even therapist. She revealed herself (though never completely, as she reminded him from time to time) and Ellis' notes ultimately became a case history which for the first time gave her illness a certain coherence. She found she could open herself to him because he did not seem to her like 'another man', but more like part of herself: 'How can I keep you from me?' she wrote. Their commitment to a scientific understanding of physiology made for an unusual sexual frankness, but their own sexuality proved to be unexpressed.

Ellis' case history documented details of Olive's work as a governess, her comments on the most important books of her adolescence, a difficulty with eating that she'd had, and references to various drugs she had taken for her chest.[69] Most significant, however, was Ellis' methodical record of what she told him of her sexual history. It revealed a terror of sexual involvement, a feeling that it demeaned her and made her feel just like a prostitute, but that it was extremely exciting nonetheless. In noting the failed outcome of one of her relationships, about which 'She says still quite calmly, "I would like *him* to tread on me and stamp me fine into powder," ' Ellis acknowledged perfectly neutrally an element of masochism in her personality. The tenor of the history as a whole was, similarly, cool and unshockable. Concerned to encourage a general sexual frankness, and to practise it now in relation to Olive's development, Ellis focused on those realities of her life in South Africa that Olive had had to keep hidden: her attraction to her employers, their sexual advances, her yearning for passionate love. At the same time he noted those basic feelings about herself that had always to be borne in mind if one would understand her: her feeling that she had something of a man in her nature; her need of men's society and her conviction of men's selfishness; her desire for the 'joyful solitude' of a soulmate, who she hoped, again, would be a man.

Ellis' commitment to researching female sexuality, his acknowledge-ment of its existence and force, enabled Olive to work on assimilating the experiences she'd had. At the same time his belief in the biological basis of character meant that a statement like 'She feels she has some-thing of a man in her nature' passed without comment. Yet here Olive made one of the most revealing statements about her sense of herself in relation to her society that a woman could make. Rejecting the powerlessness of the traditional female role, she chose an 'external' world of work for herself, yet could identify herself only as deviant within the culture: a woman who had adopted a man's pursuits: economic independence, creative work, freedom to travel, and a measure of sexual autonomy. In fact there was another part of the 'man' within her, and this a seemingly more dangerous one: the part which did indeed feel powerful, asserting its individuality and its right to experience. It was this part of herself that Olive and Ellis never fully integrated into their picture of her, however close they became and remained.

Throughout 1884 and for most of 1885 they wrote to one another daily; on occasions there were three letters a day from Olive. Ellis, though still only a medical student, followed the symptoms of her illness minutely and prescribed and monitored treatments. She was convinced that she grew stronger from the time she knew him, but a doctor she was seeing diagnosed 'nervous prostration'[70] and she went to Derbyshire to rest. There Havelock sent her his Australian diary, for it seemed easy and natural to bare his inner self to someone with her 'large tolerance and her active intellectual receptivity'.[71]

In the beginning it seemed to take 'simple easy things' to make them happy. Havelock felt delight in the strong, careless, creative powers he saw and felt in Olive; and the feeling that he was not longing for desire 'but an *immense realisation* of you'. He had never felt like this for anyone else. Olive's feelings were similar. She recalled the time she lived on a lonely farm, and, walking at night under the willow trees or on the dam walls, she had said to herself: 'One day I *must* find him.'[72]

The letters in which they explore their likeness and their responses to one another are laced with inquiry into the scientific basis of sex feeling, some of this culled from medical texts, much of it probed in self-questioning. Inevitably the scientific and the personal were joined. 'Tell me about what you feel physically that one can't understand,' Olive urged him, adding: 'How close we are to one another.' But the closeness prompted doubt and apprehension in her:

I can't explain what I mean by this fear, not even to myself; perhaps you can for me. I am so afraid of caring for you much. I feel such a bitter feeling with myself if I feel I am perhaps going to. I think that is it. I feel like someone rolling a little ball of snow on a mountain side, and he knows at any minute it may pass out of his hand and grow bigger and bigger and go – he knows not where. Yet, when I get a letter, even like your little matter-of-fact note this morning I feel: 'But this thing is yourself.' In that you are myself I love you and am near to you; in that you are a man I am afraid of you and shrink from you.[73]

Olive was staying in a cottage in Bole Hill in Derbyshire at a time when Eleanor Marx and her lover Edward Aveling were also in the neighbourhood, about a mile and a half away. Eleanor was very conscious, now that she and Aveling were living openly together, that they might be socially ostracized. The proprieties of the situation would not have occurred to Olive; she was, however, worried about Eleanor because she had a dread of Aveling that she failed to fight down even for Eleanor's sake. She wrote to Havelock:

> To say I dislike him doesn't express it at all; I have a fear and horror of him when I am near. Every time I see him this shrinking grows stronger.[74]

She did not specify her objections, and she was certainly prone to precipitate judgements; in this instance they happened to coincide with other people's opinion of Aveling. He was widely castigated for his recklessness about money and women, and many of Eleanor's friends anticipated the deep unhappiness which he would cause her.

A noteworthy letter from Eleanor to Olive written the following year demonstrates the closeness between the two women, though it is described by Eleanor Marx's biographer, Yvonne Kapp, as 'an incontinent love letter'.[75]

> My Olive, I wonder if I bore you with my stupid letters – as I wonder if, one of these days you will get horribly tired of me altogether. This is no figure of speech. I really *do* wonder, or rather fear. I have such a terror of losing your love . . . I keep wanting to hear you say you love me just a little. You do not know, O, how my whole nature craves for love. And since my parents died I have had so little *real* – i.e. pure, unselfish love. If you had ever been in our home, if you had ever seen my father and mother, known what *he* was to me, you would understand better both my yearning for love, given and received, and my intense need for sympathy . . . Edward is dining with Quilter and went off in

the highest of spirits because several ladies are to be there (and it just occurs to me, that you may be one! How odd that would be!) and I am alone, and while in some sense relieved to be alone, it is also terrible . . . I would give anything just now to be near you . . . How natures like Ed's (i.e. pure Irish and French) are to be envied, who in an hour completely forget anything . . . With all the pain and sorrow (and not even you, my Olive, know quite how unhappy I am), it is better to have these stronger feelings than to have practically no feelings at all. It is too bad of me to go on scribbling like this. But you would forgive me if you knew the help it is to me. Writing to you I see your dear face before me and that gives me courage and strength. Write me a line. Just one line – say you love me. That will be such a joy, it will help me get through the long miserable days, and longer, more miserable nights, with less heavy a heart. There is so little in me to like or interest people. That *you* care for me is one of those mysteries that remain for ever inexplicable. Good night, little girl . . .[76]

Kapp has made strong insinuations about the relationship between Olive and Eleanor, on the basis of this letter and other rather slight evidence. She maintains that Olive 'preferred women'; that she was 'possessive and domineering' in her friendships with them; that Eleanor for her part had been 'captivated', almost 'captured' by Olive; that Eleanor had lost her usual restraint; that 'something in Olive's over-powering personality had reduced her to pulp'.[77]

Biographical covetousness apart, these judgements of the relations between the two women do raise the issue of Olive's attitudes to women, which we discuss elsewhere in this chapter, but also of a possible alternative context within which Eleanor's emotional reliance on Olive, however occasional, might be seen. If the friendship was unique for Eleanor, so it was for Olive too. She had other close women friends, South Africans like Mrs Cawood and Mrs Brown, but they were older, and her patrons if not surrogate mothers; her letters to them, although affectionate, were comparatively dutiful. There was her friendship with Ellis' sister Louise, with whom she exchanged an unselfconsciously 'feminine' correspondence about clothes and sewing.[78] She was also making contact with a growing number of other women, whom Ellis called her 'commonplace' friends, perhaps because they deferred to her as a celebrated novelist and daring talker.

Eleanor and Olive were different together, and there is no doubt that in Derbyshire the women rediscovered an empathy that had been present since they first met. Whatever else they discussed they found it possible to lead on to the subject of their sexual feelings. By Olive's own account, Eleanor was the first woman with whom she could raise the issue of emotion before and after the menstrual period, and while this was a scientific concern of hers, Eleanor's appeal to her in the letter of 1885 suggests that they also confided in each other a great deal of their private lives.* Olive's practice of intermittent self-revelation may have initiated their intimacies, but Eleanor was receptive if more restrained; more than this, she needed Olive's affirmation of love and support in exchanges between them which – if the letter is any evidence – were immediate and raw but deeply touching. Whether or not Olive and Eleanor were sexually attracted to one another at some level – in fact Olive appears not to have recognized the existence of lesbianism† – Eleanor's letter testifies to her basic warmth and understanding, and, equally, to Eleanor's need of these qualities in her, perhaps precisely because they were absent in her other relationships, including her political life. Certainly if Kapp is right and Eleanor rarely lost control, Olive, on the contrary, was in continuing emotional crisis; but if her own emotional life and judgements were precarious, she was acutely sensitive to others' needs.

Once his medical examinations were over, Ellis was able to join Olive in Derbyshire for some weeks. This is the longest time they spent together, and his recollections of Olive suggest a relationship that was in many ways uninhibited and, presumably, fairly unorthodox:

> I see her coming suddenly and quite naked out of the bathroom in the house where she was staying into the sittingroom where I was waiting for her, to expound to me at once some idea which had just occurred to her, apparently unconscious of all else.[79]

But when he returned to London in September 1884, and she stayed on

---

* Eleanor's concerns and temperament were more akin to Olive's than Kapp allows. Witness a letter to Olive from a friend of theirs during 1886: 'I saw Eleanor at the [British] Museum yesterday. She fairly danced with anger. I told her that translation of the Kama Sutra was locked up, in the Library, and refused to women. See if she don't get it!' OS to KP 7 Maruh 1886, *Pearson*.

† On one occasion she wanted to 'cuddle close up' to Louise Ellis, but she was ashamed of her feeling. See *Letters*, p. 23. Other than this, there is no mention of any kind of erotic attachment between women. *Woman and Labour* includes references to male homosexuality only.

at a nearby farm, reaction set in. Initially, immediately after his departure, Havelock sensed that she felt most passion for him. But if it was passion, it was quickly drained; she felt weak and tired, and bouts of illness once again became virtually continuous. 'It's as much my mind as my body that is ill,' she wrote, 'I never felt like this before.'[80] Walking down the road past the rock where they had sat together, 'suddenly this suffocating feeling came to me and I was crying out'. In the ensuing months 'the old madness that I thought I had conquered came over me again'.[81]

Spending as much time alone as she did, she came to fantasize an eternity in which 'we shall be wandering in the dark and trying to find each other again', and over the months her symptoms grew more persistent and more varied: dizziness, nausea, fever and cold, pain under the shoulder, spitting blood. She was dizzy when she was up; it was worse lying down. She had wild sudden outbursts of crying. There were times when she found herself 'tearing my clothes off me in the agony'.[82] Havelock wrote with tender concern and medical advice. Between the patent medicines she took, his suggestions and the drugs prescribed by various doctors, she was taking quinine, chlorodyne, bromide, even morphia by injection, though the last rarely. Havelock warned her against taking quinine more than three times a day, and only a very little at a time, or it 'will prevent you working or doing anything'. His suggestion was nux vomica, a nerve tonic to stimulate the spinal cord, and, at other times, bromide, 'for it is possible you have too much blood in your head, it is important that you shouldn't exercise your mind more than you can help'. Her symptoms and the side-effects of the various treatments must have become increasingly difficult to disentangle.* As the months went by and Olive found no relief, Havelock began to investigate what we would call psychosomatic models of her illness.

Olive appears to have called her condition asthma only from the time of her association with Ellis. In South Africa she looked for treatments for her 'chest', although a casual reference to the disease in *The Story of an African Farm* indicates that she knew of its existence. Ellis undoubtedly helped her to see it as being prefigured in childhood and the situation from which she came: he was struck by the relevance of a passage in a medical book he was reading,

---

* She seems also to have had semi-hallucinatory experiences ('I woke up last night shouting and crying. I thought Fred was going to turn into nothing'), perhaps related to the large number of drugs she was taking.

taken, of course, in connection with what you have told me. He [the author] refers to young people who had, for the most part, a solitary and unsocial life; they acquire an exalted and unhealthy ambition; they acquire the habit of masturbation; they produce premature work in literature or art. He says that physically this results most commonly in asthma or neuralgia. I had never put all these things together before.

Olive was tormented by her inability to work but she ignored Havelock's advice that it might be better not to try when she was not really able to, and she almost destroyed the manuscript of *From Man to Man*. He read and re-read *African Farm* and her new manuscripts, questioning her about her characters, studying her style, and giving advice that she was evidently unable to take up:

> I always grudge a little the work you spend on *From Man to Man*. I want you so much to begin writing what will become the true outcome of your present self. You say that the moral of this book is not what you would now make it. It is such weary work for you to be revising that.

He urged her to write an article on prostitution, helping her to order books from the London Library on social life, ethics, and the relevant data. But apart from her letters to him, she wrote nothing in this period; it was a time of trying to rework old manuscripts and of struggling with feelings.

Ellis was bewildered by them, then saddened. It was characteristic of Olive to have written to him most feelingly when they were apart, as when he had returned to London from Bole Hill; when they were together some expectancy, at least hers in him, seems to have died. He pressed her to explain the reticence and doubt he felt in her, which was hardening into rejection:

> You say that what is pure and right for me [Ellis wrote] is not so for you. I have been thinking a good deal lately about these things that you say sometimes and the way that you feel about our coming near to each other. I want to know what is good. I think that if anything was wrong it was that we did not speak openly enough at first. I *assumed* that your impulse to come near to me was strong enough to make it right for you – whether it was passionate or not (I did not ask myself whether it was that or not.)

She was too ambivalent in herself to be explicit. 'I feel as if you were part of my body,' she told him, 'then why do I feel as if to kiss you were wrong?' The passion was there, but something overrode it.

As his letters grew more insistent she warned him: 'Don't love me too much. I died three years ago.' She insisted she was happy when she thought of him, because he was 'the first human being who has been perfect rest to me'; and she maintained that all she wanted was to rest. She felt remorse at having to do unpleasant things for fear of misleading him:

> Henry my letters seem cold to you. It is because I *dare* not give way to feelings of *any* kind. If a man has a wild unbroken horse he must keep the bridle on him. You are dearer to me than you have ever been. You have become part of my life itself.

Olive tried to make this last phrase sound like an achievement; in reality it was the source of their failure. They were absorbed, even exhilarated by their sense of likeness to one another, but in the course of their exploration of themselves each projected on to the other their own sense of self to the point of obscuring and then obliterating the other's personality. Olive loved Havelock in that he resembled herself; he became an extension of her own narcissism, her self-involvement.

Being narcissistic, it had the quality of an infantile love. Olive had never had much opportunity to love; her most important relationship had been with herself, and this through necessity rather than choice. She needed to create a childhood that she felt she'd never had: 'You are my family to me,' she wrote to him a year after they met, and 'fill that deep part of my heart that if it were empty would make life all sad.' She thought of Ellis and herself 'as only children together to help each other to grow'; he addressed her as his 'sister-child'. At the same time, the feeling of being a child, in the context of the late-Victorian revolt, also represented a desire for the assumed spontaneity of the child. The idea went back to Rousseau's conception of the child as pure and man in his natural state as good, then corrupted by society. Ellis and Olive believed they could escape their social constraints by representing themselves to one another as children, and childhood as a time of simplicity and sweet intimacy: trying to define their relationship when she rebuffed him, Ellis insisted on the sweetness of their being 'quite simple and childlike with each other'. The juxtaposition expressed, at source, an idea about sexual innocence, and a typically pre-Freudian one: the notion of an innocent childhood undisturbed by sexual feeling.

The sexual part of their relationship, however, cannot be completely defined. Ellis believed, with Hinton, in the 'firm showing of what is beautiful in the human body'. At the same time his sexual language was fey. The best kind of union, he told Olive, would be 'a sort of camaraderie' in which the two were 'going the same way, and can walk arm in arm, and kiss and encourage each other on the way'. He did also say that he would 'have the passion thrown in' but the statement has the quality of an afterthought. His autobiographical account of their relationship, written many years later, is more explicit. He describes Olive putting her arms round him a couple of months after they met, and 'from that moment our relationship became one of intimate and affectionate friendship'. He adds, however, that 'it scarcely passed beyond that stage':

> It is necessary to be precise. She possessed a powerfully and physically passionate temperament which craved an answering impulse and might even under other circumstances – for of this I could have no personal experience – be capable of carrying her beyond the creed of right and wrong which she herself fiercely held and preached . . . For a brief period . . . there passed before her the possibility of a relationship with me such as her own temperament demanded. But she swiftly realised that I was not fitted to play the part in such a relationship . . . I on my side recognised that she realised this . . . We were not what can be technically, or even ordinarily, called lovers.[83]

The picture that Havelock gives in his autobiography, bearing in mind his remark that nocturnal emissions with no awareness of orgasm were almost his only sexual outlet till his marriage at the age of thirty-two, is of a relationship in which Olive's straightforward sexual assertiveness conflicted with his absence of desire. But their correspondence indicates that Olive's sexuality was itself very conflicted. When she came near or kissed him she felt she was 'cruel' and 'untrue' to him, and suffered agony. It was an experience at considerable variance with the powerful and almost simple temperament Ellis describes; passionate she probably was, but she had great difficulty in accepting her own sexuality. The complexity and pain of their sexual relationship derived from the interaction of their personalities and their turmoil on issues of sexual morality; the two were internalized in Olive's fears and Ellis' uncertainties.

After a while Olive became as sexually reticent as Ellis had once been; indeed it was he who became the more outspoken and forthcoming. After the Derbyshire holiday when he felt there was something different between them, he wondered whether 'it may be ignoring sex'. Since she had said that 'the form of love without the reality was the one impurity', he had taken it for granted that she cared enough to make it right for herself. But subsequently he felt her 'gradually slipping away from me and I couldn't stop you or save you'. For himself, he declared that 'though not the best possible thing it is good for me (even physically good)'. 'It' could here refer to their coming near each other in general, or to the explicitly sexual part of the relationship. But it is still clear that Olive's rather theoretical insistence on a progressive morality made it impossible for Ellis to know what she really wanted for herself. Now he made a direct request. 'I want to know how it is for you. *Quite apart from the question of what may or may not be good for me.*' The relationship was poisoned for him if it was not good for her. Ellis had always found that loving was 'torture' to him, the more painful the more he loved someone. Where there was openness, however, there was no pain, and he had felt that freedom with Olive at the beginning. Now that there was 'something different', she had the power to hurt him 'by *not* speaking openly'.

Olive was actually struggling with very violent feelings and fantasies, her language expressing a terror of invasion as she referred back to a previous experience that was such agony it simply had to die: a man thought, she said, that when he 'touches a woman it is only her body he is touching, it is really her soul, her brain, her creative power. It is putting his fingers into her brain and snapping the strings when he draws her to him physically, and cannot take her mentally.'* She was striving to 'crush and kill all that side of my nature', and had been for the previous three years. Had she been shaken by her own sexuality to the point that she dared not allow herself to respond again? Her retreat was to a selfless relationship without passion.

Both of them needed a relationship to express their notion of a higher morality, and from Hinton they projected an ideal of a life of service. The relationship with Olive gave Ellis something very important – 'to be *able* to long' – but the desire for companionship was always anguished. 'As soon as I begin to want things for myself my strength goes and I am

* Olive reproduced this idea almost word for word in *From Man to Man.*

miserable,' he wrote. So he sought to give comfort and to lose himself, for only in loss of self could motives be pure; according to Hinton the slightest vanity or hope of salvation for self altered the whole character of giving up for others. Ellis' selflessness even created a romanticism about other relationships which Olive might form, as when he considered the possibility of her marrying someone who could help her to work: 'even if I wasn't happy I should be saved from being unhappy, by knowing you had what was best for you.'

Olive saw Ellis as morally good, and herself as striving after that same goodness. He thought her image of him a 'purely ideal creation', but she never ceased to torment herself over the imagined discrepancy between the two of them. She felt she should be away from him: 'I want to be good for you, and I think I can be better far away writing to you than near you talking and interrupting your life.' She felt her desire to see him was 'purely selfish'; she had no way of accepting her own needs as valid for her.* While the morality of assumed or projected selflessness was something of an ideological position for Ellis, Olive's tendency to self-denial was the less ideological but the more neurotic; she was locked in a conflict between her fantasy of herself as unworthy and her awareness – but active suppression – of her needs.

Although her illness forced her to rest, enforced passivity became her choice. Perhaps this passivity could somehow, unconsciously, be equated with virtue?[84] She wanted physical nearness but no excitement; perhaps she was frightened of real closeness. It certainly seemed to make her ill. Now her illness virtually never left her. And although Ellis was achieving some important insights into it, there is evidence of some collusion. He wanted to be with her when she was sad and ill, since that enabled him to love her unselfishly:

> When you are ill I am sad and also happy, then you belong to me. When you are well, I am glad and miserable; you don't belong to me, my heart aches.

Implicitly, then, he needed her to be ill in order for him to be unselfish. Indeed, there were times when he did not seem able to tolerate her wellbeing and happiness – it made him feel 'like a cloak that you'd thrown off on to the floor when you felt warm'.

* On one occasion, in fact, Ellis wrote shrewdly and forcefully to Olive about the mystifications inherent in the model of a selfless involvement. But the awareness was never integrated into the relationship.

She and Ellis seem to have held a similar view of the place of illness in personal relationships: in order to relieve suffering one had to be suffering oneself. In part this explains Ellis' willingness to engage more or less indefinitely with Olive's symptoms and to endure a relationship in which he described himself as tortured. The degree of suffering which both experienced served to reassure them of the relationship's potential for service and selflessness. Neither of them, however, suggested an explicitly psychosexual explanation for Olive's symptoms. Perhaps the complexity of their bond – as doctor/patient and lovers/children – made this impossible. To have done so would have exposed the sexual difficulty of their relationship and forced both to confront aspects of their lives that each, for different reasons, needed to suppress. Olive's illness enabled her to try out feelings about her body without the anxiety that physical involvement provoked, and in this way the relationship with Ellis could be desexualized. It was obviously significant that she could reveal so much of her inner world, but she may have needed – and used – physical distance from him to gain the detachment of a writer.

Much given to hindsight, Olive later claimed she knew from the start that a sexual relationship with Ellis was impossible, for she had detected in him 'a strong element of abnormality':

> I felt it from the first day I met him; he never denies it; and we have often discussed it. He is only interested in the abnormal – not the exceptional, but the diseased ... To a certain extent Ellis is a true decadent.[85]

It was also later that she reflected on the relations of doctor and patient, perceptions that may have come in part from the long imprisonment of her association with Ellis, in part from other contacts and observations of friends. She knew that marriages were often the result of the influence a doctor came to have over his female patient, 'in [her] times of weakness and suffering', or a nurse over her male patient, but she had also sensed 'one very curious thing about this relation ... – the extreme shortlivedness of the attraction if they recover full robust health'.[86] Her association with Ellis was much more solidly based than the manipulative liaisons she was disdaining here; at the same time, she was making the general point that a relationship involving illness was far from neutral, indeed that power and control would be central themes – on both sides.

By the end of 1885 the relationship with Olive had become a partial one-sided thing for Ellis. He wanted something he could love for ever, that would love him entirely; after her drawing back, everything about her hurt him. He wrote forlorn pleas to her not to forsake him. Olive continued to insist that her feeling for him was the most pure and perfect she had ever had for anyone, rarer than passion; it was friendship of a special kind, like that for Willie Bertram, the man who introduced her to Spencer. Ellis remained in her thoughts and close in her heart; she did acknowledge, nevertheless, that 'somehow we seem sad in body'. Now she turned back to her manuscripts. She assured Ellis that she was happy, but happiness was being 'in a condition to master my own feelings and keep them from rending me'. She would never find health while dependent on any human creature. Her health was worse than ever, but 'it isn't my chest, it isn't my legs, it's I myself, my life', she cried. 'Where shall I go? What shall I do?'[87]

Lodgings and landladies were continuing problems. In her Hastings lodging house there were seven other women and if Ellis came to visit her they had no place to talk 'because we couldn't go to each other's rooms and the old maids are in the parlour'. A landlady at Portsea Place in London gave her notice to leave because she had so many men visitors.[88] Ellis was discomfited either by the other visitors, or, alternately, by her unease: 'I don't think I can bear to see you when every moment you are thinking someone is coming in or listening outside or something.' Still, the correspondence and the relationship continued. Olive and Ellis saw each other, though at times intermittently, up to Olive's departure for the Cape in 1889. He remained her most basic source of support, the person to whom she could return even when her affections were more strongly aroused by others. For his part he appears to have accepted the limits of the relationship very slowly; only Olive's return to South Africa freed him to develop other attachments.

During the spring and summer of 1885 Olive began to feel her mind was expanding again. Back in London after several months in St Leonards and Hastings, she received calls from Rider Haggard and Philip Marston, a blind poet. George Moore spent an evening with her, and she met Oscar Wilde. Eleanor Marx sent her a frantic appeal for assistance when Aveling fell seriously ill and she arranged for help from Ellis. She attended meetings of the Fellowship of the New Life, where discussions about the equality of women became known as 'Olive's subject', and where, according to Henry Salt, she made a deep impression on the men, with her 'passionate intensity, her frank, almost immodest utterances, her obvious sense of equality with [them]'.[89]

She was now receiving medical attention from Bryan Donkin, a sophisticated physician accepted both by the radical circle of Engels and the Marx family and by the establishment world of the Savile Club, on whose committee he had served for three years. From a classical education at Oxford he had proceeded to train as a doctor and to specialize in neurology, on which subject he contributed regularly to *Brain*. He admired Olive's writing and brought Gladstone's compliments on *African Farm*.* He was clearly in love with her, and insisted that she should not be ill again within a hundred miles of London without sending for him. Olive was touched by his 'sweet respectful manner' but could not reciprocate his feeling for her.[90] She still had lapses into a rather sad nostalgia – she heard that Julius Gau, whom she had not seen since she was sixteen, was coming to England, and she wanted to be at the docks when the Cape steamer arrived.

At the same time she was absorbing herself in the Men and Women's Club, a discussion group which gave her her first experience of a shared commitment to intellectual work on the relations between the sexes. It had a precursor in a group of the same name which met from 1879 to 1885 but which discussed a wider range of topics including art, theatre, clothes, and the influence of science on modern thought. Karl Pearson, a barrister then beginning a professional career in mathematics at University College, London, attended from 1882, but soon formed an idea for more

---

* The acclaim she found in literary circles must have been doubly needed at a time when even Fred, her dependable brother, wrote from Eastbourne to say that he no longer wanted her to have anything to do with him: 'my *African Farm* brings him into trouble.' 'I couldn't bear it,' she added, 'only I make myself quite hard and callous.' Journal entry, 15 July 1885, quoted in *Life*, pp. 170–1.

This appears to have coincided with a letter to Olive's elder sister Kate from one of Kate's in-laws:

John said he would buy a copy of your sister's book for you. Did he do so? I have read it. It is very clearly cleverly written, but I am sorry that her philosophy is so gloomy and her idea of life not brighter. She must have great talent. I fancy in Lyndall and in Waldo and the Stranger she describes what her own mind has passed through in her struggles and strivings after or rather against the truth. Let us pray that the great Shepherd may bring back to His fold and to the faith of her childhood the wandering sheep.

Maggie Findlay to Kate Findlay, Cape Town, 30 March 1885, *Findlay*.

focused gatherings, since it was 'a great loss that men and women should discuss together all subjects except those most vitally important to both sexes alike'.[91] His old Cambridge friends Robert Parker and Ralph Thicknesse, members of the original club, were interested, and he approached the Sharpe family in Highbury, middle-class intellectuals with whom he had been in contact for several years.[92] Elizabeth Sharpe, a freethinker married to Henry Cobb, a Nonconformist banker and solicitor, probably met Pearson for the first time at one of his lectures on social questions at the South Place Chapel in Finsbury in 1881, and they were now in regular correspondence. She introduced him to her sisters, one of whom, Maria, she knew would be most sympathetic to such a group.

An entirely intellectual undertaking, the club concerned itself with the status of moral judgement, moral change, fact and truth in the face of received opinion about the sexes. Its deliberate isolation from the very different world of propagandist politics invited a charge of elitism from Annie Besant, the birth control pioneer and socialist, who felt club members lived in a 'cosy nest of their own and only *hear* of the rough side of the outer world'.[93] Similarly, they put the concerns of the 'race' and the 'wide mind' above the discontents of an individual situation, expressing impatience at a suffragette reference to the economically dependent wife's feeling of degradation: surely her moral duty to her child was the more basic? At the same time, the club's project was a radical one. In a culture which had successfully refused middle-class women knowledge about their bodies while stigmatizing the prostitute as being 'outside' society, the club sought to bring men and women together in an attempt at finding an alternative to the deep split between 'animal' and 'human' that characterized the dominant mid- and late-Victorian attitudes to sexual passion.

Plans for the club were laid in the autumn of 1884, but meetings did not take place until the summer of 1885, and members were selected very carefully. It was inevitable that this second club should have proceeded with such discretion. Elizabeth Cobb, for example, contacted 'three women whom I trust, asking them to sound other women, without naming names, but vaguely, asking them if they think such discussion possible'. By the time of the first meeting a group of Pearson's associates in teaching, the law and medicine, and a number of educated – though largely untrained – women like the two Sharpe sisters had gathered. It was agreed at this first meeting, in Brunswick Gardens, Kensington, that the club should contain equal numbers of men and women, and no more than twenty in all. A paper would be read once a month, to be followed by discussion; members' notes on it would be added to the minute book. The care in selection of members was to be extended to guests, who had to be recommended by at least three members with the secretary's consent; they did not wish to run the risk of 'irresponsible strangers' interrupting their work. One of their seventeen rules stressed the 'difficulty' of the undertaking and the overwhelming importance of the men and women being animated 'by the same earnestness of purpose'; in this commitment to a high moral tone the spirit of the club – however eccentric its subject matter – was very much a part of the Victorianism whose sexual hypocrisy it rejected. Subjects were to be discussed with 'absolute freedom' – meaning freedom from what was called 'personal bias' – and disinterestedness was considered indispensable in the quest for knowledge. This searching after truth could be fastidious to the point of political censorship.

When Eleanor Marx declined Donkin's invitation to join, members' responses were revealing. 'It is a very different matter to advocate certain things in theory, and to have the courage to put one's theories into practice,' Eleanor had written, continuing: 'probably many of the good ladies in the Club would be much shocked at the idea of my becoming a member of it.' Annie Eastty, a member of the original club, felt that she had done them an injustice, and Maria Sharpe was 'extremely resentful'. Eleanor had also said that she must devote her time to 'the highest and most important work' she could do, fighting for socialism. To Maria Sharpe this was most reprehensible: it was a commitment to a course of action 'in a way that leaves her no more open to reason than the various propagandists against whose admission we almost framed a resolution'. Ellis reacted strongly, perhaps because he had a high opinion of Eleanor: if they would not persuade her they wanted her he would look upon the club as being irretrievably damned; he considered altering a favourable notice of the club in an article he was writing for the *Westminster Review* on account of it. 'Those sort of women are hateful,' he added, 'and if the Club can't control its members it'll rapidly go to the Devil.'[94]

For all the formal equality of the club, the women tended either to defer to the men – to Pearson particularly – or to belittle their own capacities. 'I can't shake off the feeling men are the leaders of women,' Elizabeth Cobb wrote to Pearson anxiously, afraid that he would 'care little for this, you will say it only comes from – for all your goodness towards us – a *woman*, and an emotionalist.' The women, while doubting how much the men would understand, seem to have been amazed that the club gave them an opportunity for discussion at all. But it took the women to point out that they should study men as well, after which Pearson's suggestion that the club be named after Mary Wollstonecraft was felt to be inappropriate. Olive's objections were strongly put, in a letter to Pearson about an omission in his opening paper:

> The omission was '*Man*'. Your whole paper reads as though the object of the club were to discuss woman, her objects, her needs, her mental and physical nature, and man only in as far as he throws light upon her question. This is entirely wrong.[95]

Olive was involved in the club from the start as one of its committee members. She met Elizabeth Cobb and Maria Sharpe for the first time in Hastings in autumn 1884 at a time when they were staying in the same part of the town. She and Mrs Cobb began a correspondence which soon became strongly feminist, at least on Olive's side. She wanted to ask Mrs Cobb a question when they next met, she said; it was about the frequency of intercourse:

> It's about a little half mental half physical fact with regard to which I should like to have other people's experience. I often think that a thing quite as necessary as that women and men should understand and know more of each other, is that women should know really and understand more of one another, and each woman not be so much shut up to generalising from her own single experience. When you try to argue with men about many things they will turn round and say, 'Ah yes, that is all very well, but you are speaking for yourself, most women do not feel or think so', etc. And one doesn't always know what to reply, does one?[96]

Olive struck the circumspect Mrs Cobb as rather worldly. She would contribute a lot to discussion, Mrs Cobb wrote to Pearson, for 'she has had much more varied experience of men than most women, I doubt if she believes in marriage at all'. But there was something 'not quite wholesome' about *African Farm*: people wanted to be 'helped to move, not to lie down and die'. In all, Olive was 'rather vivid and rapid and sparkling, than calm and solid'; Mrs Cobb agreed with Pearson's initial impression of her 'taking honey where she finds it', and she was afraid the club might lose some of its earnestness of purpose if Olive became a member. But Olive did, and Maria Sharpe missed her when she stopped coming to committee meetings as she was so often out of London: 'She had one of the most generous natures I ever came across, and a smile from her from the other side of the room was enough to reassure me when I felt frightened by the men.'

The club opened with a paper from Pearson on 'The Woman Question', later reprinted, with alterations, in a collection of his essays entitled *The Ethic of Freethought*. Whether they could follow or not, Maria Sharpe records, 'and whether we agreed or not, we felt that our work had been raised on to a high level and a tone given to our discussions which was in itself an education'. Since it was this paper which Olive felt contained the oversight that 'one half of our problem has been left out', it was due to be followed by a paper from her; she was unable to complete it in time, and it fell to one of the women to talk on 'The Other Side of the Question'. This second paper put forward the conventional argument about men being more sexually driven than women and therefore less moral, ending up exhorting women to 'accuse them of this instead of condoning it by silence'. There followed a 'desultory' discussion of possible definitions of instinct and morality.

It was becoming clear that the club should decide on the strength of the sexual 'impulse' and Pearson, who had thought the whole discussion pointless, suggested a more disciplined approach: the chairman should keep speakers to the point and ensure that the main theses of each paper were debated in order. In this style, perhaps, did the club proceed over the next four years, through sexual relations among the Periclean Greeks, the Russians in the Middle Ages, the position of women among the early Buddhists, and Ibsen's characters. But there were also papers on contemporary themes like the inadequacy of girls' education, the Contagious Diseases Acts, and the physiological basis of heredity. Pearson's 'The Woman Question' was circulated privately, but an acquaintance of the Sharpes' was horrified: it was different for Miss Schreiner, who grew up among 'coarse and brutal natures' and must have learnt it all, but for unmarried women in general, at least educated ones, the fine sense of shame which taught them to shrink from discussing 'men's passions and animal instincts with them' was 'the true and natural one'.

The club aimed to work without such value judgements, particularly when it came to consider sexual attraction itself. One member of the group took it as synonymous with a desire to perform the sexual act. Pearson managed to produce an extremely fine distinction: it was a physical attraction between the sexes, which might have nothing to do with the sexual impulse (the desire towards the act), but was often the preliminary to it. This was a minority position, although the club was in general disagreement with the suggestion of a weaker sexual instinct in women. But they thought it would be impossible to measure its strength and came up only with a reference to the migratory instinct in birds. One of the men, meanwhile, followed through the logic in the notion of impulse: if sexual attraction connoted gratification of the sexual impulse, he could not agree with the idea that there should be gratification 'only for the race–end of getting children. Are our impulses never to be enjoyed merely because they are natural and enjoyable?' Here was a hint at the possibility and importance of sexual pleasure; but it was decided that the question could be answered only by a discussion of the 'meaning of moral behaviour'. Was the individual practice of self-control at odds with the demand to consider 'the welfare of the community' – that is, the race – by increased procreation? Here the club showed the eugenicist edge to its argument that was to characterize Karl Pearson's subsequent work in biometrics and statistics.

Olive and Donkin, who joined the club during its first year, were more preoccupied with the non-recognition of female sexuality as a whole. Olive countered the suggestion of a weaker sexual instinct in women with the observation that it was difficult to judge, 'in days when women are under such control'. Donkin felt that Pearson underestimated women's 'sexual passion' and overestimated the maternal instinct; and 'here he feels sure Miss S. agrees with him', Robert Parker told Pearson, adding in parentheses: 'N. B. Lyndall in her book'.[97] Theirs was also a concern with the consequences of repressed desire, Donkin commenting provocatively that sexual inactivity was injurious to health – particularly mental health – but that no medical authority dared put it in writing. Some of the women felt that these disorders might result just as much from a lack of intellectual stimulus or outside activities; Olive developed the point and backed Donkin: 'a person might stifle sexual desire by directing their energy into other channels and yet suffer in health.'[98]

Was she, however indirectly, referring to herself? This interest in bodily health was not generally taken up within the club, which had fixed its sights on discussions of morality and definitions of terms, but Donkin did pursue the theme in an article on hysteria for a two-volume *Dictionary of Psychological Medicine* a few years later.*

Importantly, however, the club had gone beyond the idea of sexual need as intrinsically degrading. They were simply concerned about its correct expression, and were not so much censorious as bound within a heterosexual norm. Darwinist in their assertion of the sexual impulse as natural – and animal – they had to conclude that women were as animal as men. Inevitably for their time, however, they used reason to argue their case, and maintained great faith in the power of rationality alone to effect change. There was also, characteristically, an opposition of reason and feeling – a stress on cultivation of the will – which is exemplified in Olive's tone of mind. She was trying to get to a higher state, an ideal, and in that reason was culturally validated, feeling had to be controlled. Similarly, the assumption that sexual feeling was natural did not lead to a re-ordering of sexual life within the club and its circle. Members saw their work as altruistic and educational, as when Mrs Cobb wrote to Pearson about 'a poor Miss H' who had never thought 'till I was telling her the other day what I thought, that women had any animal passions as men have. She believes it now.' As for Olive, her frankness appeared to stigmatize her as a 'free' woman, although perversely she typified, to the point of neurosis, the condition of the Victorian woman seeking a sort of sexual freedom by denying her sexuality. Her assertion of women's sex needs was exclusively intellectual: she was looking, at source, for a theory of sexual evolution. In herself, as her

* Here there is a hint, a suggestion of a relationship between personality, sexuality and illness. Whereas it was widely acknowledged that an asthmatic attack could be caused by hysteria, it was the link between hysteria and sexuality that was new. Donkin was working on hysteria at the same time as Freud, but remained attached to a quasi-medical model of the disorder. Correspondingly, he wavered over and over again between moralism and critique, now pointing to the utter inadequacy of modern medicine to understand psychology, now chastising the hysterical female for her manipulative 'self-regard'. Breuer and Freud's *Preliminary Communication*, on the other hand, published a year after Donkin's résumé of the field, looked not just at sexual repression but at the psychical trauma, often in childhood, that provoked the first occurrence of the symptom. Donkin later came to regard psychoanalysis as an unscientific discipline: to him the 'Unconscious Mind' was an 'assumption', not a 'discovery'. See D. Hack Tuke (ed.), *A Dictionary of Psychological Medicine* (2 vols, 1892), vol. 1, pp. 610–27, and P. McBride, *Psycho-Analysts Analysed* (1924), with introduction by Sir H. Bryan Donkin, pp. 1–17.

personal relationship with Pearson was to show, she seemed to want
freedom from sex or the risk of being considered and treated as a sexual
object.

The club's concern not to be associated with sexual licence made for
a certain anxiety about introducing Hintonians to their meetings. Discussion centred initially upon Caroline Haddon, the sister of Hinton's
widow and Ellis' first patron, headmistress of a girls' school in Dover.
Maria Sharpe was suspicious of references in her letters to 'liberty' and
'purity'. Should she be invited to attend? Should her friends? Should
the club formally dissociate itself from Hintonism by reading a paper
against it? A committee decided not to. Pearson took it upon himself
to investigate James Hinton's alleged polygamy and there followed two
months of intensive correspondence. He resumed contact with Emma
Brooke, one of the first women students at Cambridge, by now in her
forties and associated with the Fabians, and asked her to write down for
them an account of her relationship with Hinton.

Years before, Miss Brooke had stayed with a group of people who
had been impressed by some of Hinton's unpublished writings. Hinton
had been present and she had been told to go and 'amuse' him while
the household went out for a walk:

> It takes a good deal to persuade a woman that it is her duty and her
> glory to give herself up to a man she loathes, it does not take so much
> to confuse the ideas of right and wrong in a girl's head and to set
> her out in life with the persuasion that to 'Sacrifice' herself for a man
> she loves is at once ennobling and necessary. But this was Hinton's
> method with girls and while seducing their minds with splendid talk
> and brilliant images, he helped himself liberally to such favours as
> he could get by the way.[99]

Miss Brooke was 'inexpressibly thankful' that Pearson had taken the
matter up; she offered to interview a woman who knew much more than
she. Miss Haddon, however, suggested that any mistakes Hinton might
have made in his last year were due to incipient madness; he had been
'completely unhinged' by his discovery of female sexuality:

> I can only partially account for what [Miss Brooke] says of his conduct
> by supposing that he had been misled by some recent experiences
> with other women who gave way to passions which startled him as a

new revelation. He began by being apt to ignore the existence of sexual passion in women – and it came upon him with a startling shock when on investigating the causes of our terrible social condition he found that one chief part was due to the disregard of women's needs of marriage.[100]

Olive staunchly defended Miss Haddon. In a note to Pearson she wrote: 'One must be very careful of what one says because of Miss Haddon and her school. We must not crush other human lives. It is the men Hintonians I feel so bitter against.' Even for Hinton she now felt some pity: she had heard he had repented on his deathbed, and she found something 'very pathetic' in it. After nagging Ellis with her doubts about Hinton's sexual philosophy and its implications, Olive had done something of a volte-face, but she had a spirited reason:

I'm going to stick up for Miss Haddon like old boots. Compared to those white-washed sepulchres, the Hintonians are simply saints.[101]*

Mrs Cobb was vexed by Olive's apparent blindness about 'dear Miss Haddon', and expressed her annoyance in a letter to Pearson:

I do not think she can *know* the things you tell me in your letters. I asked her once point blank what she knew of Hinton's relations to women, and she told me as far as I can remember he used to touch their hands and so on, because he thought it a mistake to be so distant.[102]

Miss Haddon's communications with Pearson became increasingly bad-tempered. In a 2000-word letter she told him he had been wrong in calling Hinton a sham:

He *never*, as far as I can remember, approached the subject of polygamy except from the woman's side. He *hated* the idea of its being supposed to be *claimed* as a privilege by man – what he insisted upon was that our modern European harem has all the tyranny of the Eastern without even the poor protection which the latter accords to women.

She felt he was mistaken as to her influence over her students:

If ever I have talked to them about women it is to make them feel how we are all bound together and how the idleness and luxury of one class inflict the poverty, hard work and misery upon another. Sexual subjects are not suited to their age.

* She does not identify the sepulchres.

And she concluded revealingly:

> I am indeed rather surprised that you should speak with such scorn
> of the emotions. Surely when you come to deal with sexual matters
> they are as much *facts* that demand consideration as any physical
> conditions.[103]

The issue of personal feeling was a significant one, in which the women
were generally on the defensive. 'Do you know [Mrs Browning's]
Aurora Leigh?' Mrs Cobb wrote to Pearson. 'Perhaps it seems foolish
to men who read Homer and Plato and Dante. But I think it has helped
many women in their revolt against slavery.' One of the other women
spoke with more defiance in a discussion of prostitution: members had
been asked to contribute notes on the subject and she began hers 'under
protest that it is deliberately reducing our discussion to a lower level'
by bringing herself and her responses into it.

A couple of women left the club, one of them, Henrietta Müller, a
South American Spaniard educated at Girton College, giving her reasons
in a letter to Pearson. The men had spoken dogmatically on the Contagious Diseases Acts 'being medical only', and none of the women who
saw the regulation of prostitution, by contrast, as a moral question spoke
at all. It was the same old story: 'the women resenting in silence, and
submitting in silence'. She would start a rival club, for women only.
'This is prejudice,' Pearson would say; she would not deny it. The problem of women's silence mattered more than impartial discussion. Women
must 'learn to hear their own voices pronouncing the terrible words of
"prostitution" etc. before they can enter into a debate with or against
men'. We don't know how much impact she made when she told him
that: 'Man cannot know her [woman] nor do her justice until she has
spoken, and he has listened'; Olive and Mrs Cobb maintained a much
less critical attitude – Mrs Cobb the more obsequious, Olive always
advocating cooperation.

Another woman felt that Pearson showed an 'inclination to lay down
[women's] duty for them. This women's question,' she continued,
would not be solved unless women were allowed to work out their 'duty
and ideal' for themselves. 'This women's question' was usually taken to
mean the sexual relationship between a man and a woman. Although
everything was to be frankly discussed, members' letters indicate the
limits of their reference-point. The model of friendship, for example,

was exclusively male: 'Surely . . . the attraction of a man to a woman need not be all of one kind, and based on specially sexual feeling,' Mrs Cobb wrote to Pearson, 'it may be as the attraction of a man to a man.' Here male camaraderie was seen as both enviable and asexual: the fact that the term homosexuality only became current when Havelock Ellis defined it in *Sexual Inversion* in the 1890s indicates that homosexual subcultures were still largely invisible.[104] Nor is there any real concept of female solidarity. Olive's rather rhapsodic description of Miss Müller's 'very wonderful mental growth', then, becomes significant for its feminism: she didn't want anything hard said against her as she was a 'plucky, fearless, brave, truthful little woman', and that was a great thing to say – 'of any woman'.[105]

The club began meeting at the same time as crusading journalist W. T. Stead exposed child prostitution in a series of articles in the *Pall Mall Gazette* in July 1885, 'The Maiden Tribute of Modern Babylon'. Stead, a believer in 'government by journalism',[106] had mounted a six-week inquiry into the 'crimes which spring from vice' to save the then Criminal Law Amendment Bill from falling. No opponent of prostitution *per se*, but of unwilling assent, force, fraud, and the arbitrary powers of the police on the streets, Stead had the support of many prominent religious and moral influence groups, including the Salvation Army, in this attempt to get the age of consent raised from thirteen to sixteen. Deriving his title from Athens' annual tribute of seven youths and seven maidens to King Minos of Crete, he proceeded to create an extraordinary under-world of degradation peopled by the most respectable members of parliament, the clubs, and the professions. 'The maw of the London Minotaur is insatiable,' he began, 'and none that go into the secret recesses of his lair return again.' Here were fantastic revelations of underground rooms with boards and chains at their windows making girls' screams inaudible; girls being taken into prostitution by their employers after obtaining a position in an emporium or a theatre; men going into the country to cajole a girl up to London on a pretext of showing her the sights; procuresses picking out nursemaids pushing prams in Hyde Park. Their aim was always to secure virgins, and in the course of his researches into the extent of unwilling seduction, Stead interviewed brothel-keepers, procuresses, and ex-prostitutes. To establish the veracity of their accounts, he arranged to 'buy' a young virgin himself

with a view to her being seduced by anyone he pleased. Stead's reports
did lead to the passing of the Criminal Law Amendment Act, but he
was tried at the Old Bailey in November 1885 on a charge of complicity
in the girl's purchase, and sentenced to three months in prison.

The Men and Women's Club's response to the exposé took the form of
writing to the *Gazette*, collecting signatures for their letter, and following
the controversy that the articles generated. A letter of thanks to Stead
was drafted by Olive:

> To some of us your words have come as a revelation. They have shown
> us what lay behind our smooth lives: they have filled us with remorse.
> Have we not too been guilty? Have we not made it easy for man to
> smite down with the right hand, while he honours us with the left?
> Have we cried out, 'All women are one. In the saddest girl-child that
> is wrong I too suffer?' *Have we been content to be ignorant?*[107]

Mrs Cobb suspected that Pearson would find Olive's letter 'too emotional,
too sensational', but she endorsed it as a 'protest from the free thinking
socialist side. I *like* Olive's "All women are one!" ' The club were hostile
to Stead's religious fanaticism, but thought it important to show public
support: when they sympathized with the poor, Mrs Cobb felt, 'we are
helping to bridge the gulf between us'. She had been canvassing support
all week: 'Perhaps you could get some men's names still,' she asked
Pearson, 'but it is such hard work.' When she consulted her husband
before putting her own name to the letter she found that he objected
strongly; he disliked such excessive thanks, mistrusted the Salvation
Army's involvement in Stead's campaign, and felt his wife should guard
against 'immature speaking'. (He was then contesting a safe Conservative
seat in Warwickshire for the Liberal party.*)

The *Gazette* articles – which were translated within a year of their
publication into French, German and Portuguese – brought up intense
discussion about prostitution as a whole, and enabled club members
to circulate their own ideas. 'I do not know if you will at all sympathise
with me,' Olive wrote to Pearson, 'but my feeling is not one of hatred
to the men who do these things.'

---

* He won, and sat for the Rugby division of Warwickshire until his retirement from
the Commons in 1895. F. W. S. Craig (ed.), *British Parliamentary Election Results,
1885–1918* (1974), p. 409.

One is irresistibly drawn back to look at the women who bore those men, and in whose hand they lay for the first twelve to fourteen years of their life . . . we come back to the old point, that we cannot hate anyone. Man injures woman and woman injures man. It is not a case for crying out against individuals or against sexes, but simply for changing a whole system. When we have pure strong mothers able to see the beauty and importance of the sexual side of life, we will have pure strong men able to guide themselves nobly . . . It seems a long way off, but I always feel that it must come at last and I *do* think the *Pall Mall* letters have been wise if they have awakened only a thousand women.[108]

The issue of prostitution was central in the Men and Women's Club just as it was in the Victorian discussion of sexuality as a whole. The club read the available literature on the Contagious Diseases Acts, which required prostitutes in selected garrison towns and ports to submit to physical examination and detention in 'lock' hospitals but in no way penalized the men involved, considering it imperative that both sexes study it in detail. Characteristically, however, they still found it impossible to define a prostitute after meeting for four years. Not that they viewed the prostitute in a conventional light: at least, for Ralph Thicknesse, she was not kept in ignorance of the sexual function. He sat on a Minors' Protection Committee investigating the workings of the new Criminal Law Amendment Act, and was struck by the way in which public opinion on the *Pall Mall Gazette* reports made no distinction between free and criminal intercourse; it should be a voluntary act in all cases, he felt.

For Olive all individual relationships were sullied by the existence of prostitution, but she wrote nothing systematic on the subject. She was still working at *From Man to Man*, and in general seemed to despair of the women's question: was it possible that women 'are absolutely and altogether the inferiors of men?' she asked Havelock.[109] But still their suffering was real and something had to be done for it. She read up on venereal disease in preparation for an article and went out of her way to meet prostitutes and to talk to them. And she narrowly escaped being arrested as one herself during a midnight walk round Portsea Place with a male friend. A policeman came up to them and said to her friend: 'I don't want you, sir, I want *her*.'[110]

At the beginning of 1886 Donkin proposed marriage. Olive turned him down: 'I must be free, you know, I must be *free*. I've been free all my life.'[111] Marriage could not be right for a nature like hers:

> All I know is that I am not a marrying woman; when it comes to the point my blood curdles and my heart is like stone.[112]

Yet she also felt increasingly that 'no kind of sex relationship can be good and pure but marriage'. Donkin was tender and reverent, but she would marry only when she found a man stronger than she was – not physically but 'mentally, morally, emotionally, practically' stronger. She did not think there was such a man, and it was a rather confused ideal. She also blamed herself for the fact that Donkin loved her, since she had continued to see him even though she knew his feelings for her. It was strange, she commented at a later stage to Karl Pearson, 'that the most wrong things I have done in my life I have done from pity'.[113]

Feelings of being persecuted by her landladies – 'the only kind of woman being I don't like'[114] – combined with her despair at Donkin's dependence on her to cause a fresh bout of illness and depression, and she went to live at a Dominican convent in Kilburn, and then another at Harrow-on-the-Hill. Here she drew ascetic satisfaction from 'my books on the shelf, and my portraits and the old worm eaten floor, and the brown paper and my little white bed in the corner'.[115] She got a chunk of bread and butter for breakfast and supper and a scanty meal in the middle of the day, and she found life beautiful and rich, 'not in spite of the senses being robbed but because of it'. Edward Carpenter, whom she had met with Ellis through the Fellowship of the New Life, was making one of his frequent visits to London and came to spend a 'long restful morning' with her in the Harrow countryside. Carpenter was then involved in a project of simplification of life inspired by Thoreau's *Walden*: he was living in a cottage eight miles outside Sheffield and engaged in full-time manual labour there.[116] His yearning to realize the mood of 'exaltation' which the *Bhagavad Gita* had created in him and his hatred of capitalism and its obsession with material wealth meant that he understood very well Olive's retreat to the austerity of a convent. Both were preoccupied with questions of personal life, and talked of the need for 'institutions taking the place of the old monastic system [which] might absorb and give human ties and interests to those not fitted or not willing to enter on marriage and not strong enough to live alone'.[117]

*   *   *

It was now becoming particularly important that she prove her independence, not least emotionally. The summer before, Elizabeth Cobb had introduced her and Karl Pearson to one another, and there is evidence that Olive felt a strong personal attraction to him: when they began to meet outside the Men and Women's Club she tried to reassure Havelock, then very dejected about their changed relationship, that her feeling for him could not be touched by any new thing that came into her life, any feeling of passionate love she might have.

Karl Pearson was two years younger than Olive. He sported impressive academic qualifications: mathematics at Cambridge, physics at Heidelberg, Roman law in Berlin, engineering back at Cambridge, and medieval languages in London. Between being called to the Bar and taking the post in mathematics at University College, London in 1884, he lectured to working-class audiences in Soho and Finsbury on socialism and freethought. He was a member of the Savile Club. Whereas other women in the Men and Women's Club deferred to him, Olive did not. Her letters were from one colleague to another, with Olive as a working writer, wishing he had time to brood over his ideas, 'to let them grow of themselves'. Pearson was collecting material for a scientific study of women, and Olive gathered information for him, contradicted him with findings he wrote into a paper for the club, and on one of his absences abroad sent him her own plan for a book on women that she had had in mind for several years. Was his at all similar, she asked? With the experience of her previous writing, she imagined it would take him three or four years to do a first draft, another two or three to rewrite and condense. At the same time she felt he would do it much better than she, and she was glad.

Pearson quickly became Olive's intellectual reference-point. She for her part impressed him with her serious intelligence – he had been very struck by Lyndall's thoughts in *African Farm* – but at the outset he drew the limits of their partnership and specified them to her. 'It should and could only be the free open friendship of man to man', he stipulated, since he had already experienced the 'danger, perhaps evil' in men-women friendships 'however cautious and self-controlled one might be oneself'. He did not elaborate but to Olive it suggested treatment as an equal; this was her unceasing personal struggle as well as her guideline for women's emancipation; more than this, of the perfect character, in her ethic involving the absence of need, even complete self-containment.

She tried to theorize her ideal:

Yes, friendship between men and women is a possibility, and our only
escape from the suffering which sexual relationships now inflict . . .
But is there not always a possibility of the consciousness of sex
difference and the desires which spring from it creeping in, and soiling
the beautiful free frank friendship? *No*, not when the friendship is
true.

At the same time she conceded that:

The most ideally perfect friendship between a man and a woman that I
know is of one where the man in addition to sympathy with the
woman's whole intellectual nature, feels that she is to him also sexually
perfect; without friendship such a feeling would disturb and bring
intense bitterness and sorrow; with friendship the fact that such a
feeling exists on one side only adds to the quiet beauty of the relationship. If I so loved a man that I felt he were the only human being it
would have been possible for me to love wifehood under; yet it would
never touch my friendship for him, I should never even wish that he
should know it . . . That friendships are possible between men and
women without the least sex feeling on either side I have proved over
and over again; the only question I have ever asked myself has been –
does 'sex attraction' kill friendship? I think not.[118]

She thought the old lover's question: 'Will you love me for ever?' had
to be changed to: '*If* you feel I press on your individuality will you let
me go?' But though she made valiant efforts to suppress them, the old
ambivalences persisted. She needed to be treated, and to project herself,
as intellectual rather than as woman; at the same time her ideology
undermined the differentiation. To Olive intellectual rapport was
indistinguishable from emotional involvement. 'I wish you would define
what you mean by the intellectual and the emotional', she wrote to
Pearson. 'It seems to me very hard to draw a scientific line of demarcation
between them. There are intellectual emotions just as there are un-
intellectual. I can't see how you will do it. I have tried and failed.' It was
difficult enough to make a 'scientific' differentiation of feeling; it was
bound to undermine the split she made between the scientific part of
herself that she showed Pearson and herself as a woman.

At the beginning of their correspondence, however, during the first half of 1886, Olive's letters to Pearson were vivacious and lighthearted, even playful and humorous at her own expense, as when she referred to the women of the club as a group of 'old maids and man-haters', or asked him to meet a woman she knew:

> (*Professor K. Pearson, to himself*) 'This benighted individual wants one to go running about after every fourth woman in London; and at the same time expects one to produce work that shall stand the test of the ages! Humph!' – *The Professor's remarks become inaudible here.*)
>
> Do you ever have a sudden great longing to see a particular one of your friends? I have often. Sometimes it is my mother. I get the feeling I *must* see her little bright intellectual old face . . . I feel I must run down to the docks and take my place in the steamer . . . Last week I had that kind of longing to see you; but it's gone now. (*Professor K.P.* 'Ill regulated mind!!')[119]

By contrast with the excessive formality of the correspondence of the time, her letters bubble with audacity. Hers was a very spontaneous expression, unfettered by Victorian notions of decorum. In part this must have been a product of her colonial upbringing, distant from the middle-class conventions of London society, but also, during her adolescence and after, from family constraints. To a woman like Elizabeth Cobb, managing a household of four stepchildren and six of her own in Stanmore, Olive was a 'curious psychological study', her hands, for example, saying 'much more than most English women's'; all in all, she was 'very unique'. In the main *African Farm* lent her authority within the club as a mercurial if rather unreliable participant, perhaps the only woman who could meet Pearson on his own level.[120] She was in England not only as a rebel against convention – Edward Carpenter recalls the 'pretty woman of apparently lady-like origin who did not wear a veil and seldom wore gloves, and who talked and laughed even in the streets quite naturally'[121] – but as an outsider, and her provocation in discussions on emotional and sexual matters comes over less as calculated than as an innocent inquiry after truth. At the same time her thoughts and writing on what she hoped were scientific questions betray the eclecticism of her self-education. She borrowed freely from religion, philosophy, ethics, Darwinism, novels, biography, her perception of others and her reflections on her own experience. Her letters are bursts of polemic punctuated by good ideas, her opinions formulated almost impromptu.

It was only now, during the years in England, that she was in stimulating company, sought out for her percipience and flair, as well as her reputation. Pearson, as the man of rationality and science, offered her the cerebral absorption she sought. Her letters were addressed to 'My dear Mr Pearson', even 'K.P.', the sign of a colleague rather than a more formal acquaintance. From time to time during the body of the letter she addressed him as Karl. One was signed 'Your man-friend OS'. Whereas to Ellis she exposed herself as fragile, doubting and ill, to Pearson she was a disinterested researcher, and to that end had to be seen as a man rather than a woman, as she emphasized in one of her postscripts: 'I'm not a woman, I'm a man, and you are to regard me as such.'

It was true to their pact but it was undermined by two things. Protestations about the interdependence of intellect and emotion meant that the notion of objectivity was itself suspect. Though she never allowed herself to admit it to him, others, or herself, she wanted more than a working partnership, and it was this confusion about her needs that crippled their relationship and almost destroyed her. Conscious of their agreement, she was tentative and nervous in her inquiries about his health:

> Karl Pearson, there is something I want very much to ask of you, and yet I dare not. I felt that you had physical suffering in your life and then when you told me of your health that night you only expressed what I had felt vaguely before . . . Won't you help me by telling me?*

Later in the letter she drew back anxiously, almost panic-stricken:

> If in this letter I have passed the bounds of what our friendship allows, please put me back by a letter however short a one.[122]

It sounded an innocent enough inquiry, but it threw Olive into an uncertainty close to despair:

> I suppose I have ended for ever your feeling of friendship for me by the letter I wrote on Monday. To you it seems brutal, intrusive, or that most horrible of all things, an expression of pity. You can't understand and I can't explain to you. You have had so many friends in your life, and intellectual sympathy has been such a common thing to you, that you cannot understand what it is to me, something so much more precious than all sexual feeling or even family love. If I were a man friend you would forgive me for asking such a question, but you never

* According to Olive, Pearson told her on one occasion that he was dying of a terrible incurable disease. *Letters*, p. 271.

forget I am a woman. I am always conscious that I am a woman when I am with you; but it is to wish I were a man [*sic*] that I might come near to you.[123]

The correspondence between Olive and Pearson is one-sided – his letters to her do not appear to be extant – and since many of hers to him are allusions to ongoing or previous conversations, threads are missing and others are difficult to piece together. The general picture during these first months of 1886, particularly when she was at the convent in Harrow, is of Olive striving to avoid giving any impression of emotionality; of her strength, far more evident in this correspondence than in the letters to Ellis, in arguing a whole range of topics; but also of her irrepressible frankness on what were bound to be suggestive issues. As with Ellis, so in the letters to Pearson: scientific inquiry into the condition and responses of women prompted comments on her own as well as other women's experience; yet she recorded them as impersonal and 'objective' evidence. Was she too ingenuous – or too self-deceiving – to conceive of the degree of provocation she offered?

For a while the relationship appeared to work as a collaboration. Olive was approached by a publisher to introduce a new edition of Mary Wollstonecraft's *Vindication of the Rights of Woman*; could they work on it together, she wondered? 'The relation of Mary to Godwin gives one such a splendid opportunity for treating of the ideal form of marriage.' By contrast the blighted Hintonism posed the alternative, or so it seemed from a case in which James Hinton's son Howard was prosecuted for alleged bigamy. Olive attended the trial at the Old Bailey in October 1886, and took it upon herself to look after Maud Weldon, the woman for whom Howard Hinton had abandoned his wife and by whom he had had two children. She was perplexed about the extent of Mrs Weldon's complicity in Howard's deception of his wife, but she had to stand by her. In the Men and Women's Club the case set off interminable speculation: had young Hinton's behaviour anything to do with his father's doctrine? Was retribution for the sins of the father being visited on the son? Was this the final condemnation of the probity of Miss Haddon, she who had denied that Hinton would have carried his theory into practice, while here was the proof in his son? Elizabeth Cobb rehearsed all these conjectures in a long and respectful letter to Pearson, written after a conversation with Olive, whom she found in 'really great trouble' about it. Olive still rejected Hintonism vehemently, for 'double sex-relations whether on the part of the man or the woman' were 'utterly opposed to the deepest laws of human nature'; however she had to succour Maud Weldon, who was in need. The reverberations of the case in the circles of the club can only be explained by a fear that their own behaviour might be dubbed Hintonian.

Olive wrote to Pearson urging him to 'combat' Hintonism, but her letter also pleaded for the truth, for she feared he might be 'fighting for himself'. She had heard others describe him as a Hintonian; was his bitterness the desire to right himself?

> It would be such a terrible thing if while you seemed to be fighting only for abstract truth and right there was an element of self in it. I can't bear to think of this. You must be so absolutely pure and fleckless. My life is so broken and ... it is always far from the ideal but you must keep close to it ... You must look into your own heart, and see if all your hatred against Hinton is abstract.[124]

What suspicion Olive was harbouring is not clear, and at this point relations between Olive and Pearson are fogged by the interventions of Elizabeth Cobb. It appears that Pearson asked Mrs Cobb for her impressions not only of the facts of the bigamy case but of Olive's reactions to it. Mrs Cobb had reservations about her, but concluded with worry on her behalf:

> She teaches me much, but she is so different from me I feel it is difficult to know her thoroughly. I never could count on her entire truthfulness right through ... Poor thing she was so happy all the time at Harrow, and the other day she seemed perplexed and distressed. She said she had never before had to do so much with so many people in trouble.[125]

The letter continued with some oblique remarks on Mrs Cobb's feelings for Pearson, mostly of admiration and respect. It was the letter of a follower who assumed the right to reflect on their relationship and on Pearson's with Olive. They had known each other for six years, after all; Elizabeth Cobb was twelve years older than Pearson, and perhaps saw herself as his patron. In one of her early letters to him she had written enthusiastically about the 'immense power an intellectual and cultivated woman may have in inspiring cultivated men'.[126] But she also felt entitled to cite Pearson's views to Olive, and hers to him. To Olive this was a betrayal of the trust she and Pearson shared and a wounding invasion of her privacy. It was the signal for a complete breakdown of her health.

There followed a tortuous set of letters and telegrams between Pearson, Olive and Elizabeth Cobb during November and early December. Face to face with Elizabeth Cobb questioning her about the Hinton trial on the strength of information from Pearson that she, Olive, had given him, her initial reaction was not to make an answer, but simply to look at her, 'because I could not feel her right to ask it me'. But in a note written to Pearson during the early hours of 9 November, she repented:

Please, feel with regard to anything I tell you or write to you that you may do with it exactly as you would with information you had gained for yourself; if you used it in a way I did not approve of I should think it an error of judgement; I should never question your purity of purpose.

A telegram and then a second letter sent the same day were even more stoic:

The gentlest impulse in your heart to Mrs Cobb is the manliest. Follow it, I will not write again. Work. I will work.

She returned, unopened, a letter from Elizabeth Cobb.

A month followed in which there was no communication between Olive and Pearson. Olive struggled to work on a story – which was a failure – an allegory, and the essay on Mary Wollstonecraft. She was in torment. Had he forgotten to write? Had he changed towards her? Had he seen something unworthy in her which he could not tell her? She had cut off relations with Mrs Cobb: 'If you feel that this step makes a change in our relations necessary or necessitates my leaving the club speak frankly,' she asked Pearson.

On 11 December there was a tremulous last appeal to him:

My man-friend write to me. Find fault with me please if I am doing wrong, oh my soul is so little so little. Can't your larger one for a moment put out a hand to me? My man-friend some day when your spiritual life is burning low and dim I will put out my hand and help you if you will help me now.

Two days later Olive was seriously ill in her rooms at Blandford Square.

Olive Schreiner

Donkin found her 'utterly smashed' and remained in constant attendance for a week, dropping everything else for fear of leaving her alone. In the club he had suggested a relationship in women between hysteria and the repression of sexual desire; now he telegraphed Pearson and then wrote a letter, begging him to see her:

> I found her this morning in a state of complete temporary madness – and being without her normal control, I gathered from her words for the first time what I have known of myself for long; that she loves you . . . I was afraid to leave her, as she was dangerous, to herself. Even now, I am in fear and hastening back. Now it is not for me to give you counsel, but let me say this as one man to another, on a subject on which I at least feel strongly. If you love her as she loves you – or at all (I don't want to ask you any questions) go to her *and soon* and whatever your feelings may be, speak – don't write . . . I cannot answer for the consequences if she goes on in the state she has been lately. I have read between the lines. She has said nothing – but it is only you who can do anything with her.

Through Donkin, Olive sent Pearson her childhood Bible. Pearson appears to have seen her once during this week; he also wrote her a letter which is not in existence but which caused her more pain and prompted an immediate denial of Donkin's interpretation of her collapse:

> If [Donkin] told you I loved you with sex-love it was only a mistake on his part. You will forgive him. I do.
>
> . . . I have *never* misunderstood you, *never* for one moment thought, you loved me as a woman. You are drawn to me intellectually and I am of great interest to you.[127]

She had a deeper feeling for him than for anyone she had ever known, 'but it is not *sex*-love . . . You will say "O.S. you are deceiving yourself that is sex-love". *I deny it*.' She was drawn to him, she said, because his mind worked in the same way as hers. But there followed an extraordinary piece of body-imagery, in which all sexual feeling was displaced onto work.

> If I could I would open a vein in my arm and let all my blood run into your body to strengthen you for your work. Your work is mine.

If ever he had seen an element of sex creeping into her thought or feeling for him, she continued, why didn't you tell me of it, and crush it. See, I love you better than anything else in the world, and I have tried to keep far from you that nothing material might creep in between my brain and yours, and you have not understood me.

This was perhaps the most painful letter Olive ever had to write. She admonished Pearson for not crushing any sexual feeling he might have observed in her; but implicit in her complaint was the belief that it would take another person to recognize it. Her own picture of what had happened was extremely naïve. She took ill, her letter to Pearson ended, 'walking about in my wet lanes at Harrow and sitting in my wet clothes in the train. I am better now.' To Ellis she wrote a self-justifying letter about the impossibility of man-woman relationships and then sank her unhappiness into the general misery of the world.[128]

There are no signs that she tried to probe her own despair. Donkin had to do that for her and he tried, very delicately, to enlist Pearson's understanding and to create a new basis of trust between them. Perhaps it was because of her extreme, almost pathological sense of privacy in personal relations that

> if she thought only that there was a close friendship between any man and woman that she knew that could in any way be hurt by herself, she would be affected by that thought . . . if the lady we mentioned [Mrs Cobb] has what is called popularly a sentimental friendship for you, such even as hardly Mrs Grundy would object to, she might possibly . . . have said something to Miss S. or to others which Miss S. felt was wronging her.[129]

This would cause her inexpressible pain. Olive herself confirmed this hypothesis a few years later in a story of a younger woman retreating because of an older woman's possessive attachment to the man she loved.[130] Her impulse was to withdraw from any relationship less than ideal, for it meant her disinterestedness had failed her. The moral obsessions of her missionary background became fused with an identification with others, even when they involved her denial or sacrifice of herself. Her instinct now was to flee.

Those who had seen her during the days of her collapse found her in great agitation and distress. Just as she had always planned to leave South Africa for England, so she had thought many times of returning to the

Cape once she reached London in 1881. Now she decided to leave England for Europe. Donkin did what he could to protect her from visitors, arrange her travel, and find a nurse-companion for her. On the eve of her departure she sent a brief and rather distracted postcard to Maria Sharpe: 'Please tell Members of Committee that I am leaving London. Every success to the club. Wish I had heard your last paper.' She left Donkin and Pearson exchanging rebukes and then formal apologies, and Mrs Cobb speculating with Pearson about Olive's character. This Mrs Cobb considered perfectly natural, for had she not introduced Pearson to Miss Schreiner, and the whole time of the acquaintance 'been mixed up in it', and constantly hearing of each from the other? Pearson, evasive during Olive's illness, had tried to use Elizabeth Cobb as an intermediary, and Donkin, out of loyalty to Olive, had asked him to beg Mrs Cobb not to write to her since it only caused her more pain.

Elizabeth Cobb was close enough to Pearson to query his behaviour in the relationship. He considered that in the last month Olive had 'broken [their] agreement that no sex element should enter'.[131] Mrs Cobb pondered the question:

> Thinking it over I find that I did not exactly understand from you there was *no* reciprocal feeling on your side – if it is possible there may be, *why* should you struggle against it?[132]

She did not want to stand in the way of his happiness, and it grieved her to hear Pearson say after this experience that friendship between women and men was impossible, though

> My sisters have always felt that O.S. thought too much that purely animal feeling *must* sway, and could not be resisted . . . They have said that she lived in sensationalism.[133]

The notion of Olive's abandonment to animal feeling was totally at odds with her stated position in letters to Pearson, where she decried its 'aberrant effect on the intellect'; and with the reality of her lonely celibacy, longing for loving relationships but retreating from them. It was a significant discrepancy, nonetheless, for it showed how Olive's perception of herself still differed so radically from that of other people.

Very little is known about Pearson's feelings in the episode. Years later, in letters to a former secretary, he expressed great admiration for

Olive, considering her to have had the 'greatest mind of any woman he had met', but equally concerned as to the appropriate behaviour for a man facing a woman 'who has a sexual passion for him which he does not reciprocate'.[134] This suggests an unresolvable tension in the relationship which the correspondence, since it contains only Olive's letters to Pearson, cannot explain. Both were also conscious of an inevitable distance. Pearson told Mrs Cobb of the 'unfittingness of her character, the want of perfect mutual sympathy'.[135] Olive, in rather less cautious vein, told Edward Carpenter that she could never get on with his friends and was always the 'element of division'; to Mrs Cobb she described herself as 'too unrestful a soul ever to be a good friend' to him.[136]

During the four weeks leading up to her collapse in early December 1886, Pearson apparently made no reference to the situation. Only on a couple of occasions, one of sarcastic anger, the other of some agitation, did he reveal how much stress he was under. He made a point of telling Maria Sharpe just how differently from Olive he felt about a possible speaker for the club whom the three of them knew: it was only because she could 'apparently reach "das Innere" ' that he had suggested Olive contact the repulsive man.[137] On 13 December, the day he received Donkin's letter spelling out Olive's feelings for him, he was 'rude' and 'dogmatic' at the club and wrote to apologize the next day: he had had 'very painful news' the day before, he told Maria Sharpe, 'which rendered it impossible for me to be equable and clear in argument'.*

* The fact that Pearson produced a very emotional poem to commemorate Olive's death in 1920 does not detract from the image of him in the Men and Women's Club as undemonstrative and formal in personal relations.

> You taught the creed we longed for; I half believed awhile
> That inbred human wrangling must vanish at that smile,
> Which solvent played on discord as sunbeams calm the sea;
> Creeds sate, unsate insatiable, that cursed trinity,
> Would stricken fall abyssward, when Woman grasped her share
> In freedom, mart and council, Man's equal everywhere.
> . . .
> Childlike in form with upward gaze you stood,
> A seer beyond your age, beyond my mood.
> You turned, you saw my doubt, you felt its chill,
> You drank the bitter cup which cramped your will.
> Came hoarsely: 'I would gladly plunge my knife
> In there.' Thus scorn killed Love, thus Doubt maimèd Life.
> Our friendship died, each poorer sought the goal,
> On diverse boards each played self-chosen role.

See 'In Memoriam', poem submitted to the *Manchester Guardian (Pearson)*.

Pearson married Maria Sharpe in 1890. Whereas his involvement with Olive had been intense and short-lived, his feeling for Maria Sharpe developed slowly, over the four years of their association in the club. They met for the first time in 1884, when Pearson, through Mrs Cobb, offered to number and catalogue the Sharpe family's rather valuable collection of German prints; he then got the family an introduction to the British Museum, who were keen to purchase some of it. Maria Sharpe, then thirty-three, had been brought up to dance, play croquet, and appreciate the great cathedrals of Europe. She was gifted at watercolour and well read in the literature of the day. Pearson asked her to be the club's secretary and from then on they worked closely together. In both class and cultural terms the relationship made sense.

Olive's old hostility to women was reinforced by the Pearson episode. Women became predators again. 'She seems to have thought,' Elizabeth Cobb told Pearson at the end of December 1886, 'that I feared any intimacy between her and you, and that in some underhand way I was working to divide you.' But Olive's was a confused response. Only three weeks before, she had written Mrs Cobb a 'stormy letter' telling her how 'passionately' she, Olive, loved her.[138] Later she defended Pearson's friendship with Mrs Cobb, comparing it with that of Dante for Beatrice.[139] Mrs Cobb considered Olive to have misunderstood her throughout the affair: she did not think their relationship merited such protestations of affection on Olive's part; she also felt, though not unsympathetically, that Olive had 'invented' much of her own pain. She saw how easily Olive's suspicions of women were stirred and then entrenched: as she pointed out to Pearson before Olive left England, 'she has accused me and will not hear me'.[140]

If suspicion was involved, as Olive's subsequent behaviour shows, it had to be quickly suppressed and the experience rearranged in her mind. Hostile feelings had to be replaced by generous ones. The year before, she had told Ellis that if someone wanted something she herself had, she felt only the impulse to give it up: now she applied that maxim to Mrs Cobb's involvement with Pearson, and gave up her relationship with him. When she was recovering from the immediate impact of the break, she tried to conceal her resentment of Mrs Cobb, from herself as much as from others, and to represent Mrs Cobb as something of a saint. Once out of England, moreover, she was struck with a vivid sense of her own culpability. She was remorseful at having refused to see Mrs Cobb in the days before her departure for Europe; had she turned to her 'with love and wide impersonal sympathy, her sweet sympathetic nature would have been the first to turn to mine'.[141] But the feelings rankled; perhaps the conflict between her intuitive, even unconscious mistrust of women and the sense of sisterhood she found obligatory had helped to make her ill.

After leaving England Olive first spent several months at Vevey and Clarens in Switzerland, changing her address frequently, and then went to Alassio in Italy. She disliked Geneva, but found Clarens even worse. By May 1887 she was in Paris, where she stayed briefly with Eleanor Marx's sister Laura Lafargue. She had no sooner left England than she felt she had been away from it for many years, and in hell all the while. She needed absolute solitude, where there was no living soul, scarcely an animal. She wrote several allegories, and in a deliberately casual tone sent them to Pearson, through Donkin, for an opinion about publication: 'I don't value them, have many; can write any number.' The manuscript of 'A Dream of Wild Bees' which she sent him was signed Ralph Iron.

She felt an immense sense of relief at working again, and asked Pearson not to write to her, 'for life is very short and we are *burning* up'; he had 'comically misunderstood' her but it was a trivial matter. However, letters passing between Pearson, Olive, Donkin and Elizabeth Cobb, and also between Olive and Ellis, carried on attempts at interpreting the episode for some months. Olive, making herself more inaccessible than ever, insisted to Ellis that it was the absence of sexual feeling for Pearson that had drawn her:

> All that my sexual nature had to give I gave years ago . . . I have tried hard to feel sexual to you and Donkin and you don't know how it hurts me.[142]

Towards Mrs Cobb she was placatory and forgiving; towards Pearson distant and dignified. Pearson showed her letters to Mrs Cobb, who diagnosed her 'very very shattered and weak' and wondered whether 'some thought for others' could not rouse Olive from morbidly dwelling on her own state of mind. Perhaps Olive could use her great influence with Eleanor Marx to make her break with Aveling? Mrs Cobb recalled Olive talking of Eleanor as the one woman with whom she could live; could they be together abroad?

Charlotte Wilson, an anarchist and friend of Olive's who had maintained an amicable correspondence with Pearson for a number of

years, summed up the affair most acutely after one of Olive's return
visits to England in the next two years. She wrote to Pearson:

> I think that O.S. is well on the way towards crushing the emotional
> element in her. It is that that pained me so. I do not see why it need
> pain you. I consider that her energy is being wasted in the process –
> but, on your hypothesis, that hard schooling should be the way to
> rescue mental growth from the foes who would destroy it. In a few
> years she will be purely the woman of intellect – less than her best self
> I think – but a human being as you would have them be.[143]

The novel on which Olive worked more or less continuously during her
years in England was *From Man to Man*, the story of two sisters, one
deceived in marriage and one reduced to prostitution. It was a work which
she felt compelled to return to again and again – often incorporating
ideas from her correspondence and reading – though she never finished
it to her own satisfaction, and it was published posthumously. She
regarded it as her most important work, picturing *The Story of an African
Farm* as crude and youthful in comparison. In that it remained unfinished,
it came to symbolize everything that was unfinished about Olive's life.
Melodramatic and derivative, it was also a serious attempt to explore the
nature of sexual deception.

In *From Man to Man* Olive attempted to present women's predicament in relation to one another. Where *African Farm* described spiritual
isolation and an apparently inevitable death, *From Man to Man* explored
the possible relations of women as a sex. Here women were presented as
sisters, mothers and wives confronted with the reality of prostitution.
Olive saw herself, however, as having no authorial role. 'I make no comment throughout the book, I *never* speak in my own person, the characters
simply act and you draw your own conclusions.'[144] But the book's form
belies her statement about her characters. She rejected the form she
had used in *African Farm* – of 'the life we all lead, [in which], nothing
can be prophesied', in favour of a more didactic, propagandist text.
Where *African Farm* focused on the development of an inner world,
From Man to Man sought the relationship between external and internal
events. Most importantly, it tried to come to terms with the social
relations of sexuality; in doing so it set up an extreme polarization of the

sexes. The male world was brutally, callously sensual, and the female a retreat into a passionate motherhood or social ostracism.

Olive began *From Man to Man* in 1873, and worked on it concurrently with *Undine* and *African Farm*. It developed alongside her reading of W. E. Lecky's controversial *History of European Morals* in 1879, which was the first thing she 'ever knew or heard' about prostitution.* The passages in it which showed that it was the existence of the prostitute that enabled the monogamous family system to be maintained struck her with all the force of her earlier encounter with Spencer. 'Is it *necessary* there should be prostitutes?' she asked herself simply. 'Then let them be set on high, as other good and useful things are. But it is not necessary, and, by God, it shall not always be.'[145]

Once in England she turned again to this novel. With *The Story of an African Farm* successful and her reading public assured, she strove to complete a work which, as she herself later suspected, was of less artistic than social value.[146] The novel follows the lives of two sisters from a Karoo farm. The elder of the two, Rebekah, a great reader and naturalist, marries and lives in Cape Town, giving birth to three sons; her husband deceives her time after time, and even though she is presented with the evidence she persistently denies it and blames herself for doubting his love. Eventually, however, his relationship with their coloured servant girl humiliates her to such an extent that she demands a separation or a fresh start, this time with complete honesty between them. Her husband ridicules what he sees as her obsession with other women; now only death has any appeal. She buys a wine garden in the country and retires to it with her children and her household, while her husband Frank continues his travelling and seductions. She begins to come to life as she repairs the house, works in the garden, and attends to her sons. As the novel ends she is developing a strongly intellectual rapport with a married man called Drummond, but the relationship obviously has no future.

Bertie, the beautiful, innocent and unskilled younger sister, has meanwhile been seduced by her tutor on the farm. Her attempts at putting the episode behind her are constantly frustrated by women's gossip, and she is never able to make anything of her life. She ends up travelling to

---

* Olive was at the Diamond Fields when the South African Contagious Diseases Act, modelled on the British, was repealed in 1872. There is no reference to it in her correspondence, however, perhaps because the agitation against it was concentrated in the coastal towns. See E. H. Burrows, *A History of Medicine in South Africa* (Cape Town and Amsterdam 1958), pp. 304–5.

England with a rich Jewish moneylender,* who so traps her with possessions that she grows fatter and fatter, becoming alternately listless and
hysterical. Her protector is led to believe that she has seduced his young
cousin, and she is thrown out in disgrace. She leaves London, only to be
pursued by the cousin, and is last heard of in a brothel in Soho.

Olive created two possible endings for the novel, one of which her
husband added as a postscript to the published version. According to
this, Bertie returns to South Africa and is found by Drummond in a Cape
Town brothel, dying from a terrible disease (presumably syphilis). Since
Rebekah and Drummond know that their marital situation makes it
impossible to realize their 'undying love', Rebekah takes the children
away with her into the Karoo, and lives alone with them there, experiencing a kind of solitary, intense joy. The other ending she confided to Karl
Pearson.[147] Here an English traveller, presumably Drummond, leaves
Rebekah after scorning her for clinging to her husband; Rebekah finds
the dying Bertie, and paints what she sees as the future of love, principally
a time of sexual expression. When Rebekah's husband chides her for
burying Bertie openly, Rebekah at last speaks the truth: that for the last
fourteen years she has been living as a prostitute herself.

This second ending was the more defiant, particularly since it involved
a woman's acknowledgement of sexual need. But the critique of prostitution within and outside marriage which Olive followed in the novel as it
stands was primarily a moral one. It focused on the exploitation of
women's bodies, the inequity of a social system which derogated women
while allowing men to pursue chance encounters with no obligations. This
critique of prostitution was unable to take in questions which have
become central in the feminist movement today: what is women's
sexuality? How does it differ from men's? In *From Man to Man* as it
stands, although it was written from a subculture which was trying to
come to terms with the sexual instinct, Olive did not refer to or discuss
specifically female sexual feeling at all. Male sexuality was constantly
acknowledged in the themes of seduction and betrayal. But what of those
very 'animal' feelings that some of the women in the Men and Women's
Club acknowledged they had?

From Man to Man reveals all the ambivalences about women and

---

* Olive's Jew in *From Man to Man* is a disappointingly racist stereotype, though
twenty years later in Cape Town she took a public stand in defence of the Jews and
their contribution to culture and radical politics. See *Letters*, pp. 392–5.

womanhood that had pursued Olive since adolescence and were to appear in her writing and her correspondence for the rest of her life. Of all her works it is the only one to be set in the traditional round of domestic labour, of embroidery, darning, and lacework; there are loving descriptions of jam-making, kneading, and the preparation of medicines for a sick child. It is a novel about the solidarity of sisters, capable of participating in an unspoken domestic tradition. It asserts – if rather mystically – the spiritual understanding that women share, by virtue, it sometimes seems, of their being women. But this presentation of women's work in the home was an ambiguously critical one. 'The worst of this book of mine is that it's so womanly,' she wrote. 'I think it's the most womanly book that ever was written, and God knows that I've willed it otherwise!'[148]

Rebekah, too, willed it otherwise, when she thought:

> How nice it would be to be a man. She fancied she was one till she felt her very body grow strong and hard and shaped like a man's. She felt the great freedom opened to her, no place shut off from her . . . no law to say this and this is for woman, you are woman; she drew a long breath and smiled an expansive smile. Oh how beautiful to be a man and be able to take care of and defend all the creatures weaker and smaller than you are.[149]

But the attraction that men actually hold for Rebekah and Bertie is almost unintelligible. Men are coarse, hypocritical and cowardly, defined only by their sexual needs, which are seen as limitless and degrading. Here Olive followed the contemporary bourgeois view of the male sex drive as uncontrollable and the maternal instinct its only counterpart – paradoxically, since she insisted in her correspondence on the beauty of sex, making no differentiation between men's and women's needs. Many of the most significant parts of the novel are therefore unwritten: Bertie's life as a prostitute, Frank's courtship of Rebekah, Rebekah's feelings – other than intellectual ones – for her English traveller. Rapport with a man, to be meaningful, can be only a communion of the soul.

Olive was caught up in the dominant debate of her period. Lecky, along with many others, believed that the force of the sexual appetite was far greater than the wellbeing of man required in terms of reproducing the species; prostitution must inevitably emerge. At the same time he saw the prostitute as the 'eternal priestess of humanity, blasted for the sins of the people', and her stigma as hypocrisy. His basic assumption, however, was of a permanent conflict between soul or 'reason' and body or 'appetite'. Did sex intercourse make

> the animal part of our nature more or less predominant[?] We know, by the intuition of our moral nature, that this predominance is always a degraded, though it is not always an unhappy condition.[160]

While he provided Olive with progressive ideas about the social relations of prostitution – that is, the integration of the prostitute into the Christian system of family life – he was adamant that 'the sensual side of our being is the lowest side, and some degree of shame may be attached to it'.[151] If so, then control was imperative, and control was seen as dependent on strengthening the will. But was prostitution an expression of some immovable difference in need between the sexes? Apologists of prostitution saw it as a means of gratifying men's appetites in situations of deferred or unsatisfactory marriage, regularly assuming that female sexual desire was neither spontaneous nor inherent. Olive's confusion on this point is expressed in the novel's handling of sexuality as much as in its remaining unfinished.

Rebekah, once married and reliant on a notebook and a study in which her privacy gives her space for fantasy, pleads for an exact knowledge of all reality, laments all suppression – as in the fig leaf on the statue – and searches for the truth of sexual emotion. She places her thoughts within a disquisition on the survival of the fittest:

> Lust, divided from all love and inborn self-forgetfulness, is so dominant within thousands of us (making the world of sexual relations, which in our ideals are the highest, often the lowest, in life), because age after age the most brutally lustful has perpetuated himself, where the less lustful and brutal has failed to rape and force the women or kill the opposing males.[152]

This is forceful enough. But it is only by fantasizing herself as the man that she can imagine lying in bed with a lover:

> It seemed she was lying on the earth, on mats in the hut, and beside her lay the woman she loved, fast asleep . . . (She was him now, not herself any more.) And such a great tenderness came over him, and he drew her close and bound his limbs about her so that she was quite wrapped about.[153]

Bertie, too, is utterly incapable of any active understanding of – let alone participation in – her relationship with her tutor, demonstrating the fact in a confession to a subsequent admirer:

> 'I – I – liked him – I liked him very much – He was very kind to me . . . I did not know – he said he would be very angry with me – I did not want him to be angry with me – I didn't want to – I didn't know, you see! – Oh, what shall I do! What shall I do!'
>
>   . . .
>
> 'Bertie, do you mean that you gave yourself to him?'
> She nodded.
> 'My poor cousin!' he said slowly.[154]

Perhaps Olive was doing no more than document the absences in women's language. There is certainly an ambiguity in her presentation of Rebekah's relationship with her husband and Bertie's treatment at the hands of a series of prejudiced up-country and Cape Town women. Both women are creative, though in different ways: Rebekah reads and works with a microscope, Bertie sews, wallpapers and cooks. Both are capable of great energy and of great lassitude. Yet each is silenced by men: Rebekah when her letters to her husband about the truth of their relationship are ignored or torn up, and Bertie when the rich Jew renders her mute with loneliness in a house of fabulous wealth. The balance between description and prescription is a very fine one and the tensions over female sexual energy are never resolved within the novel.

It may have been because of these tensions that Olive could never finish *From Man to Man*. It was not only that she grappled with her plot. She was attempting to find a fictional form that allowed her to explore female psychology and to rehearse her moral position. She found it easier to do the latter in her allegories, written at the same time as *From Man to Man*, and, to a certain extent, a reformulation of it. Her way of writing fiction was to write long and then to condense. By 1885 she had written over 500 pages of the novel, but she was 'not adding' to it. 'It grows smaller and smaller,' she told Ellis, 'I am sure that all I am doing is improvement. Condense, condense, condense!' Again, this time with an element of compulsion to it: 'I can't help myself. I am driven on to make it smaller.'[155]

It was with her allegories that Olive presented herself as working most unconsciously. As she moved further and further away from the demands of characterization and of a coherent narrative, she used the flexibility of the allegorical form as a way of living more fully in the imagination. It was now, at the end of the Pearson episode, that she sought a publisher for these 'Dreams'; her novel remained a most private possession. Her stated position on publication was that it was abhorrent to her – how could she expose Bertie's or Rebekah's inmost workings only for them to be 'trodden underfoot'?[156] The allegories, on the other hand, were deep abstractions that it seemed legitimate to bring out in print. It was also the case that the slow chronology of a narrative – at least of the kind she used in *From Man to Man* – gave rise to a most unwieldy novel, as she herself was aware. Rebekah's speeches and notes on evolution, race, and the position of women occupy a full fifth of the text.* The impulse to 'condense, condense' indicates Olive's need to experiment with her form: now expanding, trying to deal with dialogue; now contracting into the admittedly rather precious symbolism of Joy, Wisdom, Truth, and the Ideal.

In letters to Pearson in 1887 Olive insisted on the importance of their relationship only in so far as it might have given him data for his work. She also used her allegorical writing as a means of symbolizing the affair in terms of archetypal conflicts and needs. But most of 1887 and 1888 were spent trying to recover from the involvement. From Christmas 1886 to October 1889, when she sailed back to South Africa, she spent less than a year in England. It was a desolate period, recorded in letters to Havelock Ellis and Edward Carpenter; in fact it was principally to Carpenter that Olive, without confiding any of the detail of the affair, turned for comfort. She moved first about Switzerland, then Italy, in a 'wild restless state'; a terrible melancholy came over her when she'd been a few days at any one place, and she had to move on again.[157]

She must have cut a pathetic figure. At Santa Croce in Italy women at the hotel laughed at her clothes; she burst into tears and went up to the grounds of her favourite church with some food and her writing. It was not the men who troubled her, she said, but middle-class women. Two

* Though sarcastic at Olive's expense, and patronizing about the novel's feminism, Hugh Walpole's comments on Rebekah are apt: 'As she is "forever raising a long low cry like a stricken dog" [Frank's] attempts at freedom are not too astonishing'; her letter to him 'goes on and on and one's sympathy with the husband increases and increases'. 'The Permanent Elements in Olive Schreiner's Fiction', *New York Herald Tribune* Books Section, 1 May 1927.

well-set-up women, whom she nicknamed the swells, asked her to go out with them but she returned from the expedition feeling sad: 'You know the feeling when you've been with people who are asleep and whom nothing will ever wake,' she told Carpenter. In part she was reliving the tangled relationship with Pearson as she insisted that it had been doomed by her sex: 'I wish I was a man that I might be friends with all of you,' her letters to Carpenter continued, 'but you know my sex must always divide. I only feel like a man but to you all I seem a woman.' Then she shifted her ground: 'One will never find a man to love,' she mourned, 'that some other woman does not desire.' It made personal life a great battlefield; 'those who enter it and will not fight get riddled with bullets. The only thing for them is keep out of it and have no personal life.'

The problem of being a woman was an old preoccupation, which Havelock Ellis had raised more than once. 'I wish very much that you didn't dislike me [*sic*] being of different sexes,' he had written, but the refrain persisted: 'I wish you were a woman.' At times this was simply an acknowledgement that it would be easier for them to meet at her lodgings if he were; at others a despair at the prospect of men and women ever understanding each other at all. Now, damaged by the Pearson affair, she accused herself of being the conventional female. Carpenter reminded her that she had driven round Paris the previous year surrounded by luggage: 'You mustn't hate us women so much,' she rebuked him, although humorously, 'though I do it myself.' Then she became resolute again: 'I won't be a woman in a couple of years.' She had begun to be one when she was only ten, she continued – perhaps in a reference to menstruation – 'so I daresay I'll leave off being one in about two or perhaps three more, and then you'll think I'm a man, all of you, won't you?' Then Pearson and everyone would be comrades with her. Meanwhile, she would work, harden herself, and learn the discipline of a life lived completely alone.[158]

At this time especially, but throughout her life in general, her experiences and stated views on women are markedly contradictory. There were the suspicious landladies, who dogged her attempt at living an independent life; the gossips and scandalmongers; the uncultivated and ignorant. But there were also the dependent and suffering women, especially prostitutes, whom she wanted desperately to support even when she could barely come to terms with her own needs. They made her glad to be a woman, for 'being a woman I can reach other women, where no man could reach them. A growing tenderness is in my heart for them.'[159]

Pearson had shown her that in living at the beck and call of every woman
who chose to make a demand on her, '*I was simply bleeding to death*'; he
stopped it by questioning this sacrifice of herself and giving her the
strength to resist. She had learned from him that when she sat up at
night writing she served the prostitute better than when 'I took her in
from the streets and laid her in my bed, and sat up all night watching her
sunken face in terror and agony'.[160] But if she realized that self-sacrifice
on occasions like these was of doubtful value, she remained divided in
her judgements on women. She understood, perhaps better than most,
the reasons for women's enforced pettiness, yet women's failings enraged
her. When it came, in particular, to the women who invaded her privacy
she railed against them:

> Oh it is awful to be a woman. These women are killing me . . . I wonder
> if I shall ever come back to England among these women again. One
> must die at last, eh Harry? Oh, please see that they bury me in a place
> where there are no women.[161]

Havelock Ellis was still her other-self; Carpenter the only person she
felt she'd like to see, and he joined her in Alassio, where she was living in
1888. She went to visit him at his Millthorpe home near Sheffield on one
of her return visits to England the same year. At Millthorpe she met Alf
Mattison, an engineer from Leeds whom Carpenter had supported when
he was victimized for his part in organizing the gasworkers. Olive and
Mattison felt an immediate affinity, for in such company Olive was
always able to subdue personal unhappiness to exalt the claims of labour;
what she learned about working-class organization was probably absorbed,
in her unsystematic and instinctive way, as much from Mattison as from
anyone else in England.* With Bob Muirhead, a young mathematics
teacher from Glasgow's Socialist League, with whom Carpenter had been
involved in a triangular relationship, she formed a special bond. So great
was her friendship for him that while days might go by without
remembering him,

> as soon as I met him the deep still joy and delight and satisfaction which

---

* In 1889 Alf Mattison wrote of the Leeds branch of the Socialist League that: 'Our
business was to make socialists and to go on making 'em until we had roped in all the
human race.' The Leeds branch went ahead because local leaders like Mattison and
Tom Maguire were organizing unskilled workers as well as making real use of the
trade unions. Alf Mattison's papers and notebooks quoted in E. P. Thompson, *William
Morris: Romantic to Revolutionary* (1955), p. 496.

his presence gave me came back, and I am quite sure that, if ever I had
been compelled to live in the same house with him for six months or
a year, it would have ended in my loving him so desperately I would
have been obliged to marry him.[162]

It was to Carpenter that she made nervous, tentative inquiries about
Pearson; the two men did not meet until 1889. She was then overjoyed
that they knew one another, but implored Carpenter not to bring her and
Pearson together: 'Don't ever mention me to him, unless he speaks of
me, and then turn it off.'[163] She herself was still trying to take distance
from him. In January 1888 she received a copy of his *The Ethic of Freethought*, which she valued because it was the peculiarity of his mind that
he 'stimulates almost to agony; it is not at all the result of knowing him
that makes one feel this'. Her enthusiasm was, as usual, disproportionate;
she compared Pearson, not necessarily favourably, but the comparison
was made all the same, with Mill, Spencer and Tennyson. Ellis apparently
had differences with her on the merit of the work; she then changed
ground and argued his bravery, as a university professor, in publishing
such views, even if he were tested not for genius or originality 'but as a
social thinker and teacher . . . [of] views we can sympathise with'.[164]

In Alassio Olive tried to finish her introduction to Mary Wollstonecraft's *Vindication*, but her letters to publisher Ernest Rhys, whom she
had met in London to consult about her contribution, show that she was
divided about its form. What she had already written had cost her, she
claimed, four times as much labour as had gone into *African Farm*, but it
was because she was trying to gather into it the result of 'my whole life'.
She wanted to do fresh research and asked Ellis to tell her about women
mill hands in the north of England:

> Do you think I am too strong in saying that they are equal (almost?)
> to the men, that motherhood in them does *not* prevent their working
> and being jolly, etc? . . . Don't exaggerate, let it have the exact truth.
> This is so important in social questions when one can so easily put
> things too strongly without being conscious of it.[165]

Still, the problem was to condense the immense volume of material she
already had, and the terms in which she describes the introduction to
Wollstonecraft make it difficult to distinguish it from the allegories she
was writing at the time: 'Sometimes I find that by throwing a thing into

the form of an allegory I can condense five or six pages into one, with no loss but a great gain to clearness.'[166]

Alassio found her, when she was not also living with her characters in the unfinished *From Man to Man*, in 'the allegory state'. These allegories, which were published as *Dreams* at the end of 1890, were already largely written. Some dated from London or St Leonards-on-Sea. Some were still to be rewritten and polished into final form when she was back in South Africa, where she sent them to Eleanor Marx and deputized Ellis to negotiate with a publisher on her behalf.[167]

Of all the writing Olive was engaged on now – allegories, *From Man to Man*, the introduction to Wollstonecraft – only the allegories were completed. She had been preoccupied for a long time with 'dreaming' as an optimum way of working (a trance-like state which she probably induced, in any case, when she worked for twenty-four hours without eating) and with finding a form that could express 'the passion of abstract ideas . . . humanity, not merely this man or that'.[168] Neither fiction nor the data of science really allowed her to develop her idea of life as a moral journey. By now, for example, all she cared about in *African Farm* was the allegory of the Hunter. Preoccupied with the vicissitudes of a contingent world, she sought their resolution in a series of transformations: from exploitation and oppression to goodness, repentance, union, and bliss.

The promise of a future heaven on earth sustained Olive at a time when she was in 'a state of despair such as I have not known since I was a girl of fifteen'.[169] The *Dreams* convey a sense of absolute desertion, yet at the same time the freedom of living in a different future: an ideal world in which problems of sex love will not occur. Most of the allegories, in fact, were set in the desert of Olive's childhood, and they gave her a way of freeing herself, of letting her consciousness drift over her own past.* Replete with Biblical images, they reflect the intensity of her religious upbringing; she still preferred the statement and cadence of a parable to the logical detail of an argument. In her main dream of socialism, for

---

* This was also the period when the 'Prelude' to *From Man to Man* 'flashed' on her. Apparently wholly autobiographical, and very dear to her, this short account of a child's day followed a five-year-old girl's persecution at the hands of African servants and the frustrations of her relationship with her mother, a weary, distant figure who has just given birth. Through a fantasy of mothering a child of her own, the child Rebekah discloses the psychological abuse which she has suffered and tells her child that she will never treat her this way; she will be the 'good' mother that she herself never had.

instance – 'The Sunlight Lay Across My Bed', a vision of a capitalist
palace and its downfall – she followed the Revelation, where Babylon fell
'because she made all nations drink of the wine of wrath of her fornica-
tion':[170] here she made exploiters repent when they saw the bloodless,
wine-pressed hands of their slaves. At the same time, the desert, the star,
and the 'Far-Off World' evoked her old sense of release in the Karoo and
remained her self-definition and her source of peace. 'Dreaming' was a
way of transcending pain and fictionalizing her experience.

Olive's characters are always simply 'a man', 'a woman'; she, as
narrator, is simply 'I'. Thus 'the woman' in 'Three Dreams in a Desert',
whose function of continuous childbearing through the ages has rendered
her weak and dependent, confronts 'the man', who she hopes will understand her need for freedom. The narrator speaks to her companion:

> And I said, 'Surely he who stands beside her will help her?' And he
> beside me answered, 'He cannot help her, *she must help herself*. Let her
> struggle till she is strong. Let her once stagger on to her knees. In that
> day he will stand close to her, and look into her eyes with sympathy.'

The woman rises an inch from the earth and sinks back. The 'I', the
dreamer, cries out:

> 'Oh, she is too weak! Can she never move?' And he answered me, 'See
> the light in her eyes.' And slowly the creature staggered on to its knees.
> And I awoke: and all to the east and to the west stretched the barren
> earth, with the dry bushes on it.

The dreamer falls asleep in the fierce heat, and dreams once more: this
time of a woman on the banks of a river, on the other side of which lies
the land of Freedom. Frightened of crossing on her own, she hears the
sound of all those who will follow in her footsteps; Reason, an old man,
reminds her how locusts cross a stream, their bodies piling up in the form
of a bridge so that some, at least, can cross. No matter that many are
swept away, Reason tells her, for

> 'They make a track to the water's edge.' 'They make a track to the
> water's edge' [she repeats]. And she said, 'Over that bridge which shall
> be built with our bodies, who will pass?' He said, '*The entire human
> race*.' And the woman grasped her staff. And I saw her turn down that
> dark path to the river.[171]

Olive was the observer of a dream; and the maker of it. She could not 'see' a dream, and so was both within and outside the imagery. The part of her which could stay outside could be free, impersonal and, at times, productive. 'Never come back to myself sometimes for a couple of days,' she wrote to Havelock Ellis from Alassio, 'and that is the only way in which work can be done.'[172] Preoccupied with Nirvana and the extinction of self, her state of mind was almost placid. Elizabeth Cobb, who saw Olive when she was in London during the summer of 1889, felt that she was making peace with the world. 'She told me that she did not publish anything,' Mrs Cobb told Karl Pearson, 'but was getting many things into order, so that if anything happened to her, "all will be ready for other hands".'[173]

Mary Brown describes visiting Olive in London at the same time, when she was writing the first part of 'I Thought I Stood', an allegory of two fine ladies who had failed to notice the women they trod on as they made their way to heaven.

> She told me she had written it in the night and I could read it; I did so. I had long felt that women were protected through the degradation of other women, and this allegory brought it forward in a most forcible manner. When I said, 'Why did you write it? What does it mean?', she replied, 'I had been at one of those infernal gatherings of women. I did not know what I was going to. I hate to be asked out and then find that I am expected to talk.' 'Well,' I said, 'did you talk?' 'No,' she said, 'they talked.' 'And what did they talk about?' Striking her fist in her hand, she said, 'They talked about the degradation of women and the selfishness of men.' And then after a pause, added, 'The selfishness of men and the selfishness of women – that is why I wrote this.' I glanced again at the paper and read, 'Therefore I picked my way, and God said "On what?" '[174]

Olive did not always find the allegories easy to write, though when they were finished she could talk of them in a tone of 'deep conviction and serene calmness'. The words are those of Arthur Symons, who visited her that summer in her rooms at the Ladies' Chambers in Chenies Street, Tottenham Court Road, a few months before she left England for South Africa. He found her in

> a bare little room, yet pleasant, only two chairs – the cane armchair in

which she sat by the fire, and another, and the sofa covered with a rug of light brown fur, pleasant to stroke. Two little tables, on one a few books, and a few more on the narrow chimney piece, with a large framed portrait of a man, sturdy.[175]

Here Olive talked to Symons with 'incredible ardency'; he stayed for eight hours. She was still agonizing over 'The Sunlight Lay Across My Bed', feeling there was more of herself in it than anything she had ever done; it had 'all her socialistic strivings and thus at present, her soul'. For, commented Symons, she was in her altruistic phase, and lived only in others.

It was this elevated purpose which *Dreams* conveyed to more than one generation of readers. Women before and during World War One found it expressed the aspirations of feminism, whether in terms of the vote or the Co-operative movement.[176] Constance Lytton recalls a literary evening in Holloway prison that a group of Freedom League suffragettes organized, at which 'Three Dreams in a Desert' was read out. It scarcely seemed an allegory to her now:

> The words hit out a bare literal description of the pilgrimage of women. It fell on our ears more like an ABC railway guide to our journey than a figurative parable . . . We dispersed and went back to our hard beds, to the thought of our homes . . . to the groans and cries of agonised women – content.[177]

Olive had always seen *African Farm* as a book for working people, and she wanted to feel sure that boys like Waldo could buy a copy. *Dreams*, she claimed, was intended for the rich – capitalists, millionaires and middlemen in England and America – and all high and mighty persons.[178] The 1890 edition, from Fisher Unwin, was sold at two shillings a copy, and by 1930 had been reprinted twenty-four times. Whether she had intended it or not, she had reached a popular audience across classes. Not that its critical reception was all favourable, of course. One American reviewer took 'The Sunlight Lay Across My Bed' to be a 'blasphemous temperance tract'. The *Catholic World*, a New York monthly, while welcoming the emphasis on injustice done to women, felt that 'the great name of God is handled more colloquially and freely than necessity required or reverence and good taste would sanction'.[179] Arthur Symons, on the other hand, writing anonymously in the *Athenaeum*, provided a

Front cover of *Dreams*, first published in 1890.

beatific account of a book in which 'the words seem to chant themselves to a music which we do not hear'.[180]

Now that she was back in England Olive was sought after for meetings and social gatherings; she declined them, or, alternately, left before the end. She refused to go near the Men and Women's Club, though both Maria Sharpe and Elizabeth Cobb tried to interest her in attending. For a while she fled to the East End of London to escape callers. It was also, as Oscar Wilde commented, 'because that is the only place where people do not wear masks upon their faces, but I have told her that I live in the West End because nothing in life interests me except the mask'.*[181] She

---

* Oscar Wilde was then editing the *Woman's World*, which had printed one of Olive's allegories.

Top: Wittebergen mission station, the birthplace of Olive Schreiner.
Bottom: Olive's mother, Rebecca (centre), in her cottage in the grounds of
the Convent, Grahamstown, after her conversion to Roman Catholicism.

Top: The Great Karoo in the area of Cradock, the landscape that always gave Olive a 'sense of perfect freedom and wild exhilaration'. *Bottom:* New Rush, *c.* 1872, when Olive, her brother Theo and sister Ettie lived there in tents.

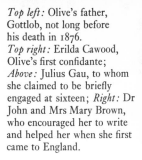

Top left: Olive's father, Gottlob, not long before his death in 1876.
Top right: Erilda Cawood, Olive's first confidante;
Above: Julius Gau, to whom she claimed to be briefly engaged at sixteen; *Right:* Dr John and Mrs Mary Brown, who encouraged her to write and helped her when she first came to England.

Fred Selewino, Wilfred & Fred's Wife
Olive and W.P.S.

April 1881.
Eastbourne

Above: The Cawoods'
farm at Ganna Hoek,
Cradock, at which Olive
completed the first
draft of *The Story of an
African Farm. Left:*
Olive at Eastbourne in
April 1881, shortly
after her arrival in
England. Left to right:
her brother Fred,
Fred's son Wilfred,
Olive (standing), Fred's
wife, Olive's brother
Will, later Prime
Minister of the Cape.

Olive's closest friends during her years in England in the 1880s: *Above:* Havelock Ellis; *Top right:* Eleanor Marx; and *Right:* Edward Carpenter (seated, right, with George Merrill, standing).

Top left: Elizabeth Cobb, a leading member of the Men and Women's Club during Olive's involvement with it in the 1880s. *Above:* Karl Pearson, co-founder of the Club, shortly before his marriage to Maria Sharpe in 1890.
Left: Bryan (later Sir Bryan) Donkin, Olive's doctor and unsuccessful suitor. *Below:* Elizabeth Cobb's younger sister Maria Sharpe (foreground) and Ralph Thicknesse, a friend of Pearson's, on a Club picnic.

Left: Cecil Rhodes, Olive's chief adversary in Cape politics.

Top right: Olive's main South African women friends in adult life, Betty Molteno and Alice Greene, teachers at the Collegiate School for Girls in Port Elizabeth. *Above:* Cronwright Schreiner and Olive at Krantz Plaats, his farm in the Karoo, shortly after their marriage in 1894.

Below: Olive during one of her walks with a young African servant, date unknown. *Bottom right:* Olive in 1915, five years before her death at sixty-five.

Above: Olive's leather medicine case. The writing reads: 'Will be rewarded. Please return to Olive Schreiner 30 Mary Abbot Terrace Kensington.'

lived at Gore Road, Victoria Park, where crowds gathered on Sundays to hear speakers from the National Secularist Society and the Social Democratic Federation; an observer concluded that East London working men appeared extremely well read in the sceptical literature of the day.[182]

By the middle of 1889, however, Olive was finally determined to go back to South Africa. She needed a few years of complete concentration on her work, she said, and asked Ellis to return copies of her manuscripts in his possession; leaving England would be leaving him, and she minded this most. She was still a celebrity; she was taken to see Gladstone, whom she compared to a Bengal tiger, and Spencer, in whom she was badly disappointed.[183] She was on her way to meet Robert Browning when she was taken ill in the cab and had to be driven home again. W. T. Stead came to see her, and she attacked him violently for his shortcomings as editor of the *Pall Mall Gazette*, though hoped he would understand that fault-finding was the truest form of friendship.[184] She was also doing things for others: trying to raise a loan for a medical student who had nursed her during one of her spells of illness in London in 1887, and to comfort Amy Levy, a depressed young woman who was just beginning to make a name for herself as a novelist. Levy committed suicide. Olive had been with her at the seaside the month before and had urged her to read Edward Carpenter's 'Have Faith' in *Towards Democracy*, but the woman had written: 'Thank you, it is very beautiful but philosophy can't help me. I am too much shut in with the personal.'[185] Three years later the *Pall Mall Gazette* carried a scurrilous paragraph suggesting that 'two literary ladies', one rather famous and both with gloomy views of life, made a suicide pact which the younger carried out but not the elder. Olive was back in South Africa when she read the newspaper report. She wrote to Ellis:

A funny idea has struck me about the enclosed cutting, that perhaps *I* am meant. So many lies have been told about me already that I now wonder at nothing . . . What makes it likely that I am meant is that it is exactly *opposite* to the truth . . . I was always trying to cheer up Amy Levy (if it be intended for her) and protesting that *I* found life so delightful and worth living. I've often felt since that if I'd been more sympathetic to her melancholy mood, I might have done more for her.[186]

The month before she sailed she went to the East End to be close to the great Dock Strike when casual labour, feared as 'the mob' by the propertied classes, won the right to unionize. In the opening month of the strike Eleanor Marx addressed a meeting of 100,000 people in Hyde Park. For Olive there was a renewed surge of hope. She wrote to Carpenter:

> Isn't the strike splendid. You ought to see the East End now. The strange earnest look on the people's faces, that sort of wild-eyed look. You look straight into their faces and their eyes look back at you. They are possessed with a large idea. It's very wonderful. I went yesterday to the place where the Salvation Army are giving away tiny packets of tea. About 500 men were there standing in rows waiting. The curious silent elate [*sic*] atmosphere, the look in the face of the most drunken old man was wonderful. I think I have never felt so full of hope as yesterday.[187]

One last futile act: before she left she tried to see Pearson in the distance. Waiting in the rain outside University College she hoped to catch a glimpse of him as he passed, but didn't. It felt like when her father died.

CHAPTER FIVE

South Africa 1890–1894

Olive arrived back in South Africa on 6 November 1889. She was thirty-four years old. She had left it eight and a half years earlier, nervous about living in a larger world, but determined. Now she returned acclaimed as a writer but, by her view of herself, unfulfilled; so much work begun was as yet unfinished. As keenly as she felt her failures as a writer, she was even more shaken by the incompleteness of her emotional life. She could not get over her fright at her part in the Pearson affair; she took refuge in cryptic letters to Havelock Ellis about 'feeling dead'. Her illness was close to chronic. But she had hopes that coming back to Africa would revive her.

She had been in the country for less than three weeks, however, when a doctor telegraphed her that her mother was dying, and she travelled for three days and nights to Rebecca's convent in Grahamstown, fighting for breath all the way. She suffered such an acute attack of asthma there that she had to hurry away as soon as her mother was out of danger. She spent the New Year with her brother Will and his family in Cape Town, and during that stay climbed Table Mountain several times, wearing 'a costume appropriate for the work, loose knickers with stockings and a coat that came well over the hips'.[1]

Still dogged by asthmatic attacks Olive moved in March 1890 to Matjesfontein, a settlement little more than a railway station on the main railway line from the Cape, three thousand feet above sea level. It was a dry, semi-desert region, and might relieve her asthma. The land around the station was owned by Jimmy Logan, a friend of Cecil John Rhodes who later became a member of the Cape Legislative Assembly and was heavily implicated in the corruption charges that brought down the

Rhodes cabinet of 1893. He imported London lamp-posts to light the
streets and erected a pretentious hotel which became a winter resort for
the wealthy;[2] Matjesfontein was an important stopping place for travellers, and for Olive the event of the day came when 'twice in the twenty-
four hours the railway train sweeps by; in the morning the Cape train on
its way to the Diamond Fields and Gold Fields stops about 9 o'clock
and the people get out to have breakfast here, and they leave our mails;
again, about six in the evening, the train from the Diamond Fields passes
and stops for half an hour.' This mixture of 'civilisation and the most
wild untamed freedom' was curious and very attractive to her: 'The
barren mountains and wild Karoo and the railway train. I know that at
any time by leaping into it and travelling twenty-four hours without
stopping I could cover the 500 miles between this and Cape Town' (she
had the distance and the time wrong). If only her asthma kept away, it
was the 'ideal place I have so long been longing for'.[3]

    She was exhilarated at being back in the scenery she knew so well from
her girlhood. The sounds reminded her of Ratel Hoek, and her descriptions
of living in the Karoo once more evoke the opening passages of *African
Farm*. By day it was 'the motionless Karoo with sunlight shimmering on
it; the stainless blue, with just one little cloud floating in it like a ship'.[4]
She felt when she went out alone that the last ten years had been a dream,
and was conscious only of an all-powerful desire to drink in through her
senses: perhaps it was after long years 'buried in abstract thought, that I
turn with such a keen kind of relish to the external world'.[5] The scenery
made her silent, strong, and self-contained: 'It is all so bare, the rocks and
the bushes, each busy standing separate from the others, alone by itself.'
Physically, too, she was much better, feeling in perfect health for the first
time in ten years. The colour had come into her face; she felt pretty again,
and people said she looked so.[6] She was especially glad to have found a
'walking up and down place' under some large trees in the dry river
course.

    Now that she had 'got the old muscle back', she was slowly maturing
plans to travel in the interior, getting letters of introduction to travellers,
traders and others who might help her on her line of march.[7] Perhaps
Ellis would journey with her? But first to writing. If *Dreams* was a success
she would have enough money to travel. She gave Ellis a free hand with
publishing arrangements since she hated business and could 'command a
fleet, govern an army, head a nation, write an epic, sooner than make a

bargain about seven-and-sixpence.'[8] The one thing she stipulated was that the book's dedication should read:

TO

A small girl-child; who may live
to grasp much, that for us is sight,
not touch.

O.S.[9]

Another story, 'The Buddhist Priest's Wife', was written in Matjesfontein in 1891 and 1892, though it was only published posthumously in the collection entitled *Stories, Dreams and Allegories*. Though the idea for it came into her head early one morning in Cape Town just after her return to the country, 'the substance of it is that which I have lived all these years to know, and suffered all that I have suffered.'[10]

Although Olive was given to exaggerating her attachments to one or other of her writings, she was always consistent about her special feeling for this story. She thought it much the best thing she had written, and told her brother Will that if everything else she had produced were put in one hand, this in the other, and one handful had to be burnt, she would let the others go, so that 'The Buddhist Priest's Wife' was left behind her when she died. Of all her stories, it is the least abstract or displaced in time, and the most personally revealing; she seems almost deliberately to have avoided an allegorical form. The action takes place in a London room of the nineteenth century, its atmosphere created in sparse detail – the fire in the grate, the woman with a silver cigarette case, her bags packed ready for the departure abroad.

Olive summarized the story in a letter to W. T. Stead:

A woman scientific in tendency and habits of thought but intensely emotional loves a brilliant politician; she is going away where she will never see him again, she invites him to see her the last night, and they discuss love, the ideal of marriage, prostitution, and the evils of celibacy.[11]

It was as though Olive was rounding off the Pearson episode in a rational discussion with him rather than in flight, and at last had the opportunity to explain to him the radical differences between men and women on questions of love and sex. These she believed to be part of a natural order.

The conversation between the man and the woman in the story proceeds with more élan than anything in *From Man to Man*:

> You see [the woman says], sex love in its substance may be the same in both of us; in the form of its expression it must differ. It is not man's fault; it is nature's. If a man loves a woman, he has a right to try and make her love him because he can do it openly, directly, without bending. There need be no subtlety, no indirectness. With a woman it's not so; she can take no love that is not laid openly, simply, at her feet. Nature ordains that she should never show what she feels; the woman who has told a man she loved him would have put between them a barrier once and for ever that could not be crossed; and if she subtly drew him towards her, using the woman's means – silence, finesse, the dropped handkerchief, the surprise visit, the gentle assertion she had not thought to see him when she had come a long way to meet him, then she would be damned; she would hold the love, but she would have desecrated it by subtlety; it would have no value. Therefore she must always go with her arms folded sexually.

It sounded very much as though Olive was the woman in the story, asking herself whether she had ever loved

> anything absolutely, this woman whom so many men loved, and so many women; who gave so much sympathy and never asked for anything in return! did she ever need a love she could not have? Was she never obliged to unclasp her fingers from anything to which they clung? Was she really so strong as she looked? Did she never wake up in the night crying for that which she could not have? Were thought and travel enough for her?[12]

In this story and in the letters written to Havelock Ellis, Olive seemed still to be living through the agony of her relationship with Pearson, partially resigned but, at times, desperate. She heard from Edward Carpenter that Pearson had married Maria Sharpe, and at last felt free to write to him herself; he would have misunderstood her before, she claimed resolutely – indeed: 'You have never understood me, Karl, my dear brother, never!'[13] She told Carpenter that she was pleased about Pearson's marriage: it was the best thing that could have happened to him. She wrote to Ellis, too, asking him to tell her all about it if ever he fell in love. As for herself, she had begun to feel that she could be married now. It would not impinge on her individuality too much. But 'no one could reach me now. You know what I mean. I know I shan't marry, but now for the first time in my life I feel I *could*.'¹⁴ She had given up the thought of finding a husband she could love and look up to. 'Now that I expect so little from any personal relation or from marriage, whether of mind or body, I could marry safely, there would be no disappointment.'

She began to feel remorse at her treatment of Ellis, and asked him to forgive unkind things she had said or done to him. News reached her of his friendship with Edith Lees, whom he had got to know through the Fellowship of the New Life and was to marry at the end of 1891. She did not appear to be jealous of her, only rueful at losing Ellis; she acknowledged that she needed continuing contact with him, he who knew her 'better than anyone else'. She asked him to name one of his children after her, if his wife were willing.¹⁵ It was not an egotistical demand on her part, but rather a reassertion of the bond between them. For she saw herself as a childless, solitary old woman,¹⁶ and she valued Ellis' affection and understanding.

While the experiences of the years in England continued to impinge on Olive's feelings, she was now having to grapple again with the problems of life in Victorian colonial society. Solitude in the country she loved brought tranquillity and the power to work, but it also brought a loneliness greater even than when she was a girl.¹⁷ It was not that Olive went unrecognized. She was a celebrity, much sought after in social circles, and she was touched by the respect and admiration of people who knew that she was the author of a famous book even if they had not read it. But the feeling of utter separation from the people about her – 'so good, so kind, so nice – and yet not a common bond between us' – made her feel like a live white elephant.¹⁸ On her return to the country she had been struck by the slow pace at which people lived, by 'their peaceful cattle-like lives. It seems to me as if all the streets were full of cows and sheep. All the men stand at the door with their arms folded; if they are doing anything it seems as if they were doing nothing; they do it so slowly that you can't see the movement.' She was, of course, describing the small insular towns of the interior where white men supervise and black men labour, the further out of sight the better. The measure of her alienation can be gauged by the savagery of several of her outbursts to Ellis: 'Fancy a whole nation of *lower* middle class people.' And again: 'Fancy a whole nation of lower middle class Philistines, without an aristocracy of blood or intellect or muscular labourers to save them.'[19] It was an impressionistic but accurate tirade against the social composition and mores of an English-speaking society which, appropriating the notions of social Darwinism then current in empire-building England, flattered itself with its civilizing mission.

In an attempt to place herself politically in this society, Olive wrote a set of essays on South Africa and its people, later to be published in book form as *Thoughts on South Africa*.* The opening essay, one of the few to appear contemporaneously in a South African newspaper, was a nostalgic, sentimental and even patriotic statement of her love of her native land after a long absence from it. She described the sense of suffocation she had felt in England. Like other South Africans she had yearned for waves that were larger than others, rivers fiercer, skies higher and more intensely blue. She recalled a journey in South Africa with an English-woman in a post cart. They had travelled all day up through the bush, and at noon came out on a height 'where before us, as far as the eye could reach, over hill and dale, without signs of human habitation or break, stretched the bush'. The Englishwoman began to sob and could only reply to the questioning: 'Oh, it's so terrible. There's so much of it. There's so much.'

Much of the country Olive described in the essays she had moved through as a child and as a young woman; other parts were filled out from history and geography books of the day, their popular prejudices included: Natal's small English population thus appeared to be 'rather above the Colonial average intelligence and culture'. From the land she turned to the 'marvellous diversity of races among us', using the organic metaphor to argue for a unified nation. 'A nation, like an individual, is a com-bination of units; in the nation the units are persons, in the individual body they are cells. The single cell, alone and uncombined, is capable only of the simplest forms of development.' Likewise, alone and divided from his fellows, she argued, the individual man was capable of only the very lowest form of development. Great men, great actions, great arts, great developments were impossible without those closely united, inter-acting organic combinations of men we call nations. It was a matter of

* *Thoughts on South Africa* (1923), was mostly written between 1890 and 1892, and published as separate articles in a variety of English and US journals between 1891 and 1900. For a full bibliographic history, see below, p. 376.

necessity. If the South Africa of the future was to be eaten internally by race hatreds, then its doom was sealed.

This plea against segregation, like her conception of a nation state, was highly generalized, inspired mainly by her preoccupation with the divide, within white South Africa, between Boer and Briton. And although the first essay on the need for union was intended as a prelude to chapters on the different races, and the conditions and individuals then influencing the future of South Africa, the essay on black Africans was never written. Such references as there are to South Africa's indigenous people are firmly rooted in the racist stereotypes of contemporary ethnology which she was clearly unable to transcend. She credited the Hottentots, for instance, with preternaturally keen senses and quick perceptions, but judged them incapable of bearing consistent intellectual or emotional strain.

The thrust of the essays is Olive's advocacy of the Boers. 'The Wanderings of the Boer', 'The Boer and his Republics', 'The Psychology of the Boer', and 'The Boer Woman and the Modern Woman's Question' are a tantalizing blend of impassioned political polemic sustained by shrewd personal observation and insight, and fiercely protective, almost Jesuitical argument in their defence. She was concerned to explain how the Boer, 'a pure-blooded European, descended from some of the most advanced and virile nations of Europe', often a wealthy landowner with flocks, herds and crowds of dependants, governing states as large as European countries, should yet, in this latter half of the nineteenth century, possess on many matters a Calvinist faith 'which has been outgrown by a London or Paris gamin'.

Her answer was that the Boers, in their geographical isolation, spoke a cramped little dialect – the Taal (or Language, by which Afrikaans was known before its successful battle for recognition). It was this language which had cut the Boers off from the Age of Enlightenment, that 'awakening of human reason in the eighteenth century', with its stern demand for intellectual tolerance and its renunciation of universal brotherhood. A young Boer, growing up on an African farm and speaking nothing but the Taal, could not even imbibe a world culture from books, in solitude. But if the isolation of the Boers cut them off from the cultural mainstream, it also left them untouched by the 'god of commerce' – capitalism. For Olive the life of the up-country Boer farmers fulfilled a need in her, heightened perhaps by her sympathy with the life style of Edward

Carpenter's Millthorpe circle, for a retreat from urbanism and industrial life, a reaction against the 'vast accumulation of material goods, for under it the human spirit is being crushed'.

Olive went on to tackle the charges that were commonly made against the Boer: that he had practised slavery, that he did not regard the African as his brother, that his forefathers had exterminated the Bushmen. It was all very well, she wrote, for the idle and luxurious in their drawing rooms to indulge in philanthropic sentiment. What of the Voortrekker mother, who 'lay awake at night in her wagon with her baby at her breast, listening with strained intensity . . . for a stealthy step approaching, or for the sound of the loosening of the oxen tied to the wagon, on whose continued possession the lives of her husband and children depended?' To her the 'little dark figure' was no record of the past but an awful actuality of the present: the stern pressure of the primitive necessities of life had stepped in and made brotherly love impossible.

But she was convinced that the Boers would change. In time the old Boer would be no more:

> Like those minute creatures, who, at a certain stage of their existence, form about themselves a hard coating, and in that condition may lie embedded in the animal tissues in which they are found for weeks, or years, without undergoing any change or growth; but who, if at any moment their cast be ruptured, start at once upon a process of rapid evolution, developing new organs and functions, and bearing soon no resemblance to the encysted creature that has been – so the true old Boer has lain, encysted in his Taal, knowing nothing of change or modification; yet from the moment he breaks through it, evolution sets in rapidly; the child of the seventeenth century departs, and the child of the nineteenth century arrives – and the Boer is no more.

She admitted that a more important question, 'involving as it does, the world's greatest problem', was how the 'primitive and aboriginal peoples are to be brought into our social system', and that this was being obscured by the divide between the white groups. But in that divide Olive was on the Boer side, emphatically and without reserve. To those who charged that she loved the Boer because she had Dutch blood, she described her parentage and her training, which had been 'exclusively and strongly English'; she claimed English as her mother tongue and England as her mother land. She had started life, she wrote, with insular prejudice and racial pride, profoundly convinced of the superiority of the English, their government and their manners, over all other peoples. She had broken these attitudes in herself as a result of contact with other peoples.

Read as a whole the essays in *Thoughts on South Africa* offer a curiously ambivalent exposition. At times Olive seems to be looking to a transformed society free of race oppression; at others she seems to endorse the ideological justifications of white conquest. In her accounts of Boer life there are passages of vibrant social history, of the domestic life of up-country farming homesteads, of courtship and marriage practices, acutely observed and tenderly described. Yet there is also the apologia for the treatment of the African peoples which was to help sustain Afrikaner nationalism in its fiercest anti-African as well as anti-British expression. For by the early 1890s Olive Schreiner was formulating the position which was to generate the contradictions confronting radicals during the Boer War a decade later. Her defence of the Boer was a critique of the purposes of capitalism in South Africa; at the same time, an allegiance to the Boer ignored the condition and claims of the majority of the population, the Africans, whose exploitation was common cause between the contending whites. It was to be some time before Olive turned her attention to this latter question. Meanwhile she was preoccupied with a need to dissociate herself from the English-speaking pro-British establishment, and to justify her advocacy of the Boer.

Not that these articles had much public impact in her own country. With the exception of the first general essay on the land and its peoples, and part of one of the essays on the Boer – which was later, to Olive's deep distress, savaged by an Afrikaner newspaper* – they were not published in South Africa till three years after Olive's death. She claimed in 1896 that this was deliberate. She had withheld publication because she had been concerned to reveal not the 'coarse external shell' of the Boer, but rather his 'finer-fibred kernel within'; but praising the Boer at the time would have been interpreted as part of the wooing of Afrikaner votes by Cape politicians. Lest her voice be mistaken for that of the flatterer, she had not published them in South Africa. She had, however, asked Havelock Ellis to place the essays, without revealing their authorship, in an English review.

Only eight months after her arrival in South Africa she was feeling acutely deprived of intellectual companionship. 'It may be good for one's

* See p. 225.

work,' she wrote to Stead, 'but there are times when one longs to rub one's brains up against another human's. There are plenty of women and children and niggers' – she might have added Boers – 'to love here, but sometimes one wants the other side of one's nature satisfied, that *thinks*.' Women drew close to her but they seemed unable to talk impersonally. 'I get so weary of personalities, always that, nothing else, between women. They don't want to discuss a man's public character, even his policy, but want to discuss all the smallest little personal things about them.' She continued to be surprised at the way people discussed her: 'Am I engaged to this one or that, have I quarrelled with so and so that I don't go to see them, when they might discuss my writings and my view of life which would be far more interesting.'[20]

The response to her writings was equally vapid. Mrs Cawood, one of her oldest friends, did not like her allegories. John Pursglove, a close friend when she was at the Diamond Fields at eighteen, thought one of them was about drinking. Her mother, Olive commented, didn't know *what* it was about, adding: 'that's rather encouraging!'[21] When people were silent to her face about her allegories, she sensed their hostility. The misunderstanding or rejection of her work made her feel 'absolutely isolated'. Except once, when her brother Will put his head against her and spoke kindly to her, no one had said anything gentle to her since she had left England. She doubted that she would live fifty years in Africa and make even one friend. There was, however, one man whom she thought she would like to meet. This was Cecil John Rhodes, 'the only big man we have here'.[22]

It was inevitable that Olive should meet Rhodes. Though she lived quietly in Matjesfontein for almost three years, she made fairly frequent journeys to Cape Town, where her own reputation and Will's carried her to the centre of Cape politics and would have carried her, had she wished it, to the pinnacle of social life in the Colony. Will had returned from studying in Cambridge to rise high in the Cape legal profession, and then go into politics. He acted as legal adviser to Rhodes' diamond syndicate and to him as governor of the Cape, and he was later to serve Rhodes' politics with devotion. Before she met Rhodes, influenced perhaps by press eulogies of the man, she admitted to a mysterious attraction – not love or admiration, a deliberate feeling that 'this man belongs to me'.[23] It meant that she had an 'almost painfully intense interest in the man and his career', as she told Stead.[24]

In November 1890 she had dinner with him when he came to Matjes-fontein. He reminded her of Waldo in *African Farm*: 'the same, curious, far-off look, combined with a huge, almost gross body'; she thought of him as a man of genius who was a sort of child, so that she felt curiously tender to him.[25] But then she entered a reserve, and one reminiscent of a similar anxiety vis-à-vis Pearson: though he himself was higher and nobler than she had expected, they could never be friends because their milieu was so different. There is no doubt, however, that Olive and Rhodes were drawn to each other: she admired his energy and he was enraptured by *African Farm*.[26] When he entertained Lord Randolph Churchill at Groote Schuur, after he had become prime minister of the Cape in 1890, he disregarded conventional protocol and had Churchill take Olive in to dinner.[27] They would often meet at dinner parties – it became a social coup to have them both present – and on the station platform at Matjesfontein, when Rhodes would use his stopping-off point as an occasion to talk to her.[28]

But by 1892, as Olive watched his performance and that of his political colleagues in the Cape parliament, the political differences between them became more apparent, and she began to insist that her name should not be mentioned in connection with his 'in any way whatever'.[29] She was also reacting against a report that had come to her ears that she wished to make Rhodes marry her. She was already feeling hounded by rumours of her romances: a Kimberley newspaper had announced her engagement to the governor's secretary, Seymour Fort, a French one had engaged her to a leading French politician whose name she did not even know. Olive denied both reports, protesting that she hated publicity and that if ever she loved a man and was going to marry him it would be a source of agony for her that people should discuss it; if anyone proposed to her not even her mother or brother would hear of it.[30]

Rumours of her emotional involvement with Rhodes served to compound an already complex relationship. Even as she insisted that her personal and political feelings were distinct, that it was not inconsistent to combat Rhodes' policies and yet to sympathize with him, there is no question that for at least a year after they met, at a time when Rhodes was at the height of his power as a financier and politician, she thought him a man of genius and one of the most remarkable men of the century, bestowing tributes on him among her English friends. In spite of the arguments she had with him she seemed to believe that she had the power to save him from his policies. They were really strongly opposed in their views. Five months before she had met him, Rhodes had voted for the Flogging Bill in parliament which imposed lashes on Africans for minor offences like absence from work and disobedience of a master's orders.* Olive had been outraged, writing to Carpenter:

> Edward, you don't know how bad things are in this land; we flog our niggers to death and wealth is the only possible end and aim in life . . . There are money-making whites and down-trodden blacks and nothing in between. And things will have to be so much worse here before they can be better.

She returned again and again to the flogging measure. In 1891 she wrote a skit on parliament in which Rhodes was damned to hell as a capitalist and upholder of the bill, but when he could not gain entry there because he was too large by far, God made room for him in heaven 'through grace, not merit', since 'with God all things are possible'.†

For a while she was dazzled by his power and force. When Stead, who saw Rhodes as an Elizabethan statesman born out of his time, put her on a par with him, she protested that he was 'much greater than I . . . Any accident to him would, I believe, mean the putting back of our South African development for fifty years.'[31] And she agreed with Stead that Rhodes seemed to enlarge the horizon: 'How he has enlarged it in South Africa it would be impossible for you to judge unless you had known the South Africa of ten years ago.'

About the changes Rhodes and his policies were producing in South Africa there is no dispute. The move of the Trekboers away from the Cape had led to the consolidation of two Boer republics, the South African Republic, also known as the Transvaal, and the Orange Free State. Between these two states, and the British-controlled colonies of the Cape and Natal, African principalities were being squeezed until, by the end of the century, few remained independent; instead they became vassals of one or other white power. The completion of the conquest of the African peoples coincided with mineral discoveries that were to

---

* Known in Afrikaans as the Strop Bill, this was the Masters and Servants Bill, introduced in the Cape parliament in 1890 and again in 1891.

† 'The Salvation of a Ministry', subtitled 'Children, how hardly shall a politician enter into the Kingdom of God', reproduced in full in *Life*, pp. 202–5, does not appear to have been published.

transform the economy. Until the discovery of diamonds, the Cape relied on wool, wine, cattle and sheep, a little wheat, some tobacco, ivory and ostrich feathers. When a single diamond was found in the Cape in 1867, alluvial diggings spread along the Orange and Vaal rivers, and at one point diggers proclaimed their own free republic. But the real diamond wealth was mined not from alluvial, but from deep, 'dry' diggings, and individual claimholders – like Olive's brother Theo – could not undertake underground mining operations. The organization of diamond mining as a highly capitalized and concentrated modern industry, and the establishment of a world monopoly of sales through a London diamond syndicate, was Rhodes' first major achievement. After an epic struggle for power between competing owners and syndicates, he dominated the industry with his De Beers Consolidated Mines.

Rhodes' interests went far beyond his diamond cartel. He was the creator, too, of the Chartered Company, later the British-South Africa Company, which was authorized to annex territory, raise and maintain a standing army, and make war. The Charter was granted by the British government because Lord Salisbury and others felt that although the extension of Britain's interests from the Cape into the interior could probably be better accomplished by government, the House of Commons would not vote money for the purpose. If expansion had to be organized on the cheap, the Chartered Company would have to be given a virtually free hand. Rhodes used it. In the words of William Plomer, the South African poet who wrote a blistering book against Rhodes in the tradition of Olive Schreiner's parable of 1891, he was inspired by 'a vision of Britannia wearing seven-league boots and carrying a pot of red paint'.[32] Rhodes used the Company's forces to provoke war against the Matabele and the Mashona, and to confirm the British settlers in their possession of nearly half a million square miles of land.

Rhodes thus played several related roles. He helped to organize the financing of the mining industry, and this laid the basis for the capitalist transformation of the South African economy. After diamonds, gold came to be mined in the Transvaal in the 1880s: the gold-bearing ore was found along the Witwatersrand in the shape of a great horseshoe stretching for hundreds of miles. Widespread but not very concentrated, these ores posed deep-level mining engineering problems. It meant that the industry required huge inputs of capital, developed technology, and virtually unrestricted supplies of cheap labour. The industry was developed by foreign capital at great speed, so that by 1888 forty-four mines were in operation. By 1890 the industry was employing over 100,000 men. It was an industry that relied on a world market which had made gold the basis of its currency, and on international capital – though the diamond industry had generated some capital for gold-mining, and Rhodes subsequently controlled one of the eight giant mining houses.

This highly capitalized gold-mining industry found its growth constrained by the limits of the Transvaal economy and state, and here Rhodes played his next role. Capitalist production required a unified economy and a unified state; Rhodes, as prime minister of the Cape, controller of De Beers at Kimberley, the Goldfields Company on the Rand, and the Chartered Company which named Rhodesia after him, was able to orchestrate these changes. After 1895 the conflict of interests between the Boer republics and the needs of an influential sector of mining capital were to precipitate the Anglo-Boer war, as a result of which the industrial revolution in South Africa took place under the direction of a ruling class in control of a national state rather than the separate entities which it had comprised until then.

With the mining and industrial revolution, the Cape, although it boasted the longest history of white settlement and administration, was to find itself marginal to the economy. But in the 1880s and 1890s, when Olive was starting to find her way in Cape politics, and Rhodes was using his premiership of the colony to pursue larger imperial and business aims, Cape politics were still parochial and sectarian. Merchants and farmers; urban, rural and imperial interests; and competing market towns were all trying to bargain within a parliamentary framework organized on British lines.

English-speaking politicians, local associations and newspapers were trying to create an 'English' party. At the same time an Afrikaner nationalist movement was forming, prompted by Britain's annexation of the Transvaal in 1877. This latter nationalist movement, the Afrikaner Bond, had as its objective a united South Africa free of British control. But though church and language served to cement Afrikaner solidarity, the Bond's Pan-Afrikaner aims came to be whittled down under the leadership of Onze Jan (Jan Hofmeyr) when the Bond worked as a kind of political party within the Cape parliamentary system.

Until 1889 it was the only organized party in the colony. Yet it never held an absolute majority, and though individual Bondsmen sat in cabinets, no Bondsman was ever prime minister. Instead Hofmeyr marshalled his supporters behind factions of politicians in government as long as that government complied with his wishes, and the demands of Bond congresses broke the government when it did not. Hofmeyr himself, and the Bond generally, found no difficulty in accepting the imperial connection, providing the British government did not directly interfere in the internal affairs of the colony. By the 1880s not only English-speaking but also Afrikaner interests in the Cape – despite their linguistic, religious and emotional connections with the Boer republics – were upholding that colony's concerns over those of the other South African states. For instance, the interests of the Cape, including its Afrikaner farmers, diverged from those of the Boer republicans; the Transvaal government imposed duties on Cape agricultural products entering the Transvaal and Hofmeyr's conversion to Rhodes' policies had come in 1889 when the Transvaal Volksraad had rejected a customs agreement with the Cape.

It was upon this divergence of interest that Rhodes, who became prime minister of the Cape in 1890 with Bond support, played so expertly. He might have appeared to be the obvious force behind a predominantly English-based party, but he had a distinctly different set of interests to assert. For while Rhodes' plans were laid in the context of British investment in South Africa and of international competition to exploit and control areas far further afield, his achievement was to assert his designs with the political support of Hofmeyr's Bond. He took care to secure even more than this: he offered shares in the Chartered Company to leading Bondsmen, and promised their followers land in the company's territory; Hofmeyr himself received shares when these were not yet being offered on the London market. Thus Rhodes used his political base in the Cape to annex and control the territories to the north. It was imperialist expansion in the interests of British capital but under the direct aegis of the government of the Cape Colony and the Chartered Company.

It was through these intricacies of Cape politics that Olive had to find her way. Rhodes' achievement as prime minister in 1890 was to assemble a Cape government with strong Bond support but into which he also introduced three men who were to achieve a reputation as liberal politicians and who until then had been implacable opponents of the Bond and its farmer support. They were John X. Merriman, J. W. Sauer, and James Rose Innes. Merriman was probably one of the few

South Africans to read *Dreams* shortly after it came out. He described it in his diary as 'short rhapsodies by a very clever woman who would be happier if she believed in what the rest of her sex believe'.[33] In her 1891 skit of the Cape parliament debating the Masters and Servants Bill, Olive had the angel present Merriman to God as a man who held anti- quated views with regard to women and who despised them. God ruled that irrelevant: 'Many men feel so, and most women deserve it.' Olive had hopes that despite his views of women, Merriman and his associates would take a principled stand in the cabinet on matters of African policy, and that 'anything would be better than that they should go out'. Within two years she had changed her mind and was trying to persuade Rose Innes and Sauer to 'come out of the City of Destruction'.[34] She was to make intermittent representations to Merriman over the years, and her close friendships with Mary Sauer and Jessie Rose Innes prompted Rhodes to charge her with having done everything in her power to induce their husbands to leave him during the cabinet crises of 1892 and 1893.[35] Olive wrote extensively about Cape politics to her women friends, but also about her own life and feelings, especially to Mary Sauer, in whom she was especially confiding on personal questions and of whose husband she had great hopes as a liberal politician.

In the cabinet the principal controversies were over the 'native' policy fostered by the Rhodes-Bond alliance, which included the annexation of the last independent African territories adjoining the Cape and the imposition there of a labour tax; the Flogging Bill; and the franchise. The qualifications for the Cape franchise had enrolled large numbers of Afrikaners, but had also enfranchised some Non-Whites, especially Coloured voters. White politicians, for the most part, were opposed to a non-racial franchise; on the other hand, because the Non-White voters tended to vote for English rather than Afrikaner candidates, the removal of Non-Whites from the voters' roll would have put the former at a disadvantage.

The dilemma of the liberal politicians can be seen in Merriman's view of the franchise proposals put forward by Bond leader Hofmeyr in 1890, which raised the property qualification and introduced a literacy test. Merriman thought that these 'would not be differential, nor would [they] be so high as to exclude the decent European or the superior class of native, but . . . would minimise the Coolie and the barbarian'.[36] The liberals could not make a unified stand, and a compromise on the franchise question became inevitable. When the break in the cabinet did come and the three liberals were jettisoned, it was over a scandal involving, coincidentally, Olive's former landlord Jimmy Logan. The affair highlighted the jobbery of a government based on Rhodes' money-power. It was over the same scandal that Olive broke off personal relations with Rhodes. One day on Matjesfontein station, finding him and Logan together, she refused to shake hands with Rhodes, rounded on her heel and went back to her house. This was the last time they talked together, though Rhodes was to make attempts at a reconciliation.

By the end of 1892 Olive was heavily disillusioned with Rhodes' politics; yet old anxieties lingered. In part they stemmed from her initial sense of deep identification with him. She was prey to 'very terrible dreams', as she had told Karl Pearson at the start of their friendship in 1886, 'like visions, you almost fancy they're real'. On that occasion she dreamed that a servant boy of hers had drowned Pearson in a large dark pond of water.[37] Now, one night in Matjesfontein, she dreamed that Rhodes was walking by with his big old felt hat on, drawn down very low on his head, an overcoat with the collar turned up and his head sunk between his shoulders. She ran up to him and stood before him. He did not speak a word, but opened his overcoat and as he turned it back she saw his whole throat and chest covered with blood and his face ghastly pale like a dead person's.[38]

In a long letter to her brother Will she tried to come to terms with her feelings about him.[39] She found Rhodes great, sincere, and without 'a spot of hypocrisy'. Rhodes himself never called his diplomacy principle, she said: he had told her that his actions were 'all based on policy, all policy', when she had tried to argue with him. It was other men who made capital out of high principle and who became hypocrites when they played Rhodes' game. 'In a sense,' she added, 'Rhodes is the sincerest human being I know; he sees things direct without any veil. There is no man in the world to whom I could show myself so nakedly and who can at times show himself so nakedly to you.' It was a suggestive phrase, but meant only that Olive responded to Rhodes, however reprehensible his politics, because she could treat him as an equal. Politics in South Africa was the business of men; Rhodes at least acknowledged Olive's reputation and intellectual capacity, and her relief at finding at least one statesman with whom to engage tempered her instinctive rejection of him.

But when it came to politics and public life, she warned Will that she would have to fight Rhodes at every step. This had no influence at all on Will. He was a strong moralist, but a white politician through and through. Like Olive in the beginning, he was mesmerized by Rhodes; she at least was early disillusioned, because she was anti-capitalist and recognized Rhodes' force for that system. Will worked in conservative politics as a constitutional lawyer, attentive to detail but uncritical of the larger economic and political processes of the time. When in May 1893 Rhodes formed a new ministry without Merriman and his colleagues he included W. P. Schreiner as his attorney-general. Will must have consulted Olive about joining a Rhodes cabinet, for she wrote: 'I should like to see you working with Rhodes, but only if you could stand perfectly erect – so we shall not see it, I fear.' Olive was dismayed when Will joined Rhodes in government, and sailed for England the day before he was sworn into office. By then she had deep personal considerations to weigh.

Olive met Samuel Cron Cronwright, whom she married at the beginning of 1894, on a visit to Ganna Hoek, the home of her old friends the Cawoods, in December 1892. Cronwright, an ostrich farmer and free-thinker who managed the adjoining farm, had persuaded them to send word immediately Miss Schreiner arrived so that he might go over and meet her, although he felt that his relationship with Olive had already begun, with his reading of *The Story of an African Farm* in 1890.[40] The genius of the writer had choked him with emotion, especially the allegory of the Hunter, for he too had 'suffered the agony of tearing from his heart the untruths planted there in his childhood'. He had thought, and said aloud, that when he met Lyndall he would marry her. He had written to Olive at the time to express his admiration of the book, describing himself as Waldo listening to the sweet voice of his Stranger.

Cronwright's grandparents were pioneering British settlers. His maternal grandfather came to the Cape in a British regiment in 1817 and married the daughter of an 1820 Settler family. His paternal grandfather Peter Wright, a member of the London Missionary Society, succeeded Gottlob Schreiner at Philippolis and became an important aide in John Philip's missionary diplomacy. Cronwright's father was first a farmer, then a businessman in Grahamstown, where he became a luminary of the city, serving as mayor for four years and as its member of parliament. Cronwright himself had thought of entering the Church but changed his mind after becoming a freethinker in his last year at college. Instead of taking his final examination he left to go farming, taking his clothes – including a pair of yellow corduroy trousers, 'about which I had to stand some chaff' – but not much else 'except my health, my physical aptitude, strength beyond the average, the love of a rifle, keen eyesight and a passion for reading'.

After receiving Mrs Cawood's note, Cronwright 'rode over, an easy hour, through the mountain pass. My horse was taken and attended to at Ganna Hoek, and I entered the front room. I was in riding breeches and top boots, was sunburnt nearly as dark as mahogany, my hair was jet black and I wore a clipped black beard.' He had never in his life been so nervous, so curious, about meeting anybody, and when Olive entered and he saw her for the first time, 'I shall never forget the quick glance and the strangeness of her presence.' The room seemed to pulse with light and energy.

Olive was then almost thirty-eight years old, eight years older than Cronwright. Twenty years of asthma had told on her, raising her shoulders and leaving her with a wheezy cough, but to Cronwright she conveyed the impression of youth, even the spontaneity and vitality of a child. She gesticulated freely when she spoke; she had a quick walk, frequently running with short steps from room to room; her face was always animated, 'and the compelling force of her genius, the rapidity and brilliance of her intellect, simply blazed through it'. Cronwright remarked that she spoke in a ringing vibrant voice, 'modulated to every emotion, arresting and strangely thrilling'. She was a big person in a small compass, not quite five foot in her stockings. Her neck was 'full and somewhat short; she used laughingly to recall Balzac's rejoinder when asked why his neck was so short: that God Almighty had made it so in order that his head and his heart might be close together'.

She dominated their conversation together and he was almost angered to find nearly everything he said contradicted; he was not accustomed to that. During their second encounter a few days later on Cronwright's farm, he conceded that he was outclassed, but 'like the high-metalled soul she was, the clash of mind only made her more brilliant and deadly'. According to Cronwright's account they were soon deeply engrossed in one another. She encouraged him to write an article on the ostrich which subsequently appeared in the *Zoologist*. They discussed the 'native question' and she tried to persuade him that he was mistaken in thinking that she had 'any affection for the Native', but that she saw it as the 'labour question which does not differ materially from the labour question all over the world'. She gave him some of her most treasured books. She wrote him little notes about the joy their encounters gave her, asked for the story of his early life, was moved that he was bound up with Krantz Plaats where Waldo had lived, and then bestowed the ultimate sign of approval: 'Yes, it is curious how like Waldo and Lyndall you are. The curious feeling I have towards you that you are a part of myself; it's such a curious, curious sort of feeling.'

She told him about her attempts to write her sex book, and how the previous year she had thrown most of it, or it had thrown itself, into 'The Buddhist Priest's Wife', which had given her more bliss than anything she had written. She explained that only when the woman asked her man visitor to kiss her did he realize that she loved him, but by then she had left the room. Lest he conclude that because all her stories ended with her ideal characters remaining unmarried she thought the celibate life the ideal, she told him that this was not so. 'Neither physically nor mentally does it lead to the fullest health or vigour. I find it one of the bitterest evils of our transitory condition that the best men and women in Europe have now so often to remain single.'

It was now patently a courtship, however tentative. Olive was introduced to Cronwright's mother and was moved that she put her arms round her and kissed her. 'My mother has never been a mother to me; I have had no mother,' she told Cronwright. 'She is a brilliant little woman, all intellect and genius. The relation between us is a very curious one; it is *I* who have had always to think for, guide and nurse her since I was a tiny child. She seems to me like a favourite brilliant child of mine.' At Olive's suggestion Cronwright visited Rebecca, who was still living in her Grahamstown convent; she approved of him, admiring his 'physical manliness, his muscular prowess'. It corresponded closely with Olive's impression of him: she asked him to have himself photographed in his shirt sleeves with the sleeves rolled up to show his arms.

Towards the end of March 1893 Olive chose to revisit Wittebergen, which she had last seen when she was six. It would be nice to be there on her birthday, she said. The white thatched house perched among the great rocks on the edge of the cliff was just as she had pictured it. She remembered the 'great flat stone by the house on which I was making a house when I heard that my little brother Will was born, and . . . the bushes with the funny smell under which I sat alone the first time I ever realised my own individuality and the mystery of existence. It was all so entirely unchanged.'[41] Back at Matjesfontein Olive confided in her journal 'I am his', and, a few days later: 'I have given myself in my thoughts to Cronwright for ever, in as far as a human woman can give herself to a man. I feel such peace when I think of him.'[42] Yet other diary entries and some letters suggested that she was not yet sure: 'There is just a possibility that I may marry Cronwright. We shall see.'[43] For by this time Olive had decided to return to England: she had promised herself a few years in South Africa in which to work, and they were now up. But perhaps the trip would give her distance in which to make up her mind about marriage; perhaps Cronwright would follow? In the last letter she wrote to him before her departure she wished a good happy life to 'my friend, my brother, my boy. I know we shall never meet again and I am quite satisfied if you only are glad to hold by the right . . . Think that I am an unchanging friend, a part of yourself as you are a part of me.'[44] It had begun to sound like the relationship with Havelock Ellis all over again.

During her six-month stay in England from May to October 1893, Olive wrote regularly to Cronwright, including a thirty-six-page letter which he does not appear to have preserved. She went first to visit her brother Fred at Eastbourne, then to London, where she met Havelock Ellis and Edith Lees, and seems to have been at ease with them. After that she travelled to Millthorpe in Yorkshire, where she rented a cottage to be near Edward Carpenter and his friends: George Merrill, Carpenter's lover, though they were not yet living together; Jim Joynes and Henry Salt, ex-Eton schoolmasters; Joynes' sister Kate, who later married Salt; and Bruce Glasier, the Glasgow socialist propagandist, and his wife.[45] This was a circle within which she could discuss her indecision. She confided in Carpenter that in Africa there was

> a man who I love and who loves me, but I'm not quite sure marriage would be right; the curious thing is I want to marry that man, to be always where he is, see him when I go to bed and when I rise in the morning, and everyday at the table and all day long and all my life long till I'm an old woman.

She had never felt like this before. She had loved Ellis, and Karl Pearson, and so many men and women, but had never felt 'I want to be with you always'. She found Cronwright a 'fiercely strong passionate impulsive kind of man', and she had to be gentle and meek when she was with him 'to make up for it'. Yet even after this frank expression of her need, she left the decision open: 'I left Africa because I wanted to feel I was removing from him any undue fascination I might be exercising over him and I don't suppose we shall ever see each other again.'[46]

One evening during this visit to England she was with women friends who, according to Cronwright's account, were averse to her marrying at all; when asked what sort of man it was she contemplated marrying, she produced his portrait and said 'That is the man!' and danced round the room, brandishing her fists in mock imitation of a boxer and boasting that he was 'a man who can knock eight men down with his fists one after another', as her friends broke into laughter.[47] Though she was clearly strongly physically attracted to Cronwright, and both of them badly wanted a child, she told Carpenter that there were other important considerations: it would never have done for her, for example, to marry Bob Muirhead, the young mathematics teacher and socialist to whom she had been attracted towards the end of her last stay in England. Muirhead was too good; she knew she needed 'the type of man most removed from our divine Bob, a man compared to whom I shall be a saint, a sort of small Napoleon'. It was those natures that drew her, she added, not the men of thought and fine-drawn feeling like Bob and Ellis and Karl Pearson, intensely as she loved them. For Olive, the wish to marry came only with 'the man of *action*, yes the philistine within me'. Indeed, all the men she thought she could marry were of that one type: 'men I felt needed me for their moral education'.[48]

A few months after first meeting Cronwright, perhaps when she was trying to come to terms with her attraction to him, Olive confided in Jessie Rose Innes that 'this loneliness of women's lives is very terrible, our unused emotional and intellectual energy lying unused within us, that breaks out in force as though it would overpower us at times'.[49] On her return to South Africa she had a severe attack of asthma that confined her to bed. It appears that she had agreed to marry Cronwright in a letter from Millthorpe, and she now felt able to confess to the conflicts she felt about the prospect. These related to her ideal of perfect, unselfish love, and her doubt that she was equal to it. She asked Cronwright to solve the problem:

I have not the strength to walk. Cron, will you think it all out with that brain of yours so clear and strong, and tonight when we are in the train explain to me just what is right . . . Oh, Cron, with that clear moral sense, with that direct sight of yours, lead your little Olive . . . Where another soul is concerned such a terrible doubt comes on me . . . Can I trust you to find the ideally right path and lead me in it.[50]

In the next letter to Cronwright Olive referred to Tolstoy's *Kreutzer Sonata*, which she had just read on Ellis' previous advice that she would find her own views in it.[51] But she did not find him

wide enough and full enough. You see Tolstoy was a libertine in his youth, and nowhere in his works does he grasp or understand or even catch glimpses of that *sympathy* which is 'the perfect love' between man and woman. He says the only ideal which suggests itself to a pure girl is the desire for children; now, long before that, in many of the noblest natures, comes the *instinctive* yearning for an absolute sympathy.

Tolstoy had seen the

hideousness of the conventional sensual idea of 'love'; but the nobler holy possibility beyond he does not see; his nature never thirsted for it because in his youth he had sullied sex feeling in himself.

It pained Olive that Tolstoy did not see

sexual intercourse as a sacrament to be partaken of between two souls; not only for the production of children, but sometimes going even further and consecrating the two who partake of it to a life – the highest fellowship in production, mental and spiritual, of the highest good and beauty. To me sexual intercourse would have failed, if it were not something[which]both tried to be pure and great enough to be worthy of, and which did not stimulate and strengthen them for a holier, broader, more unselfish love.

The months immediately before their marriage are obscured by Cronwright's censorship. She consulted a doctor twice, once in Grahamstown, to undergo 'several slight operations', the nature of which is not revealed;[52] and again in Kimberley two months later, where the doctor pronounced her perfectly healthy. She revealed subsequently that she feared she might transmit her asthmatic condition to a child, but she was told that this fear was unfounded. In between the visits to the doctor she wrote Cronwright a letter which is inexplicable without further information:

> Dear one, I love you as I never, never loved you before. Help me to do right . . . Cron, I have taught you the little I could, try and teach me a little now I am in this great weakness and darkness . . . Oh, love, I can give you up, I can part from you for ever, if only you are helped by me in some way. If only life is better for you, because of me. Cron, it was *all* my fault about . . . [deleted]. You must know this. Your Olive was so weak and she's so ashamed.[53]

It suggested Olive's need to expiate some wickedness by her devotion to him.

Once her decision to marry was taken, Olive, in a state of high excitement, sent Ellis three letters in four days. The marriage took place on 24 February 1894. It was a short civil ceremony at which Olive wore an old blue-black serge dress and hat and Cronwright his everyday clothes. Olive's brother Theo was one of the witnesses. Cronwright agreed that she should keep her name and he changed his to Cronwright-Schreiner. Olive wrote to Ellis that the most terrible part of the ceremony was sitting down at the table to sign her name; she did not elaborate. The couple went to the Krantz Plaats homestead near Cradock which Cronwright had renovated for her, and on the following day he showed her how to use the loaded revolver that hung at the head of their bed in case she needed it during his absence at a remote kraal on the farm where the ostrich-plucking was under way.

Olive's letters from Krantz Plaats make her new life sound idyllic.[54] According to Cronwright she had no household duties except to give the servants orders; he continued to run the house and the dairy. She spent some of her time horse-riding and bathing in the river in front of the house. Her dear husband, she wrote, 'grows closer and dearer to me daily. I am much, much more happy than I had hoped to be.' Yet at Krantz Plaats Olive's asthma began to attack her every night. Cronwright concluded that the site of the house was deadly for her. He saw her insensible from the attacks: at times there was no way to give her relief except by a small injection of morphia, which she disliked because it gave her severe headaches. Next morning her vitality would return, but Cronwright could see that the 'mental distress' her attacks caused made writing impossible.

Three months after their marriage Olive proposed that she leave Cronwright at the farm to go and live in Kimberley, where she had last stayed in 1873 when it was still New Rush. It would be a bitter separation, but Cronwright had no other means of livelihood and the farm was doing well. Cronwright has recorded how he struggled to reach a decision about their future. In the end, believing that 'in Olive I had a sacred trust and that it would be almost criminal if any act of mine should prevent her writing', he terminated his agreement with the farm owner and was paid out his share. When the time came to leave he 'gazed chokingly at the beautiful Angoras and cows I had bred and at my good servants',[55] apparently unaware of the juxtaposition. It was unquestionably a painful wrench for him to give up farming, and one to which he probably never reconciled himself. As for Olive, she reasoned that two years at Kimberley would give her time to finish 'her two "big" novels' (*From Man to Man* and 'The Buddhist Priest's Wife', though this is the only time the latter is referred to as a novel, or, indeed, as unfinished), which she calculated would bring in £30,000 and make them independent. Cronwright clearly had misgivings about the move, but 'for my own sake, I, the man she loved, should not be the destroyer of her genius'.[56]

In Kimberley the Schreiners bought a small cottage of corrugated iron, The Homestead, in a neighbourhood that Cronwright thought 'would seem uninviting to most people' – it was unlit and unpaved[57] – though among the visitors in 1894 was Tengo Jabavu, the editor of the African newspaper *Imvo*, who came to urge Cronwright (unsuccessfully) to contest a parliamentary election.* For the greater part of that year Olive was well, and as far as Cronwright was concerned there was nothing to distract her from her literary work. As her husband, Cronwright had assumed the role of protector, but also of taskmaster. He was supportive but at the same time proprietary, and though he was proud of her reputation, and sympathetic to her sufferings from illness, he was insensitive to her struggles for expression either as a woman or as a writer. At this time she was unable to complete any work, despite his expectations and her financial calculations.

She was, however, expecting a baby, and felt the anxieties about childbirth appropriate to the time. She wrote to a woman friend that she was preparing a little book for her child: 'Every day I write a little to it, so

* Rudyard Kipling also visited the Schreiners in Kimberley on his first trip to South Africa, in 1898.

that, in case I should die, it will still have that, and I am writing out a list of all the books I want it to read. I don't think I shall die, you know, but it satisfies me to think it will have that.'[58] Olive did not die, but the baby girl did. The labour was attended by Kimberley's leading doctor and a trained nurse, with Cronwright present throughout since he had insisted on remaining in the room. It was an instrument delivery under chloroform, and the baby was taken into the nurse's room so that Olive could have a good night's rest. In the morning the baby was found dead. No explanation was given, and perhaps none was available. She had lived for sixteen hours, and Olive insisted on holding her in her arms for ten hours afterwards.

For months Olive could not write or speak about the event. When she did write it was to Dr and Mrs Brown:

> One day I will tell you of my child. Such a great, beautiful strong creature. It weighed 9lb. 9 ounces when it was born with, oh, such a calm strong face. It seemed as though the curious joy and calm I have felt the last four months had settled in it.[59]

CHAPTER SIX

The Boer War and Union

The death of the baby was a deep hurt. In her letters Olive handled the loss with something of the stillness with which she had made Lyndall deal with her dead child. Olive did not want anyone to call on her; she was better alone. She and Cronwright had difficulty in talking about it: 'Neither Cron nor I dare ever say to each other what is in our hearts. There are some thoughts we shall carry with us to our dying day.'[1] At the same time she could not write about the baby. But as though to test the shock of the incident Olive wrote a letter to Cronwright some years later in which she recorded the facts:

> Our little baby was born at a quarter past twelve on the morning (i.e. noon) of the 30th April 1895. I was put under chloroform and became insensible at a quarter past 11. When I became conscious at half-past three on the afternoon of the 30th she had been born a couple of hours. She lived that night. The last time I heard her cry from the other room was at a quarter past four. When I woke at nine you told me she was dead.[2]

Olive had the baby buried in their garden, and abandoned a projected visit to England rather than leave it: 'You don't know what that little brown heap is to me.'

The hurt grew into resentment, however. Olive came to hate women who had children over whom they 'groaned' when other women would give years and years of their life and hard work to have one. But her hostility frightened her and she deflected her sense of personal loss and inadequacy onto moralizing about marriage and child-bearing in general. Women who had children should feel that they were receiving a great reward, and those who did not feel so should never have children at all. It was like writing a book:

> It may be a great labour and half kill you but if you don't feel it's a great joy to suffer the agony of writing it, and a reward in itself, you're not fit to write it. Women would never have too many children or more than they wanted if they made it a rule to think they couldn't marry till they'd made provision even if small, for every possible child they might have, and for themselves had at least a sure mode of earning their own livings, however small.

She was also convinced that husband and wife should share equally, or almost so, in the care of the children.[3]

Now Olive began to expound a theme she was to elaborate fifteen years later in *Woman and Labour*. Modern, wealthy, middle-class married women tended to become selfish and to fall into a complete state of mental and moral disease.

> The women of old, even if their husbands were wealthy, worked in the fields (like Homer's princesses who washed clothes, and fed and reared their children themselves). But the modern middle-class woman has servants and governesses and all sorts of single women to do her work, and then she sits and howls that she hasn't everything she wants, and that she's badly off, because she has to bear children. It's this kind of woman we want to do away with, and turn into a *working woman*. At the present day I think one of the saddest things is that so many, I might almost say *most* of the noblest and best specimens of woman-hood do remain unmarried and so bear no offspring, while the worst breed.

Perhaps because of his previous concern with child prostitution, Olive wrote W. T. Stead more than one emphatic letter on the subject, and by contrast, on the ideal of married life which had 'haunted' her since she was a child.[4] She objected fiercely to Stead referring to a particular woman as the man's 'mistress', since there was nothing to infer that the man supported her. To Olive the purity of a sex relation lay finally in the fact that it was 'not a matter of material considerations'. Nor, ultimately, of physical attraction.

To me it appears that in highly developed and intellectual people, the mental and spiritual is more important, more truly the *marriage*, than the physical. I should feel it (and I think any person who has reached a certain stage of growth) a much more right and important reason for terminating a union, that the person to whom I was united had a fuller, deeper and more useful mental union with another than that there should be a physical relation. Just the mental union, 'for the begetting of great works' to me constitutes marriage. Of course there are millions, even in the most civilised communities, for whom physical attraction, affection and fidelity must constitute marriage. But for natures more highly developed I believe such a union to be wrong. Continuance of the physical relation when the higher mental relation is not possible, and when the affection is given elsewhere, seems to me a more terrible because a more permanent prostitution than that of the streets.[5]

As for Edward Carpenter's pamphlet on the subject, *Marriage: A Retrospect; A Forecast*, which Olive received at this time, she thought it splendid except that not enough was made of the need for financial independence. In a long letter to Carpenter[6] she drew parallels, from her vantage point in a colony, between man-woman relationships and relationships between white and black. In the same way that the black man needed economic equality with the white, so the woman needed monetary independence, because otherwise 'old unconscious traditions' would show. The newly freed slave, whether black or woman, had to 'stand a little on his dignity'.*

Carpenter found the human male polygamous, while woman, 'by her more limited sexual needs and her long periods of gestation found one mate physically sufficient'. But the long historic serfdom of women had exaggerated 'the naturally complementary relation of the male and female into an absurd caricature of strength in the one and dependence on the other.' This was Carpenter's ivy and oak marriage, parasitism on the one hand and strangulation on the other.

Olive always claimed that her own marriage to Cronwright satisfied her

---

* *Marriage: A Retrospect; A Forecast* was one of three pamphlets on sex questions that Carpenter wrote in 1894. Their success – each sold three or four thousand copies – encouraged him to put them together and add new material; this became a book, *Love's Coming-of-Age* (1896). See Carpenter, *My Days and Dreams*, p. 195. It was perhaps in response to Olive's comment about dignity that the book asserted that the free woman 'has to stand a little aloof'.

high ideal: a 'curious moral and spiritual comradeship' held them together, and their feeling for nature, 'the whole religious side of our
being', was entirely one.[7] Long before she married, in fact, Olive had
specified – to herself and to others – what she needed in a husband. She
had a physical image of a strong male partner; Ellis had been too uncertain about his own needs. Yet it was partly from Ellis that she had
derived this notion of conventional masculinity and virility. His assertion
of the biological basis of character, and thus of the essential distinction
between male and female, had produced the stereotype which he himself
could not imitate, but which Cronwright, in Olive's expectation, would.
By fulfilling the assertive male role Cronwright was expected, whether
Olive was conscious of it or not, to settle her own moral turmoil, to
assuage her sense of sin in her sexual responses.

But precisely because recognition of her own sexuality was so
problematic, marriage had to be idealized as an eternal and blissful union
of two like souls. Was this, as Jane Graves has suggested in an imaginative
interpretation of Olive's asthma,[8] because her awareness of her sexuality
and its passion appalled her? Intellectual companionship had to come before
sexual desire – for Olive the second was out of the question without
the first. Rebekah in *From Man to Man*, for example, told her children
that the greatest longing a being could have was to find another who
'thinks and feels alike'; when they met it would be like 'two drops of
water that run into one another as soon as they touch'.

In the early years of her marriage Olive's involvement in politics was
expressed vicariously, through her attempts to influence two men: her
husband and her brother Will, by then attorney-general in a Rhodes
cabinet. There had been a general election in 1894 after the break-up of
the Rhodes ministry which excluded the liberal parliamentarians, and
Will had contested, and won, the Barkly West constituency for Rhodes'
party. Deeply fond of him and critical of his politics, though believing
that Will had none of the vices indispensable to a successful politician,
Olive told him firmly that she would like to see him out of party politics,
just as she would never like to see Cronwright in them. Cronwright,
however, was trying to make an entry into politics and involved himself
in the attempts of local Farmers' Associations to form an English party
as an organized political alternative to the Bond. When Progressive
Committees emerged as a precursor to the Progressive Party, Olive saw

little difference between their politics and those of the Bond. She was, in fact, more sick of the Progressives than the Bond, if this were possible, and the overtures made to Cronwright to enter Progressive politics seemed to her distinctly politically immoral. Their electioneering tactics were not one bit cleaner. The place for the strong, straight men was to stand free, rousing and directing public opinion; if Cronwright did go into parliament, he should be content to stand absolutely alone.[9]

In August 1895 Cronwright delivered a public address on 'The Political Situation' to a meeting of the English Farmers' Association in Kimberley. The address must have been written in the months immediately after the death of Olive's baby. It bore clear marks of her draughtsmanship, though its first appearance was as Cronwright's speech; and only in the following year did it appear in England as a small book under both their names. It was the first time, apart from private letters, and in spirited conversation with politicians, that Olive committed herself not on general moral issues of race and colour, but on the political issues of the day.

The Political Situation was a warning of the danger of the monopolists' control over South Africa's resources. Adopting the perspective of English liberal democratic theory, it perceived the trend 'in all civilised countries' towards a broadened electoral basis, the consideration of the welfare of the labouring classes, and the abolition of the lash as punishment. In South Africa, by contrast, a civilized people was deliberately undoing the progressive work of the previous generation. 'While the wheels of legislation in other civilised and Anglo-Saxon communities are tending to propel the car of state forwards, ours are slowly but surely running us backwards.' But far from retrogressive policies in South Africa being the work of the Bond alone, extraneous forces had acted upon it:

> There came to South Africa certain men from Europe of great shrewdness, and with large abilities for speculation. Slowly but surely, the wealth of the country passed into their hands. Today a small resolute and keen body of men amalgamated into rings and trusts are quickly and surely settling their hands round the mineral wealth of South Africa.

The same monopolists and speculators were gaining control of the political machinery, they were acquiring political power so as to increase their wealth, to extend their exploitation into adjoining territories. It was the monopolists who had 'taken advantage of the childlike simplicity which is at once the weakness and the greatest charm of the Boer'. The coalition between the Bond and the monopolists was corroding public life till the principle that every man has his price and can be squared, if only you can find his figure, was becoming established dogma.*

How was retrogression in South Africa to be stayed? Three test principles were needed to unite the progressive elements: taxation, the franchise, and the labour question. On taxation the booklet was strongly anti-protectionist, since the prevailing tax policy, under Rhodes' influence, gave protection to the monopoly-controlled diamond industry at the expense of the farmers. On the franchise the booklet coined a vague though significant demand for parliamentary representation on the basis of 'individuals rather than property', and for 'the man as the woman, the wealthy as the indigent'.

It was on the question of labour that the essay formulated a view unique to Olive Schreiner at this time: that the South African labour question included the whole of what was popularly termed the 'Native Question'. For that question was 'indeed only the Labour Question of Europe, complicated by a difference of race and colour between the employing and the propertied, and the employed and poorer classes', and Cape political parties regarded 'the native labouring class only in terms of the manual labour which can be extracted from him at the cheapest rate possible'. But from this promising beginning, the rest of the paragraph subsided into a patronizing plea for those 'with superior intelligence and culture' to consider 'the welfare of the Native, and to raise him in the scale of existence'. The boundaries of white politics and electioneering once again enclosed the issue.

At the same time the essay was uncompromisingly anti-Charter monopolist and, as the *Cape Times* made clear, 'for monopolist read capitalist'. Its leader commented that it was a little absurd to ignore the fact 'that the world is at present organised on a capitalistic basis, and that

* *The Political Situation* attacked not only the influence of the monopolist in Cape Politics, but also the Chartered Company by name for its activities further north, where Mashonaland and Matabeleland were being taken over as the future Rhodesia.

this particular continent is just now in the full flush of material development'. The wealth of the country had to be developed by individual enterprise. 'Brain, organisation, energy, all are at a premium; it is and must be a riot of individualism. While the fever lasts it is certain to have its unlovely side.' But as long as a capitalist did not stretch the laws of the game, 'as long as you can bring up against him no dirty trick, it seems hard to condemn him merely *qua* capitalist'.[10] It was the standard apologia.

By the following year, 1896, Olive's suspicions of Rhodes' machinations were confirmed in the Jameson Raid. This was a plot to achieve a British take-over of the Transvaal Republic as the result of the entry of a military force under Dr L. S. Jameson, Rhodes' subordinate, at the same time as a rising was staged within the Republic by the white immigrant *Uitlander* population, in ostensible protest at its exclusion from republican franchise. The plot to take the Transvaal from within and from without, referred to in mysterious telegrams as the flotation or the polo tournament, failed, but was subsequently traced back to Rhodes and officials of the Chartered Company and of De Beers.*

After the failure of the Raid, Olive believed that Rhodes had fallen for ever and her feelings were a strange mixture of 'intense personal sympathy with him in his downfall, and an almost awful sense of relief that the terrible power which was threatening to crush all South Africa is broken'.[11] She was in immediate demand as a political commentator but she turned down offers to write for English newspapers: 'I can't strike Rhodes as he is utterly broken down.' She wondered whether he was drinking himself to death, whether he would face parliament. 'I have seen this fall coming for so many years, but no one could save him from it; he had to rise to it.'[12]

The Raid did indeed force Rhodes to resign as prime minister, and it also had an extraordinary effect on Cape politics, which Olive anticipated clearly. 'The Raid and all it revealed and brought into being has entirely altered the entire body of South African problems,' she wrote to Will. 'The questions of Bond or not Bond, Progressive farmer or non-Progressive,

---

* The Jameson Raid created the climate for the Anglo-Boer war four years later when the interests of empire and mining capital converged. A sector of mining capital needed the economies of large-scale production and an ample supply of cheap labour; these labour needs competed with those of the farmers. The chief plotters inside the Transvaal were two of the largest deep-level mining companies, one of which was Rhodes' own Consolidated Goldfields.

have all been washed away. They were all important; they are nothing now. We want new men and a new party based on the new conditions.'[13] The resultant division in Cape politics now began to anticipate the coming alignments of the Boer war. On the one side was the pro-Rhodes party, advocating British intervention for British supremacy, and on the other those whose sympathies were with the Transvaal. The Bond turned solidly anti-Rhodes and pro-Transvaal, and drew allies from the small but prominent group of parliamentarians, Merriman and Sauer among them, who had previously been outspokenly anti-Bond. Cronwright was drawn to Bond leader Onze Jan Hofmeyr, the founder of Afrikaner nationalism; Olive confided in Will that it was with difficulty that she had restrained her husband from writing him a long letter of congratulations and approval; apparently she failed, for the letter went to Onze Jan, congratulating him on his 'signal service'.[14]

The controversy over Rhodes' part in the Jameson Raid was the subject of two official commissions, one British and one South African, and it split the Schreiner family. Olive and Cronwright, according to Cronwright, saw at once that Rhodes was behind it, and said so. And it was because Cronwright feared that the anti-Rhodes reaction would in turn provoke a strongly anti-Boer reaction from the English community that he wrote a letter to the South African press[15] which he hoped would demonstrate that one could oppose the Raid without falling into the hands of the Transvaal. Olive shared his reaction, and told Will that Cronwright had written because they were anxious to do anything that would show the Dutch throughout the country that 'there are some Englishmen who can rise above race prejudice'.[16]

By trying to rise above (white) race prejudice, Olive opened herself to the suspicion of English-speaking South Africans, including her mother. Rebecca, like her son Will,[17] was a devoted admirer of Rhodes; in her view to be anti-Rhodes was to be anti-British. She defended Rhodes to the hilt and Will with him, insisting that an accusation made against Rhodes was made equally against Will. Olive, who did not believe that Will had been party to the Raid plot, tried to convince her that Will was 'in no danger of being hanged or something of that sort!!' But Olive's attempt to comfort her mother in this way was misjudged. Up to now she had been writing to her mother every other day but without mentioning politics; her attempt to defend Will now prompted from Rebecca a series of vehement letters about Olive's political views, and Cronwright's.

Ettie and Theo were also fanatical Rhodes supporters, and the combined effect of all this hostility 'made a hell of Olive's life' for a time.[18] Such a family divide was typical of the hardening of pro-British opinion in the Cape, but while Olive was quite capable of pitting herself against adversaries in public debate, she was painfully vulnerable to disagreements with her mother, and within the family.

After her death Cronwright found a foolscap envelope among Olive's papers in which were copies of 'Letters to Ettie and Mother about Rhodes'.[19] Cronwright was instructed to print them if false statements were made after her death. The letter to Rebecca, of which she had also enclosed a copy to Ettie, but about which Cronwright appears to have known nothing, is the longest letter Olive wrote. These were considered letters, written over a period of six weeks in which Olive had brooded over her relations with her mother. 'During the last fifteen years,' she wrote to Rebecca:

> both in England and here, my work and my interest in life have been mainly political, yet I do not think that six times I have, in all these years, mentioned politics to you, because I felt that you were not sympathetic to my view; and I believe that where, with regard to either *religion* or *politics*, parents and children, or even brothers and sisters, are not agreed, they should avoid these subjects. I have held this all my life. The tender love existing between mother and child and brother need surely never be ruffled by these things.

Rebecca had made wounding accusations: that Olive's and Cronwright's opposition to the Raid had been directed at Will; and that Olive was allowing Cronwright to warp her mind and degrade her character. This prompted Olive to set out the story of her relation with Rhodes to explain how, Cronwright's influence or no, she had consistently opposed Rhodes' politics. This took her back to Matjesfontein days, when if 'we got on to the native question, we ended by having a big fight, and Rhodes getting very angry'. She had liked Rhodes for the same reason that he liked her, because of his *life* and energy; 'but we never once met without a royal fight'. She had given up hope of him at the time of the Logan corruption affair of a few years earlier, the letter continued. When he called at her house and she heard him knock at the door, she had not opened it. She had declined his dinner invitations. Sauer had brought her a message to ask what was the matter and she had told him to tell Rhodes that 'in political matters I was absolutely opposed to him, and was going to fight him on every point'. Far from Cronwright having formed her attitude to Rhodes, in the two years since she had married she had taken no part or interest in political life, except for the little pamphlet on the political situation. Since the Jameson Raid she had received requests from overseas papers asking her to cable her views 'and I could have made much money, of which I am in need. But I attacked Rhodes frankly and fearlessly and endlessly when he was in power, and therefore I can afford to be quiet now'. So far from hating Rhodes, she wrote Rebecca, she had the greatest sympathy with him on many questions. 'Surely, my dear little mother,' she pleaded, 'you can distinguish between *personal* feeling and political opinions. Have they anything to do with each other ?' Life to her would not be worth living if she felt her love for friends grow less on account of their views on public persons and political situations.

The letter to Ettie went over much the same ground but revealed Olive's view of Will and her opinion on the sources of his political reaction. Olive believed that 'poor old Will, with his lack of imagination and creative insight, but so good, so simple, so pure', would be betrayed by Rhodes, as Rhodes had betrayed all men who had trusted and loved him. Now she was 'bitterly opposed' to her brother on the 'Native Question', but 'if ever his intellect is enlightened, as it seems to me, and he takes another view, he will hold it honestly and truly'.

At the time that these secret letters were being written Olive asked Ettie and Theo not to communicate with her any longer, nor to discuss her with their mother: she suspected that Rebecca, if left unprovoked by others, would not violate a lifelong tenderness and friendship for abstract political views. She told Ettie that she would continue to write to Rebecca almost every day, about books and the weather. She was an old woman and Olive wanted her to be surrounded 'by no feelings but those of love and tenderness for all her children'.

Not long after the accusations by her mother, Olive found herself attacked in a leader in *Ons Land*, organ of the Bond. Her essay 'The Boer', written a few years earlier on her return to South Africa, had just been printed in the London *Fortnightly Review*, and the *Cape Times*[20] published an extract. 'The Boer' was a characteristically elevated peroration about the Afrikaner, his religion, language and love of his country. To Olive, the Boer represented the true South African. Her defence of him was necessary now that he was so vulnerable to the British political offensive. But *Ons Land*[21] charged that she presented the Afrikaners as an unattractive people; that she had taken as typical of the Boer 'the most contemptible white frontiersman'; and above all that she ridiculed their religious beliefs because they did not agree with the ideas of freethinkers. Olive's was the hand, the paper reminded its readers, that had drawn Tant Sannie in *The Story of an African Farm*; and that book, however accomplished and brilliant, would never make its way among Afrikaners. 'We could not more than cry out,' *Ons Land* concluded, 'Afrikaners: show that you do not have the bad features that are attributed to you . . . Afrikanerdom will flourish, and become great and good.' Olive's attempt at pathos had failed. 'The Dutch papers to attack me!' she exclaimed, dizzy with surprise.[22] She expected the English papers and the Jingo Englishman to attack her, 'but that the Dutch papers should attack me seems to me impossible. I feel like a man who goes to help another whom he feels is unjustly treated and the man he is helping jumps up and gives him a blow between the eyes'.

Rhodes' culpability in the Jameson Raid had yet to be demonstrated officially before the commissions of inquiry set up by both the Cape and Westminster parliaments, but in the immediate aftermath of the episode he was busy in Rhodesia, where the Matabele and then the Mashona rose against Chartered Company rule in 1896.* When he returned to the

---

* Rhodes and Jameson had planned the eventual conquest of Matabeleland from 1890 but the clash had been postponed largely because Lobengula, king of the Matabele, had gone to such lengths to maintain the peace. The Chartered Company had banked on finding a new Rand north of the Limpopo; this would have made Charter territory, and not the Transvaal, the coming economic centre of South Africa, capable of dictating, together with the Cape, the terms of the new economic federation for which Rhodes planned. Mashonaland had been occupied by 1890, but not Matabele country, though the infamous Rudd Concession of 1889 had given Rhodes the monopoly of all the minerals in Lobengula's kingdom in return for 1000 Martini-Henry machine-guns, 100,000 rounds of ammunition and an annual grant of £1200 and a steamboat to ply on the Zambesi. In 1893 a pretext was found for the war and Jameson marched on Bulawayo with white volunteers who were paid in land and captured cattle; Lobengula was dead within the month. Over the following three years Matabeleland experienced a dispossession of Africans and the penetration of white settlement on a scale as yet unparalleled in central and east Africa; virtually the whole of the land formerly occupied by the Ndebele and by far the greater part of their cattle passed into white ownership. The volunteers of the Company column had to be rewarded; as well, important sections of English society were given a stake in the success of the new colony; this was the arrival in Rhodesia of 'youngsters of the la di da class'. The result was that in 1896 first the Ndebele and then the Shona rose in rebellion against Company rule.

Cape it was as the triumphant pacifier of the new colony named after himself. Olive was unimpressed. She wrote to Alf Mattison, her gas-worker friend in Leeds:

> We have been having terrible times here. You people in England don't know what the heel of a capitalist is when it gets right flat on the neck of the people. We have an awful struggle before us in this country. It's no case of not being allowed to fish in somebody else's ground. We won't be allowed soon to have even a soul of *our* own. Now we are busy killing the poor Matabele.[23]

Olive wrote her long parable *Trooper Peter Halket of Mashonaland* while Rhodes' Company and imperial troops were 'pacifying' Rhodesia in 1896 and 1897. She had been ill and depressed and she and Cronwright had taken a short holiday at Kowie where they bathed and walked bare-foot on the sand. One morning as she woke and opened her eyes 'there was an allegory full fledged in my mind: a sort of allegory story about Matabeleland'.[24]

Trooper Peter Halket is an English soldier in a company putting down the Mashonaland rebellion. One night in the veld Christ appears to him, and there ensues a dialogue in which the men of the Chartered Company are indicted for rape, pillage, atrocity, murder and enslavement.

> . . . Peter said, 'Did you see any niggers about yesterday? I haven't come across any in this part.'
> 'There is,' said the stranger, raising himself, 'an old woman in a cave over yonder, and there is one man in the bush, ten miles from this spot. He has lived there six weeks, since you destroyed the kraal, living on roots or herbs. He was wounded in the thigh, and left for dead. He is waiting till you have all left this part of the country that he may set out to follow his own people. His leg is not yet so strong that he may walk fast.'
> 'Did you speak to him?' said Peter.
> 'I took him down to the water where a large pool was. The bank was too high for the man to descend alone.'
> 'It's a lucky thing for you our fellows didn't catch you,' said Peter. 'Our captain's a regular little martinet. He'd shoot you as soon as look at you, if he saw you fooling round with a wounded nigger. It's lucky you kept out of his way.'

'The young ravens have meat given to them,' said the stranger, lifting himself up; 'and the lions go down to the streams to drink.'

'Ah – yes –' said Peter; 'but that's because we can't help it!'

They were silent again for a little while. Then Peter, seeing that the stranger showed no inclination to speak, said, 'Did you hear of the spree they had up Bulawayo way, hanging those three niggers for spies? I wasn't there myself, but a fellow who was told me they made the niggers jump down from the tree and hang themselves; one fellow wouldn't bally jump, till they gave him a charge of buckshot in the back: and then he caught hold of a branch with his hands and they had to shoot 'em loose. He didn't like hanging. I don't know if it's true, of course; I wasn't there myself, but a fellow who was told me. Another fellow who was at Bulawayo, but who wasn't there when they were hung, said they fired at them just after they jumped, to kill 'em. I –'

'I was there,' said the stranger.

'Oh, you were?' said Peter. 'I saw a photograph of the niggers hanging, and our fellows standing round smoking; but I didn't see you in it. I suppose you'd just gone away?'

'I was beside the men when they were hung,' said the stranger.

'Oh, you were, were you?' said Peter. 'I don't much care about seeing that sort of thing myself. Some fellows think it's the best fun out to see the niggers kick; but I can't stand it: it turns my stomach. It's not liver-heartedness,' said Peter, quickly; anxious to remove any adverse impression as to his courage which the stranger might form; 'if it's shooting or fighting, I'm there. I've potted as many niggers as any man in our troop, I bet. It's floggings and hangings I'm off. It's the way one's brought up, you know. My mother never even would kill our ducks; she let them die of old age, and we had the feathers and the eggs: and she was always drumming into me; – don't hit a fellow smaller than yourself; don't hit a fellow weaker than yourself; don't hit a fellow unless he can hit you back as good again. When you've always had that sort of thing drummed into you, you can't get rid of it, somehow. Now there was that other nigger they shot. They say he sat as still as if he was cut out of stone, with his arms round his legs; and some of the fellows gave him blows about the head and face before they took him off to shoot him. Now, that's the sort of thing I can't do.

It makes me sick here, somehow.' Peter put his hand rather low down over the pit of his stomach. 'I'll shoot as many as you like if they'll run, but they mustn't be tied up.'

'I was there when that man was shot,' said the stranger.

'Why, you seem to have been everywhere,' said Peter. 'Have you seen Cecil Rhodes?'

'Yes, I have seen him,' said the stranger.

'Now *he's* death on niggers,' said Peter Halket, warming his hands by the fire; 'they say when he was Prime Minister down in the Colony he tried to pass a law that would give masters and mistresses the right to have their servants flogged whenever they did anything they didn't like; but the other Englishmen wouldn't let him pass it. But *here* he can do what he likes. That's the reason some fellows don't want him to be sent away. They say, "If we get the British Government here, they'll be giving the niggers land to live on; and let them have the vote, and get civilised and educated, and all that sort of thing; but Cecil Rhodes, he'll keep their noses to the grindstone." *I prefer land to niggers*, he says. They say he's going to parcel them out, and make them work on our lands whether they like it or not – just as good as having slaves, you know: and you haven't the bother of looking after them when they're old. Now, there I'm with Rhodes; I think it's an awfully good move. We don't come out here to work; it's all very well in England; but we've come here to make money, and how are we to make it, unless you get niggers to work for you, or start a syndicate? He's death on niggers, is Rhodes!' said Peter, meditating; 'they say if we had the British Government here and you were thrashing a nigger and something happened, there'd be an investigation, and all that sort of thing. But, with Cecil, it's all right, you can do what you like with the niggers, provided you don't get *him* into trouble.'

The stranger watched the clear flame as it burnt up high in the still night air; then suddenly he started.

'What is it?' said Peter; 'do you hear anything?'

'I hear far off,' said the stranger, 'the sound of weeping, and the sound of blows. And I hear the voices of men and women calling to me.'

Peter listened intently. 'I don't hear anything!' he said. 'It must be in your head. I sometimes get a noise in mine.' He listened intently. 'No, there's nothing. It's all so deadly still.'[25]

Peter is converted; when he rejoins his company he helps an African prisoner to escape and is shot for it.*

Olive was in anguish as she copied out the small book. She was sure that Rhodes and the Company would proceed against her and that the matter would kill her, 'as it did to a very large extent. There was all the other possible work I might do, my box of manuscripts lying unrevised and on the other hand the great doubt whether, whatever the book meant to me, it might have any effect in increasing justice at all commensurate with the price I was paying.' At last the matter decided itself within her:

> Don't think I mean anything supernatural takes place, though that decision which our nature gives when one tries to silence the lower and purely personal interest to allow the higher elements in it to adjudicate amongst themselves *is* what the ancients call the 'voice of God', and it is to a certain extent, because it is the highest and for each soul within itself the most ultimate injunction it can receive. And this thing is certain, that when one acts in obedience to it, one never regrets, even though absolute failure in the eyes of the world follow on it.[26]

Although she was preparing for the Chartered Company to attack her, she also said that she did not feel anything as much as the attacks from members of her own family.[27] During 1896, in letters to Betty Molteno, a school teacher in Port Elizabeth, Mary Sauer and Will's wife Fan, Olive wrote of sustaining three miscarriages after the death of her baby. She put the first down to being thrown from a horse, the second to

* The first, 1897, edition of the pamphlet carried a photograph of Africans hanging from a tree said to be outside Bulawayo, but this picture was dropped from the subsequent editions and reinstated only in the 1974 edition introduced by Marion Friedmann. The photograph appears to have been supplied by Frank W. Sykes, who served on the campaign and wrote *With Plumer in Matabeleland*. According to his account of the garrison which relieved Bulawayo, 'troopers would go out early in the morning, shoot some rebels and return for breakfast, all in a day's work. Rebel spies who were caught were summarily tried and hanged. The hanging tree to the north of Bulawayo served as a gallows.'

The same photograph makes its appearance in Percy M. Clark's *The Life Story of Percy M. Clark of Victoria Falls*, the autobiography of an old drifter published in 1936 by George Harrap and Co. Clark was a Cambridge-born man who took up a post as a photographer in Bulawayo (the date is not given) and who used the picture opposite an account of a trial of an African who raped a white woman and whom Bulawayo citizens seized as soon as the verdict was announced by the magistrate. They put a rope around his neck and took him to an electric standard opposite the Bulawayo Club. He was apparently rescued by police so that the authorities could do the hanging themselves.

mental agony, and the third to a letter from her mother and family (not Will) that kept her awake for nights – 'the attacks from my family, ever since I wrote on the political situation two years ago, kill me'.[28] She wished for a woman doctor who had 'gone through everything herself', she wrote to her sister-in-law after the third miscarriage, which had left her very weak. 'I've had two doctors here and neither has given me any consolation except to tell me I must lie on my back for six months if ever I want to have another child, which of course I can't do.'[29] But by the end of the year she and Cronwright, together with the Misses Greene and Molteno, were preparing to sail for England.

The Schreiners were carrying the manuscript of *Trooper Peter Halket*, and Cronwright's book *The Angora Goat*. Rhodes was also a passenger on the *Dunvegan Castle*, on his way to give evidence to the parliamentary commission into the Jameson Raid. Olive feared that it might be an unpleasant voyage: although 'Rhodes and his sister would of course act with perfect refinement' she was apprehensive about 'the low fellows who generally follow in his wake. And Cron may make it very unpleasant for them if they insult me.'[30] They decided to keep to themselves as much as possible; they refused to speak to Rhodes. Cronwright's biography describes the curious incident when Cronwright claimed that he found Rhodes' manservant prowling about in their cabin; Cronwright presumed he had been sent to look for the manuscript.[31]

By the time that Will Schreiner arrived in London to give his evidence about the Jameson Raid, *Trooper Peter Halket* was in print. Fisher Unwin gave it prominence in its listing of new books, and it attracted a good deal of press interest. Most of the provincial dailies and the London papers revered its style and ignored its politics, however: the *Athenaeum*, invariably one of Olive's main supporters, for example, saw it as a most successful experiment in the 'writing of a modern gospel'. Only *Blackwood's Edinburgh Magazine* came out and called it a 'political pamphlet of great bitterness, linked on to the very smallest thread of a story that ever carried red-hot opinions and personal abuse of the fiercest kind into the world'.[32] In the Cape parliament, Will had been prepared to condemn the Raid but not Rhodes, and he considered the book unfair. His principal had used wrong methods but he had high aims; he tried to distinguish between Rhodes as conspirator and Rhodes as founder of Rhodesia. Will did refuse to join Rhodes' post-Raid cabinet but it was a full year before he broke with him and they went their opposite ways: Rhodes to lead the

Progressives, and Schreiner to cooperate with the moderate wing of the Bond and increasingly be seen as leader of the opposition to Rhodes.[33]

Olive tried to alert Will and others to the danger of the war which she was convinced Rhodes would provoke in order to gain control of the Transvaal. If once Rhodes and his party could get 'only two English women, nay only one, shot, say in the bombardment of Johannesburg, the whole English nation will stand up', she told Will.[34] *Trooper Peter Halket*, she pointed out, was addressed to the British public, for 'if that public lifts its thumb there is war, and if it turns down there is peace; if as in the present case they are indifferent and just letting things drift there is no knowing what they may be surprised into at the last moment'. But a year later she was forced to acknowledge that the book had apparently been a dead failure. 'In spite of its immense circulation,' she wrote to Will, 'I do not believe it has saved the life of one nigger, it had not the slightest effect in forcing on the parliamentary examination into the conduct of affairs in Rhodesia and it cost me everything.' And yet she had never regretted publishing it. 'When I had that bad attack of the heart in Naples and they carried me into a chemist shop and I believed I was dying, the one thought that was with me was "Peter Halket".'[35]

During their visit to England Olive and Cronwright spent some time trying to meet people of standing to warn them that the powers behind the Jameson Raid were working for war, 'but all seemed to think we were in error in our judgement; the forces, especially the financial forces, they said, which were working in South Africa were not operating in English political life'.[36] Those few people who did express sympathy with her fears were 'so afraid of Rhodes' party' that they begged her not to mention them. When things reached that point, she wrote to Mary Sauer, one should 'end existence itself in some expeditious way; life can't be worth living any more'.[37] Her meeting with J. A. Hobson was an exception; the following year he was in South Africa to study the causes of the war, and his *Imperialism* tried to document the workings of precisely those 'financial forces' behind Rhodes.

Back in South Africa and based in Kimberley, Cronwright involved himself once again in Cape politics. In a new round of elections Rhodes contested Barkly West again but now came out as a Progressive and lost, and Will Schreiner, parliamentary leader of the Bond, though himself no Bondsman, became prime minister, with liberals Merriman and Sauer in his cabinet. Cronwright campaigned for the Bond candidate in Barkly West, where his job was to campaign for African votes;* and he sent Onze Jan Hofmeyr, the Bond leader, explicit instructions not to mention the Bond in election propaganda directed at the Africans. 'All work regarding Natives had better be done by me,' he wrote. 'Don't mention the Bond. The appeal to the Natives must be directly against Rhodes as their Oppressor.' There followed detailed suggestions:

1. Compare your Native policy with that of Rhodes. (Rhodes' oppressive Native Policy to be the heading.) 2. Quote Rhodes' proposal to reduce Native wages and his statement 'preferred land to niggers' and 'slavery in Rhodesia'. 3. Drive home the point that Rhodes, and the League are trying to oust all friends of the Natives from Parliament. 4. Photograph in *Peter Halket* – excellent idea to disseminate it widely but don't mention *Peter Halket* or my wife. Just say this photo shows how Natives are treated in Rhodesia *and don't mention Transvaal*. 5. Circulate copies of *Ons Land* among the Dutch of the Division.[38]

This was election propaganda of the worst sort, in which Cronwright manipulated the evidence to conceal the Bond's and the Boer republics' policy on African questions.

Cronwright was immersed in electioneering, but Olive's health became so bad that there was talk of her going to a sanatorium near Beaufort West; she refused to allow friends to visit her until she was well, and for a while Cronwright had to take over as correspondent. On one occasion she had been out on a 'raw and cold afternoon' and had a prolonged attack of asthma that night; it lasted through the next day and into the following night; yet another attack followed soon after and she became 'quite broken down'.[39] Cronwright found her unnecessarily despondent about herself, but he was coming to the conclusion that unless a radical change came over her, she could not continue to live in Kimberley. It was decided that she should go to Johannesburg, which lay at an altitude of 6000 feet, to see if she was better there. Even so, it would be an awkward state of affairs unless he could get work there.

At the time money was a central consideration. Cronwright's biography indicates that by 1898 his funds were exhausted and that, to his mind, Olive had not made use of the two years' writing time she had

_____
* There was a property and educational qualification for the vote which few Africans met.

asked for. She did not seem to remember, he wrote, 'that I had taken the grave step of giving up my livelihood at her special request so that she might finish writing and publishing'. They were rushing on to ruin, for he was earning little and they were exhausting her capital. 'Yet she seemed quite oblivious of this and could not see the approaching catastrophe.'⁴⁰ Contrary to Cronwright's impression, Olive was always concerned about money. For her the issue of financial independence in marriage and, by extension, her work as a writer, was so basic as to need no discussion. 'The first step towards true and beautiful marriage,' she wrote to Betty Molteno, 'seems to me always that marriage and material interests should be severed, as friendship and material interests should be severed.'⁴¹ Cronwright had plenty of money, she thought, but she made him promise before they married that he would go on spending all his spare money on his mother and sister, just as he had done before.*⁴²

Four years after his marriage Cronwright was still convinced that Olive was a great genius – 'the completion of her work would have been a far better service to mankind than anything I could possibly do' – but he was beginning to wonder whether she would ever finish *From Man to Man*. He thought that perhaps with the exception of the last two years, she had never had conditions so suitable for her work as when she was governessing; then she had had intellectual solitude without severance from people, without the personal and social problems that destroyed her capacity for work when she was in England.⁴³ He had begun to believe that she could not live anywhere permanently, and Kimberley was certainly unsuitable. But there was no way for him to earn a living except in a town, so he would qualify for the Side Bar and article himself to an attorney in Johannesburg. Olive's worsening health meant that she would leave immediately.

By October 1898 Olive was living alone in a Johannesburg boarding house. It had been hard to part from Cronwright but, she explained to

* Olive told Will that the dream of her life was that she should have earned enough before their mother died to make her last years free of money problems, 'but it seems more likely I won't be able to support myself'. At the time Rebecca was receiving £60 a year from her children. 'Ah Will when I think of what other mothers demand from their children you don't know how heroic our little mother seems plodding on on her £60 and never asking for more. Cron's mother when getting £25 *a month* was always grumbling, and Fan's mother had £300 a year. Mother feels an intense pain from taking the £5 from Fred alone and I know she has to pay £1 a month for rent, this leaves her only £4 for food, clothes, stamps, medicine etc. Be careful when writing to her not to tell her that I sent you her letter but that I asked you to pay £24 towards the £60.'

her friends, she had to get well somewhere. This was the first time since their marriage in 1894 that they had been apart, and although Cronwright joined her within a matter of weeks, it was to set a pattern of separations. In her letters Olive was as loving as before, and there is no suspicion of a decline in their relationship. It remained a matter of great pride to Olive that her marriage be a triumph; whether it was sexually fulfilling or not is a complete unknown, since Olive was idealistic and now deeply reticent about such things. If the passion had drained from the relationship, she would have been unable to concede it.

In Johannesburg she did not find it easy to live alone. The city itself was intolerable. Writing to Carpenter she described it as a 'great, fiendish, hell of a city which for glitter and gold, and wickedness, carriages and palaces and brothels and gambling halls, beat creation'.[44] Only to a woman's eye could it be opened to all its full hideousness, she wrote to Merriman.

> It is the women that are the most terrible thing here; but doubtless the mass of ill-gotten wealth obtained without labour and squandered with all recklessness is the true source of the evil. It attracts the worst class of women to Johannesburg; and it demoralises those who were not demoralised before. It is not the poor outcast women who are the most terrible thing here, by any means; it is the apparently respectable women. I have lived on various places on earth, Monte Carlo, London, Paris; I have worked among the outcast women and drunken sailors in the East End; but anything so appalling, so decayed I have never seen. One realised in Johannesburg what the tone of society must have been in the reign of Charles II. The *whole* moral fibre relaxed.[45]

Johannesburg crushed her power of thinking. The doctor said 'the same old things' about doing no writing and taking complete rest, 'but they don't see that it's the consciousness that I can't work that is killing me'.[46]

South African politics after the Jameson Raid pivoted on the Transvaal, and the Schreiners came as celebrities who had opposed the Raid and espoused the cause of the Republic. They had ready access to its notables, including President Paul Kruger. Olive was offered an annuity by the Transvaal government of £300 a year[47] but she turned it down and was hotly indignant about the rumour – which she pinned on Rhodes – that the Transvaal government had paid her to write *Trooper Peter Halket*. 'The only thing the Transvaal government could do for me would be to enfranchise all wives and daughters of the burghers,' she wrote angrily to General and Mrs Smuts.[48]

Olive could not throw off the feeling she had had before the Jameson Raid that the blow was about to fall. For Rhodes to 'right himself now' he must plunge South Africa into war, 'and he will do it'.[49] Will shared her premonition that a provocation would be staged. When they tried to convince the Chief Justice, Sir James Rose-Innes, his disbelief prompted Olive to say: 'If it were from a woman one would say "See how unfit the female mind".'[50] Yet Olive believed that access to and persuasion of the right public men might avert the crisis. She believed that Sir Alfred Milner, the British governor of the Cape, who was later to be high commissioner of a unified South Africa, meant to do the right thing 'if only he knows the true state of South African feeling', and she would not give him up until she saw what his advice was to Chamberlain, Britain's colonial secretary.[51] She consulted Smuts about the advisability of her trying to see Milner to explain the resistance Britain would have to face in a war with the Boers.[52] Yet at the same time she believed that 'we can't win the capitalists to our side but we can try to win the mass of thinking English people'.[53]

Accordingly, during the first half of 1899 Olive produced *An English South African's View of the Situation*.* Written for those who 'love Africa, but love England also', it was an eve-of-war appeal to England and the English to stop the coming conflict. For:

> who gains by war? What is it for? Who is there that desires it? Not England! She has a great young nation's heart to lose. She has treaties to violate . . . Not Africa! The great young nation, quickening today to its first consciousness of life, to be torn and rent . . . Not the brave English soldier. There are no laurels for him here. The dying lads with hands fresh from the plough; the old man tottering to the grave, who seizes up the gun to die with it . . . Who gains by war? Not we the Africans whose hearts are knit to England. We love all. Each hired soldier's bullet that strikes down a South African does more; it finds a bullet here in our hearts.

This sentimental plea to English patriotism and pride was followed by a tremulous vision of the scale and aftermath of war:

* This essay appeared in June 1899 as 'An English South African's View of the Situation: Words in Season' and was published with Merriman's assistance in the *South African News* in the same year. A version was translated into Dutch by Francis Reitz, President of the Orange Free State from 1887–96. An English edition was published by Hodder and Stoughton in 1899. See also below, p. 375.

It may be said: but what has England to fear in a campaign with a country like Africa? . . . she can sweep it by mere numbers. We answer yes – she might do it . . . There is no doubt that England might send out sixty or a hundred thousand hired soldiers to South Africa, and they could bombard our towns and destroy our villages; they could shoot down men in the prime of life, and old men and boys, till there was hardly a kopje in the country without its stain of blood. When the war was over the imported soldier might leave the land – but not all. Some must be left to keep the remaining people down. There would be quiet in the land. South Africa would rise up silently, and count her dead and bury them. Have the dead no voices? In a thousand farmhouses black-robed women would hold memory of the country . . . There would be silence, but no peace. You say that all the fighting men in arms would have been shot? Yes, but what of the women? If there were left but five thousand pregnant South African-born women and all the rest of their people destroyed, these women would breed up again a race like the first.

Olive was astonished that several English-speaking *Uitlanders* in Johannesburg thanked her for the article. 'But I haven't heard yet what *one* South African Dutch person thinks.'[54] When the book containing the article appeared in Britain, the 3000 copies printed were sold out in five days.

She had written a ringing warning that Britain would not fight an easy war, yet she feared that the Transvaal burghers were going into war too hopefully and that the first big reverses would be very depressing.[55] She herself was ill again; she had yet another miscarriage, a fourth; she was fighting for breath and unable to lie down at night. Cronwright wrote:

She had the best medical advice of the Rand, but it did not help her. With the wind in one direction she went down; with it in another direction she got better; you could tell at once, without going outside, merely by her asthma (which produced bronchitis) as soon as the direction of the wind changed.[56]

In August 1899 her doctor insisted that she leave Johannesburg. She refused time after time in what Cronwright found a most stubborn manner; later she told him that she thought that if she went away and war broke out, he would join the Boer commandos and fight. Eventually he decided that he had to take her away. They bought return tickets from

Johannesburg in the hope that the war would be averted, and they went to the Karoo in the Cape where a cousin of Cronwright's had a farm.

Karee Kloof was a refuge after Johannesburg. Cronwright joined the men on horseback rounding up the ostriches; Olive rode each evening under the stars. But she felt she had a knife in her side.[57] She sent cables to newspapers abroad and to public meetings in Britain appealing for peace and protesting against Chamberlain's provocative foreign policy.[58] The *New York Journal* cabled her to serve as their war correspondent and she wrote to Smuts, then attorney-general of the Transvaal: 'Will Transvaal authorities give me facilities for gaining information? Where should I be – Bloemfontein or Pretoria or the Natal Frontier?'[59] She asked Smuts to show President Reitz of the Orange Free State a copy of her article on the Boers and to get from him a letter of safe conduct through that territory. But a week later an illness which she diagnosed as a heart attack persuaded her that she might break down if she went to the front with the Burghers as she wanted.[60] Instead she went to Cape Town to live with Will and Fan. She was in Cape Town when the war broke out in November 1899.

At the suggestion of J. A. Hobson, who was in South Africa for the *Manchester Guardian* as hostilities began, Cronwright went to Britain for six months to campaign against the war. Organized anti-war agitation was coming from several sources: the nonconformist churches; Liberal MPs bucking against the policy of the Liberal Party leadership which, though critical of the government's handling of the pre-war crisis and of its military mismanagement, virtually committed the party to the war; and the Social Democratic Federation and the Independent Labour Party. Cronwright's speaking tour was under the auspices of the South African Conciliation Committee (SACC), whose moving spirits were Liberal politicians and solid, respectable middle-class and business circles.*

---

* SACC President was Leonard (later Lord) Courtney, a Liberal MP and former deputy speaker of the House of Commons; its secretary was Frederick C. Mackarness, and its vice-president F. C. Selous. Committee members included liberal journalists, clergymen, Herbert Spencer, Gilbert Murray, the classicist, and prosperous businessmen like Alfred Mond and George Cadbury and members of the Rowntree family. As the war advanced the aims of the SACC were clarified: to assist war-sufferers; to promote goodwill through the recognition of both Dutch and English claims; and to work for a peace settlement through restoring Republican independence. *Cape Argus*, 22 March 1900.

Liberal anti-war campaigners objected to the war as diplomatically unnecessary, and thus immoral and unjust; they were not against empire, but wanted an 'imperialism of service' inspired by a sense of duty, not acquisition.[61]

In these Liberal circles Cronwright seemed to find a natural home. Not that it was an entirely comfortable one. His speaking tour coincided with a frenzy of patriotism during the initial setbacks suffered by the British army in South Africa.* During his tour of Scottish towns, Cronwright was the target of jingo crowds. His manhandling in Edinburgh was reported to Olive by Keir Hardie, who alone at that meeting got a hearing; it was also the subject of debate in the House of Commons, when the Liberal MP who raised the matter referred to Cronwright as

> an Englishman who married a German lady, and who came over to this country as a loyal British subject, with no desire except that of reasoning with the public with regard to the best method of preserving the South African dominions to this country.[62]

Preserving South Africa for the British Empire was by no means an inaccurate description of Cronwright's political position. In a speech to the Liberal Association at Penistone, Cronwright opened defensively by trying to persuade the audience that an anti-war stand did not mean championing the Boer cause. He was concerned to safeguard the 'permanent interests of Great Britain and the Empire' not only because he wanted to see justice done to a smaller people, but because he wanted to see 'his own people do the great, and the large, and the statesmanlike thing'. It was not for a 'free and generous people like the British to crush small nationalities which, if left to themselves, would grow and be a benefit to humanity at large'. Cheers issued from the audience.[63]

When this report reached Olive it was too much for her to stomach. His speech, she wrote him,

> is undoubtedly clever . . . so clever I would never have said it was yours! It's more like Rosebery† or some old English politician. And

---

* In the initial period of war, Republican forces carried the war into the Cape, swept into Natal and besieged Mafeking (and Rhodes, then in that town). The patriotism whipped up during these defeats later culminated in the 'khaki' election of 1900 when the Conservative Party swept into power with a larger majority.

† Lord Rosebery was a senior member of the Liberal Party's pro-war leadership. The Cape Liberal politician J. X. Merriman called him an imperialist grandee (Lewsen (ed.), *Merriman Correspondence*, p. 242).

yet on the whole I don't like it. If Rosebery had made it I should have said it was magnificent, but I don't like it from you, as I shouldn't from myself.[64]

While Cronwright identified with the SACC and its 'constructive imperialists', some of his meetings were also supported by Stop the War Committees and by the Social Democratic Federation, for at the local level anti-war campaigning by Liberals, nonconformists and socialists were enravelled. The inspiration for the Stop the War Committees was Olive's friend W. T. Stead, who had recently embarked on a series of cranky crusades, and who now idolized Rhodes, charging Chamberlain, not Rhodes, with responsibility for the war.[65] To Stead the war was unjust because Britain, as the superior and civilized power, should have acted differently. Himself the son of a Congregationalist minister, Stead believed that God's work in an Anglo-Saxon imperialism should consist in Christian arbitration.[66] The appeals of the Stop the War Committees rallied considerable nonconformist anti-war feeling and Olive was quick to point the contrast between this and organized Church response.*

The Social Democratic Federation manifesto *War in South Africa*, put out in January 1900, was uncompromisingly anti-war; it branded the war one of 'aggression waged on behalf of cosmopolitan millionaires'.[67] The columns of the SDF paper *Justice* show that there had been an internal debate in the organization about whether it should support the war or not, with one side determinedly pro-Boer and another arguing that Britain would have to fight for supremacy in South Africa one day, so why not now? When the anti-war stand was adopted, the monthly review of the Federation carried factual articles on the Boers and Boer leaders, together with their photographs.[68]

The issues of the war which had been ventilated in the SDF had been debated within the Second International as a whole. The Paris Congress of the International in 1900 took a resolutely anti-imperialist stand. Rosa Luxemburg formulated a resolution which bracketed militarism and colonialism as a new phenomenon that threatened the world with

---

* Olive wrote to Betty Molteno on 1 May 1900: 'Yes, Christians have not come out well over this matter . . . It is notable but not strange that nearly all the people in England who are on the side of the Republic are freethinkers and not Christians – Herbert Spencer, Sarah Grand, Ed Carpenter, Ellis, Morley, Courtney etc etc all the workmen of the Socialist and Independent Labour parties who are solid on our side are free thinkers.' UCTJ.

permanent war. H. M. Hyndman of the SDF sided with the militants against Eduard Bernstein, the German socialist, who called for a 'realistic attitude' towards colonial policy, but shortly after the Congress Hyndman changed his position. The SDF, he insisted, had devoted quite enough time to South Africa, and anyway its business was to spread socialism.[69] As for the war, it was only a 'struggle between two burglars'; seventeenth-century piracy and slave driving were no better than twentieth-century capitalism, and the only people worth agitating for were 'the splendid native tribes'. It was a rare position on the Boer war, and it seemed to go unnoticed. Within the SDF the debate that ensued concentrated on trying to reconcile, in rather abstract terms, the fight for socialism and against imperialism, and Hyndman's defeat in conference was seen as a victory for internationalist class consciousness; the anti-war agitation would be carried on, and an anti-war stand meant a pro-Boer stand.

Hyndman's advocacy of the Africans as the only genuine cause in South Africa was capricious, but if he arrived there by unaccountable means, hardly any other tendency in the anti-war movement got there at all, whether in Britain or in South Africa. The anti-war movement, whether nonconformist, Liberal imperialist or socialist, was trapped in a view of the war as a conflict between British and Boers. Furthermore, it was symptomatic of the conditions of the debate that ideological positions bore little or no relation to social class and political affiliation. There was a considerable if unorganized body of working-class dissent over the war, but working-class spokesmen and Liberals analysed the war in similar terms.

The most influential and closely worked out position on the war was J. A. Hobson's *The War in South Africa*, which appeared in 1900 after his researches in South Africa, and from whose data Lenin drew.* In its simplified form Hobson's thesis described the war as the product of a 'small confederacy of international mineowners and speculators' whose war policies were dictated by a need to secure for the mines a cheap and adequate supply of African labour. It was a thesis Olive not only agreed

---

* Hobson, by contrast with Lenin's *Imperialism: The Highest Stage of Capitalism*, published in 1916, adhered to a simple under-consumptionist theory: imperialism arose from the unequal distribution of wealth under capitalism, which limited the home market and therefore made inevitable a search for external markets, which led to colonial annexation. Unlike Lenin, Hobson envisaged a non-imperialist capitalism based on the increased consumption of the working class. T. Kemp, *Theories of Imperialism* (1967), p. 82.

with but must have helped to inspire; the book included a six-page interview with her.

Variants of a simplified version of this conspiracy of international finance were current among war critics of diverse politics. The SDF's *Justice* described the war as being fought for 'gold-greedy ghouls' and having been engineered by the Stock Exchange gang. Liberal MPs who fought the 1900 'khaki' election in working-class constituencies linked the war with the 'selfish intrigues of the Capitalists'.[70] J. X. Merriman, who identified most closely with British Liberal spokesmen, thought the Boer republics 'in a very grotesque fashion were really fighting . . . imperialism, militarism and stock-jobbing capitalism'.[71] This was the basic case against British imperialism: money-capitalism had attacked the Transvaal for its wealth.

The case for the Boers was noticeably influenced by Olive's idealistic portrayal of Boer society as simple and defenceless. Edward Carpenter published a pamphlet on New Year's Day 1900 which was almost a paraphrase of Olive's earlier essay on the Boer. Here were a pastoral people who had fled from English occupation of the Cape into their promised land, which was now being snatched from them.

> Religious, almost puritanical (for they descend from much the same puritan sources as we do) simple in their lives, loving their land, their cattle, their homes they have only asked to be left alone in their country.[72]

Keir Hardie wrote in a similar vein:

> As a pastoral people the Boers doubtless have all the failings of the fine qualities which pertain to that mode of life; but whatever these failings might have been they are virtues compared to the turbid pollution and refined cruelty which is inseparable from the operation of capitalism.[73]

The Boer republics were not capitalist, and were therefore freer. 'As Socialists,' Hardie wrote in *The Labour Leader*, 'our sympathies are bound to be with the Boers. Their Republican form of government bespeaks freedom, and is thus hateful to tyrants, whilst their methods of production for use are much nearer our ideal than any form of exploitation for profit.'[74] The war was thus seen as a conflict between two social systems. But if the pro-Boers exalted the one – the simple rural economy – the choice could be turned on its head, as it was by those who, like Olive and Edward Carpenter, adhered to an evolutionist ideology with its conception of distinct societal stages, but who chose to side with the march of 'civilization'. Karl Pearson went furthest in justifying the war as a step towards the fulfilment of a Darwinian plan.*[75] Leading Fabians like Sydney Webb saw the war as 'wholly unjust but wholly necessary'. George Bernard Shaw used a similar historical parallel to Hyndman: although the Boers were on the right side, Kruger, president of the Transvaal, stood for the seventeenth century and the Scottish seventeenth century at that, and his conclusion was not to reject both sides, but to opt for Britain's:

> ... the fact remains that a Great Power, consciously or unconsciously, must govern in the interests of civilisation as a whole; and it is not to those interests that such mighty forces as goldfields ... should be wielded irresponsibly by small communities of frontiersmen.[76]

The apologists for the imperial side argued, then, from the historical logic of the triumph of an industrial system over an antiquated society. Some on this side further justified themselves as protectors of the Africans against Boer inhumanity. Coincidentally, another Schreiner was on hand to flesh out this case: during Cronwright's speaking tour of Britain, Olive's elder brother Theo challenged him in public in a series of pamphlets which denounced the record of the Boer Republics on 'the native question'. However, the denunciation of the Boer republics' record necessarily prompted Theo's unqualified defence of Rhodes'

---

* At the end of December 1900 Pearson wrote very angrily to Olive about her stand in the war, but Cronwright intercepted the letter and returned it to Pearson with the words: 'Mrs Cronwright-Schreiner has not seen this. It is quite unnecessary that she should.'

'Dear Olive Schreiner, I know nothing which has given me, from the side of any I esteem my friends, so much pain as the "speech" which you send me in the South African News ... You use the great power of words you have to incite all the racial passion you can, and you do it by working yourself into a state in which you lose sight of one half of the truth ... It is men and women like you, who are capable of influencing large masses of men on whom the responsibility for the bloodshed and the bitterness which have accompanied and followed this war will largely rest. And I believe that one day when you realise your responsibility, it will be as if a great gulf opened beneath your feet. You speak as if a moiety of the South Africans in South Africa today had sole right to that land now and for ever. But my children and the children of all the crowded lands of Europe have a right in all new lands and the conditions must be such or be made such that they can live in them ... It is the old half knowledge, which is the bane of human life and leads to most of the fanaticism and oppression in this world. Sorrowfully yours, Karl Pearson.' 22 December 1900, *Pearson*.

policies on the same question.* In 'Some Aspects of the Native Question', a pamphlet published under the auspices of the Imperial South Africa Association, Theo charged that Cronwright had been 'unfair' in his attacks on the mining capitalists; when it came to Rhodes, Theo wrote, 'there was a philanthropic purpose in all his schemes for making money'. For his part Theo saw the Afrikaner Bond as the cause of the war. He denounced the 'terrible wrongs' of his Dutch countrymen who sought to substitute the supremacy of England for Dutch domination. For domination it had to be: 'The Boer looks on the Coloured man as a mere animal,' Theo wrote.

The two sides, for Britain and the Boer republics, here advocated by two members of the Schreiner family, thus projected themselves as diametric opposites. Yet they had far more in common than dividing them. Both white sides in the war fought to determine the terms of white power over South Africa; the majority African population was to be subject to the authority of the victor. Olive castigated imperial policy without reserve and had shown an acute perception of its southern African strategy in the hands of Rhodes, but she blinded herself to the record of the republics on everything except their anti-British agitation. In her revulsion from imperial policy she committed herself to its antagonist in the white man's war. Her political – and sentimental – attachment to the Boer, later the republican, cause had not been an easy adherence for an English-speaking South African. The more isolated she was for her heretical views, the more committed she grew. She had always lived as an outcast; one had to stand outside the mainstream for the sake of principle. The trouble was that in this case the central principle – the African question – was excluded by the force of white politics. Allowing for the monopoly of politics by competing white causes, and their total exclusion of the majority African population from political life, it was nevertheless a failure of political intellect for Olive to refuse to see the republics for the racially bigoted despotisms they were, and for

* The first blow in the pamphlet war between the two Schreiners was struck by Cronwright's article 'Some Vital Facts about Kimberley and Johannesburg for the Workingmen and Friends of the Natives'. It was a criticism of the closed compound system instituted by the mining industry for its African labour. In pamphlet form this article was published by the SACC in 1900. In the same year Theophilus Lyndall Schreiner wrote 'Some Aspects of the Native Question in South Africa: a reply to an article by Mr Cronwright-Schreiner in the *Manchester Guardian* of 30 October 1900'. Theo Schreiner also wrote *The Afrikaner Bond and Other Causes of the War* (Imperial South Africa Association, London, 1901).

her to identify with republican politicians and policies merely because they were not British. She was pilloried for siding with the republicans and this victimization served to obscure her error of judgement both to herself and to her supporters.

At the same time it must be said that if Olive Schreiner failed on the Boer war, who did not? Perhaps only Rosa Luxemburg. Analysing the historical conditions of capitalist accumulation and the tendency for capital to overwhelm pre-capitalist methods of production, Luxemburg illuminated this process through the example of the Boer war.[77] It was 'on the backs of the Negroes that the battle was fought between competitors who had precisely the same aim: to subject, expel, or destroy the coloured peoples, to appropriate their land and press them into service by the abolition of their social organizations'. The methods of exploitation of capitalism (represented by Britain) and the peasant economy (the Boer republics) were different, and the domination of capital was a foregone conclusion, which made it hopeless for the republics to resist.

It was a brilliant thesis – but it appeared more than a decade after the Boer war. Olive Schreiner did not have the advantage of this time distance nor of Luxemburg's theoretical strength and involvement in the debates of Marxism. But if she lacked prescience at the time she anticipated the latter part of the Luxemburg thesis: that when the new South African union incorporated the republics within a great modern state as envisaged by Rhodes' imperialist programme, the conflict between British and Boer would be superseded by the new conflict between capital and labour. Then, Luxemburg wrote, 'one million white exploiters of both nations sealed their touching fraternal alliance within the Union with the civil and political disfranchisement of five million coloured voters'. Olive Schreiner was in the thick of all this. The Boer war was no sooner over than she distanced herself from both white sides to espouse the cause of the Africans; at the height of the war, however, she spent her passion for the republican cause.

The Boer war was fought in two phases. In the first, the British and two republican armies of the Transvaal and the Orange Free State fought battles of position in which, initially, the British army suffered reversals. During 1900 the tide of war turned. By the middle of that year there were a quarter of a million British troops in the country, who swept northwards. The Free State Republic was annexed in March 1900; Johannesburg was entered in May; Pretoria a week after; and in September the Transvaal was annexed. The republics tried to sue for peace on the basis of their continued independence, but Britain insisted on their unconditional surrender and their acceptance of annexation. There followed the second phase of the war, of mobile, guerrilla warfare. Even during the phase of regular warfare, republican commandos had struck into the British-held areas and had sparked off local rebellion among Afrikaners, especially in border districts, some of which went over almost entirely to the republican cause. In the latter months of 1900 and during 1901 the war of movement was extended by commando actions. The British forces advanced up the rail line; the commandos became masters of scouting, of rail-line sabotage and of survival as they foraged for supplies in friendly communities. Britain countered with martial law, farm burnings and concentration camps to stamp out rebellion and cut the commandos off from their sources of support.

Living in Will's house in Cape Town during the opening months of the war, Olive must have had an inside view of the attempts of the Schreiner cabinet to keep the Cape neutral. But it was an impossible task for a British colony. The Cape was a base for imperial troops, and when commandos from across the Orange River brought Cape Afrikaners out in rebellion, the Schreiner administration was responsible for administering martial law. Olive took a cautious position at first, hoping that the

> Freestaters and Transvalers will have the wisdom *not* to come into any of the colonial possessions. It will ruin their cause if they do. If they fight on their own ground they may yet get or keep their independence.[78]

But annexation was another matter, and she was astonished to hear that Will was in favour of Britain's annexation of the republics. 'I can't make out what the politicians are about in Cape Town,' she wrote to Fan.[79] By then she had left their house and was moving about several small Karoo towns until Cronwright returned from England and they could set up a more permanent home. She found it difficult in this period to speak up and act because her brother was prime minister, and advancing Britain's policies. 'I don't agree with him. I just express my views and leave them to work. That's the best way with him.'[80] She said that she would rejoice to see Will out of office,[81] and soon afterwards, in June 1900, the Schreiner ministry did fall on account of an internal crisis on the annexation of the republics, the administration of martial law, and the trial and punishment of Cape rebels.

Despite her protestations of restraint on Will's account, Olive plunged into a series of popular congresses summoned in the Cape against annexation and, especially at congresses of women, against farm burning. The Conciliation Committee working in England for a negotiated peace thus had its counterpart in the Cape, where conciliation committees found active Afrikaner Bond support, though they were not directly associated with the Bond.[82]

To the British authorities these congresses were 'in reality meetings of conspirators, engineered by agents of the Boer governments'.[83] Olive was the principal speaker at the first, in Graaff Reinet in May 1900, and when she appeared the air vibrated with cheers.[84] After the fall of the Schreiner ministry, three anti-war congresses were held within seven weeks. In Cape Town she spoke again, and writer H. W. Nevinson heard her:

> I described her at the time as a short heavy brown-haired woman, but when she began to speak she was transfigured. Indeed, though she stood perfectly still, she was transfigured into flame. Indignation can make the dumb speak and stones be eloquent. But this woman was not dumb, and was no stone. I have heard much indignant eloquence, but never such a molten torrent of white-hot rage. It was overwhelming. When it suddenly ceased, the large audience – about 1500 men and women – could hardly gasp. If Olive Schreiner (for, of course, it was she) had called on them to storm Government House, they would have thrown themselves upon the bayonets.[85]

At Somerset East, where two thousand women gathered under 'tall pollarded oaks in full foliage', a letter from her was read to the assembly: 'Now England is dead to me,' she lamented.[86] (She wondered afterwards if this message had been too strong.)[87]

The congresses of women persuaded Merriman – if he needed persuasion – of the unfitness of women for public life.[88] Olive as orator was 'illogical, appealing to feeling rather than reason'. He called on her the morning after the Cape Town meeting and had an hour's talk with her; he found her 'excited and visionary as ever, full of vague schemes without any practical means of carrying them out. Beautiful sentiments but they do not carry us much further. She is one of those persons one admires more at a distance.' Yet he conceded that oddly enough the women were exercising a great influence. He found their influence 'odd' because they were so utterly opposed to the modern view of women's rights, and were such a contrast to the 'shrieking sisterhood who write on sex problems and scream out for votes'.[89] To Merriman Olive must have represented this 'shrieking sisterhood'; she, of course, would have rejected the description with contempt, and continued to identify with the women's protests. Sent for on one occasion by a British officer to be questioned about her republican sympathies, Olive told him it was the spirit of the women that would bring back the independence of the Transvaal and the Free State. 'Yes,' the officer agreed, 'the women are something too awful; they are not afraid of anything.'[90]

By September 1900 Cronwright was back in South Africa and the Schreiners were living in Hanover, a village in the Cape interior, almost 5000 feet above sea level where the air was cold and sharp. It was also an appropriate political climate. Cronwright described in his biography how during the war there were many places where for Olive to go was to court disaster, for she was almost incomprehensible to most people, and while many were rude to her, she alienated almost as many.[91] In Hanover she was spared the strains of a hostile community, for practically the whole district held her opinion as to the rights and wrongs of the war, and they (he included himself) were looked upon by the Afrikaner townsfolk as their leading champions.

In Hanover the war was close, 'raging about me in sight and sound', as she wrote to the Browns.[92] Hanover was only nine miles from the railway along which the British had built blockhouses to prevent commandos crossing the line, and when in December 1900 Free State commandos again invaded the Cape, martial law was reimposed on wide areas, Hanover included. The town was fortified by barbed wire and was closely guarded by night.* Olive had to get a permit to walk beyond the village limits, and to burn a light in her bedroom at night. From time to time cannon fire could be heard. On one occasion Olive claimed that in drizzling rain and mist, she could hear members of a commando singing psalms

---

* Accounts of the guard over her during the war are not consistent. Newspaper accounts – and the foreword to *Woman and Labour* – claimed that she was heavily guarded, but she wrote to Betty Molteno on 8 March 1901: 'No, it's not true that I have a guard permanently round the house. A guard of six men is here every night, just outside the windows but they are supposed to be guarding the town generally.' Cronwright's account makes it clear that the whole town was fortified with barbed wire fencing and she lived in one of the outside houses (*Life*, p. 328).

from a rock outcrop near the town. 'They are a strange people these,' she wrote, 'how little the world knows them.'[93]

Despite the confines of her situation, Olive became a partisan, and an organized one at that. Through the network of her women friends like Betty Molteno and Alice Greene, another Port Elizabeth schoolteacher, and her contacts with Marie Koopmans de Wet, an organizer of the women's congresses, and Emily Hobhouse, niece of the Liberal jurist who had organized the SA Women and Children's Distress Fund and got authority from Chamberlain to visit the concentration camps, Olive collected funds and provisions to allay the hardships martial law had caused in Hanover. 'There is much want here in many ways,' she wrote to Betty Molteno:

> We have four men now in prison to whom the village people have to send meals daily, different people taking it in turns; we have a lot of Free State people here turned out, whom the village people have to help and we have besides many people impoverished by martial law. For instance, one family close to me, the man made his living as several poor people did, by bringing in the loads from the station for more than two months since martial law came in, they have not earned one penny. They have bright, intelligent children whom they would have had to take from school, but I went to see the Committee about it.[94]

When three young men suspected of working for the republican cause were held under martial law and then shot at De Aar, Olive's accounts of the episode were troubled, but carefully composed and articulate. She wired the British commanding officer to ask for a permit to travel to De Aar to plead their case but he wired back that the men 'were to be shot tomorrow, and that he was acting under superior orders. You see I am so tied here under martial law I can't get to him'. The men had been charged with an attack on a train; according to Olive they were undefended; she was convinced that the principal witness, who had turned Queen's evidence, was lying;[95] the men died protesting their innocence. After the war Olive and Cronwright pursued the De Aar shooting into a murder trial in July 1902 when the principal witness in the case was the man on whose evidence the three men had been executed. In the absence of an official shorthand writer Olive sat next to Cronwright in court and took notes: 'I think I got every word down.' When Cronwright was elected to parliament after this, he managed to have the shooting sent for review; the widow of one of the men was recommended for a pension and the remains of the three shot at De Aar were exhumed and reinterred in Hanover's graveyard.[96] Olive was deeply distressed at the farm burning and capturing of women and children but in some ways the execution of the three young men upset her even more, perhaps because she was powerless even where she thought she could use her influence to get access to higher authority.

Olive did not write much during the war years, but one of her short stories was a rather maudlin account of the sufferings of women in war-time. 'Eighteen-Ninety-Nine'[97] was about a grandmother and a mother whose men had fallen in battle or been wounded lion-hunting and whose remaining grandson of eighteen was called up on commando, and then left for dead after a sortie with 'khakies'. Without their menfolk, the women were left to run the farm on their own, with the war all about them. By 'Nineteen Hundred and One', the tailpiece to the story, the women lay in graves near one of the concentration camps, buried side by side. The older woman had died first, the younger had been unable to live without her. On their graves 'no stone and no name . . . to say who lies there . . . our unknown . . . our unnamed . . . our forgotten dead'.

Though she had always claimed to need solitude, the war brought confinement. Now Olive could not even walk freely without a permit; news was irregular and her mail stringently censored. She was lonely for intellectual sympathy and emotional tenderness; her letters were cut off and distressed. Both the Schreiner and Cronwright families were divided by the war, and Olive suffered not only at the long spells of time without a letter from her mother, but also at the thought that Cronwright's relations were against her, 'thinking that I am making Cron pro-Boer'.[98] She continued to write regular dutiful notes to Rebecca, describing her pet animals, the weather, and the books she was reading, and visited her at least once a year in Cape Town. Then news came that Fred, her caring elder brother, had died after a short illness; Olive declared that a large part of her died with him.[99] She was still distanced from Ettie, who had married a Rhodesian, John Stakesby Lewis, in a baptist ceremony and later opened a home for inebriates in Cape Town; Olive found much that was great and beautiful in her older sister, but thought that religion had warped her.[100] When Ettie brought Rebecca from Grahamstown to Cape Town in 1901, the presence of their mother helped to bring the sisters somewhat closer. But with Theo there was still no reconciliation: the issues of the war had driven them far apart.

The war lasted two and a half years. By the middle of 1902 a peace treaty was signed, and Olive was able to visit Johannesburg, where she searched for bits of her manuscripts in the charred remains of their looted house.[101] But after a brief visit to Rebecca she returned to Hanover, and this time it was the exigencies of Cronwright's work which made them decide to continue living there. In all, seven years of Olive's life were spent in this small country town. Cronwright had been frustrated throughout the war period by his inability to register his law articles – they could not be transferred from the Transvaal to the Cape – but now he opened a business of his own, acting as insurance agent, town auctioneer, sworn appraiser, and justice of the peace. In June 1902 he was elected MP for Colesberg in the Cape parliament, and a member for Beaufort West the following year. Olive spent much time alone, since Cronwright was frequently away from Hanover to tour his constituencies and to attend the parliamentary session in Cape Town.

There are great gaps in Olive's published letters and diary entries for these years. Her most frank and expressive letters were written to her women correspondents: to Betty Molteno and Alice Greene in Port Elizabeth; to Will's wife Fan; to Isie Smuts, wife of the Boer general who, after the war, joined hands with Lord Milner's 'kindergarten' of young administrators to shape the unified state. Her letters to Cronwright were brief and matter-of-fact. He was absorbed in his work and his parliamentary career; she had an increasing horror of politics as they showed themselves in parliament, and would rather he had not contested a parliamentary seat, but 'each soul must do as it thinks right'.[102]

Life in Hanover after the war was still stern; in the immediate aftermath there was typhoid, and panic on the farms and in the town about the spread of the epidemic. Cronwright fell ill, and Olive nursed him. In the summer the heat rose to 104 degrees in the shade, there were clouds of dust and no sign of rain, and Olive had no one to help her fetch water. Hanover had neither baker nor dressmaker; Olive made her own bread and saw herself as shabby and old-fashioned – 'a backveld *tante*'.[103] Her companions were Nita, her dog, and a collection of mierkats, one of whom she named Sancho Panza; she went for long walks with them on the veld. She had learned to nurse herself during these years, taking her pulse, monitoring the fluctuations of her heart rate,[104] and reflecting that her symptoms were indicative of a nervous breakdown. She felt that she had lost her hold on life, and never felt quite alive.[105]

She was self-pitying, and pretended to be reconciled to her baby's death. 'At last I am glad my own little girl died.' Olive's life would have been different had she lived, 'but what of her'? One felt differently about boys, but the longer she lived the more she sympathized with the African woman who said to her: 'God cannot be good, otherwise why did he make women?'[106] Perhaps one day it would be beautiful to be a woman, but not now.

After the war she would have liked to leave Hanover, never to see it again. The kopjes and the hills were terrible to her and recalled wartime tragedies – 'if you go out you will see the market square where our men were sentenced to death' – and sometimes she woke at night fancying the town guard was firing.[107] The worst of it by far was her disappointment at the post-war settlement. Once again she felt rejected by all sides. After the war, as during it, she felt hounded by English-speaking 'jingos' for her republican sympathies, but now she no longer found a place on the republican side either.

> They all loved me so in wartime, now they are beginning to remember that I am English, and don't go to church, and [am] a 'liberal' in religious matters, and it makes life very lonely. One gets such a curious yearning for one's own, the people who understand one.[108]

For a short while after the end of the fighting she had been accepted. She cherished a brooch which Boer prisoners of war on St Helena had sent her.[109] She was a member of the delegation that carried the wreath from Hanover to the state funeral in Pretoria in December 1904 of President Kruger, and while in Pretoria she was visited by a group of the commandos who had operated in the Cape near Hanover; there was even a plan for her to help one of them write a book about his war experiences.

But the sense of belonging soon passed with the post-war settlement in which both sides, imperial and republican, were committed to creating a system of unrestrained white power. Military government by Britain was followed by a period of self-government during which the character of the future unified South African state was determined. Both the British side and the republican, headed from 1907 by former Boer generals Louis Botha and Jan Smuts, pursued a strategy of conciliation between the whites. Presiding over the reconstruction of the economy, Milner, until then, had concentrated on getting production on the mines back to pre-war levels and then surpassing them, and on securing dependable supplies of cheap African labour. This was the time during and after Milner when the ideology and the structures of segregation were formalized in order to block access to political power by the African majority and the Coloured and Indian minorities. Smuts' address to Chamberlain during the formative years of this policy was explicit on this question:

> It is necessary by a firm administration of the law to make it plain to the natives that the war altered the relations between the two white races but not between the white and coloured population of the country.[110]

Olive recorded with considerable bitterness the changes that were coming over everything. Her initial reaction was one of personal resentment: she had been rejected by those with whom she had previously identified:

> People who were everything to me during the war, more than my brothers and sisters when I had to try and help them get out of prison, or to get food, seem nothing to me now, and I am nothing to them. They pass me in the street almost without saying 'good morning'.[111]

This time she found the conviction to reject feelings that the fault was in her, understanding that the issues she had espoused in the war were dead. There was no sharp dividing line between the white parties, they merely divided on smaller issues. 'It is the Boers who are top dog now,'[112] and by 1908 she was writing of herself as 'the last of the Republicans, sick of empire and Union Jack'. Smuts was getting more like Milner; she told him so and added: 'Don't be cross, what must be said, must be said.'[113] What she called her apostolic days had passed. Her thoughts and anxieties had long passed from the Boers. If there was any public fight worth fighting in the country it would be in defence of the Africans and the Chinese.*

The conflict between Boer and Briton had indeed been superseded by the conflict between capital and labour, as Rosa Luxemburg had anticipated. The rise of South Africa's labour movement coincided with the importation of skilled white labour. Immigrant engine drivers, mechanics,

---

* In 1904, before the supply of cheap African mine labour was regularly secured, Milner imported indentured Chinese labour; there was an ensuing hue and cry in both South Africa and Britain, and they were repatriated with the advent of the Liberal government in Britain.

miners and builders took advantage of the official policy of colour discrimination, and the crop of trade unions that sprang up after the Boer war combined class militancy with colour bars.[114] Olive's perspicacious letter to the Johannesburg Shop Assistants' Union in 1905 warned against this policy: in the spirit of international unionism

> . . . There must be organised union of all workers; union among all workers in different branches and in the same society; and a yet larger union between the workers of all nations and countries, without which our labour problems can never be solved. For as long as there is an Italian girl willing to take the work for five shillings which a French girl did for ten, or a Chinaman who will take the miner's work for half that the Englishman or Kaffir demanded, there is always a hole in the bottom of the boat through which the water will ultimately creep in.[115]

When a Social Democratic Federation was founded in Cape Town, Olive sent a written message;[116] she always considered that socialists looked upon her as 'one of their folk'.[117] She made a point of protesting against attacks on labour, generally white organized labour at this time, at the same time as she propagandized whenever she could on the importance of labour unity irrespective of race and colour. She wanted to read a paper to white workers to point out that the 'Native Question is really the labour question complicated and made virulent by the question of colour' and urging them to stand by the African in the coming years.[118]

Only her circle of correspondents, many of them politicians' wives, and her annual trips to Cape Town kept her in touch with national politics, but when she sensed that principles were at stake she was quick to take issue, especially against race bigotry. At a protest meeting in Cape Town in 1906 against pogroms against the Jews in Russia, Olive's 'Letter on the Jew' was read out by Cronwright.[119] The cry 'Keep out the Jew' because he corrupted finance and commerce was raised not by those seeking to save the community, Olive wrote, but often by those very financial and commercial interests themselves. In defence of the Jews she pointed to their presence among social and political reformers in every country in Europe; she need only mention the name of Karl Marx, 'the great German socialist and leader . . . who chose poverty and exile to benefit mankind'.

As in this message, the allusions she made in her speeches and articles were often remote from the experience of South Africans, for though she followed the country's politics closely, many of her reference points were not national or South African but British, European or international. She still wrote, though less regularly, to her friends abroad; visitors from abroad sought her out. Emmeline Pethick Lawrence, one of the leading suffragettes, came to stay in a small Hanover hotel and visited Olive daily. She gave her W. E. B. Du Bois' book *The Souls of Black Folk*; Olive wrote enthusiastically about it to Carpenter and loaned it to Will. Keir Hardie also visited her and she held him up as an example to Will of the only man she had known in political life for many years who yet retained the 'singleness of mind and directness of method' that marked him in private life.[120]

The vigour of her political opinions was not, however, a reflection of how worn Olive felt in herself at this time. She was still sad about the distance from her family. When Rebecca died in 1903 she was relieved that it was peaceful and sudden, with no pain, and that Ettie and Will were at her deathbed. The following year Olive and Ettie travelled to-gether by ox wagon to Bedford to exhume Gottlob's remains. Four days were spent sinking trenches on each side of the grave and Olive felt a 'kind of resurrection as the early sunlight came and shone again on the dear old head that had been buried for 28 years'; then the coffin was taken to Cape Town and reburied in the same grave with Rebecca in a family ceremony of children and grandchildren which Olive was sure 'the old man would have liked'.[121] While concerned with reuniting Gottlob and Rebecca, Olive also gave Cronwright instructions about her own death. Her baby and her favourite dog, Nita, were to be buried with her; all private letters from her mother and from Will were to be burnt.[122]

This was an administrative rather than a morbid preoccupation. Olive had come to accept her chronic illness, and was becoming almost matter-of-fact about it, even when she wrote to Cronwright about 'pains in my heart' and a sense that 'I don't think it can go on very long'. She sounded calm, almost resigned, and had taken to reflecting to her women friends on issues of love and friendship. She admired and envied the bond between Betty Molteno and Alice Greene, who had lived together for seventeen years; she no longer felt any such closeness in her life 'nor any terrible strength of human affection'. 'One gets such a hunger for your own flesh and blood sometimes. Of course in England where I have so many dear beautiful friends I don't feel it so much,' she wrote, 'but here I am terribly lonely.'[123] Cronwright was away more than ever, not only in Cape Town for the parliamentary sessions, and touring his constituency but also in De Aar where he was preparing to open a branch of his business. His routine left little time for her:

> He goes to his business as soon as he is up in the morning after a hurried breakfast, comes back at one for a hurried dinner. When his office closes at 4 he always has to see people. There is tea about six and then he goes to his room to write or lie on his bed to read, or goes out to see people. I wish him goodnight at half past nine or ten and that is all I see of him. On Sunday we sometimes go for a little walk but he cannot bear going for walks and I walk too slowly for him.[124]

Her irritation at seeing so little of him was ill-concealed, yet she tried to rationalize it by turning it on herself; what good was she to him? But: 'I can't leave him, he might be ill and need me.' She thought of going away to write; if not for him she would have gone to Italy to work, certainly would have left South Africa, yet something told her that she could not live away from him.[125] It was the old conflict about her need to write and be independent, and her sense of obligation to others. As for being unable to be away from Cronwright, this was becoming self-deception in that they were living apart for longer and longer periods.

When she did leave Hanover it was to move to De Aar, where Cronwright's branch business interests had been very successful: he was now the valuer for the government Land Bank, secretary to the municipality, and deputy sheriff to the Supreme Court. She had made earlier attempts to join him at De Aar, then not much more than a railway junction, but 'the smell of the engine smoke and the dust completely breaks me down',[126] and anyway she could only see to Cronwright's comfort when they had a proper home for her to keep. When the house was built, Olive joined him in October of 1907, bringing furniture from their former Johannesburg house, and the baby's remains from its Kimberley grave.

Olive lived in De Aar for the next six years, escaping from the height of the summer heat to Cape Town between November and March, and sometimes visiting other favourite places like Matjesfontein. Except for the war years when she could not leave Hanover, this restless movement was the pattern of her life. She acknowledged herself to be a wanderer, and put her restlessness down to the climate, in other words, to the demands of her asthmatic condition. This way of life meant that she lived a great deal not in her own home but in the homes of others and frequently in boarding houses, and her friends were put to work to choose amenable landladies and rooms. When she was in De Aar she felt as lonely as in Hanover. The difference was that the commercial travellers at the hotels and the train coming across the plain 'from the great world of things and men . . . kept away that terrible shut-off feeling' she had suffered in Hanover. But Cronwright's account of her years in De Aar suggest that she did little writing, and was increasingly difficult to live with.

> . . . Olive would often sleep both morning and afternoon and then go to bed early. She would have enough sleep by midnight and would then get up to walk about the house. She would slam doors behind her as she passed in and out of the rooms.[127]

Cronwright had to remonstrate with her: she did these things quite unconsciously, he conceded, but she did them just the same.

While this account of the years in De Aar suggests that Olive was sunk in personal weariness, it was during this time that she summoned political energy reminiscent of her battles with Rhodes to engage in the public debate about the future South African constitution. On this occasion she and Will drew close to one another in a lonely and defeated minority. After the fall of his premiership, Will had kept his distance from the white parties and, for reasons which are unclear, had shed his previous position to emerge as an advocate of 'no colour bar in politics'.[128] Olive had maintained her elder sister role, monitoring all his speeches[129] and writing critical but concerned letters to prompt his radicalism. She was finding white politics 'loathsome' and thought 'with terror' of the future;[130] now she saw Will as some last hope. She still wrote to him rather patronizingly: 'With regard to capitalism', he was at least as advanced as any man in the SA Party (the leading Cape party); and 'I *hope* as advanced on the native question'.[131]

It was the so-called 'native question' which was again the pivot of all politics. The self-governing constitutions granted to the former republics after the Boer war had given the franchise to whites only. In the Cape there had been a non-racial qualified franchise since the 1830s, though it had been made more restrictive, especially during Rhodes' ministries; still, the voting qualification was legally on grounds not of race and colour but of property and education. In the Cape alone of the four colonies, there was thus a tiny minority of non-white voters, some Africans, but more Coloured persons. The peace treaty after the war had made the enfranchisement of the non-white people subject to the decision of the whites. During 1908 a National Convention of delegates – whites only – from all four colonies met to negotiate the terms of the constitution including the franchise of the future unified state. During the discussion the African question was obscured in a contest between the advantages of a federal or unitary constitution; a federal system would have allowed for a somewhat greater diversity between the constituent parts of government. Will was a pronounced federalist; so was Olive.

She expounded her reasons publicly as the National Convention met behind closed doors in October 1908, when she answered a set of questions submitted to her by the editor of the *Transvaal Leader*.[132] 'What form of Closer Union do you favour – Federation or Unification; and for what reasons?' she was asked. A federal system, she replied, on the grounds that small states were more favourable to liberty and good government than large ones. The danger of centralized states was their falling prey to 'the tyranny of sections, of large interests, or of strong individuals'. The advocacy of the small state was probably a ploy to protect the autonomy of the Cape, with its more liberal franchise system.

Asked to discuss problems of revenue allocation, railways and debts as handled within a federal system, she waved these aside as details to be worked out when the general issues were decided. She was, however, prepared to expand on the issue of the franchise and on the African question. Here she veered uneasily between constitutional proposals tailored to enlist support from the least reactionary lobby of the time, that of the Cape liberals, and a portentous and deeply pessimistic declaration about the disaster into which South Africa would plunge if the rights of Africans were not recognized.

Her general principles were unequivocal: 'I am of the opinion that . . . no distinction of race or colour should be made between South Africans. South Africa must be a free man's country.' Yet when it came to detailed proposals for a system of political representation, she advanced no further than the qualified franchise of the Cape:

I hold it should be adult franchise with a high educational test. This would tell heavily against the natives, most of whom the educational test would exclude. I therefore think that, where natives are still living in large masses, under a tribal tenure, some arrangements should be made for their electing a certain small number of direct representatives to the Federal Parliament, but all natives not still living under tribal tenure would of course come under the ordinary law for all citizens.

The greater part of her interview was an impassioned and verbose declaration. The Native Question, she held, was the root question in South Africa, and 'as is our wisdom in dealing with it, so will be our future'. The Africans 'are the makers of our wealth, the great basic rock on which our State is founded – our vast labouring class'. 'If,' she continued,

blinded by the gain of the moment, we see nothing in our dark man but a vast engine of labour; if to us he is not a man, but only a tool; if dispossessed entirely of the land for which he now shows that large aptitude for peasant proprietorship for the lack of which among their masses many great nations are decaying; if we force him permanently in his millions into the locations and compounds and slums of our cities, obtaining his labour cheaper, but to lose what the wealth of five Rands would not return to use; if, uninstructed in the highest forms of labour, without the rights of citizenship, his own social organisation broken up, without our having aided him to participate in our own; if, unbound to us by gratitude and sympathy, and alien to us in blood and colour, we reduce this vast mass to the condition of a great seething, ignorant proletariat – then I would rather draw a veil over the future of this land.

Blemished by its expectation of 'gratitude' from labour, and couched in the patronizing tones of a political system which saw Africans as objects, not makers of policy, this was none the less an ominous and prophetic vision which set her apart from her contemporaries. And while her constitutional scheme was not distinct from the model of the Cape liberal franchise, its makers were now scrapping it. When Will Schreiner fought the clauses of the draft colour-bar Union constitution in its passage through the Cape parliament, Merriman found him 'intolerably wearisome'; the draft was adopted with a majority of ninety-six votes to two. Sauer, another member of a previous liberal team, was shortly to pilot through the Union parliament the Land Act which dispossessed the Africans of their land and thus formed the bedrock of the system of segregation.* If Olive had once encouraged the Cape liberals like Merriman and Sauer for the lengths to which they were prepared to go, they now abandoned the field to her.

She was in Cape Town to watch the proceedings of the parliamentary session when the draft constitution was finally carried, and saw the Cape's representatives as 'they squirmed and lied and each gave the other away, and all gave away principles'. All the while, however, there was Dr Abdurahman's 'drawn, dark, intellectual face looking down at them'.[133] Abdul Abdurahman was the president of the African Peoples' Organization, and when a delegation from the APO and from the South African Native Convention went to Britain to try to have the colour bar clauses of the constitution overruled by the British parliament, Will Schreiner was invited to head it.

By now both he and Olive despaired of influencing the shape of white politics, and were searching for ways to identify themselves with African political struggle. Will's faith in white supremacy politics had failed at last. Olive had always believed that he was good, simple and pure, if unimaginative; now that he had experienced a crisis of conscience and was changing sides, the stubborn, guileless and self-denying commitment that had once served Rhodes was transferred to the fight for African rights. Will, indeed, had decided to surrender his seat in the National Convention because he had committed himself as defence counsel in the trial of Dinuzulu, the Zulu chief charged with murder, sedition and other crimes as a result of a series of conflicts over Natal's break-up of the Zulu nation to allow the penetration of Zululand by land-hungry whites. It was Harriett Colenso, oldest of the five children of the famous Bishop Colenso of Natal, who had persuaded Will to act for the defence;[134] and Olive applauded his decision. When Dinuzulu was acquitted on the major charges but sentenced to five years' imprisonment for 'sheltering rebels', she reflected on how she and thousands of others had done much the same during the Boer war.

She was going through 'one of those dark times of depression and crushing loneliness that I suppose come to all sometimes',[135] and admonished Will to 'fight on, quite alone. Any man can fight in a

---

* Olive wrote on this occasion to Will Schreiner, 25 July 1913 from De Aar: 'What a tragedy his last act should have been that Native Land Bill. Our men in some sense liberal are dying out and there are none to take their places unless it is possible to arouse the working men to see their duty to *all* labour.'

company; only a great man fights quite alone'. The men who had participated in the Convention 'know that the real force hurrying them on is to crush the Native – cheap labour, mines, the native territory'.[136] It was a shorthand description, though a perfectly accurate one. She was deeply worried about the outcome of the National Convention, and she set the reasons out to Edward Carpenter:

> If the plan of this miserable convention is carried out, we stand at the beginning of a long steady downward course of 20 or 30 years. There is no hope of even that little shred of justice to the natives there has been in years past. The capitalists and the retrograde Boers are going to dominate the country. We shall have native wars which for injustice and horrors will make the Boer war an innocent little game, and we have no working class to fight with because *our* working class is the natives themselves who will have no votes and who, if they strike or move in any way, will be shot down like dogs . . .[137]

From this time on she barely concerned herself with white politics or white politicians, except to nag or attack those she knew personally. When Smuts as Transvaal colonial secretary tried to break the Indian passive resistance movement and to push through restrictions against the Indian minority, she wrote his wife Isie Smuts: 'Tell Jan I say he's not to go on dancing on the head of my Indians like he does.' When she died, she continued almost humorously, he would have to take care of 'all my black people for me. I shall leave them to him in my will'.[138] It was excessively patronizing because she asserted herself as the protector of the underdog, possibly because these may have been the only terms which white politicians could fathom. For she had no illusions about the Botha-Smuts government. When the mine owners cut white wages and broke strikes of miners, the government called imperial troops in, as Olive said, 'to shift the bloodshed on to British shoulders'.[139] At the same time she perspicaciously saw labour, too, divided by the colour bar and the Africans under attack not just by the state but also by 'white working men who are trying to get a law passed that natives shall not be allowed to do skilled work'.[140] She continued to feel hopeless about the treatment of the Africans and, when additional discriminatory laws were framed, confided in Will that nothing surprised her, and a little more or less seemed to make no difference. Of course the whites would pay in the long run but that would not prevent the wrong being done first.[141] She had been convinced since the days of the National Convention that the only hope for the Africans was that the politicians would fall out over the spoils, 'and when the oppressors fall down, the weak sometimes come by their own'.[142]

During all these years the women's movement was also Olive's continuing concern. When the political parties reformed after the Boer war, she impressed on her circle of women friends the importance of women being admitted to them as equal members. She knew full well, however, that many supporters of votes for women were concerned less about women's rights than about using women's votes to ensure the preponderance of their party or community – Afrikaner or English-speaking – over the other.

The debate about the shape of the new Union constitution automatically raised the issue of the franchise for women, and in 1907 a League was formed 'for the sole purpose of promoting women's enfranchisement'. It began with forty members, with Olive as a vice-president together with Mary Brown. That year a Bill to enfranchise women was brought before the Cape parliament, seconded by Cronwright, and lost, with the parties dividing both ways.

The Women's Enfranchisement League were proud to have Olive as a member. They produced a compilation of her *Thoughts about Women*[143] from *African Farm* and *Dreams*. She was hailed as the genius of the suffrage movement in South Africa, and speeches from or about her were often 'the chief event of the meeting'. They were proud, too, of Olive's influence on women in England, and this link gave them a sense of affinity with the suffrage movement in Britain that Olive, in close contact with radicals Constance Lytton and Emmeline Pethick Lawrence, cultivated. On one occasion she received a postcard from Bow Street police station where a Mrs Griffiths, one of the League members in the Cape, was among the suffragettes arrested. 'I'm very glad one of our women was with them,' Olive wrote to Betty Molteno.[144]

Indeed the two campaigns were to split in not dissimilar ways. Votes for women on the same terms as men in South Africa was not a demand for adult suffrage, for only white men were being enfranchised. When a split occurred in the Transvaal branch of the WEL, Olive put it down to autocratic control, and claimed that divisions in societies were a sign of life;[145] but whatever the source of this divide, she could not overlook the real crisis in the movement. This, predictably, was over the colour bar. The alignment in national politics was replicated in the League, with the Transvaal and Natal societies insisting on votes for white women only. The more radical members in the Cape League were isolated, and bound to be overruled in the national society. This was the case for Olive.

When the Women's Enfranchisement League published its object as being to advocate the granting of the vote to women on the same terms as men, Olive resigned and later scrawled over a leaflet on which this was printed that it was '*not* a personal matter that made me leave the Society'. She underlined the phrase about women being granted the vote on the same terms and added: 'The women of the Cape Colony *all* women of the Cape Colony. These were the terms on which I joined.' She was obviously very angry:

> And no one had the right without telling me [word illegible] or giving me a *hint* so that I might either come down and fight the matter or resign.[146]

She could not compromise on this issue.* She had, in any case, another reserve about the limited franchise. She was anxious for women to keep on fighting for the vote, for it was the struggle that educated, and all women should have that experience: 'a degraded and subject class or race gains much more by a fight for freedom than by having it given them.'[147]

In fact Olive's dissatisfaction with the WEL may have done no more than confirm a feeling about political organizations that she already had. Adela Villiers, who met Olive in 1890 as a girl of nineteen in Cape Town,† remembered her showing 'scant reverence for the reforms, leagues, communities established to improve mankind', and saying repeatedly that 'nothing can be of permanent value nor bring lasting peace to the world until the heart of man changes'.[148] Olive's commitment to the heart of man was, at source, expressed primarily as a search for the 'woman of the future', and pleasure in her wherever she was to be found, whether the 'new Cape girl of the 20th century', or 'those dear suffragettes'

---

* Interestingly, in fact, visiting British suffragettes were not more radical. Mrs Henry Fawcett and Mrs Pethick Lawrence came to speak in South Africa, and Mrs Pethick Lawrence was actually in the country when white women were enfranchised in 1930. Where a few South African women fought for representation of Coloured and African women as well, Mrs Pethick Lawrence made no comment at all.

† Adela Villiers and Lady Constance Lytton were nieces of the then governor of the Cape Colony, Sir Henry Loch.

Women's Enfranchisement League,

CAPE COLONY.

OBJECT.—To promote an intelligent interest in the question of the political enfranchisement of Women in Cape Colony, and advocate the granting of the vote to them on the same terms as men.

President: Mrs. A. N. MACADVEN Plumstead.
Hon. Treasurer: Mrs. SOLLY, Sir Lowry's Pass.
Hon. Secretary: Mrs. CHANDOS PRINGLE, Rhine Road, Sea Point.

WHY SHOULD WOMEN DEMAND THE FRANCHISE?

Because it is unjust that those women who are taxed equally with men should have no direct representation in the Parliament which decides how the public money should be raised and how it should be spent.

Because women, no less than men, must obey the laws.

Because some laws affect the interests of women specially.

Because women as a class must be the best judges of their own interests.

Because political experience shows that no large class of citizens is fully protected without a share in the making of the laws which affect them.

> "The Woman's cause is man's:
> They rise or sink together,
> Dwarfed or godlike,
> Bond or free."   —Tennyson.

Olive's hand-written comments on her departure from the Women's Enfranchisement League (*Ruth Alexander Collection*), transcribed opposite in England. Her constituency was no single movement, but an imperative, a presence, a set of beliefs that gathered momentum from place to place. The globalism of *Woman and Labour*, the book on which she was working during these years, did no more than reflect that concern with the development of a new kind of woman, and, by extension, a new kind of life. For now *Woman and Labour* was finished at last. Cronwright had taken to calling the unfinished manuscript 'the Encyclopaedia that is to be finished in the next century'.[149] She had been working on it spasmodically in Hanover and De Aar, and in 1911 it was published in London.

CHAPTER SEVEN

Woman and Labour

Woman and Labour, published in 1911, was Olive Schreiner's exposition of women's relationship to work and war; for social commentator Vera Brittain and many of the early twentieth-century feminists it became the 'Bible of the Woman's Movement'. To *Woman and Labour*, 'which sounded to the world of 1911 as insistent and inspiring as a trumpet-call summoning the faithful to a vital crusade – was due my final acceptance of feminism', Brittain wrote in 1933. She had been lent the book soon after its publication, and could 'still tingle with the excitement of the passage which reinforced me, brought up as were nearly all middle-class girls of that period to believe myself pre-destined to a perpetual, distasteful but inescapable tutelage, in my determination to go to college and at least prepare for a type of life more independent than that of a Buxton young lady: *"We take all labour for our province!"* '[1]

Woman and Labour was Olive's definitive work on the female condition, variously referred to in correspondence over the previous thirty years as her 'sex book' or her 'sex paper'. She maintained that what she published was only a fragment of a much longer manuscript destroyed during the Boer war, and in an introduction that is, for her, unusually forthright and detailed, she explains the history and circumstances of the book.[2] During the Eighties, she says, she wrote up reproduction and courtship practices in the animal kingdom and the condition of women in primitive society, including the African society of her own time. She had the chapters typed and bound and went on to deal with the causes and probable outcome of the contemporary movement. By 1899, when she was living in Johannesburg, further chapters were finished and similarly typed and bound; only some revision and the addition of a preface remained to be done.

The Boer war broke out while she was away from Jonannesburg, she continues, and since martial law was proclaimed almost immediately she had no access to Johannesburg and could do nothing to ensure the safety of her possessions. In 1900, when the British had taken Johannesburg, her brother-in-law Robert Hemming was able to visit her home and found it looted, her desk forced open and broken up, its contents set on fire. Although a few remnants of paper had survived, she felt sure the book had been destroyed.

As the war continued, appalled by the 'horror of the world around me', Olive forced herself to dwell on 'some abstract question' and rewrite what she could recall of one of her original chapters. She was then hundreds of miles from Johannesburg in a small country town, under close martial supervision; she was allowed out only at certain times of the day and was denied access to books, newspapers or magazines. In 1902, when the war was over, she obtained a permit to visit the Transvaal. She found the 'leathern back of [the] book intact, the front half of the leaves burnt away; the back half of the leaves next to the cover still all there, but so browned and scorched with the flames that they broke as you touched them'. She destroyed the remains of the book herself, thinking that she might rewrite the whole thing at some future time.

None of this would be at all contentious if Cronwright, in his biography, had not denied the existence of the original work; on matters of fact this is the single most important difference between them. Discounting immediately the notion that the book was begun when Olive was in her thirties, he considers the possibility that it originated from Karl Pearson's suggestion, in 1886, that she make what use she wanted of his historical and anthropological material. Referring to Pearson only as 'her friend, an eminent man of science', he claims that 'such a book would have meant hard, exact, systematic reading and study, and a collection and tabulation of exact scientific facts, a kind of labour she was incapable of'.[3]

There are only five references to 'the sex book', he says, and all in letters to Ellis: in 1888, suggesting it would do for his Contemporary Science series, since it was a purely scientific collection of facts; in 1889, thinking of dedicating it to him; in 1890, comparing it with the volume that Ellis did publish – hers would have been 'much more profound and original . . . but it'll never be finished now, I'm so tired'; again in 1890, despairing of how little she has to show for her life 'in sex work'; and in 1911, again in despair: 'Oh, I do wish the part of the book on sex-relations was not destroyed. I can never write it again.'[4] In addition, he says, it was inconceivable that she should have left any significant manuscript in their undefended house at Johannesburg since their personal luggage always included her work. Referring to 'a few papers' being burnt in an 'insignificant fire', Cronwright says that the bulk of the things were stored for them until after the war.

In support of his position Cronwright reminds his reader that *Woman and Labour* is 'an argument, a setting forth of her long brooded-over thoughts on the Woman Question . . . it is thought, and on this subject she had been thinking from her "early youth".' But Cronwright is himself confused about the relationship of work and thought. Acknowledging that Olive was 'constantly absorbed in thinking, in constructing creatively; and such thought is really hard work, demanding a far higher faculty and exercise of the mind than go to close reading and tabulation of facts', he insists that writing and systematic reading are something else, and concludes, with scrupulous bad temper:

> I have several times dwelt upon the fact that imaginative beings and events were often more real to her than hard fact. It seems to me she may have dwelt upon the thought of this imaginary sex book until, for her, it assumed objective form, and then that the only way in which she could account for its disappearance was that it was 'lost' at Johannesburg.[5]

Repeatedly describing Olive as a woman of genius, Cronwright was actually very unsympathetic to her discontinuous, almost passive way of working – the Prelude to *From Man to Man* 'flashed' on her, her book on sex evolution 'threw itself' into 'The Buddhist Priest's Wife'[6] – and his literalism over the manuscript says more about his irritation with her failure to produce than it does about the 'facts' of the situation. Katie Stuart, one of Olive's nieces, actually felt he had destroyed Olive's capacity for work by his ambition for her and his 'planning for her to write'. 'Could you? Could I?' she wrote to Ruth Alexander in 1924, 'write a word if someone was ceaselessly planning, arranging and cajoling us to do so? – and then bitterly disappointed because we couldn't!'[7] D. L. Hobman, in her commemorative biography of Schreiner, points out that Cronwright did not know of the existence of *Undine* until Ellis gave it to him after Olive's death; she could certainly have done other work without mentioning it to her husband.[8] Even this interpretation, however, has to be qualified in the light of a letter written a year after Olive died in which Mary Brown claimed to have received a letter from Cronwright acknowledging the existence of 'a sex book ms'.[9] If so, Cronwright's evidence is so contradictory as to be worthless, and his attempt to show how 'her capacity for stating hard, objective facts was often conditioned by her powerful imagination' invalidated.[10]

This much can be said. It is true that there are no references to *Woman and Labour* as such before 1909, when Olive was getting it ready for her publisher. On the other hand, her correspondence with Karl Pearson in 1886 alone indicates that much of the subject matter of the book was already in her mind, and that few of the ideas she was working with then were to alter with time; indeed, when she thought she might die with the thoughts on sex and social questions that she wrote at night 'left un-worked' she made a will leaving them to Pearson that he might work them up.[11] Her correspondence between 1890 and 1911, particularly with women friends in England, shows how consistently the ideal of the New Woman, elaborated in *Woman and Labour*, had informed her thought for years. Quite legitimately, then, did she say of *Woman and Labour* that 'the work had occupied a large part of my life'.[12]

Woman and Labour addressed itself to the contemporary feminist demand for work. '*Give us labour and the training which fits for labour!*' Olive put it. '*We demand this, not for ourselves alone, but for the race.*' Women, she wrote with some pride, had always worked. 'We wandered with the naked savage, we carried the race on our shoulders, we gathered as men hunted, and we were contented. Later, in settled communities, we worked the land, built dwellings, wove, made pots, and studied the properties of plants.' Time had passed, and it had become unnecessary that all men hunt or fight. Men had begun to share in women's work, and women moved indoors, though retaining their traditional tasks of spinning, embroidering and brewing.

At the present time, however, a further change was under way. Technological innovation meant that the 'culture and activity of man's brain and nerve' were becoming dominant, and an increasing body of men for whom there was no labour at all was forming – the Great Male Unemployed. In ancient societies they would have been valuable as warriors or toilers – now they were useless as society made more and more demands on the intellect and the machine. At the same time, an army of scientists, engineers, clerks and skilled workmen was required to invent, construct and maintain the new machinery, and never before had the male sex, taken as a whole, been so fully and 'strenuously' employed.

Olive saw the consequences for women as very different. Modern civilization had tended to rob them of practically all their traditional labour. Bread, beer and clothes were now made outside the home, and the 'army of rosy milkmaids' had been replaced by the cream-separator. Year by year there was a 'determined tendency for the sphere of woman's domestic labours to contract itself, and the contraction is marked exactly in proportion as that complex condition which we term "modern civilisation" is advanced'. Even in the traditional area of child-rearing, since children were now taken off into technical education, a woman of almost any class might 'yet in early middle age be found sitting alone in an empty house'. More significant still was the change in the practice of child-bearing. In primitive societies and the European Middle Ages continuous child-bearing had been imperative: the rate of infant mortality was high, and there was always war. Now, general social advance and an increasing understanding of sanitation and disease had combined to diminish infant mortality and lengthen human life; a race could maintain its numbers and even increase them 'with a comparatively small expenditure of women's vitality'. In addition, the demand now was not only for mere beasts of burden, but 'for few men, and those few, well born and well instructed'. So the woman who 'merely' produced and suckled twelve children was rightly seen by her community as unproductive; and a state whose women 'recklessly' produced under-nourished, under-instructed children would deteriorate.

This, then, she saw as the 'great fact, so often overlooked as the propelling force behind the vast and restless Woman's Movement': not just that the years of child-bearing and suckling had been so reduced, but that three-quarters of the entire field of women's traditional labour had shrunk away for ever. Not that today's women sought a regression to an earlier society, or to one where every woman was a child-bearer: she knew that 'the past material conditions of life have gone for ever'. The demand was rather that women should have their share of 'honoured and socially useful toil'.

All this was Olive's preamble to the introduction of her central concept, and the one by which the book was to be remembered, that of sex parasitism. Male and female labour problems were quite different, she felt. Society would not tolerate idleness in a man – he must find new fields of labour, or perish. But women had an acceptable alternative to new forms of labour – in sex parasitism, a peculiarly insidious form of inactivity which led to a decay in vitality and intelligence, first in women themselves, then in their descendants and in society as a whole; and only now had it become a danger to the mass of civilized women. Sex parasitism, the argument continued, was historically possible only when the dominant race or class was so supplied with material goods – through slave labour, for example – that female 'physical toil' became unnecessary. It meant that women became parasitic on society and on men, existing through the 'passive performance of sex functions only'. And since 'mental industry' had not taken the place of the woman's physical labour, she came to look with distaste on 'life-giving' itself, dressing finely and seeking dissipations and amusements to fill up the blank left by the lack of productive activity.

Olive attempted to give her argument a historical dimension, though it was predicated on a fairly conventional view of 'perversion' as a product of decadence. The decay of any dominant class or race was often heralded by the full development of sex parasitism, she added. Among the upper classes of ancient Greece, men came to absorb the intellectual labours of life, slaves and dependants the physical. It resulted in an increased division and dissimilarity between men and women which could not even be bridged by sexual love, indeed led inevitably to the 'abnormal institution of avowed inter-male sexual relations'. But the decline of a society, of course, did not spring only from the sex parasitism of the female; behind it lay the subjugation of slaves, subject races, or classes. The debilitating factor was the accumulation of unearned wealth in the hands of the dominant class, rather than wealth itself; unlaboured-for wealth possessed the power to rob the individual of the incentive to exertion. And sex parasitism was now tending to reach the 'large mass of women in civilised societies, who form the intermediate class between poor and rich'; in the next fifty years even the domestic labour of the poorest woman would be replaced by labour-saving machinery.

In support of her view of the essential difference between contemporary male and female problems, Olive reminded her readers of the fact that the most 'short-sighted' opposition to the attempts women were now making to enter new fields of labour had come from male handworkers, both as individuals and in their trade unions. They had tried to exclude women not only from new fields but from their traditional occupations of textile manufacture and handicraft. This was a valid enough comment. But for the rest, Olive's sense of the two movements was rather stereotyped, even pejorative of the men's: the men's labour movement originated in the poor and hand-labouring class, the women's in the 'wealthy, cultivated and brain-labouring classes'; the male was material and self-seeking, the female could only be attained 'through personal suffering and renunciation'. It was this 'over-shadowing consciousness of a large impersonal obligation' which, she felt, gave the women's movement something of the quality of a vast religious movement sweeping across humanity, and enabled us to forgive the woman who, waving her 'poor little Woman's Rights flag', represented women's suffering as 'wrongs intentionally inflicted . . . where they are merely the inevitable results of ages of social movement'. It enabled women to survive sexual isolation and the renunciation of motherhood, or the lonely, self-denying student to survive and fight on.

A woman – like a soldier – might not be conscious of the causes of her action; she might not be able to express them logically. But that did not make her action any the less inspired; in any case each woman did have 'a vague but profound consciousness' of the basic truths involved. 'Mere intellectual comprehension may guide, retard or accelerate the great human movements; it has never created them.' The fact that women in the movement today acted as a result of the immediate pressure of the conditions of life, that the movement took forms 'divergent and at times superficially almost irreconcilable' showed how vital, spontaneous and 'wholly organic' was its nature. Indeed, the New Women were not even new:

> We have in us the blood of a womanhood that was never bought and never sold; that wore no veil, and had no foot bound; whose realised ideal of marriage was sexual companionship and an equality in duty and labour.
>
> The banner which we unfurl today is not new: it is the standard of the old, free, monogamous labouring woman, which, twenty hundred years ago, floated over the forests of Europe.[13]

Having argued the case against sex parasitism, Olive proceeded to a theme, three years before the outbreak of World War One, of immediate contemporary concern. In war, too, women had always been involved:

Olive Schreiner

not only as nurses or as tillers of fields destroyed by battle, but as creators of life. 'We have made the men who destroyed and were destroyed.' The day when woman was involved with man in government would be the day that heralded the 'death of war as a means of arranging human differences'. This was not because she was morally superior to man, however, but because 'she knows the history of human flesh; she knows its cost; he does not'. It was this fact, she emphasized, which constituted one of the few differences between man and woman as such, for almost all 'psychic' sex differences, if compared with other cultures, were found to be purely artificial creations.

Olive's style was to state her case rhetorically. What, she asked, of the objections to be made to our argument? That the labour of child-rearing was enough for the woman? But did the lofty theorist in his spotless shirt-front always remember this? When the elderly house drudge brought his morning tea late,

> Does he exclaim to her, 'Divine child-bearer! Potential mother of the race! Why should you clean my boots or bring up my tea, while I lie warm in bed? . . . Henceforth I shall get up at dawn and make my own tea and clean my own boots, and pay you just the same!'[14]

No, he was disturbed by the woman doctor with an income who spent the evening smoking and reading, or receiving her guests. It was the imagery of 'The Buddhist Priest's Wife'.

What if woman proved to be inherently mentally incapable in the new world? Where accident of birth or marriage had enabled women to govern, they had done well; the new generation of women graduates showed the same. What if woman's entry to new fields of labour should lead to a loss in the mutual attraction of the sexes? Supposing her 'new intelligence and width . . . should render the male objectionable to her, and the woman undesirable to the male'? But sexual attraction was universal and ineradicable in life, from the amoeba [*sic*] to mankind; changes in forms of labour were superficial compared with it. Indeed, in any society in which the female was highly valued, it was safe to infer her comparative social freedom.

Now Olive reiterated her old idea of the appalling consequences of prostitution. Probably three-quarters of current European 'sexual unions' – whether in marriage or in prostitution – were dominated or influenced by the sex-purchasing power of the male; in that sense relations between the sexes even now were not determined by attraction or passion. But it was inevitable – though she did not spell out how – that prostitution would become extinct, and the relationship between men and women a 'co-partnership of freemen', for the modern woman's movement was one of 'the woman towards the man, of the sexes towards closer union'. The New Man, similarly, would no longer find that he could improve his standing by drinking, boasting about sex, or gambling. She was stating Rebekah's hope in *From Man to Man* as if it were already becoming fact.

But how was it, she asked, that if close reciprocity *was* developing between 'advanced' men and women, there was so much 'disco-ordination' and struggle in sexual relations? It was because the conflict was part of a general upheaval, a conflict between old and new ideals that had become inevitable as society became so complex.

> The sexual tragedy of modern life lies, not in the fact that woman as such is tending to differ fundamentally from man as such; but that, in the unassorted confusion of our modern life, it is continually the modified type of man or woman who is thrown into the closest personal relations with the antiquated type of the opposite sex; that between father and daughter, mother and son, brother and sister, husband and wife, may sometimes be found to intervene not merely years, but even centuries of social evolution.[15]

But was it all a dream, our conviction of fellowship between the sexes? She ended optimistically:

> The ancient Chaldean seer had a vision of a Garden of Eden which lay in a remote past. It was dreamed that man and woman once lived in joy and fellowship, till woman ate of the tree of knowledge and gave man to eat; and that both were driven forth to wander, to toil in bitterness; because they had eaten of the fruit.
>
> We also have our dream of a Garden: but it lies in a distant future. We dream that woman shall eat of the tree of knowledge together with man, and that side by side and hand close to hand, through ages of much toil and labour, they shall together raise about them an Eden nobler than any the Chaldean dreamed of; an Eden created by their own labour and made beautiful by their own fellowship.[16]

Vera Brittain's response to *Woman and Labour* is characteristic for someone of her class position.* Olive was, in fact, more alert to the specificity of working-class experience than most contemporary feminists, indeed to its value and strength – witness her letter to Ellis in 1888 about the mill hands in the north of England and her interest in the textile mills of Lancashire.† But the logic of her argument, based as it was on a picture of the 'modern woman' as being outside social production in comparison with earlier epochs, involved her in generalizations and fantasies about women and their social possibilities that were appropriate only for the professional and academic strata of the middle class.

On the other hand, *Woman and Labour*, though the product of more than twenty years of thought, nearly half of them spent in Europe, was finally written in South Africa, at a time when white women's lives *were* overwhelmingly domestic and confined, in Olive's words, to the 'passive exercise of the sex-function'. With black women starting to work as domestic servants, the white woman's chief role became that of administrator within the home.‡ This arrangement was still in force two generations later, in the 1940s, when Doris Lessing's fictional radical Martha Quest took on the task, in *A Proper Marriage*, of managing a large house in Rhodesia, four servants, her daughter and her husband in a colony which she felt was like a Victorian novel, where women 'talk about their servants at tea-parties, and . . . even go so far as to pay them twelve pounds a year, like our grandmothers' – those very turn-of-the-century women about whom Olive wrote – 'and say they are spoilt'.[17] The picture created is one of a pervasive cultural emptiness, while an equivalent sense of personal impoverishment and fragility was expressed in Martha Quest's case as envy of the black woman, whose dignity deemed to make her absence of material wealth almost insignificant. Martha thought of

* *Testament of Youth*, in which *Woman and Labour* is mentioned several times, was an attempt to draw a self-conscious picture of middle-class England. Brittain wanted to 'write something which would show what the whole War and post-war period – roughly, from the years leading up to 1914 until about 1925 – has meant to the men and women of my generation, the generation of those boys and girls who grew up just before the War broke out. I wanted to give too, if I could, an impression of the changes which that period brought about in the minds and lives of very different groups of individuals belonging to the large section of middle-class society from which my own family comes.' Brittain, *Testament of Youth* (1933), p. 9.

† See above, p. 181.

‡ Olive emphasized this point in a letter to Edward Carpenter in 1914 in which she described an old friend of hers, who, though rich, 'has never had a servant in her house. They cook, wash, etc. as you can see from the letter. In Africa where no white person does anything this is considered *quite mad*.' Carpenter MSS.

the simple women of the country, who might be women in peace, according to their instincts, without being made to think and disintegrate themselves into fragments. During those first few weeks of her marriage Martha was always accompanied by that other, black woman, like an invisible sister simpler and wiser than herself; for no matter how much she reminded herself of statistics and progress, she envied her from the bottom of her heart.[18]

The more general response of white to black women was to despise them for their difference. Olive admired them – in part because they were workers still, unlike the women of her own class – and something of Martha Quest's respect and awe comes across forcefully in the introduction to *Woman and Labour*. Here Olive attempted to find a social explanation for black women's acceptance of oppression. When she was eighteen, she says, she had a profoundly important conversation with an African woman 'still in her untouched primitive condition', who spoke of the sufferings of the women of her race with passion and eloquence. Olive was struck by her account of

the labour of women, the anguish of woman as she grew older, and the limitations of her life closed in about her, her sufferings under the condition of polygamy and subjection.

But she was equally impressed by the fact that

there was not one word of bitterness against the individual man, nor any will or intention to revolt; rather, there was a stern and almost majestic attitude of acceptance of the inevitable; life and the conditions of her race being what they were.

It was as a result of this conversation, she says, that she arrived at the belief that

the women of no race or class will ever rise in revolt or attempt to bring about a revolutionary readjustment of their relation to their society, however intense their suffering and however clear their perception of it, while the welfare and persistence of their society requires their submission.

It showed an early awareness of that connection between the emancipation of women and broader social change that socialist feminists point to today. Given her Spencerian social perspective, however, the determinism of her position was inevitable. Her conclusion was that

> wherever there is a general attempt on the part of the women of any
> society to readjust their position to it, a close analysis will always show
> that the changed or changing conditions of that society have made
> women's acquiescence no longer necessary or desirable.[19]

Within the feminist movement of her own time, *Woman and Labour* was very influential. Historian Alice Clark, writing during World War One about the working life of women in the seventeenth century, derived much of her argument from it, saying that it 'first drew the attention of many workers in the emancipation of women to the difference between reality and the commonly received generalisations as to woman's productive capacity'.[20] Constance Lytton, a suffragette, believed that Olive had succeeded in her interpretation of the women's movement 'more than any one other author'.[21] In the USA Floyd Dell, writing just before the war, took Olive as one of a number of 'women as world builders' including the American feminist and economist Charlotte Perkins Gilman, dancer Isadora Duncan, and social worker Jane Addams, and the Swedish thinker on sexual questions Ellen Key.[22]

How much did *Woman and Labour* create a new field, however, and how much did it clarify a pre-existing one? For it to make the impact that it did required a constituency of women already concerned about female powerlessness. In addition, its own radicalism was not unusual for the period: in stressing the social recognition and elevation of motherhood Olive was following Havelock Ellis and Ellen Key,[23] and her influence on this subject was less innovative than inspirational. Her demand was that women be prepared for motherhood as a field of labour like any other – Olive called George Sand a 'complete human creature' because she was a great mother as well as an artist and a lover of science[24] – that their vitality be preserved, that their bodies and minds be nurtured.

The social context for these ideas, however, was an extremely complex one. The birth rate was declining and the physical condition of recruits to the Imperial army was a great cause for concern. Issues of fitness for motherhood and eugenics generally were at the forefront of political discussion; indeed, campaigns around infant mortality and maternity in the years leading up to World War One united Liberals, Fabians, conservatives and extreme right-wingers.[25] To the right this 'surge of concern about the bearing and rearing of children' was a concern for the next generation of soldiers and workers; to a feminist and socialist like Olive Schreiner, though her position on race was made ambiguous by her attachment to social Darwinism, concern for motherhood was essentially a cry for personal dignity.

Olive saw motherhood, almost non-politically, as one of the glories of life. At no point in *Woman and Labour* did she either endorse or question the institution of the family. Where middle-class convention took it for granted that 'the proper context of childhood was the family, and the person most responsible the mother', Olive had once stated simply that every unmarried woman over the age of thirty should be allowed to bear a child without disgrace. It was her right, and a necessity for the proper health of her bodily functions.[26] It was inconsistent, however, with her repeated insistence on the deathless union of two persons in marriage, and she carried no further any investigation of the place of motherhood outside the Victorian family. For those who did, ambiguous issues arose in connection with the relationship between the family and the state. The reforms of the first decade of the twentieth century, in which the state intervened in the protection of national and child health, drew out the potential contradictions in the confirmed establishment position. A Liberal MP, proposing school canteens, free transport and baths for schoolchildren in 1905, knew that

> All this sounds terribly like rank Socialism. I'm afraid it is; but I am not in the least dismayed. Because I know it also to be first rate Imperialism. Because I know Empire cannot be built on rickety and flat-chested citizens.

The situation of motherhood similarly lent itself to ambiguous uses, and superficially there is little difference between many of the formulations of right-wingers or of radicals. For many of the activists, however, like the Church of England Mothers' Union, founded in 1876 and growing fast by the turn of the century, issues of the liberation of women were tangential. To the Mothers' Union, women were charged with that special moral duty of the mid-Victorian period: to restore a 'high tone in the homes and among the people of this country'.[27] The Mothers' Union regarded motherhood as an object of holy reverence: in the words of its founder, Mary Sumner:

> As I gazed with rapture at my little baby, it struck me how much I

needed special training for so great a work as the character-training of a child . . . I felt that mothers had one of the greatest and most important professions in the world, and yet there was no profession which had so poor a training for its supreme duties.

Compare this with a description of Olive provided by her close friend in England, Adela Villiers. It has some of the same sentiment.

Olive always said she envied men and would rather have been a man than a woman; nevertheless she was the first who woke in me the knowledge of the glory of womanhood, which has never since left me. She showed me the force and the power possible to women; she taught me how high was their mission and she revealed to me the knowledge of the sublime love of motherhood – rich gifts to have given and which few were able to offer.[28]

As positions on motherhood, so too beliefs about the 'new woman' served conformist and radical notions alike. In 1911 a doctor wrote in the *Eugenics Review*:

There is no doubt that the new woman is a more interesting companion than her predecessors, and that she has made great progress in the arts and sciences, in trades and professions, but the question of questions is – is she a better mother of the race?[29]

No, these new women were less fit to become the mothers 'of a stronger and more virile race', he felt, and the notion of virility remained unquestioned throughout the period. It was a key word in eugenics, which was, in the words of its originator Francis Galton, a 'virile creed'.[30] It became a key word in *Woman and Labour* as well. To Olive, in whose mind an uncritical use of 'virility' could be counterposed to the 'effeminacy' of Gregory Rose in *African Farm*, the new woman was the 'labouring and virile woman, not the always fainting and always weeping, always terrified Emily or Sophia'.[31] Still, there was a difference, even though the terminology is the same. The *Eugenics Review* went on to endorse all conventional notions of masculine and feminine.

Womanliness is disassociated in men's and also in most women's minds with either intellectual power or physical development, but is . . . rightly or wrongly associated with certain passive qualities, such as sympathy and tenderness . . . which best find their expression in the

domestic sphere and more particularly in the roles of wife and mother
. . . may it not be that the manliness of men and the womanliness of
woman are . . . but the modern expression of Natural Selection ?[32]

Olive's own position on motherhood was rather different, even though
there is some similarity, in her concept of civilization, to the mainstream
social thought of the period. On the surface she appears to be saying no
more than that the virility of the race demands better educated and
trained mothers, a position which could be seen as entirely instrumental,
overlooking the needs of women to make their own lives. In fact, she was
emphatic in *Woman and Labour* that child-bearing and rearing could not
satisfy all the modern woman's need for social labour and activity,
although she felt, characteristically, that the hunger for motherhood lay
'deep and over-mastering . . . in every virile woman's heart'.[33]

Nevertheless, she recognized and emphasized the labour that women
performed in socializing their children; she commented, perhaps too
romantically, on the high esteem in which the labour of reproduction was
held in primitive societies and in the Middle Ages, when women's
intelligence and ingenuity were taxed in order that they might provide
sufficient numbers of labourers to maintain the life of the society as a
whole. She used the facts of reproduction as similes within her argument
as a whole, as though to demonstrate, within her writing, the all-
importance of women's work: she reminded her reader that

with each generation the entire race passes through the body of its
womanhood as through a mould, reappearing with the indelible marks
of that mould upon it, that as the *os cervix* of the woman, through
which the head of the human infant passes at birth, forms a ring,
determining for ever the size at birth of the human head, a size which
could only increase if in the course of ages the *os cervix* of woman itself
should itself slowly expand; and that so exactly the intellectual capacity,
the physical vigour, the emotional depth of woman, forms also an
untranscendable circle, circumscribing with each successive generation
the limits of the expansion of the human race.[34]

Olive saw her picture of the 'over-producing' woman and the 'incompetence' of the modern mother as a purely scientific assessment, rooted in
a view that the speed of social change – which, for her, was a primarily
technological matter – was making it impossible for women really to train

their children. But again there was an inevitable ambiguity in this position, in that it could be read as a eugenicist plea for more selective breeding. The time would come, Olive felt, when child-bearing would come to be regarded as a 'lofty privilege' because it was so expensive, in terms of technical and moral resources, to rear a child.[35] Still, her advocacy of training for women to be fit for instructing the next generation contained no proposals for actual change; it was rousing rather than strategic. The condescension to 'incompetent' women (working-class or leisured parasite?) was in some way defused by the fact that her concern, unlike that of establishment figures who allocated blame, was rather to explain the 'great' historical forces acting on her own time.

Olive's position on women as mothers was less compromised than Havelock Ellis', who had been thinking about these issues for a long time. For a just society, Ellis believed, each sex must follow the 'laws of its own nature'.[36] A study of evolutionary patterns showed, he claimed, that: 'Woman breeds and tends; man provides; it remains so even when the spheres tend to overlap.' Fundamental 'feminine' characteristics – fairly similar to those proposed in the *Eugenics Review* – were associated with women's capacity to reproduce; and the biological imperative of motherhood and the debilitating effects of menstruation combined to prevent women from successfully competing with men in men's sphere. He argued for a moral equality based on the separation of roles; but he also believed that women should be better educated for motherhood, and proposed fairly detailed state involvement. Against the socialist tradition which, theoretically at least, favoured the socialization of housework and childcare, he believed that individual child-rearing was each mother's basic responsibility, and organized in this way with state support would best serve the interests of healthy childhood.

Olive disagreed with this position, again phrasing her own as a truth of evolution:

> Every attempt to sever the procreator and that which he creates is a distinct step of retrogression towards that savage condition in which the woman was supposed to be more nearly related to the child because her relation was more grossly palpable: scientific knowledge, and the necessities of developing human nature, will negative every such attempt.[37]

The notion of the inseparability of men and women in parenthood was atypical for her period. She reminded Ellis of the point in a letter in 1912, where she told him that to be a real mother – emotionally and intellectually – was the highest function in life, 'except to be a real father'.[38]

The basis of the difference between them was, in fact, derived from different uses of animal data. Ellis took his position from the 'laws of nature'; so did Olive. But in order to oppose the idea that the current division of labour was natural, she used different material. All forms of 'psychic variations', she stressed in *Woman and Labour*, were to be found in the animal world, giving examples of different forms of affection, courtship, care of the young among birds and mammals; she pointed to the existence of sex-parasitism in both male and female form in the lower animals. At the same time she acknowledged that variations existed as soon as one approached the sphere of reproduction itself, though not that of the 'intensity of initial sex instinct', and she returned to the passion of her description: of course there must be a 'distinct psychic attitude' between the

> man who, in an instant of light-hearted enjoyment, begets the infant . . . and the woman who bears it continuously for months within her body, and who gives birth to it in pain, and who, if it is to live, is compelled, or was in primitive times, to nourish it for months from the blood of her own being.[39]

None of this, however, should exonerate women from obligations in labour or government; she was merely arguing that women's specialness should not disinherit them. Similarly, where Ellis felt that sexual activities became abnormal when they interfered with the 'race-end of getting children', as lawyer Robert Parker had termed it in the Men and Women's Club, Olive always maintained that there were distinct ends in sexuality besides reproduction, indeed that the technical and social changes of modern civilization were such as to make it possible, for the first time in history, for sexual love to develop. Like the Men and Women's Club, too, Ellis considered female economic independence to be less important than moral equality, a position that Olive had never held: 'Let love bind you,' she wrote, 'not a common account in the bank.'[40] By this she meant that marriages in which the woman had no independent career or source of income were a form of bondage for both partners. But at the same time, Ellis saw that if women were to be fitted for their role as socializers they needed access to reliable contraception and abortion, a frankness in discussion which Olive never reached, though she did, apparently, contribute to Margaret Sanger's *Birth Control Review*.[41]

These, in a sense, were matters of detail. *Woman and Labour* appeared three years before the outbreak of World War One, and taken as a whole it became a powerful reference-point in the argument for a specifically female pacifism. Maude Royden, writing in 1916 about the prospects for international understanding, believed that it deepened women's conviction of the horrors of war. 'Expressing with a noble idealism the right attitude of women towards war,' Royden wrote, 'Olive Schreiner gave to an emotion its philosophy.' It was the phrase, 'No woman says of a human body: "It is nothing",' which,

> like the whole chapter in which it appears, became the classic of the Woman's Movement. It was believed to express the true, the inevitable attitude of women as a sex, whether in or outside the progressive ranks. It was assumed to be so 'natural' to them, that to put power in their hands, was to forge a weapon against war. It was not denied that they might still feel that war might in some cases still be a national duty; but it was believed with conviction that women, from their very nature, would approach the question with an unspeakable reluctance, that war would appear to them in all its naked horror, shorn of glory, that they would be free from the 'war fever' to which men so easily fall victims.[42]

The exposition of women as a force against war was variously argued. Some, like Maude Royden, believed that to work for women's rights was to work against militarism. Here the destructive creed of militarism was juxtaposed with the spiritual force of the women's movement; and women were implicitly seen as creative and constructive. Royden's reasoning was that the Woman's Movement was an assertion of moral force as the supreme governing force in the world; women had understood that a claim to share in government could not be entertained if government rested on physical force, so had 'rightly based their demand on the great principle that government rests upon consent'. Thus they were 'forever asserting a principle of which war is a perpetual denial'.

For all the force of this argument about women's natural pacifism it was always to be a minority position. The suffrage movement in Britain was split by the war and its majority support taken into war work by Mrs

Pankhurst. Olive's radical suffragette friend Emmeline Pethick Lawrence, although she acknowledged that the movement had indeed been split, nevertheless thought that the international solidarity that had been developing between women 'could not be shaken even by the fact that men of many nations were at war. The principles that had inspired our great struggle for women's emancipation came back to remembrance.' Was not the main vocation of all women one and the same – the 'guardianship and nurture of the race'?[43]

If women were natural pacifists in consequence of their place as guardians and nurturers, then surely they could influence society in the direction of a morally progressive 'soul-culture'. Ellen Key, in *War, Peace and the Future*, addressed herself to women in their role as mothers and caretakers of animals and the elderly – not mentioning their work outside the home – and reminded them of the 'age-old division of labour' – that women gave life, men took each other's. A soul-culture, to be striven for ceaselessly, was the only basis on which women could slowly hinder future war and further future peace. Like Olive's, her ideas expressed an eternalism about history and culture, the conviction that the new spirit among women was emerging among the educated women of the race. Rejecting the use of ideas about the survival of the fittest as a justification for domination and slaughter, Key believed that mothers should educate their children in the naturalness of cooperation; she also hoped, again rather romantically, for a world conference on motherhood:

> The concern of the two great preserving and upholding powers of life –
> the mother and the earth – must some day be given the foremost place
> of attention in the community.[44]

Woman and Labour may have been as influential as it was in the early years of the century because its ideas about war were rooted in a determinist logic about the inevitability of change in women's role. In that Olive failed, at least in the published text, to take cognizance of women's growing participation in industry, Olive's argument could be used to endorse this new role of women as 'scientific' educators, able to take 'informed' decisions for the community as well as the home. Her ideas about women's special relation to life could be invoked to legitimate the early twentieth-century version of the old 'two spheres' position – namely the idea that the collective influence of women in the home could be as nationally important as men's in the public domain. It was a departure from the mid-Victorian assertion that each woman belonged in the privacy of her husband's 'walled garden';[45] the new role of women after the turn of the century and the war was part of a new consumerism.

In work on the emergence of woman as a consumer in the United States, Christopher Lasch points to contemporary social concern over the discontented woman of leisure, seeing the influence of Olive's term parasitism on other writers as illustrative of this trend.[46] He suggests that it was in answer to the problem of the emptiness of their lives that a 'progressive' position on women emerged: with the shift from domestic labour to factory production of domestic goods, the argument ran, women's role became primarily that of a consumer, and they should learn to use this new position as a strategy through which to influence and finally control the national destiny. This Lasch terms a pseudo-feminism, for it conceived of family management as a profession, with women's future lying in the vote *and* the home. Equally, when feminists asserted women's right of entry to the world outside the home, he continues, they tended to argue that women would bring with them special qualities. Olive was no different. She too felt that women had a particular instinct for 'conserving and preserving'; and that as the ages to come would be not mainly destructive but conservative, women would have an all-important part to play.[47] It left her with a concept of 'the woman' which was at odds with her demand for freedom of work and self-expression.

Indeed one testimony to the confusion about the 'new woman' in the period before World War One is that the assumptive framework of both feminist and non-feminist argument tended to be the same. The view that the family had lost its economic functions, for example, was extremely widespread at the end of the nineteenth century, and not just among feminists; it did not necessarily lead to feminist conclusions. There is also confusion in the writing of the period. The terms female, feminine and feminist are rarely defined by contemporaries or indeed by later commentators. Arabella Kenealy, an English writer on sex questions whose *Feminism and Sex-Extinction* was written explicitly in response to *Woman and Labour*, managed to catch at one of these problems amid a mass of anti-feminist dogma. She pointed to an anomaly in the feminist argument: on the one hand, feminists asserted with great pride that motherhood was woman's most valuable function and 'her greatest claim on the community' in the days of barbarism (the 'simple society' that Olive had characterized in *Woman and Labour*); but at the same time they denied that it was her most important function in civilization. The eloquent defence of maternity could be confusing.

Woman and Labour was rooted not in the feminist activism of the pre-war period but in the evolutionism of the 1880s. Olive's ideas were developed in relation to Karl Pearson's, and though she was critical of his, and never arrived either at his eugenicism or at his theory of state organization, the influence of the Men and Women's Club ran very deep. 'My sex paper is purely scientific in principle,' she wrote to Ellis in 1887. 'It is an attempt to apply the theory of evolution to elucidate sex problems.'[48]

In April 1886 she sent Pearson a sketch of her proposed work on sex, a classic of evolutionism and presumably the outlines of the work whose first chapters, she claimed, were completed by 1888. The whole of the first volume was to be a consideration of comparative historical material, juxtaposing 'savages' and the 'modern civilised world'. He replied, full of enthusiasm for the project:

> The field is so novel that one wants a first class philological power to get at the facts that one requires. Otherwise, one would just slip the very points one wants. Every step I have taken in early history shows me how easy it has been for people to miss the key to the whole primitive system. I seem to have got now all the early customs, all the extraordinary practices of witchcraft, primitive law and philology into harmony, and most absurd things have become significant and intelligible. . . .
>
> Now what I propose is that when it is sifted and organised I hand it over in the mass to you, and you make what you like or can of it. Such a work as you have planned wants the entire energies of an individual; mine partly by calling, partly by wilfulness, must perforce go off in other channels . . . Add to this that a book which shall strike a blow for women on strong scientific grounds would be ten times more valuable if it came from a woman, above all from one who has sufficient emotions left to be capable of influencing her fellow men.[49]

By the mid-Eighties, when Olive was in contact with him, Pearson had formulated much of his intellectual framework in biometry and statistics, and there is indeed a sense in which she wrote more from the response to Darwin than from within a feminist movement. She followed Pearson in seeing Darwin as a force for scientific work, freeing men from the 'fetters' and 'bondage' of the Christian model of the origins of life.[50] In that she was concerned with axioms of evolution, moreover, she was looking for a social model which would allow for progress and perfectibility. From Pearson she absorbed a peculiarly all-embracing concept of science as well, in which the term had connotations far wider than the practice of science itself. For Pearson,

> science, no less than theology or philosophy, is the field for personal influence, for the creation of enthusiasm; and for the establishment of ideals of self-discipline and self-development. No man becomes great in science from the mere force of intellect, unguided and unaccompanied by what really amounts to moral force. Behind the intellectual capacity there is the devotion to truth, the deep sympathy with nature, and the determination to sacrifice all minor matters to one great end.[51]

Science demanded and created a world of morality by means of which individual choice became possible. But science as such was also to provide a way into moral strategies for the future. It was in lectures to the South Place Chapel in the early Eighties that Pearson laid out his basic position.

What was man's relation to the whole, he asked? Religion grew up in answer to this questioning, but mythology had supplied the place of true knowledge. This latter was to be attained by

> the rejection of all myth explanation, the frank acceptance of all ascertained truths with regard to the relation of the finite to the infinite, [which] is what I term *freethought* or true religious knowledge.

Freethought was difficult to attain, he believed; perhaps more of an ideal than an actuality. The freethinker must possess the highest knowledge of his day:

> he must stand on the slope of his century and mark what the past has achieved . . . still better if he himself is working for the increase of human knowledge or for its spread among his fellows.[52]

Few individuals could contribute to the stock of accumulating knowledge, he acknowledged, and it was an explicitly élitist position. For if few individuals were so placed as to make a contribution, then few would enjoy the 'discovery of new truth' which provided the 'highest pleasure of which the human mind is capable'. It was the basic contradiction of moral socialism – the notion that social progress would flow from the example of morally superior individuals.*

Science had thus become bound up with notions of personal integrity and the advanced individual. Similarly, Pearson's view of the woman question was that it called for study by impartial minds, rather than platform appeals, for social problems would not be solved if they were subject to the 'passion and prejudice' of the market place. The 'scarcely perceptible influence of enthusiasm of the study', moreover, might have more effect over the centuries than the 'strong eloquence' of the street. Such political gradualism, steeped as it was in Darwin and Spencer, was integral to an evolutionary model of social change.

Olive, too, used the vocabulary of an evolutionist social science. But – and this was inevitable – scientific terms have a confused status in *Woman and Labour*. Her phrasing was intentionally 'mathematical': the contraction of women's domestic sphere, for example, was 'exactly proportional' to the advance of civilization.[53] At the same time the term 'civilization' remained a fairly subjective one. Her ideas about the dominance of race and class never or rarely applied to contemporary society. For her notion of change, of order out of chaos, was predicated on an assumption of continual progress from the beginning of time to the present day, just as it more or less defined civilization, as Spencer had done, as being a function of an increase in the 'degree of complexity' of the society.[54] She was thus unable to move outside the boundaries of a classically Victorian notion of progress. Is it perhaps significant that of the body of material she amassed for *Woman and Labour* most was used to demonstrate the inevitability of such progress, and that the material on the conditions of women of her day, though it may have been lost, was not reinstated? She grasped a good deal about the conditions under

* Engaging in the controversy over socialism and natural selection in the eighteen-nineties, Pearson also gave full expression to the scientific racism of contemporary anthropology. Here the dominant issue was whether the 'inferior races' could legitimately aspire to improvement. Hence the imperialism of his formulation: 'No thoughtful socialist, so far as I am aware, would object to cultivate Uganda *at the expense of its present occupants* if Lancashire were starving. Only he would have this done directly and consciously, and not by way of missionaries and exploiting companies.' He wrote this only six years before the outraged letter to Olive about her partisan stand during the Boer war. See above, p. 242, Marvin Harris, *The Rise of Anthropological Theory* (1969), especially Chapter 4, 'The Rise of Racial Determinism', pp. 80–107, and Karl Pearson, 'Socialism and Natural Selection', *Fortnightly Review* 56 (1894), p. 6.

which working women were living, but her framework could not integrate it.

But if her model constrained her in the same way as Pearson's, her politics did not. It was far more radical. Where Pearson was scathing about Mary Wollstonecraft, regarding her as over-emotional,[55] Olive saw her work as basic to the feminist position, and tried hard to finish her introduction to Wollstonecraft's *Vindication of the Rights of Woman*. Cronwright, who deposited it at the Albany Museum in Grahamstown after Olive's death, marked it 'not for publication'; he considered it had been 'dashed off and left; it was read with great difficulty', and 'some words beat the typist'.[56] The manuscript does not really end, and, interestingly, it is not really an evaluation of Wollstonecraft at all.

Olive remarked that the *Vindication* appeared to have had little influence on the women's movement, that it lacked genius, that it would convince no one;[57] it was a somewhat brusque beginning. At the same time Wollstonecraft was 'one of ourselves', for she had seen the necessity and end of the women's question: that change in women's position revolutionized society, and that the movement was not of class against class but of sex towards sex. She went on from there to make a rather hurried résumé of the ideas about human evolution that she had been working on in the Men and Women's Club, rehearsing the view that women and men, after a period of complete differentiation in agrarian systems supported by slavery, were at last coming nearer one another.

In this introduction Olive presented herself as an educated observer of primitive society, but she also took as exemplary the strengths of the African woman in a description of a conversation almost identical to that reported in the published introduction to *Woman and Labour*. Here her sympathy was with the African as a woman rather than as a black – she was writing in the eighteen-eighties – and she tried out a concept of 'social instinct', an attempt at an explanation of submission which was more than individual. It was a notion of a collective culture that operated independently of the woman's capacity to express it, and it was in the context of that silence that the woman demonstrated her strength. How could the African kraal be explained, where the man lay, apparently lazily, and the woman toiled unceasingly?

What lies behind this awful calm, this dead resigned nature like that of man to death? I think it is even more than a mere perception, that, under her social circumstances it is as hopeless for her to strive against oppression, as it would be for one wave in the sea to rise up against the tidal current. I believe that deeper yet than this, lies the perception that it is her duty to *submit*. I believe the social instinct which formulates right and wrong, distinctly acts within her, and that her 'moral sense', unable as she may be to formulate it exactly, acts as a mighty force upon her urging her to submission.

Although she identified herself as an intellectual worker she never assumed the political disengagement of a pure theorist. Her sense of herself as a feminist was always near the surface, as in her review of Pearson's *The Ethic of Freethought* in 1889. This was a collection of his lectures and papers from the previous five years, ranging from the development of social theory in medieval Germany to the modern women's question. She considered it to be the 'most valuable contribution' to the solution of the woman's problem since J. S. Mill's *Subjection of Women*, and liked the integration of work on women and on other themes, but she had a pertinent point to make:

The book is published at 12s., practically a prohibitive price, especially to the woman public, and there is nothing in the title of the work to suggest that it deals with this question.[58]

She also disagreed with Pearson, who had adopted Johann Bachofen's theory of mother-right, on the question of matriarchy. She never elaborated her objection, but referred to it several times. In her review of Pearson's *Ethic*, after a lengthy peroration on the diversity of opinions on women's emancipation and history, she stated simply that she disagreed with the cause of women's subjection as Pearson presented it. Pearson maintained his position relatively unchanged; in *The Chances of Death*, published in 1897, he recounted having traced 'Mother-Age civilisation' in folklore, philology, and fairy-tales in order to demonstrate that 'primitive women had a status widely divergent from that of woman in the present or in the patriarchal age'. Olive doubted there was evidence to support the theory of primitive matriarchy,[59] and tended to tease Pearson about it, even when she was back in South Africa in 1890. Could she investigate the Africans for him? She was learning one of their languages so as to do this. She could tell him 'of the wonderful relics of what you would call "the mother age" which are to be found among them'.[60] She had always wanted to investigate the Africans; perhaps the fact that she had grown up alongside the 'primitive' cultures social theorists were so prone to categorize, and had a sense of the subordination of their females, enabled her to be wary of the matriarchal model. Describing the name for the external organs of sex in an unmarried girl in an African tribe – 'your-father's-oxen' – she noted that the word father meant as much ruler, chief, king; oxen meant *all* wealth.

> Another kaffir word *ky* means the sex organs of the woman, but is used to mean woman. Suppose the same happened to the first – then we'd have a word whose two roots were 'ruler and property, signifying woman' . . . I feel so strongly the way in which the early history of the race is buried in words, but I feel also the great difficulty there is in digging it out.[61]

She reminded Pearson of the investigator's task: if she returned to the Cape, she wrote to him in 1886, she would send a paper for the Club 'being the views of Hottentot, Kaffir, Bushmen and Basuto men *and women*'.[62]

Olive's views of sexuality were developed at a time when female sexuality began to be divorced from the maternal 'instinct'. It was only at the end of the century that changes in material conditions – in particular, through advances in contraceptive technique and the management of childbirth and venereal disease – made it possible for the question of sexual autonomy even to be considered.[63] Earlier in the century feminists had accepted the idea of the sexual drive as being present in both sexes, but as a 'base' instinct to be kept in check by the higher, moral instincts. It had also been felt that women were congenitally less sexual than men, and that female sexuality, being weak, was easily controlled by an act of will. In this sense feminists followed the orthodox bourgeois view of male sexuality as a driving force in which women acquiesced with no really active sexual consciousness of their own. In the writings of feminists like doctors Elizabeth Garrett Anderson and Barbara Bodichon and suffragette Millicent Fawcett, for example, there is no evidence that sex might be pleasurable; harmony in a relationship was described as a matter of emotional, political or intellectual rapport. Still, and as recent analytic work on Victorian sexuality shows, one cannot conclude either that feminists (or women in general) were ignorant of their sexuality, or that the 'prudish puritanity we lend to the Victorians, and rather lazily apply to all classes of Victorian society' was not a 'middle class view of the middle class ethos'.*

For women to assert that their sexuality was normal was to take up an emphatically radical stance, for they were challenging the social dominance of the medical profession. By the end of the Victorian period the assertion began to be made. It ran counter to the ideas of a book like *The Evolution of Sex* – one in Ellis' Contemporary Science series – which believed that menstruation bordered on the pathological; one of the first textbooks on the physiology of reproduction, twenty years later in 1910, maintained this idea. In the eighteen-nineties, for example, the Women's Emancipation Union began to advocate sex education and distribute pamphlets on the subject. Later *The Freewoman*, brought out in 1911 and committed to creating a 'new morality', included articles on homosexuality as well as feminism.[64]

Olive herself acknowledged the power of female sexuality, and actually felt that sexual isolation was 'more terrible' for women than for men, though she did not explain in what way. In 1911 she wrote to Ellis from Cape Town about a friend of hers

> who thinks it's wrong for people, even if married, to have any sex relations with each other except just when they want to make a child. She says her husband feels just the same! I would base all my sex teachings to children and young people on the beauty and sacredness and importance of sex.

It was one of her simplest statements, and the least caught up in the vicissitudes of her own sexual life.

> Sex intercourse is the great sacrament of life . . . but it may be the most beautiful sacrament between two souls without any thought of children.[65]

But she was appalled by what she saw of *The Freewoman*: it ought to be called *The Licentious Male*, she felt.

> Almost all the articles are by men and not by women. It's got the tone of the most licentious females or prostitutes. It's unclean, and sex is so

---

* John Fowles, *The French Lieutenant's Woman* (1969), p. 261. Fowles' novel, set in England in the 1860s, fictionalizes this debate.

beautiful. It can be discussed scientifically, or philosophically, or poetically.[66]

Indeed, she always maintained that her thoughts on women's equality and subjection should not be interpreted as an advocacy of sexual promiscuity. She demanded simply that the relationship between men and women be freed from its corrupt, mercenary dimension – whether economic dependence in marriage or the degradation of prostitution, lust in place of love.

Further, she believed that sexuality, like other laws of nature, followed an evolutionary pattern. She suggested her model to Karl Pearson in 1886:

As war, famine and the hardship of life diminish, the number of infants who die become very small: and from this cause alone *apart from any others* the demand upon the sex system to produce becomes necessarily small. May not the surplus power naturally adapt itself to aesthetic uses?[67]

Human beings were to be distinguished from the 'most lowly animal and vegetable forms of life' in which sex served only to ensure the continuation of the physical stream of life. The sex relation between men and women, she felt, had in it

latent, other, and even higher forms, of creative energy and life-dispensing power, and . . . its history on earth has only begun. As the first wild rose when it hung from its stem with its centre of stamens and pistils and its single whorl of pale petals, had only begun its course, and was destined, as the ages passed, to develop stamen upon stamen and petal upon petal, till it assumed a hundred forms of joy and beauty.[68]

At its most rhapsodic Olive's writing about sex bears comparison with that of birth control reformer Marie Stopes, whose prose in *Married Love* had some of the same elevated tone.* For she was a determined opponent of celibacy.[69]

* cf. Stopes' conclusion to *Married Love:* 'When knowledge and love together go to the making of each marriage, the joy of *that new unit, the pair*, will reach from the physical foundations of its bodies to the heavens where its head is crowned with stars.' 1918, p. 113.

But her sexual evolutionism was as élitist as Pearson's socialism, and can only be described as racialist:

> Were it possible to place a company of the most highly evolved human females – George Sands, Sophia Kovaleskys, or even the average cultured females of a highly evolved race . . . on an island where the only males were savages of the Fugean type [*sic*] . . . it is undoubted fact that, so great would be the horror felt by the females towards them, that the race would become extinct.
>
> . . . A Darwin, a Schiller, a Keats, though all men capable of the strongest sex emotion and of the most durable sex affections, would probably be untouched by any emotion but horror, cast into the company of a circle of Bushmen females.[70]

In fact there is no perspective in *Woman and Labour* on a distinct female sexuality. This was consistent with the politics of Olive's critique of sexuality as a whole. It was the institutions of marriage and prostitution – interdependent and mutually reinforcing – which bound women's bodies. Once freed from the constraints of economic dependence, sexual love would be able to flow. Her notion of female sexuality was as much bound up with 'masculine' notions of vigour and vitality, with virility even – when she applauded the 'conquering Teutons', whose proud, monogamous women had never been subjugated – as her picture of women's relation to maternity was based on the 'feminine' qualities of tenderness and compassion. Her description of the possibility of sexual freedom that modern civilization was creating was both mystical and undifferentiated: where Ellis considered female sexuality more problematic than male and, therefore, a priority for discussion – though he came to conservative conclusions – Olive never separated the two. In a way the force of her endorsement of female sexuality may have been restrained by the demands of 'science':

> We've got to try and see what sex is exactly. For example there are three modes of reproduction in some animals: why has the sexual conquered so universally?[71]

Sex, reproduction, the sexual instinct, the 'initial attraction of sex', the aesthetic power of sexuality: she confused reproduction and pleasure over and over again. The notion of objectivity in some way served to defuse the feminism, though never consistently so, as when she used the information she had gathered from women to refute some of Pearson's ideas. She had collected a lot of evidence from married women, and 'I cannot doubt that you are wrong in saying that women feel any [underlined twice] dislike to intercourse with their husbands during pregnancy'. One woman told her that 'during the whole period of pregnancy she had the same physical desire as a woman has just after her periods! Do men feel repugnancy to a woman at this time? I do not know.'[72] Similarly she had asked prostitutes about suckling, and found that 'both during pregnancy and suckling no difference of feeling is shown in men towards them, nor do they expect less money'.[73]

But though she inquired of her women friends about their sexual life, she gave no special attention to homosexuality in her own society, even though she was so close to Edward Carpenter, who was homosexual; to Havelock Ellis, who investigated contemporary 'inversion'; and knew Edith Ellis, who was a lesbian. She attempted only to rationalize the male homosexuality of ancient Greece as a product of a society made rotten by parasitism. Equally, there is no understanding of sexuality as, in itself, conflicted. Her model of difficulty in the relations of men and women was invariably related to the 'social disco-ordination' of the 'life of our age'. She had only a rudimentary concept of intra-psychic conflict: she suggested that the unrest and suffering peculiar to her own time was also caused by 'conflict going on within the individual himself', but it was to be explained by the inevitability of suffering for the individual who 'first treads down the path which the bulk of humanity will ultimately follow'.[74] Leadership was the reward for pain.

Olive could not have read Freud, although translations of his writings were being made when she was in England at the end of her life, and a work like *Woman and Labour* must be seen in the context of a crucial intellectual transition. Olive was writing at a time when Freud's theories of the unconscious and of infantile sexuality were a very recent source of outrage to a culture which accorded religion great prescriptive powers in matters of morality. In her notion of the advanced individual carrying the responsibilities of the race, Olive had, in a sense, simply secularized this model. On the other hand, it was not the case that she addressed herself to a wholly different range of phenomena from Freud. She prefaced *African Farm* with a quote from Alexis de Tocqueville that made the same point as *The Interpretation of Dreams*:[75]

We must see the first images which the external world casts upon the dark mirror of his mind . . . if we would understand the prejudices, the habits, and the passions that will rule his life. The entire man is, so to speak, to be found in the cradle of the child.

Interesting, too, is her enthusiasm for Schopenhauer. Looking at his predecessors in the recognition of unconscious mental processes, Freud stressed that

> It was not psychoanalysis . . . which took the first step. There are renowned names among the philosophers, above all the great thinker Schopenhauer, whose unconscious 'Will' is equivalent to the instincts in the mind as seen by psychoanalysis.[76]

Olive read Schopenhauer's work and a *Life* during the eighteen-eighties, and wrote to Ellis, amazed, about his effect on her:

> If I ever read him, or even knew before I came to England, one would say I had copied whole ideas in the *African Farm* and *From Man to Man* from him. There is one passage of his on the search for philosophic truth that reads like a paraphrase of my allegory in the *African Farm*.[77]

More paradoxical, however, is the fact that although Ellis and Freud corresponded over a number of years, Ellis seems never to have referred to his work in letters to Olive. It may possibly have been intentional, although very few letters from the later period exist, for Freud and Ellis were in disagreement on important issues. Their work overlapped: both had been influenced by meetings with French neurologist and psychiatrist Jean Charcot in Paris, Ellis in 1884, Freud the following year. Ellis had known about Freud's work from 1893; writing in an American periodical in 1895 he gave an account of Breuer and Freud's *Studies in Hysteria* in which he accepted Freud's views about the sexual aetiology of hysteria.[78] This was reprinted eight years later in the second volume of his own *Studies in the Psychology of Sex*. In 1904, as the *Studies* proceeded in publication, Ellis devoted several pages to what he called Freud's 'fascinating and really important researches'.

But the differences were significant. Where Freud made the notion of an original bisexual constitution a central part of his theory, Ellis went only so far as to recognize 'elements' of inter-sexuality in the individual. If homosexuality arose through the suppression of the heterosexual element as the Freudian model of the Oedipus complex seemed to suggest, then the possibility of similarly regarding heterosexuality as the product of the suppression of the homosexual element was opened up – a position that would have been as intolerable to Olive as it was to Ellis. For Ellis, committed to the congenital basis of sexual behaviour, Freud's theory could not be part of any 'rational biological scheme',[79] and by World War One he had come to feel that Freud was an artist, not a scientist. He declined to join the London Branch Society of the International Psychoanalytical Association when it was founded in 1913.[80]

By 1911, when *Woman and Labour* was published, Freud's work was sufficiently developed for him to provide a conceptual structure for psychoanalysis as a whole. Olive's model of sexuality was part of a different stream of thought – the progressive, evolutionary, historical – in which concepts of repression, sublimation and the unconscious were entirely absent. Sexuality, once its social distortion was removed, was an unchanging given; only a free monogamy could make historical sense. The naturalness of heterosexuality was so basic to her thought as to need no emphasis. Her picture of human sexuality belonged, in fact, to the Men and Women's Club, and the Darwinism of their insistence on a sexual instinct. Breuer and Freud had challenged the existence of an instinct based on an animal model of a natural goal and a natural object, postulating a set of drives, basically unconscious, out of which normal sexuality developed, and from which perversions could develop if sexuality became fixated or regressed to one of the earlier stages or organizations it had to pass through.[81] Repression was one of the vicissitudes of the drives, and the system of the unconscious its site. For Freud, then, the concept of conflict replaced the concept of instinct, that pattern of adaptation that was a mix of morality and nature.[82] By comparison with Freud, Olive, in her 'political' writing on sexuality, lacked any substantive theory of individual psychology.

Not that she denied the existence of an unconscious mind of some sort. She wrote to Ellis about her thought processes, wondering at the apparent existence of a range of thinking quite beyond her conscious control.[83] But in that she termed this process 'unconscious cerebration' she was referring to a proposition within contemporary physiology that was to be explained purely in terms of the reflex functions of the brain.* Where Freud

---

* These were the ideas of William B. Carpenter, expounded in 1874 in a textbook for medical students, *Principles of Mental Physiology*. Olive may have been introduced to them by Bryan Donkin, who felt Carpenter's work had been grossly neglected.

postulated a dynamic relationship of conflict between conscious and unconscious needs, Olive had recourse only to an entirely neutral model of benevolent cooperation. In Carpenter's words:

> In the habitually well-disciplined nature, this unconscious operation of the Brain, in balancing for itself all . . . considerations, in putting all in order (so to speak), and in working out the result is far more likely to lead us to a good and true decision [on any important subject], than continual discussion and argumentation.[84]

As a model of personality it also accorded the will a high, independent status as an 'interior fact', placing it at the interface of mind and body. Most importantly, it emphatically assumed the ego to be a free agent. It followed logically from such a position that the individual, motivated to progressive intellectual ends, should be able to accomplish them by virtue of the controlling power of the will. For although Olive saw progress as a social inevitability, she also had to suggest a resolution to the difficulties facing the morally superior individual in a society that was not yet free. In that she relied entirely on the power of self-denial and the memory of earlier social advance to do this, she remained a basically late-Victorian thinker, untouched by ideas about the relationship of rational and irrational forces in the personality which, however contentious, go some way to explaining the individual psyche.

CHAPTER EIGHT

World War One and Old Age

Olive left South Africa for England in 1913 with a sense of her life coming to an end. She was fifty-eight. She had sorted out and burned many of her papers and letters, including all Ellis', even though it had been 'hard work'.[1] It was because she had no daughter to leave them to, and she didn't want to leave anything that could cause pain to anyone she had known; she would never have been lonely, she felt, if her little girl had lived.[2] Cronwright refused to leave his business; competition was keen and he had decided that nothing would make him pull it up by the roots.[3] She had gloomy forebodings about leaving him, and South Africa. Her brother Will and her friends had pressured her to leave on the strength of her account of her illness; she was now finding it difficult to leave her armchair even to do her few household duties. Will suggested that she take Emily Hobhouse with her, but Olive adamantly refused; Emily was a dear good woman but 'one of those masterful women who quietly crushes everyone who comes near her'.[4]

Before she left she tried to assert her financial independence. When Will offered to pay her boat fare she wanted to give him the Prelude to her unfinished novel *From Man to Man* in exchange; she had been offered £300 for it, and if Will paid her £200, he would be sure to recover more than that sum after her death. She could not borrow the money because she might die and be unable to repay it.[5] In the end, however, Cronwright appears to have paid the fare. She made her will in December 1913, just before she sailed.

She was *en route* to Italy for an 'electrical' heart treatment which had helped a friend. The voyage was exhausting – after the first day she never left her berth – but she was cheered by the 'great pile of letters from

English friends' that she received when the boat docked at Madeira.[6] Alice Corthorn, whom she had known as a medical student in the Eighties, was going to meet her at Southampton and Constance Lytton was coming to London to spare Olive the journey to Kenilworth. Once in London, she was 'overrun' with invitations to lunches, dinners and teas which she wasn't fit enough to accept; she did, however, attend a reception in her own honour. One hundred and fifty people gathered at the Lyceum, Piccadilly, on 29 December 1913, and although Olive declared that a speech was impossible, she did say a few words about her optimism about the twentieth century which touched and delighted her audience.[7] Ellis came up from Cornwall to see her, Carpenter spent New Year's Eve with her, and there was a reunion between Olive, Constance Lytton and Adela Villiers Smith; it was sixteen years since the three had been together.[8]

This visit to London, and the attention she received, did provide a temporary relief from the increasingly depressing realities of her life: her ill health, her inability to work, the deaths of family members and friends, and her growing awareness of ageing and fears of becoming a burden to others. A few weeks after the reception, when she was in Italy, Ellis wrote to say that the papers were full of accounts of the dinner they gave her. She wrote excitedly to Will: 'one paper comments on "the very youthful appearance of the author of the *S.A.F.*" Who would believe a newspaper after that! But I felt so happy when I was in London. I might have been 16.'[9]

Feelings of being sixteen were very rare now. For the most part Olive was aware that she had lost a centre to her life, and it was more than a personal loss. She was in Europe throughout World War One, she with her faith in 'progress', but with her whole historical model undermined by the 'savagery' of the war.[10] She felt entirely alone, and it was a solitude combining the sense of absolute political isolation with the necessity of coming to terms with death. These connections were illustrated in a very sad letter to Ellis in September 1914, written after a visit to Eastbourne, the town to which her brother Fred had brought her on her arrival in England more than thirty years before. She had seen Fred's grave and remarked on the 'ghosts of my dead youth', then turned to a cry against the war: 'Why has one always to stand alone? Why can one never go with the tide of the mob?'[11] She felt let down politically by many of the people who had been important to her at different times: Pearson was a supporter of Empire; although Carpenter was a pacifist he still felt that the war would 'bring the Kingdom of Heaven';[12] she considered Ellis to be hypocritical over German executions in Belgium when he made no comment on English atrocities in Ceylon.[13] It seemed that her friends were going against the very opinions they had endorsed in her 'The Sunlight Lay Across My Bed' twenty years before.[14] The worst of it, she wrote to Ellis in December 1914, was the sense of being cut off from one's own fellows – 'the people who know me and know I condemn the war – and all wars'.[15] She hoped then that it was her last year, she felt so broken.

But Olive did not die for another six years, and they were years of prolonged physical and emotional distress. Early in the war she summed up her situation in a letter to Cronwright that was more resigned than almost any other she was to write from now on:

It is funny why I have always to be out of everything. The day will never come when I can be in the stream. Something in my nature prevents it I suppose. Sometimes I don't seem to be alive at all, but only creeping about in a ghastly dream. No one wants me. I'm [in] no relation with the life or thought in England or Africa or anywhere else.[16]

On her arrival in London at the end of 1913 Olive had been anxious to see a heart specialist, an ex-partner of Dr Brown's. The man did not find her heart seriously affected and described her attitude as irrational. She left London soon afterwards, but once in Alassio developed severe internal pains that were diagnosed as kidney stone. It was to Ellis, as in the past, that she wrote about her health, though now her letters were more controlled than those of the Eighties: there was almost a neutrality in her awareness of the possibility of heart failure. She knew, simply, that she was 'walking on thin ice'.[17] Once better she left for Florence and spent a month there under one Prof. Carloni. Carloni's treatment seemed to help, but it was unpleasant and dear: she went to his consulting room every morning and got back shortly after noon, but she was so exhausted by it that she couldn't walk again for several hours. More painful, almost, was her sense of frustration – 'I don't seem to be able to die and I can't work, which is the thing I want to live for'[18] – and she asked Ellis to visit her.

Ellis was not especially anxious to go, but Edith persuaded him: she felt he 'owed it to so old and dear a friend not to neglect her wishes' and that he would never forgive himself if something happened to her. Edith, by her own account, had had to fight much illness herself and perhaps she understood Olive's needs fairly well; Ellis, however, was basically preoccupied with Edith's forthcoming lecture tour in the United States and the improvement in their own relationship: he wrote later that it was the 'honeymoon at the end of [their] life together', and Edith was obviously much more important to him than Olive. Accordingly, he writes about the Italian visit with some restraint. He found Olive in a 'large, dull cosmopolitan hotel' which he would never have chosen for himself, spent ten days with her, and returned via an 'easy and pleasant tour' of some other Italian cities.[19]

Olive returned to London in April 1914, wrote in somewhat elevated style to Cronwright about the infinite joy of Beethoven's Ninth, and then went to Bad Nauheim in Germany, optimistic that the baths would do her good. Here she was with Will – also taking the waters – and her health improved; but she had to leave hurriedly when war broke out in August. She and Will made their way to the Netherlands separately[20] and took boats from Amsterdam to London; Olive was dismayed at the cold and wet journey, the boat so crowded that passengers could not lie down. 'War is hell,' she wrote to Ellis when she was back in London.[21]

Once back in London Olive began having difficulty getting rooms, and she asked Ellis and Edith to let her know if they came across any cheap hotels that would take someone with a German name. Adela Smith found one place for her, in Manchester Square, but Olive's stay there lasted two days. She received this explanation from the manageress:

> When your friend Mrs Smith came here about your room, she did not mention that your name was Mrs Schreiner, and as I find this is either German or Austrian I wish to say that we accommodate only British and American subjects in this hotel. I regret that this should be so, but I think you will understand the reason from the state of affairs in this country at the present time.[22]

'Of course I took a taxi and my things and left at once,' Olive wrote to Ellis. She found a much more expensive place, in Kensington Palace Mansions, and remained there ten months even though she was apparently very poor; Cronwright says he sent her money every year while she was in

Europe.[23] The experience with landladies and hotels haunted her correspondence: 'Oh Emily,' she wrote to Emily Hobhouse, 'the worst of war is not the death on the battle fields; it is the meanness, the cowardice, the hatred it awakens.' She had tried another place in Chelsea, she told her, very nice and cheap, with a sweet refined-looking woman letting the rooms; when she gave her name she was asked if it was not German. Olive explained that she was a British subject born in South Africa, that her father was a naturalized British subject, and so on. The woman became abusive, and Olive, 'feeling so ill and worn out ... dropped into a chair and burst out crying', but, her letter continued, 'it seemed so contemptibly weak of me'.*[24]

Her loneliness and her feeling that 'only death gives an end' were expressed in letters to Ellis, Emmeline Pethick Lawrence and Adela Smith in England, to her suffragette friend Anna Purcell in South Africa and occasionally to Cronwright.† She was anxious to make contact with Dollie Radford, one of Eleanor Marx's close friends, to talk about Eleanor's last years; they met towards the end of 1914 but there is no record of the encounter. Otherwise she was more or less on her own, feeling there was no one left to write for, and she could not embark on a paper or a book. For the first time in her life, she lost confidence in her ability with letters, apologizing to Will's wife Fan for one that she deemed 'stupid' and describing herself on one occasion to Adela Smith as 'an uninteresting old person'.[25] Her letters became shorter and less

---

* In 1923 Constance Lytton took lodgings that Olive had had duriug her years in London. 'The landlady was dedicated to Olive Schreiner, and prepared to welcome any friend of hers. The room was large, airy and comfortable ...' This may have been Kensington Palace Mansions or 9 Porchester Place, in which Olive spent nearly three years, and which Cronwright praised on seeing it in 1920. Whichever house it was, the experience was unusual. Lady Constance Lytton, *Letters* (1925), p. 263.

† Olive never seems seriously to have contemplated suicide. She mentioned it in a letter to Ellis in April 1915 in connection with the 'atmosphere of hate and resentment from those to whom you have done nothing that blights your soul', but a letter the following year, again to Ellis, sounds a more characteristic note, in terms both of her work and of the old division between body and mind. Olive was replying to Ellis' reservations about prescribing opium:

'I suppose you wouldn't write me the order because you're afraid I may kill myself, but it always seems such a cowardly thing to do; one wants to defy God to the last bit, to show him that if he can conquer one's body he can't conquer one's mind. I never wanted so much to live as now, because I *must* just must finish my little peace and war work.'

London, 30 April 1915, *Letters*, p. 351, and Hampstead, n.d. 1916, HRC.

flowing, only rarely expressing the concentrated enthusiasm for music and books that they had always had.

Within the peace and women's movements there were disappointments as well. She wrote to Ellis that she wouldn't be going to any of the peace meetings:

> Of course they condemn all people who fight against us, and all future wars, and some even condemn just wars – but the main end of most peace speakers and writers seem always to be to wind up by showing what a good people we are and what a noble and good thing we are fighting today, and to prove how right and necessary it is we should maintain our supremacy over the *sea* and the earth. . . . 'Any' other nation which tries to build up such an Empire as we have in India and Burma (where we depopulated whole districts) and Africa and Egypt to rule the sea is a vile and wicked nation on which God's curse will surely fall. Let us pray![26]

Similarly she dreaded the thought of any League to 'enforce' peace; and only a few individuals earned her respect. One was Sylvia Pankhurst, whom she regarded as a 'fine woman' because she had helped to save Germans in the East End when they were attacked. For Christabel and Emmeline Pankhurst she had little time: 'They have lost nearly all their suffragette following so they have had to take up war to keep themselves before the public.'[27] And once before the public, she felt, it was all ' "lime-light" and theatrical'.[28]

Sylvia Pankhurst, for her part, had 'vivid recollections' of Olive as a supporter of adult suffrage and opponent of forced feeding,[29] and as an important friend:

> On account of her malady she could not endure to travel in the London Underground of those times, or I think in any train, but she frequently came to see me, making the long journey on the top of the bus to Old Ford in the East End of London where I was then deeply engaged in efforts to ameliorate the hardships caused by the war. I saw, I think, more of her than of any other person outside the immediate circle of those who were working with me at the time.[30]

This mutual respect was based on a political affinity. Olive had had enough of an entrée to the suffrage movement in England to come to fairly firm conclusions about it, and she made her position clear in a letter to a Women's Meeting in July 1918. The occasion was a commemoration of J. S. Mill, and Olive's address was very brief – six short paragraphs. Many women now had the vote, and all would have it soon, she said; but Mill had done more than labour for women's freedom. If women wished to use their new 'governing power', they should learn Mill's lesson – that the freedom of all human creatures was essential to the full development of human life on earth. She thus linked the emancipation of women with a 'larger Freedom . . . for every subject race and class'.[31]

Olive's anti-racism had prompted her support of Gandhi's *satyagraha* movement, which used the technique of non-violent struggle as a defensive strategy for the Indian minority in South Africa. Gandhi had been flattered by Olive's interest: 'Fancy the author of *Dreams* paying a tribute to passive resistance,' he wrote after Olive and her sister Ettie, then Mrs Stakesby Lewis, had come to shake hands with him when he left Cape Town for London in 1909.[*][32] In London she renewed her contact with him and with his supporter Hermann Kallenbach,[†] both of whom were in London in 1914. But at the same time Gandhi was an active supporter of Empire, first on the side of Britain in the Boer war and then in World War One. Olive was distressed to learn that he planned to do recruiting work for the British side. On opening her newspaper one morning she had been:

> struck to the heart . . . with sorrow to see that you and that beautiful and beloved Indian poetess whom I met some months ago and other India [*sic*] friends had offered to serve the English government in this evil war in *any way* they might demand of you. Surely you, who would not take up arms even in the cause of your own oppressed people cannot be willing to shed blood in this wicked cause. I had longed to meet you and Mr Callenbach [*sic*] as friends who would

---

* Gandhi remarked on more than one occasion on what he called Olive's 'simple habits' – including the fact that she knew no difference between her servants and herself. See M. K. Gandhi, *Satyagraha in South Africa* (Madras 1928), p. 281.

† Hermann Kallenbach, a German businessman, settled on the Witwatersrand in 1896. An associate of Gandhi's, he corresponded with Tolstoy and believed in vegetarianism. He gave Olive help with her diet in these years in London and also ran errands for her, especially when she was ill. Olive's letter to Gandhi about the latter's stance in the war was actually sent to Kallenbach.

understand my hatred of it. I don't believe the statement in the paper can be true.[33]

She followed this up with a refusal to attend one of Gandhi's meetings in London, giving her reason in a note to Kallenbach. It was against her religion, she wrote emphatically, 'whether it is Englishmen travelling thousands of miles to go to kill Indians in India, or Indians travelling thousands of miles to kill white men whom they have never seen in Europe. It's all hateful.'[34]

She had the same reservations about Sol Plaatje, the secretary-general of the newly-formed South African Native National Congress, later the African National Congress, when he came to Britain as a member of a delegation to put before the British Government and public the Congress case against the Natives Land Act of 1913. This was the measure which restricted the land occupancy rights of four million Africans to less than eight per cent of the country's land area, while the one and a half million whites had unlimited access to the remaining ninety-two per cent. Plaatje had toured the areas affected by what he called the 'Plague Act' and had written a harrowing account of the plight of evicted tenant families. Olive knew of Plaatje and his book, but at the time the delegation visited England she was wary of him, for 'he advocates the natives coming here to help kill'.[35] This was a reference to the decision of the Congress leadership to drop its agitation against the Land Act when the war broke out and to offer to enlist men for active service. Her pacifist convictions were paramount.

She was active where she could be, and was involved in the first public meetings of the Union for Democratic Control. She also prepared an address on conscientious objection for the *Labour Leader* in 1916. She was one of a deputation of about sixty people who went to the House of Commons to discuss conscription with MPs opposed to it. She was in wholehearted agreement with an appeal to women workers to demand equal pay for equal work in jobs where they took the place of men on active service, and said she would assist in any way she could.[36] She read widely on the background to the war, mainly on events in Russia, China, Germany and Central Europe, and took the leading periodicals; her comments on the events of the war, especially in letters to Ellis, were informed if somewhat casual: she had strong opinions though she did not always stop to justify or explain them. She returned to Euripides and to Gibbon's *Decline and Fall*, perhaps in a struggle with her morale. She published a short allegory, 'Who Knocks at the Door?', in the *Fortnightly Review* in November 1917, inspired, she told a friend, by a brief newspaper report that the Chinese had launched their first submarine. She began to write a small book about war, part of which was published after her death as *The Dawn of Civilisation*.[37]

In all these writings, which were, effectively, her public statement about the war, she summoned up her faith in history, her faith as a whole. She wanted to show conscientious objectors that they were not alone, that there did exist individuals – like herself – who were 'organically unable' to hold a position different from theirs even though, from the 'accident of age and sex', they might not be called up.[38] The allegory and the address – in which her theme was that the greatness of wealth and empire brought with it the smallness and cruelty of possession, envy, hoarding and destruction – were framed in terms of her oldest imagery: a dream in a forest, a banquet, an age-old past, a limitless future.[39] In *The Dawn of Civilisation* she returned to her insistence on the validity of the internal world, her vision of a place where the strong helped the weak, where men understood one another. She recalled herself as a child of nine on the veld one morning, moving between a feeling of absolute smallness, of total ineffectiveness on the one hand and intense mystical experience on the other. Her sense-impressions became the whole field, the whole material reality, and landscape assumed an 'almost intolerable beauty'. The vision was not part of a distant picture, 'it was there, about me, and I was in it, and a part of it'. And although as an adult she had seen the Boer war, experienced the degradation – for both classes – of class division, the 'terrible world of public life' – of diplomacy and international relations – still that consciousness of love which she carried back from the veld that morning had never wholly deserted her.[40] With *The Dawn of Civilisation* Olive was doing much more than review the events of the previous ten years. In identifying herself with the tradition of conscientious objection she was creating a continuity for herself, politically, spiritually, and personally.

Olive was especially reliant at a personal level on old friends in a situation where family members like Theo and Ettie went war-mad. With Carpenter she tended to talk about the future, with the intimacy of a common language; telling him, for example, about a woman she knew in

South Africa who lived a kind of Thoreau existence.[41] Constance Lytton, Adela Smith, the Pethick Lawrences, Havelock and Edith Ellis were all very steadfast, and for someone as ill and as demoralized as Olive was, she had a great deal of energy for the detail of their lives.

Her letters to Ellis have the quality of an old friendship, secured by the passage of time, but quietened by the existence, for both of them, of other lovers, other involvements. Havelock was 'My dear friend'; they were still talking about love and sexuality, Olive sending him a cutting about sex relations between Indians and white women. She would still ask him – partly because she could not afford a doctor – for 'that old prescription', and commiserate with him about the expense of illness, his own as well as hers: 'How dispairful [*sic*] it is we are all so *poor*. Illness sops up money like water.' There was a touch of the old intimacy when she suggested he come and spend a 'long day' with her when he was next in London, and told him – as they'd once recounted all the lovely, prosaic detail of their lives to each other – that dawn had come and she was about to draw her curtains. But for the most part there was concern about illness, their own disabilities, money, and, especially, Edith's health.[42]

Edith Ellis had been diagnosed manic depressive years earlier, but now her health was 'deeply undermined' by diabetes and a condition variously described as organic disease in the brain or schizoid temperament.[43] By 1915 Olive was 'always thinking' of her and when it came to a serious nervous breakdown the following year she was anxious to help, advising complete vegetarianism and discussing the merits and problems of an asylum in letters to Havelock. Edith died that year and Olive made the journey to Golders Green crematorium, even though she was ill, because she knew Edith would have liked her to.

Havelock Ellis' account of Olive's last years in Europe is a relatively cool one. In his autobiography he was concerned not with the feel of their meetings but with a final evaluation of Olive's personality, and he emphasized just how much she had changed over time. With increasing years and ill health, he felt, she had become 'less tolerant, less receptive', and, finally,

dogmatic and intolerant of contradiction, so positive in her inner convictions that it was only with great difficulty, if at all, that she could admit that she had made a mistake (as often happened) on the simplest matter of fact.[44]

What he did mention – and this fairly unsympathetically – was a request she made in 1917 that her friends destroy or return all her letters. He had preserved her letters carefully, he says, 'arranged in bundles and duly numbered', and was unwilling to agree to their destruction; even though he assured her of their safety and that once he died they could not legally be published without her permission or that of her representatives, she still insisted, 'even with tears'. In the end he burnt a large number of them, and for a year they had no contact with one another. Then, he says, she resumed writing and the incident was never referred to again.[45]

There was also an explicitly political dimension to the distance between them. Neither has left a record of their disagreement over the war, but the division is still fairly clear. Olive tried to set out her pacifism in a letter to Ellis in 1915. One reason for their difference, she felt, was that she could never base her opinion on anything on what had just happened; she must go back to the past. Thus one could never understand Germany without remembering that a century before, Germany was subjugated by France:

> torn and desolated, her objects of art . . . carried off from Berlin to Paris, the King and Queen of Prussia insulted . . . A nation, no more than an individual, can wash its hands of the past.[46]

Ellis, for his part, did not write openly about the war. Only by reference to Edith's position was his own expressed. It was 'spontaneously identical' with his, he says: she was always absolutely opposed to war but believed that England had played an honourable and justifiable part in entering this one. But she was 'singularly disinterested and aloof', and was never moved to take part in war work, though not because she had 'rigid pacifist principles'.[47] The impression given is one of opposition to a militant stance of any kind. Havelock's political passivity had been an issue between him and Olive for a long time – when the child prostitution scandal broke in 1885 Olive remarked on his unwillingness to get involved in the protest about it[48] – and now it reinforced her feeling of having no real allies of her own.

Very few other accounts of Olive exist from these last years. Those that there are – admittedly by people who never knew her well – create a picture not unlike Ellis', of a difficult old woman at the end of her life, in a society that she no longer understood. The London correspondent of the American *New Republic*, for example, to whom Olive wrote about simultaneous publication in London and New York of one or two of her later *Dreams*, felt all the 'early sparkle' had gone.

> I could not make her understand why, if a piece was coming out in the next number of the *Fortnightly*, it could not get into the next issue of a New York weekly . . . There was no point in my seeing her again about her stuff.[49]

To the journalist from the *New Republic* she was simply a 'stocky, elderly woman', but Olive Renier, ward of Alice Corthorn, had the special perspective of a three-year-old child.

> I remember a very dark big room full of plush furniture, probably a hotel lounge, and I was terrified of the strong, fierce face of a woman who seemed to me to be at least a hundred years old. Afterwards she stayed with us in Addison Road; it was a dismal period in that dismal war, and 'Aunt Olive' argued with my guardian about the evils of war.[50]

Alice Corthorn was a reluctant supporter of the war and the two women felt badly out of touch with one another. Olive apparently thumped the table so that the china rattled, and shouted till an attack of asthma reduced her to silence.

In a public context, like that of the Lyceum reception in 1913, Olive's 'personality and her influence' could still simply be described as magnetic. But one of the more perceptive observers, for she had intuited something of Olive's past, was a young woman, Joan Hodgson, who became a close friend of Olive's towards the end of Olive's years in London, though they first met in 1915. Hers was a very thoughtful description, unlike the adulatory or deferential appreciations that most of Olive's friends submitted for Cronwright's biography.[51]

Olive had met John Hodgson in South Africa in 1911 and then met him and his wife Joan in London in February 1915; they were friends of Dot Schreiner, Will's daughter. Dot, Joan and Olive met at a 'pretentious, dingy restaurant' in Holborn, and Joan obviously saw her as still very strong. She was struck by Olive's indifference to fashion, the way she took the lead in discussion; she left an impression of great tenseness and vitality, the capacity to enjoy as well as to suffer. And although Joan liked the wicked joy and appreciation with which Olive quoted from the Bible, she sensed a certain 'bitterness' in her freethought 'which was not known to my generation; her battle had been hard and lonely and long, one guessed. We found our feet more easily because of the pioneering that had been done.' Altogether, she came away from the meeting 'more overwhelmed than happy', and they did not meet again for several months. Joan sought Olive out towards the end of the year, when she wanted to talk over her perplexities about going into war work. Olive was then living in a private hotel and Joan and her friend were not asked up to her rooms, because Olive could never be too sure of her visitors. So they sat in the 'big, chilly, impersonal reception hall', Olive with her feet tucked up on a sofa, denouncing England's 'wicked and hypocritical' alliance with Russia.

From 1918 the relationship became closer. Joan would go in and visit Olive when she was in London, and stay about an hour; her husband had told her how lonely she was. Now Olive talked very openly, about 'the hold of South Africa on men's hearts', about her nieces and nephews, her feeling that Joan's baby would become a poet, one of the Schreiner babies (this one a girl) a prime minister. Olive visited them several times before going back to South Africa, staying two or three days, then 'on some pretext, often health, or that she was giving too much trouble, would flee back to London'. And although Olive was obviously an ageing, sad woman, she could still elicit the same responses as she had done as a young girl: her conversation seemed to be the result of 'intensive thought which she had stored up', Joan felt, concluding that: 'one often felt that she lived habitually in silence'.

Olive had begun to claim that she did not mind being on her own now. This came out in letters to Adela Smith in 1916, in one of which she told her she would never know how important she had been to her;[52] it was as though she wanted to leave nothing unsaid. She was now more or less incapacitated by illness: some time during 1916 she tried to visit Betty Molteno, then in London, but her heart was so bad she had to turn back at the bus stop. In the same letter, to Alice Greene, Olive described a social gathering at Will's, at which everyone seemed 'so utterly sad and tired':

> I just lay on the sofa, I couldn't even talk to Dot. I think the want of proper food is making us all ill and weak. It is not the dying, but the never being fully and highly nourished that is the horror of starvation. To be living and not yet alive.[53]

Will was in London throughout the war as well, as South African High

Commissioner. With his radicalization on the native question he and Olive had grown close, but when war broke out, and Will took it for granted that Britain should support France and even Russia against Germany, he and Olive differed openly, and painfully. Will claimed not to want South Africa's military campaign in German South West Africa but believed it necessary: as it was in the war, South Africa must pull its weight.[54]

Olive's position was sharply opposed. The 1914 war was even more wrong than the Boer war; and England's league with Russia was the greatest crime, she thought. Her opposition was a mixture of pacifism and anti-imperialist opposition to the schemes of the big powers and the involvement of South Africa. She was appalled that Smuts, who had once led a Boer commando, now sat in the imperial war cabinet alongside Milner, and when there was a rebellion inside the South African army led by the group still intransigent against Britain, she termed this a 'rising against the dictatorship of Smuts and Botha'.[55] She had in fact anticipated this development and told Lloyd George, when she met him, that drawing South Africa into the war with Britain would result in a Boer rebellion.[56] These emphatic opinions were all written to Will during 1914, but then she relented, and promised not to worry him again about war politics: she wanted to remain simply 'your small sister who loves you more than you know'.[57] So she drew back from discussing the events of the war itself, but tried to communicate something of her own attitude to it, letting him know what she was working on and how it was going, sending him a book of war poems by a friend of Carpenter's, suggesting books on Russia and on German social democracy that he might like to read.[58] She also seems to have asked him to deal with the correspondence over a proposed film of *The Story of an African Farm*. The general manager of African Films Ltd was waiting for an answer and she didn't know what to say.

> Long ago Wilson Barrett, a celebrated actor, wanted to dramatise it and I refused. The tragedy of Lyndall and Waldo can't be put into a picture because it is purely intellectual and spiritual. Lyndall and Waldo's story is a cry against fate, a struggle against adverse material conditions.[59]

How could this be filmed without vulgarizing it? Olive seemed to have recovered some of her old definition, her strength.

By late 1918 she was writing more frequently about angina attacks. One particularly painful bout had lasted nine weeks, she wrote to Ellis in October: 'Angina is different from anything else, it curls you up.' Even so, she hadn't written to Cronwright about it 'because I don't want to trouble him'.[60] When she did write, it was with no real confidence. She told him simply that she had taken a bus to Hampstead, and got talking to a lonely man. 'Well, that's not very interesting, but it's all I have,' her letter ended.[61]

In January the following year she wrote to Cronwright that she sat 'alone in the dark day after day', describing her life as 'walled in'. By June she was preoccupied with Will's illness as well as her own angina. Will already had a heart condition and was overweight when Olive persuaded him to take the waters at Bad Nauheim in 1914, but now, five years later, the stress of his work was telling on him. He had looked after the South African troops and war workers, saw all applicants for commissions, involved himself in a fund for soldiers' dependants and the Richmond Hospital for the South African Wounded. In addition, though Fan and he were together in London, they were separated from their children, the two sons on active service and the two daughters doing war work overseas.[62]

Now Will's heart condition was deteriorating fast and Olive wanted him to go and stay with the Murray Parkers in Llandrindod Wells in central Wales, where she herself had been three years previously. Although Will had been preoccupied with his death for two years and had given directions for his ashes to be buried beside his parents' grave near Cape Town,[63] Olive apparently wanted to keep the seriousness of his illness from him. She urged Mrs Parker not to let Will think that she was coming too because he was so bad, but because she needed a rest.[64] Will died very soon after this, however, on 28 June, and Olive went up to Golders Green a second time, on this occasion with Fan, Lord Milner, and Generals Botha and Smuts. She saw the box of ashes at Waterloo on its way out to Africa at the end of September.

With Will gone, she wrote to Betty Molteno, Betty seemed her closest link with humanity. His death seemed to have 'ended everything for me', and she wrote regular letters of condolence to Fan, supporting her decision to return to Africa.

Tomorrow will be our Will's birthday. I know what you will be thinking. I'm so glad you're going back to Africa. I feel like a ship-wrecked mariner standing in the shore of an island who sees the last of his fellows sailing away. But I'm glad you're going. Bill will be a comfort to you and your old friends will gather round.[65]

She herself was becoming so unfit that she couldn't write, she wrote to Ellis. She couldn't breathe at all, and she was sure her heart was getting larger and larger.

But there were still moments of conviction and optimism, largely bound up with the course of the Russian revolution. Olive had been interested in events in Russia since the revolution of 1905, and now followed those of the civil war, convinced that Lenin was the greatest genius of the past hundred years.[66] By autumn 1919 the White Guards were retreating and the outcome of the fighting was in no doubt.[67] Olive was evidently referring to the collapse of the White Russian armies when Ruth Alexander saw her in her rooms in London, 'pacing up and down in a terrible state of excitement. "Do you know what's happened?" she said. "Denikin's been thrown out of Russia." '*[68] By now, too, although Churchill had proclaimed an anti-Soviet crusade of fourteen nations, the opposition of Western European workers was seriously hampering British and French intervention,[69] and Olive was glad 'the labour men wouldn't load that ship with the guns for the Poles to kill the Russians with'.[70] She was also interested in the German revolution of 1918, and was moved at Karl Liebknecht's having stood up in the Prussian Reichstag 'against the whole power of militarism and autocracy'. She wrote enthusiastically to Adela Smith about his book *The Future Belongs to the People*.[71]

But it was only in letters like these that she sustained herself. 'I can't speak to anyone,' she wrote to Adela late in 1919, 'and I hardly ever see anyone.' She had been shocked by the consequences of peace. 'People seem so much more *bitter* and hard than they were before the victory.' She was depressed by the orgy of extravagance and self-indulgence that she saw around her: women were gambling as never before, to make up for the 'excitement' of the war.[72] She was sure that manufacturers were making millions: she had gone to Marshall and Snelgrove's to buy a baby's jacket for a friend, and found it cost eighteen shillings; before the

---

* Denikin, one of the White generals active immediately after the October revolution, mounted one of the three major campaigns against the Soviets at the end of the civil war in 1919.

war it would have been one and sixpence and 'last year not more than
4/-'.[73] She spelled out her concern in a letter to Fan, now in South
Africa:

> If the government can do nothing to keep the wealthy from making vast
> profits they are doing now, there will be a revolution in this country,
> and that will only make things worse. The streets are quite different
> from what they were when you were here. They are just crowded with
> motor cars filled with opulently dressed women in fur cloaks and
> dresses that cost £500 and people pay as much as £25 for a seat to go
> and see a boxing match.[74]

Now her friend Alice Greene became fatally ill. By January 1920 Olive
was sure that she was dying, but she was principally worried that Betty
Molteno, then nursing her in Cornwall, would break down over it. Alice
died that month, and Olive heard that Betty was 'well and calm, I need
have no anxiety'. But Olive was too ill to go to her funeral, and wrote
warmly to Betty, expressing affection for Alice and concern for Betty after
the long strain of nursing her.[75] Within a few days she heard that Theo
had died; they had been on different sides of the war, as they had been
for years, over Rhodes, the Jameson Raid and the Boer war, but Olive
was glad that she'd written to him when Will died. She was also glad that
he had written to her twice, but she was fully aware that she was now 'the
last of the old brigade'. It was a particularly significant death, as she told
Cronwright:

> Yes, I felt Theo's death very much. It's the last of my past – it's all
> gone. No one knows anything of the things of my childhood and youth
> any more. Here in this room where I am alone week after week I live so
> strangely with them all: Father, Mother, Ettie, Will, Theo. Some-
> times one could almost feel they were here; one hears their voices.
> Ettie and Will and I are all children playing at Healdtown. Oh, I am so
> glad to think they are all resting so peacefully and will never know pain
> any more.[76]

In a letter to Adela she pursued the theme of rest and peace: 'It's so
restful to sit still and see masses of human beings about you and watch
them and sort of live through them.' It was as though she sensed her life
was winding down and she must draw strength in observing others'.[77] She
was coming to moral conclusions, settling accounts due. In a letter to

Ellis, possibly about Pearson, she wrote that she had 'lost all feeling of sorrow about —— [Cronwright's deletion] I love to see him now. One has no right to form ideals of people, and then, because they don't justify them, become bitter.'[78] By now she had also come to feel that she could not tolerate another English winter, and must return to Africa. But meanwhile Cronwright was due to visit her 'for a little while' before he went to America, and she told him (and Fan) that she thought she would drop dead with joy when she saw him.[79]

Olive and Cronwright had now been separated for five years. Olive always maintained that she had left Africa only because there were so few places where she didn't get asthma; they both stressed that he needed to keep his business in De Aar going; he wrote to her every week[80] and says in his biography of Olive that neither of them consciously missed a single mail while apart. At the same time, this separation was part of the pattern that was established within a few years of their marriage; and although Olive claimed that she wanted to be with him more than anything in the world, her life was so arranged that she was constantly travelling away from him, constantly professing her love for him.

In December 1919 Cronwright sold his business interests, planning to sail for England in April the following year. Three factors contributed to his decision, he says in the biography: he now had enough money for their retirement; he could no longer endure the monotony and solitude of De Aar, and wanted to finish with the 'rigid and exclusive concentration on a business career begun late in life'; his health had been seriously threatened by the demands of his work. Writing about these last months as though they were something of a business deal, he says only that the financial matters keeping him in Africa until June had 'tragic consequences' – they meant he had only one month with Olive in London before she sailed for the Cape.[81]

In a file marked 'Strictly Personal' at the 1820 Settlers Museum, Grahamstown, however, Cronwright deposited the typescript of an exchange of letters between him and Olive between 1913 and 1920. This record of an estrangement was kept separate from the seemingly fond correspondence of these years to which both of them have referred. Some of the letters deal – rather acrimoniously, on Cronwright's side – with the expenses and arrangements of both their trips to Europe, but the most pertinent is a long letter from Cronwright to Olive in May 1920 about her 'unreasonable, absurd obsessions' about other women. Why Cronwright did not destroy the evidence of this episode is not known, given his collusion, in the biography, with her picture of their marriage. Possibly that 'love of *fact* and truth [which] has no counterpart in any relative that I am aware of' played a part.[82]

In May 1913, while she was still in South Africa, Cronwright told Olive that he must have a long holiday or he would have a breakdown. 'I feel that we are both getting on in years, that your own funds are low, that soon I shall have to defray *all* expenses.' She should go to Europe, but he would pay only her fare. He sympathized with her 'lonely life most of the year', but if he went it had to be on his own.[83] Concerned to affirm the relationship, Olive replied:

> If you had asked me to I would not go in the same steamer with you, because I should be so afraid of being ill and spoiling your much-needed holiday . . . Perhaps we might arrange to meet somewhere and have a little honeymoon . . . If you pay my return ticket I shall find some way of paying the rest.[84]

But two months later their relationship had become very strained. Olive hoped they would both go to Europe separately, and if they were in London, she assumed he would stay with his friends Dr and Mrs Philpot. For Mrs Philpot she seems to have had little respect:

> I would be willing to meet Mrs Philpot if she called on me *because she is your friend*; that would be necessary. She could not feel me insincere because *she* knows well that I know her, and what I think of her though I have never told her. I should be quite [partly legible only] polite to her, and that would be all.[85]

Cronwright added notes to her letter, to the effect that he hoped she would not call on the Philpots, that she had no more right to resent his friendship with Isaline Philpot or think ill or evil of it than he had with regard to her friendships with Ellis, Muirhead and other men; and that 'if she wrote to me THUS again about Mrs. P. or any other woman, the result would be *disastrous*'.

In April 1920, when he was at last planning his own travel, Cronwright wrote to Olive to say that he would take a bed and breakfast place apart from her and spend the days with her.[86] At the beginning of May he wrote to her:

Before I left De Aar for J'burg I reread the correspondence between us before you left De Aar for England. (I have your original letters and copies of mine to you.) I again grew so angry that I almost decided to cancel my trip to England, but although I was then on the point of breaking down by reason of work and solitude and although I was nearly as enraged as I had been when I received your preposterous letter about Mrs. P., I refrained from so deciding because I should not have allowed a decision so come to, although it might have meant our severance forever, and because I love and revere you and desire, as far as I can, to aid you.

I meant it then and I mean it now, and I wish to add that the result will be equally disastrous whether you so address me again in writing or verbally.

Cronwright then went on to imply the existence of a long-standing tension between the two of them.

Long ago, I found that, in all things, it was quite useless to try to put you right about myself, no matter what you thought about me. As you know, I have not swerved from that decision, and I shall not do so.

Then came a description of Olive's behaviour which, however much it reiterated Cronwright's obsession with 'objective' reality, revealed a great deal about the extraordinary power of Olive's imagination and how destructive – and self-destructive – it could be.

I am quite determined to suffer no more persecution at your hands, especially about women. You do not base your attitude reasonably on *facts*; you build up something fantastic from your inner consciousness, which may and often has no relation whatever to essential facts; then this becomes *real* to you. Mrs. Philpot's only one and perhaps the most innocent (if there be degrees of innocence) of the women about whom you have persecuted me.

Then came an ultimatum, oblique and impatient:

You may attack me *once* more; if so I shall not 'explain' (and I have never retaliated) but it will never occur again. I write this now because I shall of course see the Philpots in London and possibly stay a few days with them, and because you may suddenly and unreasonably get some absurd obsession about some other woman whom I have never even met.

Finally there was a special warning, with Cronwright frankly contemptuous of Olive's views of his friend:

> But I warn you particularly about Mrs. P. I have told her (I did so long ago) that you had written me a letter about her and that, in my opinion, she should in consequence refuse to meet you. I have of course not shown her the mad letter nor given her details, but I should do her an injustice if I did not mention you had written me a letter of such nature that, if she knew its contents, she would refuse to meet you. If you don't wish me to come over, please say so at once, Cron.[87]

Up to now Cronwright had deemed Olive 'impossible' only in the sense that she could not complete work; he had been concerned to rationalize whatever neurosis he found in her as being a necessary part of the 'creative personality'. Now it looked as though the relationship itself was very tangled, and he was anxious to protect himself. He took a carbon of the letter and sent it to his nephew Morthland. Olive must have replied promptly, for the next letter is dated 11 May. She wanted to tell him something before she died, she wrote:

> I have never thought you loved Mrs P. or that she loved you . . . – it was the things she *said* about me . . . If there were only one woman in the world and that Mrs P. I should never have dreamed you were in love with her. I have never thought she was a passionate or by any possibility an immoral woman but what she can't help doing is discussing other people and their affairs with which she has nothing to do.[88]

Mrs Philpot was apparently a friend of Elizabeth Cobb's, and Olive's letters to her date from 1885, the year after Olive and Mrs Cobb met. But before she had even met Mrs Philpot, Olive's letter to Cronwright continued, Mrs Philpot had caused trouble by her talking. Still, they developed a correspondence over the next four years,[89] in the early stages about books they were reading, and then on a more relaxed and personal basis once Olive was back in Africa, Olive sending Mrs Philpot photographs of Cronwright when she was considering marriage, and confiding her fears of being unworthy of him. Then when Olive was pregnant it was to Mrs Philpot that she described the 'little book' she was preparing for the child in case she died, telling her she was also compiling a list of all the books she wanted it to read. The published *Letters* contain nothing to Mrs Philpot from 1894 onwards, except a brief note in 1903, and it is possible that whatever fantasy Olive developed about Cronwright's attachment to this woman who had never been a real intimate of hers, Olive stopped writing to her. There is no trace of Olive's 'mad' letter to Cronwright about her.

Cronwright copied Olive's letter of 11 May as well and sent it to Morthland with a covering letter saying he had tried to find out what Mrs P. had reported about Olive: it could have been a Mrs Unwin saying Olive was an 'impossible woman' whom no one, including Cronwright, could live with. In fact, this letter of Olive's, with its sense of being personally invaded, its exaggeration, and its characteristic insistence on total, binding privacy, says something about the stress that any partner of hers would have lived under. Cronwright himself, writing in his journal three years after her death, referred to their relationship as 'so many weary years'.[90]

Olive, for her part, could never allow herself to admit that the relationship with her husband could be over. She was so ideological about personal life that to have called the relationship a failure would have meant a defeat of all her political idealism. It had certainly been sexually active – if one goes only by the number of miscarriages she suffered – but once other kinds of issues arose, of differences in temperament, politics, or choice of work, Olive had to suppress any antagonism she felt towards him, or even her awareness of distance between them. As she had written to Ellis in the Eighties, the struggle was to learn how to love:

> Neither Christ nor Tolstoy nor any one of us now living has yet seen and preached that doctrine of love and forgiveness as it will be preached in ages to come . . . The strife and agony of these last years has not been to forgive, it has not been magnanimously to overlook: that is easy enough. It is to *love*.[91]

She therefore set herself an impossible task, in which her conduct had to stand for the morality of the future, and where a basically Christian doctrine had to be transposed into a subculture which, in part, rejected it. Olive's conception of love confused relations between individuals and relations of peoples as a whole, applying fairly unearthly criteria to the first, as the last sentence of her letter to Ellis shows: 'If there be one soul you cannot love, then you are lost.'

On his arrival in London in July 1920, Cronwright went straight to Olive's rooms in Porchester Place. Olive had become a different person and he was

> shocked at her appearance. She had aged greatly. Her bright hair was gray. Her glorious eyes were almost closed and but little remained in the sick woman of that bursting elemental force which was so arresting and dominating in her tremendous personality. She was palpably very ill; any exertion brought on wheezing at once; she could walk only a short distance, very slowly, and even that brought an increasing wheezing and great heart pain.*[92]

During the month that they were together Cronwright described Olive reading the newspapers eagerly, usually taking no breakfast, but eating lunch with him. Sometimes they would meet a friend, such as Ellis; sometimes they went to a cinema near Marble Arch or to a light opera. She was pleased by 'simple things'; they would buy bread and cheese and jam for supper; the landlady's sister would make a light pudding and bring it in with tea and coffee. Then Olive would smoke a cigarette and lie down on her bed and read the papers, commenting briefly on passing events. When, however, she really began to talk, 'she would rapidly get off the bed and walk up and down the room, not with her old quick walk and vibrating voice, but in a laboured way, speaking slowly and painfully'. They went out little, but many of her friends visited her, showing a 'love and tenderness and reverence' that touched Cronwright deeply.

In his biography Cronwright avoids any comment on Olive's pacifism in the war, presumably because his own attitudes had been quite different: he had backed the British Empire against Germany. Accordingly, he describes an occasion on which he asked her to talk about what she thought the origins of the war had been:

> I said I did not want to put my own views forward or argue or discuss the matter with her, but just to understand her attitude and the reasons; one could not argue with her then; she had not the strength; she would break down and cry in great physical distress.

* According to Buchanan-Gould's biography, Cronwright reached Porchester Place, and 'enquired of the old lady who met him at the door if he might see Mrs Cronwright-Schreiner. "Don't you know me, Cronwright?" the woman asked.'

He says that he did not comment on what she said, but merely asked more questions; it was 'very interesting and informative', Olive walking up and down the room slowly, smoking cigarettes. She was 'lucid'; had read about all the countries involved and their problems.

The visit was brought to an end by Olive's departure for the Cape. She had put her name down in February for a steamer in August or September and was due to sail on 13 August. Cronwright's arrival does not seem to have influenced her plans; in fact her letters to friends about Cronwright's movements have an almost disinterested quality: she is initially 'not sure' he will come in May, he may go via Japan; she is simply glad his 'lifelong dream' of a trip to America will be fulfilled and doesn't know what he means to do afterwards.[93] In any case, other factors counted for a great deal. The war was over and it was at last possible to travel freely. She wanted to go out to the Cape, even though her doctors said it was 'madness', because she would 'rather end my life in my own country and among my own people'.[94] Finally, there was the opportunity of travelling with her nephew Oliver, Will's son, then returning to South Africa with his wife and baby daughter, his wife's sister and a nurse.

The whole trip aroused acute anxiety for her. She was afraid she might die before she left, and worried that there would be no one to arrange about her being embalmed and sent home. She had meant to be brave when she came to England and to die alone, she wrote to Ruth Alexander in May, and once in Africa, she assured her, she wouldn't trouble anyone, she would go to a nursing home. She said something of the same to Fan Schreiner, stressing that she would spend only the first days with her while she looked for a room, for she was 'always in pain and too ill to stay with friends'. At the same time she was terrified of the voyage back, wondering how she would get through the Tropics in her condition.[95]

By the time she came to leave, however, she claimed that she was ready to die now that she had had the 'great happiness' of the time with her husband.[96] She gave Cronwright her manuscript of *The Dawn of Civilisation* a few days before she left, willing for him to publish it if she died. Instead of going to America, Cronwright decided to follow later, after he had rested. He packed all her belongings and saw her off at Waterloo with a little party that included Ellis. The travelling party had a compartment reserved and Cronwright says Olive sat there 'comfortably but sadly, holding my hand most of the time'. As the train drew out and the two waved to one another, he saw her 'dark, distressed, beautiful loving face for the last time'. Then he sent her a telegram to the Docks and went back to her rooms, which he had taken over.[97]

Olive wrote to Cronwright several times on board ship, grateful for his care, glad that she could picture him in a room she knew so well, and suddenly, painfully nostalgic for Alassio as they left Madeira – at one stage her plan had been to go there to die. On her arrival in Cape Town she spent some time with Fan and her niece Ursula, Lady Rose Innes, wife of the then Chief Justice, and Anna Purcell; her nephew Oliver wrote to Cronwright that she had stood the seventeen-day journey 'amazingly well' and now seemed to be fitter than in England. Olive's first impressions were of the food – it was so good after England, 'real bread, fresh fish', and for a time, when the weather improved, some of her symptoms abated. She became much weaker fairly quickly, however,* but remained determined to be 'quite free' and moved on 25 October to Oak Hall, a large, pleasant boarding-house at Wynberg, a tram terminus in the Cape Town suburbs.[98]

Olive's last weeks were deliberately self-sufficient. She had reassured the Hodgsons on this point, presumably before she left for the Cape:

> I didn't mean when I said I was 'hard up' that my dear friends wouldn't help me. But I meant I wanted so to take care of myself till the end came, and pay for all nurses and doctors *myself*. I've always done everything for myself all my life.[99]

Ellis, and others, had found her cantankerous, but there were also the dignity and pride of an old woman who was respected and loved. She was attentive to her family and they to her; many of her letters from England were family inquiries of one kind or another.

There were still the fiery political flashes. That year there was a strike of African municipal workers in Port Elizabeth organized by Samuel

---

* Ben Farrington, who then lectured in Classics at the University of Cape Town and was married to Ruth Alexander, met Olive during these last three months in South Africa. 'I came to the interview prepared by Ruth, who worshipped Olive Schreiner,' he told Ruth First in 1969:

> 'Here she was, coming back from London . . . There was a steep hill and a steep flight of steps before you got into the sitting room. By the time Olive appeared, not only by her own steam, but with various people helping and pushing, she was completely out of breath, almost ready to collapse . . . Her skin was very leathery and folded . . . and her voice was a rusty bellows. There was not much clear resonance in it, there was so much damage done by the asthma. But she had very bright eyes.'

Masabalala of the Cape provincial branch of the African National Congress, and police action resulted in the deaths of nineteen African workers. From her boarding-house Olive collected money for Masabalala's defence. She also sent Smuts a warning: 'We may crush down the mass of our fellows in South Africa today as Russia did for generations, but today the serf is in the Palace and where is the Czar?' She followed the African women's civil disobedience campaign against passes then under way in the Orange Free State where, she wrote indignantly to a friend, one hundred women were in prison in Bloemfontein for refusing to pay sixpence for their passes. Now she felt that she knew exactly where she stood, but 'I have not met one human being who feels at all on the native question as I do. There is so much one ought to do now, and I can't do it. I would like to go among the natives and really try to enter into touch with them.' By 1920 she had given up hope of Smuts. She thought a long talk with him would make little difference since he appeared to hear little and to respond less. She was aware that he must be laughing at the 'little woman in one room, seeing no one, who fancies she sees more than men in the midst of affairs'. But, she reminded him in a sharp letter, it was no longer the nineteenth century but the twentieth, 'and the whole old world is cracking'. Then she moved from this world view to turn 'the native question' back into her personal distress. 'Oh Betty,' she cried out in a letter to Betty Molteno, 'why did I come out? I have made many mistakes in my life but this is the greatest of all.'[100]

To Mary Brown, however, she seemed at peace. Mary saw her twice after her return, once in the nursing home where Mary had gone for an operation on her eye. Mary wrote: 'She came to me there and sat stroking my hand as if trying to express all she felt in a loving, lingering touch. It was her goodbye.'[101] For all her dismay about the political situation in Africa, Olive had returned to her roots, and she was able to write equably to Mary, this woman who had been in her life since the age of eighteen:

> It is strange how slowly hope dies: if one can only accept and die gamely. After all, it has been a wonderfully beautiful thing for us to be alive, hasn't it dear? To have loved so many things, and enjoyed Nature so much.[102]

She had a small bedroom on the first floor of Oak Hall, opening onto a large balcony running along two sides of the building. She suffered from the heat, but could walk up and down on the balcony and take tram rides in and out of Cape Town, an hour's ride each day. So she was still walking up and down, to the end of her life maintaining a pattern which she herself felt could have been established in the womb. Her mother had lost two children before she was born, she wrote to Adela Smith in 1909, one when Rebecca was pregnant with her.

> She was almost distracted when the little one died three months before my birth, and said she found no comfort in anything but walking up and down by herself behind the church which stood near the little mission house in which I was born. It's curious, as all my life since I was two or three, I've always had such a passion for walking up and down.[103]

Cronwright's brother Alfred and his two sons visited her on 26 November at Wynberg. Alfred Cronwright was very impressed with her: she'd enjoyed the children and he had wanted to take her out motoring, which she loved: 'she looked well and was awfully happy . . . she kept us in fits of laughter'.[104] On 3 December she dined with Fan Schreiner, Ursula and Ursula's husband. Before dinner she talked to Ursula alone, expressing several wishes. She was anxious for a post-mortem to be held, 'as findings might be useful to other sufferers'; she wanted to be embalmed and buried temporarily at Maitland alongside her parents, Theo, Ettie and Will, until Cronwright could take her up to the summit of Buffels Kop, where they had decided, shortly after their marriage, that they would be interred. Finally she told Ursula where to find enough gold for the burial.

On 7 December she wrote to Cronwright (though he received this and other letters from these last two weeks after her death) to say that the heat was terrible; sometimes she had to get up twice in the night to change her nightdress because of the perspiration. She was trying to find a different place to live, but despaired of doing so; when she was strong she had loved solitude above all things; now she longed for human beings. On 9 December she wrote to him again, hoping he was out of the London fogs, imagining him in Rome, remembering her father's birthplace outside Stuttgart, and wishing Cronwright could get to see it. For herself she longed to see 'the stars and the veld'.

The same day she rang Ursula and had a long talk with her about Ursula's baby, who was ill; Olive also told her she was having her doctor up the next day to see if he could devise a treatment to ease her heart attacks: they had been made so much worse by the heat that she couldn't take exercise without getting one. The following day she went into town to catch the English mail. She was apparently in good spirits, meeting and lunching with a young relative. She returned to Oak Hall; the land-lady said later that she seemed very well and cheerful. Between five and six o'clock her doctor called and examined her; she said this was an exceptionally good day and he should call again, as she wanted him to see her when she had an attack.

In the small hours of the night of 10 to 11 December, a woman in the next bedroom thought she heard a moving and a slight coughing. When the maid went in with Olive's early morning tea, she found her dead, lying in her bed, just as she had gone to sleep. The hot water bottle was in its usual place under her shoulder-blade, her glasses were on, her little mapping-pen lay in her right hand, the book she had been reading lay open in her left hand on her chest, the candle had burnt down and out. There was 'not the least sign of any struggle for breath, any pain, any distress or any movement whatever'.

Olive had 'spoken much of death recently', Ursula Scott told Alfred Cronwright.[105] Although it was inevitable that as she grew older and iller she should be preoccupied primarily with physical suffering and the special anxieties of a dying person – that others should be prepared for her death, that her papers be in order and in safe keeping – her concern with death was also a thread running through the whole of her life. As a ten-year-old she had been fascinated by the 'endless existence' which claimed her sister Ellie, and, equally, by the 'annihilation of self' that she had experienced in loving her when she was alive. From childhood, then, these two issues – of the nature of self and the nature of existence in time – were closely linked and were later incorporated into an attitude to death that Olive never lost. To die was to become part of nature, to lose all boundaries, to attain the silence and peace which were so elusive in life. Death brought the possibility of rapture, of the 'greatest delight',[106] for it seemed to promise that same annihilation of self that she had felt around Ellie. It was also, of course, the greatest mystery, and would remain so: 'Oh, Anna!' she said to Anna Purcell in Maitland cemetery very shortly before she died herself, 'When shall we understand the mystery of death?'[107]

Of course, too, there were fears. Supposing death were as lonely as life, or as much of a struggle? Olive tended to express these fears in her thirties, when she was in England and most urgently absorbed in questions of personal identity and love:

> I suppose one never kills out one's personal instincts entirely till death comes and sets one free. The terrible thing will be if death comes, and instead of *rest the struggle goes on on the other side*.[108]

Or again, from her convent in Harrow and again to Ellis:

> For the first time for long, long, I thought of death, realised it, that wandering out of the soul alone; that's what I always *feel* death will be, though I know it won't be. I got that kind of suffocating feeling I used to have at Ratel Hoek, as if I couldn't bear to think of it, as if my physical heart was breaking.[109]

As she got older and needed to feel that her life had had meaning, her main preoccupation was with her unfinished work. A woman in the Free State had written to her for advice about a particularly stressful domestic situation, she wrote to Mary Brown, and it had revived 'that terrible wish' for somewhere to finish *From Man to Man*,

> that it might make such lonely and struggling women as she less lonely. Oh, it would be so beautiful a thing to think when I was dying that I had done that. I should feel then that I had done something with my life – that it was not all failure and loss. It would square life to me.[110]

For the most part, however, she wanted to accept that her death was inevitable, and that it was only one of the issues facing her in old age. 'I opposed this war,' she wrote to Betty Molteno in 1918, 'because of the evil I foresaw it would produce for generations to come. One must face the future of humanity broadly and calmly, as one must strive to face one's own death; and *not to fear*.'[111]

For herself Olive wanted a sudden death. She was appalled, and very understandably, by the rigours of Ettie's slow death; she wanted none of the inexplicit wasting that she had created for both Undine and Lyndall. She told Alfred Cronwright that as a girl she had prayed to be thrown from her horse or be struck by lightning,[112] and during World War One she wrote to Ellis that 'a bomb would be just as good'.[113] In Olive's mind, then, sudden death would bring the release and rest that illness provided in her novels but never in her own life. It would mean an end to all pain.

That this should be her attitude explains the letter to Dollie Radford after Eleanor Marx's suicide in 1898 to which Yvonne Kapp has taken great exception. Listing resolutions lamenting Eleanor's death, and referring to obituaries too numerous to mention, Kapp remarks that 'one discordant and appalling note' was struck by Olive Schreiner, writing from Kimberley 'eager to learn further details'.[114] Taking Olive's wish, should she be in England, to 'find the servant who was the last person with her and get her to tell me all she knew'[115] as evidence of her destructive personality as a whole, Kapp fastened on the end of Olive's letter as the most outlandish of all, italicizing its first sentence: 'I am so glad Eleanor is dead. It is such a mercy she has escaped from him.'[116] Olive was probably doing no more than express what a lot of people felt about Eleanor's association with Aveling, though she did it absolutely ingenuously and in a way that was bound to be misunderstood. More importantly, she was wishing Eleanor the peace that she felt Eleanor had rarely had when she was alive.

Just as Olive had chastised a particular novelist for 'fingering his characters with his hands, not pressing them up against him till he felt their hearts beat',[117] so she wanted to come close up to Eleanor's death, to understand it, if only it were possible, from the inside. She brought that desire with her to England in 1913, when she sought out Dollie Radford in person, for 'no one I have ever met' could tell her anything about it.[118] Olive wanted a perspective on Eleanor's life as a whole, and it was a life that had ended in the most basic self-destruction. In insinuating that her curiosity about the death itself was part of a morbid and insensitive prurience, Kapp overlooked the significance that death had for Olive, not just as 'data', but as metaphor as well.

News of Olive's death reached Cronwright on 13 December, when he saw a press cable about it in his morning newspaper.[119] Later that day he got a private cable from Fan, telling him that 'Olive died peacefully tenth'. He had had no warning, and during the next three weeks he received four letters and a postcard from Olive; it felt as though she was still talking to him. Immediately after Fan's cable arrived, he cabled his brother to take possession of Olive's belongings, put all her papers in a strong room, and hand over her will to one Godlonton, presumably a solicitor. The cable ended emphatically: 'Carry out burial instructions. Will return about end January. Please write fully.'

Much is unexplained in the last chapter of Cronwright's biography, and his movements, correspondingly, are hard to understand. He remained in England for a full six weeks after Olive's death – indeed his brother, who wrote to him about the funeral at length, felt it would be a 'pity' for him to come out to the Cape straight away, and so, apparently, did Fan – and gave no reason for his decision. Whereas in other parts of his book there are lengthy justifications for his behaviour, here there is none, and in a situation which calls for one. He had the special difficulty of realizing Olive's death in another country, away from the ritual of the burial; not surprisingly did it all seem 'incredible; impossible'.

First thing on 11 December the maid at Oak Hall telephoned Ursula and Dr Charles Murray, Olive's doctor. Alfred Cronwright went to the Scotts' house as soon as he heard the news of Olive's death, and he and Ursula began to make arrangements for the burial according to Cronwright's previous instructions. Ursula, knowing how much Olive had wanted a post-mortem, arranged for one, though she was anxious that Cronwright should not think 'I took a great deal upon myself in arranging at once for Dr. Murray and Dr. Molteno to perform [it].' Fan joined her later at Oak Hall and the two of them put Olive's things together and had them brought to Ursula's house; a couple of days later, when Cronwright's cable reached Alfred, her boxes of papers were put into a strong-room in town.*

After the post-mortem, Olive's body was moved from the mortuary to an undertaker's in Wynberg, where she was embalmed. Alfred told Ursula that Cronwright insisted there be no religious ceremony, and he ascertained that a burial in a cemetery was still permissible. A Unitarian minister in Cape Town, a great admirer of Olive's, said he was willing to sign the burial certificate if it had to be done by a minister, but Alfred had 'got some inkling that some ceremony or speaking might be attempted, so decided to cut all clergymen out', and the undertaker signed the certificate. It was a central issue, as Alfred's letter to Cronwright of 13–17 December indicates:

* Olive's anxiety about her papers in the week before her death indicates an awareness that she would die very soon. Her papers were all at Ursula Scott's house, where Ursula was sorting them for her, but Olive wanted them to be safe from fire and planned to have them taken into town to a strong room. In the meantime, she brought them back to Oak Hall. They were still there at the time of her death.

A minister had nothing, absolutely nothing, whatever to do with any part of the arrangements. I felt I could not be too particular about this.

His anxiety about religious intervention applied to the mourners as well:

I understand some people wanted to say or have something said at the graveside ... but I refused to have a word spoken; my reason for this being I was afraid Christianity might be drawn in and I knew that would not please you.

On the afternoon of 12 December, a Sunday, Alfred had Olive's body brought to Wynberg station, where Dr Brown, three young relatives of Olive's, and an old servant of the Schreiner family were waiting. As they proceeded along the line to Maitland Cemetery, near Cape Town, many people joined the train, although no announcement about the burial had been made. At the cemetery station the coffin was placed on a wheeled carrier and they all followed to the grave. The burial took place in complete silence, and after it was over, Fan and Ursula and some other women went back to put palm leaves on the grave. A friend of Cronwright's wrote that she had never seen so many women at a funeral before. The *Cape Argus* remarked on the simplicity of the ceremony.

Olive's will, made in December 1913, appointed Cronwright sole heir and executor. Drawn up by Will, apparently from her notes, it appears to be the only one that she ever formally completed. She had made a series of notes for a will between 1890 and 1892, some of them no more than scraps of paper, and one in Ellis' handwriting; they were basically instructions about her papers and manuscripts, variously appointing Will and Ellis as her literary executors.[120] These notes were, of course, nullified by the will of 1913. At the time of writing the biography, Cronwright was getting under way with the publication of Olive's other allegories, *Undine* and *From Man to Man*. Olive's will as such does not appear in the biography, so it is not known whether she had revised her earlier wish for *Undine* not to be published. It may be so; on the other hand, a harshly worded business letter from Cronwright to Fisher Unwin in 1926 indicates that he was using the privileges of a sole executor in a somewhat high-handed way: 'The only thing that ultimately matters is what *I* decide, and you and Ellis both know that.'[121]

His discussion of the will in the biography is much more temperate. In pursuance of his determination to do all she wished, he says, he went further than the terms she had set out. Among her papers he found one in her own handwriting, written at De Aar in November 1912, apparently notes for an intended will. If, after all expenses in connection with her burial had been defrayed, and there remained more than a certain sum she wished Cronwright to have, she wanted such balance to be used to found a Scholarship for Women at the South African College, Cape Town. Since Olive's estate was 'negligible financially', Cronwright immediately provided in his own will for the creation of a trust, the interest on which would amount to about the same sum as the 'leading South African scholarships already in existence'. Although anxious – and, as usual, obsessively so – to emphasize that his estate 'owed nothing to her money or her help, but was wholly the result of my own unaided efforts', it was still a 'great solace' to Cronwright that this wish of Olive's would be carried out. It would be a medical scholarship, and should be administered without reference to race, colour, or religion, 'poor women and girls to have preference'.[122]

The most important term of Olive's will, however, was that relating to her interment. Soon after their marriage in 1894 Olive and Cronwright, then living at Krantz Plaats, had made the ascent of Buffels Hoek. This was the mountainous part of the farm, and it was at its summit, Buffels Kop, that Olive had wanted to be buried. They had climbed the 2000 feet from the plain, Olive in some distress because Cronwright was so much fitter and faster than she, and they never went there again. But on the one occasion when they were there together, Olive was totally absorbed in the landscape around her. The mountains and kopjes of the Karoo stretched for mile after mile, and Olive 'stood and gazed at it all in an ecstasy'. She was silent, and Cronwright had never seen her so rapt; she was looking down on the veld where she had been a governess twenty years before. Before they went down, she said: 'We must be buried here, you and I, Cron. I shall buy one morgen of this top.'[123] Cronwright took the matter up 'at once'. The owner would not hear of selling the ground, but gave her the morgen on the summit.

In the will of 1913 Olive reiterated her wish to be buried on Buffels Kop, and laid it down that no one else except Cronwright, their baby and her dog Nita should be buried there. Shortly after he left De Aar in December 1919, Cronwright buried the baby and the dog in a temporary cement grave in his garden. Then he went down to Cradock, and with the owner of Buffels Hoek went up to Buffels Kop, where he had not been since the walk of 1894, and showed him the spot where the grave was to be. He drew his own will and provided for the detail of the interment in case of his own death. On his return to South Africa in 1921 he went to Cradock and made arrangements with the local undertaker to build the grave.[124]

This was to be a very difficult task. The top of the Kop was ironstone, so hard that not even a cold steel chisel could make an impression on it, and the sarcophagus had to be built on the exposed layer. In addition, there was no water, sand, or cement on the Kop and all had to be carried up by donkeys. The stonemason and his African workers camped at night on the plain and climbed the 2000 feet to the Kop each day in order to avoid the midwinter cold of the summit. In spite of these drawbacks the sarcophagus was completed in under two months, and with enthusiasm on the part of at least one of the workers – the Johannesburg engraver who prepared the brass plate and cut the letters for it had 'read and loved' *African Farm*.

Cronwright wanted the reinterment to take place on 13 August, the first anniversary of his and Olive's parting in London. Olive's coffin was exhumed a few days beforehand, and he prepared for 'Our Last Ride Together'. As the train left Table Mountain behind on its way up to Cradock, the clouds began to fade away, and

the spaces that were so much to her began to open up; the sun she so loved, that she said she could understand people worshipping it, began to shine . . . I seemed almost to see her sitting in the window corner, bunched up in her curious way, her great eyes and keen face aglow with the beauty of the mountains.

When the train passed through De Aar on the following day, the coffins containing the baby and Olive's dog Nita were placed in the funeral van with Olive's.

On the morning of 13 August, everyone involved was up early and on their way to the mountain by eight o'clock, making the first part of the journey by car. There had been no publicity, just as there had been none for the burial in December, but a number of people joined the procession, including a photographer Cronwright had hired for the occasion. All assembled at the northern end of the plateau, where the three coffins had been carried up from the first krantz in the early morning, and the party set out along the high plateau for the Kop.

It was not a 'funeral procession'; at my request all walked informally. I told them of the opening lines of *A Grammarian's Funeral*, one of Olive's great favourites – 'Let us begin and carry up this corpse, *Singing together*' – and, adding a few words in explanation of the poem, asked the people to 'carry up' Olive in the same spirit.

Near the Kop a large eagle flew overhead, one that Cronwright could not remember having seen before; to him and the woman from the neighbouring farm it seemed like the Bird of Truth from *African Farm* welcoming them to Olive's last resting-place. There were early butterflies and some early flowers along the way: to the local *Midland News* 'there was as little stir in nature as there was in the world of men'.

By midday the party was on the summit, where it was joined by the Cawood family from Ganna Hoek, who had ascended from their side of the range. When everyone was assembled at the sarcophagus, Cronwright spoke 'as well as I could', though to the reporter it was with 'obvious strain'. He thanked the workmen, and said it was most appropriate that Olive had been carried up by Africans, 'because she had always been their champion'. He described Olive's feeling for Ellie and her sense, after the child died, that 'in everything she saw the baby sister'. Similarly, he continued, nature now seemed to him almost visibly permeated by Olive's spirit. He ended by repeating, 'with almost breaking intensity', a verse from Tennyson's *In Memoriam*. There was no other ceremony. The coffins were placed in the sarcophagus together with a laurel wreath from the Browns. The *Midland News* shared in the transport of emotion, concluding its report thus:

> No fence encloses the morgen of land on which the sarcophagus stands; it is surrounded by the wild life she loved and in view of the mountains that appear to have no end.

Cronwright's biography of Olive Schreiner ends here, with the young girl that Olive had once been 'out at last on the wild Karoo, never to leave it again'. He had made her into a child of nature, for it was only as such that he was able to contain his basic disapproval of her 'strange and incredible' personality. In his mind he saw a causal chain involving her absorption in nature, her genius as being in some way untutored, and, most importantly – since it was this he set himself to rationalize – her inability to produce, or be part of the 'real' world. It gave the impression of a woman whose talents and personality had sprung from nowhere.

CHAPTER NINE

Broken and Untried?

Far from Olive Schreiner being an untutored child of nature, it is precisely her conscious struggles for self-definition, in productive and sexual terms, which make her compelling for women and the women's movement. Not that the sources of her late adolescent writing, her lapses into unproductivity after early womanhood, her deep unhappiness at virtually all times of her life, and her own sense of failure at the end of it, are easy to explain.

For the woman writer, intellectual growth and independent work were to be the way out of the feminine paralysis. Breaking out of the power-lessness of the traditional female role, she would struggle in the external world of work for economic independence. Creative work would give freedom to live an independent life, freedom to travel, the right frankly to assert her sense of self, not least her sexual needs, and the capacity to intervene in politics. These needs were pre-figured in the frustrations and the strivings of the young women of her novels; Olive herself would live and work as they had failed to do. Her characters had been caught in the predicament of the female who could experience the world, but not act upon it. She herself would act, through work and personal liberation.

Yet in the end, like Mary Wollstonecraft a century earlier, there remained that gap between her demand for her woman's rights and her overwhelming sense of her wrongs; somehow she could not throw off her sense of personal oppression. More painful than that: in fierce con-tradiction with her early self-strivings, she found that in the end she had struggled not for but against her individuality. The pursuit of self – as the Prelude to *From Man to Man* shows – had brought no gratification, only punishment. Had she not been damaged in being singled out so young?

She had then to lose herself (her self) at all costs. Through her correspondence run themes of selfless love, the role of work in creating a boundary between the self and the emotions, the desperate suffering of life – and the terror of inflicting misery with the conviction that she was bound to do so. The sense of sin which her self-education in freethought had seemed to release was never really to leave her. It imposed an ethic of selflessness – even, at times, expressed in religious terms – and an incapacity to express antagonism in personal relations.

The mission of selflessness, perhaps paradoxically, prompted a lifetime of self-absorption. The punishing sense of guilt at hurting others went back to her early childhood, and prompted a continuing reflection on it. The child of the Prelude was punished; Olive ever felt so, and her sense of exclusion, of marginality, was persistent. Her experience of rootlessness was, of course, very real. She felt herself to be a motherless child:[1] her mother had been superior, distant and severe; her father tender but ineffectual, and a foreigner, ever uncomfortable in Africa. At the age of twelve she had had to adapt to a complete disruption in the care she received. Her elder brothers and sisters could not console her sense of herself as orphaned. The young orphan was also, moreover, some kind of outcast. In her personal, private world she struggled from an early age with the charge of being odd and wicked; her freethinking prompted isolation, and at times social persecution, during much of her life in South Africa. The years in England broke her intellectual isolation, but she lived there as an expatriate. She made close lifelong friends, and with some she achieved deep, searching relationships; but she lived alone, in rooming houses, as an itinerant, without family, and with the most tenuous contact with English social life of any class. She lived as a single woman until her late thirties; as a childless woman and separated from her husband during some of the most stressful years of her life.

Living alone grew in part from her fear of forming loving relationships. At the same time it was in her living that she experimented with the ideas about personal freedom that informed her novels. As Havelock Ellis said to her shortly after they met in 1884: 'We have no code of morals which forces us to be hypocrites.'[2] This was the rationale for a frankness about sexual feeling and a commitment to a relationship that shocked landladies not because it was salacious but because it assumed that friendship as well as desire could exist between the sexes. It was a way of living that departed radically from the moral code in which she grew up, and she exposed herself to great risks. She paid a heavy price in the persistent guilts and griefs of her personal relationships and a lifelong and debilitating illness. She was forced to acknowledge that she was in no real relationship with life or thought 'in England or Africa or anywhere else', as she put it.[3]

Even back in South Africa, she was once again an outsider. She was too critical, too knowing, to fit into colonial social life. Since she was a celebrity, a certain allowance could be made for her eccentricity, and she commanded respect and recognition. Now her public place and her public role became part of her rejection of female powerlessness. At times she wrote of herself that she felt she was something of a man. In a sexist culture in which women were mystified by being objects of men's contempt as well as their reverence, how could an assertive, free woman validate herself? Perhaps by experiencing herself as a man. As a writer, for example, or as a polemicist within South Africa, Olive Schreiner was almost inevitably a 'man', given the distribution of roles within the culture; the same is true of her as a self-determining personality. But as a woman, and one more sensitive than most to the material and psychological servitude of women as a sex, was it not a real betrayal to identify oneself as a man? How could Olive Schreiner, as we asked in our introduction, 'live like a man, but like a woman as well'?

She found it impossible to do both successfully. Her sexual identity was split, and there was no way for her as a woman to integrate the powerful, aspiring part of herself (the 'masculine'). This issue of power was more than an internally terrifying fantasy of Olive's; it was an equally telling social constraint on women's freedom of self-expression. The one reinforced the other. What Olive did do, in her personal relationships at least, was to become a child and give up her claims to control. Her illness, further, was an expression of just this kind of conflict. Although in her sexual relationships the conflicts between activity and passivity, control and powerlessness were played out most acutely, they were more general issues for her. She herself wrote that the conflict between the duty to the individual (presumably she meant the duty to others) and the duty to one's talents was the 'agony' of her life;[4] and in her illness she achieved some sort of resolution of the problem. The literal duty of the asthmatic was to 'lie still'. If Olive could do this, there might be moments of relief from the contradictions of her situation.

Significantly, Olive's asthma developed in late adolescence after an emotional involvement which transgressed the code of propriety into which her mother had attempted to educate her children. Olive became a sick girl, and then a sick woman. Sickness, as it were, brought her back into society as a powerless individual; it provided a counterpoint to the force of her writing and of her unconventionality. As far as she herself was concerned, illness signified and prompted only flight, stillness, and a yearning for rest. She did not – indeed could not – interpret her illness to include the role that the pattern of her relationships played in reinforcing or colluding in it. Those concepts did not exist during her lifetime. Illness was not yet seen as an interactive process. And if the concepts did not exist, then ways of thinking and perceiving were similarly constrained. Illness, for Olive, was simply a continual reminder of her sense of utter personal failure; a failure which caused her to remark, towards the end of her life, that she was 'only a broken and untried possibility'.[5]*

Broken perhaps, but hardly untried. She tried herself unceasingly, and from these trials there emerged a peculiar but compelling constellation of weaknesses and failures as well as strengths. In her writing, although she never got beyond *The Story of an African Farm* in her fiction, she successfully freed herself from the Biblical literalisms of her childhood.

---

* These are more in the nature of conjectures with hindsight. In another way, Olive's asthma can be explained by looking at it from the perspective of late nineteenth-century attitudes to diagnosis and treatment, by finding its meaning in the meaning it was given at the time. For it was not until after the turn of the century that asthma began to be understood as a specific disease entity with a complex aetiology involving both allergenic and psychogenic factors. Until then it was not always clearly differentiated from other respiratory conditions and treatment was pragmatic, with many new inventions and endless old remedies purporting to cure. There was certainly a concept of the asthmatic personality, but it was barely distinguishable from the stereotype of the hyperactive individual whom doctors, in general, liked to pacify. Plain diet and exercise were recommended, and control of the emotions. In her own relationships with doctors, Olive experienced the full range of contemporary opinions on the subject of her chest condition. To one it was not asthma, but bronchitis; to another she should never expect a cure, only relief with narcotics; to yet another she was just a bundle of nerves: 'once you have said she is asthmatic you have said all there is to say.'

By the 1920s, at the time of Olive's death, a psychosomatic theory of asthma which has basically lasted to the present day, if only among a small proportion of practitioners, was being developed. It focused on the specific problem of the mother-child relationship in an asthmatic patient, whether child or adult. It did not, however, ever exclude the allergenic or constitutional factors predisposing to the illness. But it reiterated – and with relative constancy, if one follows mainstream psychosomatic and a good part of the psychoanalytic literature to the present day – conflicts over dependence and independence, the problem of aggression and separation from the mother, and the whole issue of a symbiotic bond. We mention it here as a way of looking at asthma consistent with the main themes of Olive's personal life.

In doing so, she created a novel whose brilliance and power have been acknowledged over and over again. As a novelist, however, her work was overtaken and her reputation suffered when fiction changed and feminism declined. Modernist criticism of the 1920s situated her as an intellectual novelist of the Victorian age, almost petulantly obsessed with the position of women. This was indeed her purpose: she wrote to change consciousness, both of and about women. When she could no longer use one form she tried another, but despite the different literary forms she chose, her preoccupations were continuously linked and reinforced. What her prose did not express, her correspondence did. In her letters to both Havelock Ellis and Karl Pearson she broke with conventional Victorian inhibition on sexual matters and demanded a frankness of expression in response that she herself was unable to achieve in her novels. Further-more, in her letters to Ellis she seems often to be writing from the unconscious, allowing delights and anxieties to come up and be joined with more abstract considerations of her situation. For all that she claimed 'feeling' was dead in her, she was immersed in it.

The continuity of her concern on the women's question was ultimately expressed as *Woman and Labour*. Olive approached women from their work as reproducers of labour power – or, in the language of the time, nurturers of the race. The work as a whole, quintessentially Victorian in its evolutionism, shows the limitations of a person who went furthest among feminists in trying to study the origins and specifics of women's oppression, but whose conceptions were overlaid by the strongly romantic notions of her time as to the specialness of women. Thus she expressed no vision of a reorganization in the social division of labour, no need to challenge the division of tasks within the family as a whole. The importance she attached in her personal life to the transformation of per-sonal relations between men and women is only rarely present in her texts.

Yet she knew that the family was a system of containment and she broke from it. She knew that the hierarchy of sex was reflected in notions of uneven sexuality between men and women, and she rejected these. She sought relationships independently of marriage, rejecting the mothering role if it was to be women's only sphere. She believed, with Ibsen's Nora, that men suffered 'as much as women from the falseness of the relations'. She was adamant that women must make efforts to under-stand their own sex, but never abandon the efforts to understand men as well. She sought involvements with men, like Edward

Carpenter and Ellis, who rejected the norms of Victorian middle-class masculinity.[6] At the same time her own emotional needs dictated a longing for the private, perfect bond between a man and a woman, and she retreated continually into her fantasy of blissful union. It meant, in fact, that the orthodoxy went unchallenged. This was one of the contradictions from which she struggled to free herself, and failed.

This personal struggle was recorded in her letters; to *Woman and Labour* was left the exposition of a materialist explanation for women's oppression – namely that women's place in society is determined by their place in production, and that women need once again to have their share of socially useful work. Even this was a rather unsustained exposition, trailing off into polemic where sharper social analysis was required. She respected theory; she relied on books and needed them. In pursuit of an alternative to theology, she read widely, but unsystematically and without discipline, even capriciously; accordingly her critiques of books and of society were more intuitive than theorized.

It was her contact in England with socialists in discussion groups and in the labour movement which made her into an adherent of the socialist cause, but she spent no time in any organized movement. Ever her politics were thus solitarily pursued. In England she was briefly within and then on the fringes of groups concerned with sexual politics; in South Africa she could identify with no organization at all, except as an occasional speaker or sponsor of a women's congress or cause. She was engrossed in political issues at a time of profound changes in South Africa, and she recognized Rhodes and the international capital he commanded as the principal instrument of these changes. She castigated him as a representative of a system; the very concept of a system was unusual at the time, let alone its identification as capitalism. There were few to understand, let alone associate with her. She refused to identify with white politics and white politicians and came to despise them. In England she had imbibed respect for trade union principles, and was a champion of organized labour, but when the white working class of South Africa connived in the operation of a colour bar against black workers, she alone recognized that the colour question was really the labour question, and that labour, both black and white, could not be free unless it was united. Her independence from organized politics earned her the freedom to assail them, and there was no more relentless critic in her day. At the same time her political aloneness caused her to make some facile judgements and several unexpected reversals. The most marked was her turnabout after the end of the Boer war when, after investing deep emotion in the Afrikaner republican cause, she threw it over for the Africans. She explained herself in highly sentimental terms: 'I'm always with the underdog, not with the top dog. When people are very big and successful (or causes either) I don't feel very much interest in them. They don't need me.'[7] It was a protective, patronizing attitude that grew as much from her isolation as her altruism.

She suffered the persistent pain of this isolation, both political and personal. Indeed the two were joined, for her sense of politics included the necessity for the individual to define her independence and make it an inviolable part of herself.[8] Lyndall's adolescent protest in *African Farm* against the life of the farm, her determination to bear her child despite the ostracism it would cause, were made possible by the depth of her commitment to herself, her refusal to compromise for the sake of social convention or the security of a loveless marriage. She would let no one possess her. Olive set herself to enlarge this conception of freedom in her own life. She made important claims for herself, and in her struggles to reach them she savaged herself. Despite the constant pain, she did not resolve those issues of personal and productive relationships – her needs and her sense of self as a woman with those of her work as a writer – and the tension persisted to the end.

Of course, too much can be made of her internal conflicts and too little of the constraints imposed on her by the times in which she lived. She took gigantic leaps – away from religion into freethinking; away from colonial racism and segregationist white politics to advocacy of the African cause; out of the suffocating limits imposed upon women and into the exploration of female psychology and sexuality. But her social science was too nervously evolutionist; her analysis of South Africa intuitive and unsystematic. Much of her melancholy and desperation were induced by the awareness that her attempts were incomplete, and her goals probably unattainable. We have written that her incapacity to finish *From Man to Man* reflected the unfinished state of her own life: for she was a product of a period of great intellectual and political change, but one of transition too, in which alternatives were stirring but as yet inchoate. In South Africa the alternatives to the politics of white domination were slowly forming within the ranks of organized African political and labour organization. White spokesmen were no longer needed to speak for and about Africans; they were ready to speak for themselves. But this African mass organization was beginning only as Olive died, and her perceptions of the special relationship between class and colour had yet to be theorized by a much later generation of analysts. For women as for Africans she was an advocate of an alternative life and politics, but like the tracts of the abolitionists pleading for the subjected, her writing on the women's question was didactic and rhetorical. At the same time, there was not yet a constituency of emancipated women advocating their own needs, and it meant that her lifelong attempt to bring together different facets of oppression – personal, sexual, material – remained an almost individual concern. For her, however, the crucial absence was not simply that of a sympathetic, active feminism in which she could test out and develop her ideas: she herself lacked a constituency. The absence of an involvement in any one community for any length of time meant inevitably that she lived at one remove from the investigative work being done at the turn of the century by socialists interested in the condition of women, or from the local work of a sustained campaign on demands that she supported like adult suffrage and equal pay. This actual distance gave to her writing on women a certain benevolence, perhaps even the benevolence of someone formed on a mission station.

It is in the context of the current women's liberation movement, however, that some of the paradoxes of Olive Schreiner's life and work can best be set out. For though she was a secular evangelist she was not a defeated woman. Though she was no political organizer she inspired those in Britain who were – suffragettes, co-operators, and socialists – both during her lifetime and after it. Though she was debilitated by illness she was fully immersed in her life. And because feminism in the 1970s set itself to explore the relationship between social, sexual and personal life, it provides a framework for linking the success of *African Farm* with the manifest frustrations of Schreiner's adult life. She lost the shelter of the adolescent self-education that nurtured her novel, with its capacity for imaginative transformations in the mind, and came up against the demands and limits of a late Victorian culture. But in tracing the patterns of her thought and work we have not tried to cut her away from the tension of her life, for she could do no more than live the contradictions that emerged. Perhaps she will always be discovered through *African Farm*; if so, it is in the relationship between the world of her novel and that of her experience that her life takes shape for us now.

NOTES

BOOKS

Books cited frequently in the Notes are abbreviated as follows:

Brown, *Memories*	Mrs John Brown, *Memories of a Friendship* (Cape Town 1923).
Carpenter, *My Days and Dreams*	Edward Carpenter, *My Days and Dreams* (1916).
Eagleton, *Myths of Power*	Terry Eagleton, *Myths of Power, A Marxist Study of the Brontës* (1975).
Ellis, *My Life*	Henry Havelock Ellis, *My Life* (1940).
Kapp, *Family Life*	Yvonne Kapp, *Eleanor Marx. Vol I: Family Life (1855–1883)* (1972).
Kapp, *Crowded Years*	Yvonne Kapp, *Eleanor Marx. Vol II: The Crowded Years (1884–1898)* (1976).
Letters	S. C. Cronwright-Schreiner (ed.), *The Letters of Olive Schreiner* (1924).
Life	S. C. Cronwright-Schreiner, *The Life of Olive Schreiner* (1924).
Lewsen (ed.), *Correspondence, 1890–1898*	Phyllis Lewsen (ed.), *Selections from the Correspondence of J. X. Merriman, 1890–1898* (Cape Town 1963).
Lewsen (ed.), *Correspondence, 1899–1905*	Phyllis Lewsen (ed.), Selections from the *Correspondence of J. X. Merriman, 1899–1905* (Cape Town 1966).
Rowbotham and Weeks, *Socialism and the New Life*	Sheila Rowbotham and Jeffrey Weeks, *Socialism and the New Life, The Personal and Sexual Politics of Edward Carpenter and Havelock Ellis* (1977).
Showalter, *A Literature*	Elaine Showalter, *A Literature of Their Own* (1977, Virago repr. 1978).
Walker, *W. P. Schreiner*	Eric A. Walker, *W. P. Schreiner, A South African* (Oxford 1937).
Walker, *Decline of Hell*	D. P. Walker, *The Decline of Hell, Seventeenth Century Discussions of Eternal Torment* (1964).

MANUSCRIPT COLLECTIONS

Manuscript sources and collections cited are abbreviated as follows:

Carpenter MSS	Letters from Olive Schreiner to Edward Carpenter, Sheffield City Libraries Archives Divisions.
Findlay	Unpublished correspondence between members of the Findlay and Schreiner families in the possession of the late George Findlay, Pretoria, now held by the Department of Historical Papers, University of the Witwatersrand Library, Johannesburg.

HRC   Correspondence between Olive Schreiner and Havelock Ellis with
                  related material, Humanities Research Center, The University of
                  Texas at Austin.
Pearson   Papers and Correspondence of Karl Pearson (1857–1936), held in the
                  Library, University College, London.
Pringle   Olive Schreiner material from the Cradock Public Library held in
                  the Thomas Pringle Collection for English in Africa, Rhodes
                  University Library, Grahamstown.
SAPL   South African Public Library, Cape Town.
Settlers   Albany Museum, 1820 Settlers Division, Grahamstown.
UCTJ   University of Cape Town, J. W. Jagger Library, Rondebosch.

Individuals quoted frequently in correspondence are abbreviated as follows:

GS   Gottlob Schreiner-
RS   Rebecca Schreiner
OS   Olive Schreiner
HE   Havelock Ellis
KP   Karl Pearson
EC   Elizabeth Cobb
CS   Samuel Cron Cronwright-Schreiner
WPS   W. P. Schreiner

INTRODUCTION

1   Elaine Showalter's *A Literature Of Their Own: British Women Novelists from
    Brontë to Lessing* (1978) has been at the forefront of this discussion.
2   Ideas in this paragraph are based on discussion with Martha Vicinus, who is
    currently researching feminist writers between 1880–1920. Showalter places
    Schreiner's allegories in the context both of the fin-de-siècle and her own writer's
    block in *A Literature*, pp. 197–8.
3   Nadine Gordimer, 'English Language Literature and Politics in South Africa',
    Journal of Southern African Studies, vol. 2 no 2 (April 1968).
4   Lewsen (ed.), *Correspondence 1890–1898* pp. 29 and 14; fn 43.
5   E. P. Thompson, 'Solitary Walker', *New Society*, 19 September 1974, a review of
    Clare Tomalin, *The Life and Death of Mary Wollstonecraft* (1974).
6   S. C. Cronwright-Schreiner, *The Life of Olive Schreiner*, London, Unwin (1924).
7   *The Times*, 7 March 1924.
8   Words in quotes are Cronwright's, taken from *Life*. Ideas about the 'hysterical
    personality' are based on entries in *Index Medicus. A Monthly Classified Record of
    the Current Medical Literature of the World* (New York, Boston and Washington,
    1890, 1892, 1898–9), and D. Hack Tuke (ed.), *A Dictionary of Psychological
    Medicine* (1892) vol. 1, to which Bryan Donkin, Olive's doctor in the 1880s, and
    French neurologist and psychiatrist J. M. Charcot contributed.
9   CS to HE, 18 May 1922, HRC.
10 S. C. Cronwright-Schreiner, *The Letters of Olive Schreiner*, London, Unwin (1924).
11 CS to HE, 10 September 1934, HRC.
12 Vera Buchanan-Gould, *Not Without Honour: The Life and Writing of Olive
    Schreiner* (1948); D. L. Hobman, *Olive Schreiner: Her Friends and Times* (1955).
13 Johannes Meintjes, *Olive Schreiner, Portrait of a South African Woman* (Johannes-
    burg 1965).
14 Charlotte Painter and Mary Jane Moffat (eds.), *Revelations: Diaries of Women*
    (New York 1975).

15 Marion V. Friedmann (Johannesburg 1955).
16 Friedmann, *Olive Schreiner*, p. 21.
17 A variety of definitions of the analytic relationship exists. Ours is taken from B. Barnett, 'Intervention, Professionalism and the Child's Rights', paper presented at the 50th Anniversary of the Child Guidance Training Centre, London (June 1979).
18 John S. Haller Jr and Robin M. Haller, *The Physician and Sexuality in Victorian America* (University of Illinois Press 1974). See also Carroll Smith-Rosenberg, 'The Hysterical Woman: Sex Roles and Role Conflict in Nineteenth Century America', *Social Research* 39 (Winter 1972). More generally, Michel Foucault, *History of Sexuality. Vol 1: An Introduction* (1978), has cast doubt on the 'repressive hypothesis' as to nineteenth-century sexual life, especially in relation to female sexuality, and looks instead at the contemporary proliferation of discourses on the subject.
19 Margaret Walters on Mary Wollstonecraft in 'The Rights and Wrongs of Women: Mary Wollstonecraft, Harriet Martineau, Simone de Beauvoir', in Juliet Mitchell and Ann Oakley (eds.), *The Rights and Wrongs of Women* (1976), p. 306.
20 ibid., pp. 304-78.
21 ibid., p. 306.

CHAPTER 1: *Early Life on a Mission Station*

We have drawn on four main manuscript collections: letters by Gottlob Schreiner to his original training institute in the Archiv der Basler Mission, Basel, Switzerland; the archive of the London Missionary Society, held on deposit for the Council for World Mission by the School of Oriental and African Studies, University of London; Gottlob Schreiner's letters to the Wesleyan Mission Society in the archive of the Methodist Church Overseas Division (Methodist Missionary Society), London; and correspondence with the Church Missionary Society held in Church Missionary Society archives, London. These sources have been abbreviated as follows: BASEL, LMS, WMS, CMS.

1 Richard Lovett, *The History of the LMS, 1795-1895* (1899).
2 ibid., p. 534.
3 See W. M. MacMillan, *The Cape Colour Question* (1927).
4 Rev. John Philip, DD, Preface to *Researches in South Africa*, vol. 1 (1828), p. xv. For a combative evaluation of Philip's role see N. Majeke, *The Role of the Missionary in Conquest* (1952).
5 Philip, loc. cit., p. x. See also W. M. MacMillan, *Bantu, Boer and Briton* (1929), p. 66.
6 Robert Ross, 'The Griquas of Philippolis and Kokstad, 1826-1879', unpublished Ph.D. thesis, Cambridge University (1974), is a brilliant exploration of the role of Dr Philip as leader of the modernizing missionaries; likewise a thesis dealing with an earlier period of Griqua history, Martin Legassick, 'The Griqua, the Sotho-Tswana and the Missionaries, 1780-1840: The Politics of a Frontier Zone', unpublished Ph.D. thesis, UCLA (1969).
7 Christian Eipper and GS to Church Missionary Society Committee, 9 January 1837, CMS (G/AC3).
8 GS to Inspector Blumhardt, London, 9 May 1837, BASEL.
9 Eipper and GS to CMS.
10 Particulars about the Rev. Samuel Lyndall are to be found in the Dr Williams Library, 14 Gordon Square, London WC1. See also H. Davies, *The English Free Churches* (1963), and Jones R. Tudor, *Congregationalism in England, 1662-1962* (1962).

11 This was the family of young Andrew Reed, who officiated at Rebecca and Gott-lob's marriage. See Andrew and Charles Reed, *Memoirs of the Life and Philanthropic Labours of Andrew Reed, DD* (3rd edn, 1866).

12 Walter Wilson, *The Outlines of an Essay Towards an History of Dissenting Churches in London and its Environs, with an Appendix relating to the Methodists*, n.d.

13 Census of 1841.

14 *Life*, p. 7.

15 Tudor, *Congregationalism*, p. 232.

16 See Geoffrey Best, 'Evangelicalism and the Victorians' in A. Symondson (ed.), *The Victorian Crisis of Faith* (1970).

17 GS's Report for Year 1839 to Rev. W. Ellis, LMS Home Secretary, Philippolis, LMS.

18 Ross, 'The Griquas of Philippolis'.

19 See letters by Dr J. Philip, 4 December 1839 and 16 April 1841, T. Atkinson, 20 February 1840 and 26 May 1840, and GS, 16 September 1840 and 7 June 1841, LMS.

20 GS's Report for Year 1841, Philippolis, LMS.

21 GS to Rev. Tidman, Thaba Nchu, 25 July 1842, LMS.

22 Dr J. Philip, 'On Case of Gottlob Schreiner', 26 May 1842, LMS.

23 GS to Rev. Tidman, 25 July 1842, LMS.

24 GS to Rev. Tidman, Beersheba, 30 September 1842, LMS.

25 GS to Inspector Hoffmann, Basel, 20 October 1843, 10 January 1844, 20 October 1845, BASEL.

26 London Missionary Society to GS, 7 July 1846, LMS.

27 GS to Wesleyan Mission Society, Thaba Nchu, 4 December 1846, WMS.

28 GS to Inspector Hoffmann, Umpukani, 3 April 1850, BASEL.

29 Joyce Murray (ed.), *Young Mrs. Murray Goes to Bloemfontein, 1856–1860* (Cape Town 1954).

30 Joan Findlay (ed.), *The Findlay Letters, 1806–1870* (Pretoria 1954), pp. 112–13.

31 GS to Wesleyan Mission Society, Wittebergen, 6 May 1857, WMS.

32 This account of Schreiner family life and discipline is drawn from Findlay (ed.), *Findlay Letters*, pp. 95–164.

33 GS to Wesleyan Mission Society, 10 April 1851, WMS.

34 See Theo Schreiner to OS, Kimberley, 19 March 1880 (?), *Life*, pp. 41–2.

35 *Life*, p. 66.

CHAPTER 2: *Governess and Freethinker*

Where no references are given, information about this period of Olive's life, including quotations from her journals, family letters, and others' recollections of her, can be found in *Life*, Ch. 2, 'Childhood and Girlhood', pp. 55–98, and Ch. 3, 'The Governess', pp. 99–148. Where verbal recollection of her as a child is involved, we have relied more on others' statements than on hers, since she was given to exaggeration and to getting her dates wrong. The other biographies, Vera Buchanan-Gould, *Not Without Honour* (1955), D. L. Hobman, *Olive Schreiner, Her Friends and Times* (1955), and Johannes Meintjes, *Olive Schreiner* (Johannesburg 1965), follow Cronwright-Schreiner's information with varying amounts of additional manuscript sources, and we have used them mainly as historiographic sources. We have used Alan F. Hattersley, *An Illustrated Social History of South Africa* (Cape Town 1969), for basic information about schooling, journalism and libraries. More detail, especially on the local libraries and their holdings, can be found in Theo Friis, *The Public Library in South Africa* (1962). On issues of Christian theology and the crisis of faith very little has been written

– at least that is available in this country – on the South African experience. We have used Geoffrey Rowell, *Hell and the Victorians: A Study of the Nineteenth Century Theological Controversies concerning Eternal Punishment and the Future Life* (Oxford 1974), especially pp. vii–viii, 2–16, for an introduction to the field of eschatology, and found very useful D. P. Walker, *The Decline of Hell, Seventeenth Century Discussions of Eternal Torment* (1964), for an overview of the doctrinal issues involved. For a flavour of evangelical teachings on practical Christianity of the kind available to Rebecca Lyndall's generation, see Anon, 'The Poetry of Death', *Tait's Magazine* XXII (1855), pp. 157–9, and the very influential Henry Venn, *The Complete Duty of Man: or a System of Doctrinal and Practical Christianity* (various edns, 1763–1838). On the context of Herbert Spencer's contribution to the debate between science and religion, see J. D. Y. Peel, *Herbert Spencer: The Evolution of a Sociologist* (1971). On Spencer's concept of progress, see J. D. Y. Peel, 'Spencer and the Neo-Evolutionists', *Sociology* 3 (1969) pp. 173–91. European women's lives in South Africa, unsurprisingly, are not well documented. Alan F. Hattersley, *A Victorian Lady at the Cape, 1849–1851* (Cape Town 1951), is invaluable, though for a slightly earlier period than Olive's. See also Lucy Duff Gordon, 'Letters from the Cape', in Francis Galton (ed.), *Vacation Tourists and Notes of Travel 1862–3* (1864), pp. 119–222, for a European woman's impressions of nine months at the Cape. All the digger memoirs contain the odd reference to women at the Fields, but the material is still scant.

1 To HE, n.d., quoted in *Life*, p. 67.
2 *Nation and Athenaeum*, 26 March 1921, quoted in *Life*, p. 222.
3 *Life*, p. 186.
4 Marion V. Friedmann, *Olive Schreiner, A Study in Latent Meanings* (Johannesburg 1955), pp. 43–5.
5 *Life*, p. 245.
6 Points about Schreiner's personality made by Friedmann, *Olive Schreiner*, and suggested by Joyce Berkman, University of Massachusetts at Amherst, in an unpublished paper, 'Olive Schreiner: Feminism on the Frontier' (1978).
7 *Life*, p. 219.
8 To Mrs Francis Smith, 22 October 1907, De Aar, in *Letters*, p. 274. Olive dedicated *From Man to Man*, her third novel, to Ellie thus:

> 'Nor knowest thou what argument
> Thy life to thy neighbour's creed hath lent.'

9 See Luke 11.10–13, 12.20–23; John 13.34; 1 Corinthians 13.1–13; 1 John 4.7–9. See also Psalms 4, 39, 41, 49 and 51 for her concern with transgression and redemption.
10 Hattersley, *Victorian Lady*, pp. 44–7.
11 Ettie Schreiner to Kate Findlay, 20 January 1868 and 16 June 1868, *Findlay*.
12 Ideas in this paragraph are based on data in Susan Budd, 'The Loss of Faith: Reasons for Unbelief among Members of the Secular Movement in England, 1850–1950', *Past and Present* 36 (April 1967), pp. 106–125.
13 Alfred William Benn, *The History of English Rationalism in the Nineteenth Century* (2 vols., 1906), vol. 2, pp. 135–45.
14 Hattersley, *Illustrated Social History*, pp. 245–7.
15 Herbert Spencer, *First Principles* (6th edn, 1911), vol. 1, p. 11.
16 ibid., p. xi.
17 RS to Kate Findlay, Hertzog, 25 August 1871, *Findlay*.
18 ibid., and OS to Kate Findlay, Dordrecht, 6 April 1872; RS to Ettie Schreiner, n.d., *Findlay*.
19 To Mrs Cawood, Bournemouth, 19 March 1886, *Letters*, p. 95.

20 *Life*, pp. 219–20.
21 See G. A. Leyds, *A History of Johannesburg* (Johannesburg 1964), pp. 47–8.
22 To Kate Findlay, Hertzog, August 1872, *Findlay*.
23 To Kate Findlay, Hertzog, 18 August 1872, *Findlay*.
24 RS to Kate Findlay, Hertzog, 6 October 1872, *Findlay*.
25 Buchanan-Gould, *Not Without Honour*, p. 39.
26 Meintjes, *Olive Schreiner*, p. 21.
27 RS to Kate Findlay, Hertzog, 28 November 1872, *Findlay*.
28 Information and quotations in this and the next five paragraphs are taken from John Angove, *In the Early Days: Pioneer Life on the South African Diamond Fields* (Kimberley and Johannesburg 1910); J. W. Matthews, *Incwadi Yami, or Twenty Years' Personal Experience of South Africa* (1887); Charles A. Payton, *The Diamond Diggings of South Africa, A Personal and Practical Account* (1872); and H. J. and R. E. Simons, *Class and Colour in South Africa 1850–1950* (1969).
29 To Kate Findlay, New Rush, 30 April 1873, *Findlay*.
30 CS to HE, 15 January 1922, HRC.
31 To HE, Aspley Guise, 3 July 1884, *Letters*, p. 25.
32 Romans 8.6 and 1 Peter 4.1.
33 To Kate Findlay, New Rush, 30 April 1873, *Findlay*.
34 *Life*, p. 43.
35 Brown, *Memories*, pp. 1–2.
36 John Brown M.D., 'Some Reminiscences of Practice in the Cape Half a Century Ago', *South African Medical Record* 14 (1916), pp. 216–18, 248–50, 321–3, 384–6.
37 E. H. Burrows, *A History of Medicine in South Africa* (Cape Town and Amsterdam 1958), p. 327.
38 ibid., pp. 237, 255–65.
39 To Kate Findlay, Hertzog, 1 March 1874, *Findlay*.
40 cf. Eagleton, *Myths of Power*, p. 8.
41 To KP, 12 June 1886, *Pearson*.
42 To KP, 2 July 1886, *Pearson*.
43 RS to Kate Findlay, Hertzog, 24 March 1874, *Findlay*.
44 HE, 'Notes on Olive Schreiner', 1885, HRC.
45 To Miss McNaughton, Ganna Hoek, 24 September 1875, *Pringle*.
46 HE, 'Notes', HRC.
47 To Kate Findlay, Colesberg, 19 February 1875, *Findlay*.
48 To Kate Findlay, Balfour, 23 July 1876, *Findlay*.
49 OS's Ratel Hoek Journal, 2 September 1876, HRC.
50 ibid., 18 September 1876.
51 To Kate Findlay, Ratel Hoek, 27 January 1877, *Findlay*.
52 To Kate Findlay, Ratel Hoek, 18 March 1878, *Findlay*.
53 To Mrs Cawood, Tarkastad, 9 December 1877, *Letters*, p. 3.
54 To Mrs Cawood, Ratel Hoek, 24 April 1878, *Letters*, p. 4.
55 To Mrs Cawood, Ratel Hoek, 9 January 1879, *Letters*, p. 6.
56 OS's (Klein) Ganna Hoek Journal, 7 April and 16 April 1879, *Pringle*. *Life* reproduces most of this journal, omitting these (and some other) lines.
57 Mr E. Cawood, son of Erilda Cawood, quoted in an interview with Winifred B. Harvey, *Eastern Province Herald*, 19 March 1955, from a collection of cuttings in the Albany Museum 1820 Settlers Division, Grahamstown.
58 To WPS, Ganna Hoek, 20 October 1875, *Pringle*.
59 Brown, *Memories*, p. 3.
60 ibid., p. 4.
61 OS's Lelie Kloof Journal, 31 December 1880, HRC. *Life* reproduces this extract, omitting the words 'and been loved so little'.

62 Application for training as a nurse at the Edinburgh Royal Infirmary, 25 November 1880, *Pringle*.

63 To Kate Findlay, Lelie Kloof, 5 January 1881, *Letters*, p. 9.

CHAPTER 3: *Two Novels*

In this chapter we have deliberately drawn on a variety of sources – biographical, literary critical, art historical, psychoanalytic, and social psychological – in an attempt to situate Olive Schreiner's fiction within a broadly marxist-feminist framework. For material on Olive's development as a writer see *Life*, Chapters 2 and 3, and for the notion of a greater sense of reality in absence and loss see a case history of D. W. Winnicott's described in 'Transitional Objects and Transitional Phenomena', *Playing and Reality* (1971), pp. 20–25. Anyone working in the field of nineteenth-century female novelists is indebted to Terry Eagleton, *Myths of Power, A Marxist Study of the Brontës* (1975), and Elaine Showalter, *A Literature of Their Own* (1977 Virago repr. 1978); Showalter has written confidently and provocatively on Schreiner in Chapter 7, 'The Feminist Novelists', pp. 194–204. See also the debate on *Wuthering Heights* in *Red Letters* (Communist Party Literature Journal) no. 2 (Summer 1976), and no. 3 (Autumn 1976), and Colin Mercer and Jean Radford (eds), 'An Interview with Pierre Macherey', *Red Letters* no. 5 (Summer 1977) for illustrations of the relationship between ideology and specific texts. The issue of women's entry into culture is a contentious one; we have used Cora Kaplan, 'Language and Gender', *Papers on Patriarchy (Conference London 76)*, Women's Publishing Collective (1976), pp. 21–37 for ideas about the restriction of women's speech and their silence. For a slightly different perspective and for comparable material on the representation of sexual difference in art history, see Rozsika Parker and Griselda Pollock, *Old Mistresses: Women, Art and Ideology* (1980). For images of loss, passivity and waiting in mid- to late-Victorian painting informing our interpretation of Undine's relationship with Albert Blair, see John Callcott Horsley, *The Soldier's Farewell* (1853), William Powell Frith, *The Proposal* (1877), and Frederick Walker, *Old Letters*, in Graham Reynolds, *Victorian Painting* (1966). On specific points in our discussion of the novels see R. D. Laing, 'Confirmation and Disconfirmation', in *Self and Others* (2nd edn. 1969), pp. 81–89, for Undine's sense of herself as being in a 'false' position; for the idea of the diffusion of female sexuality into notions of service, see Colin Gordon's discussion of Michel Foucault, 'The Birth of the Subject', *Radical Philosophy* 17 (Summer 1977), pp. 15–25; for the idea of 'ways into' a feeling or a problem, see Janet Rée, unpublished 'Notes on a women's literature group based on Doris Lessing's *The Golden Notebook*' (1977).

1 Andrew Lang, 'Theological Romances', *Contemporary Review*, vol. 53 (June 1888), pp. 814–24; Anon, 'The Story of an African Farm', *Life* magazine, 8 February 1883, pp. 107–8 for the novel as 'a *new book*'; Hugh Walpole, 'The Permanent Elements in Olive Schreiner's Fiction', *New York Herald Tribune Books*, 1 May 1927. See also Robert Morss Lovett, 'South African Novels', a review of Schreiner's *From Man to Man* and Pauline Smith's *The Beadle*, in the *New Republic*, 25 May 1927, p. 25; Mary Ross, 'The Young Olive Schreiner', a review of *Undine*, *New York Herald Tribune Books*, 9 December 1928, p. 7; T. S. Matthews, 'Fiction with a Purpose', *The Bookman*, February 1929, p. 687; and L. P. Hartley, 'New Fiction', *The Saturday Review*, 23 March 1929, pp. 410–12 for a persistent emphasis on Schreiner's Victorianism.

2 *Undine*, pp. 100–2.

3 ibid., p. 170.

4 ibid., p. 43.

5 ibid., pp. 156–7.

6 ibid., p. 236.

7 Walker, *Decline of Hell*, pp. 26–7, makes the point that the complex of ideas around redemption, original sin, retributive justice and expiation by suffering rests on this assumption.

8 cf. Eagleton, *Myths of Power* (1975), pp. 1–8, for the mythical resolution of the internal conflicts set up by the 'real' history of the period.

9 *Undine*, p. 246.

10 ibid., pp. 250, 252.

11 To HE, St Leonards, 20 November 1884, *Letters*, pp. 45–6.

12 'Ralph Iron' (Olive Schreiner), preface to *The Story of an African Farm* (Hutchinson, 1894), pp. vii–viii. All references are to this edition unless otherwise stated.

13 Dan Jacobson, introduction to *The Story of an African Farm* (1971), p. 7.

14 Doris Lessing, introduction to *The Story of an African Farm* (1976), p. 2.

15 *African Farm*, pp. 1–2.

16 ibid., p. 332.

17 ibid., p. 333.

18 Jacobson, introduction to *African Farm*, p. 21, makes the point that the blacks are simply 'extras'. See also Nadine Gordimer, 'English-Language Literature and Politics in South Africa', *Journal of Southern African Studies*, vol 2 no 2 (April 1968), and William H. New, *Among Worlds, An Introduction to Modern Commonwealth and South African Fiction* (Erin, Ontario, 1975), pp. 28, 54, 63.

19 *African Farm*, p. 85.

20 See, in particular, the Bible illustrations of John Martin (1789–1854), showing tiny figures in vast landscapes and a prominent, ominous sky. Martin's originals were shown in an exhibition at the Victoria and Albert Museum, London, 'The Bible in British Art', January 1978. William Vaughan of University College, London, gave us additional references based on a lecture at the V & A to coincide with the exhibition entitled 'Realism and Religious Fervour, 1840–80', in which he traces the attempt to reconcile devotional paintings with the growing knowledge of the historical Christ and the life and terrain of the Middle East.

21 *African Farm*, pp. 132, 146.

22 Showalter, *A Literature*, p. 199.

23 *African Farm*, pp. 198–202.

24 ibid., p. 208.

25 ibid., p. 264.

26 ibid., pp. 268–9.

27 ibid., p. 317.

28 ibid., p. 319.

29 ibid., p. 324.

30 Showalter, op. cit., pp. 198, 201.

31 We owe this idea to Michelene Wandor.

32 *African Farm*, pp. 212–13.

CHAPTER 4: *England 1881–1889*

Gareth Stedman Jones, *Outcast London* (Oxford 1971), has been important in the reassessment of class relationships in the late nineteenth century. On Britain as a declining industrial power, see E. J. Hobsbawm, *Industry and Empire* (1969), p. 127, and on positivism Royden Harrison, *Before the Socialists* (1965). Beatrice Webb's autobiography, *My Apprenticeship* (1926), especially pp. 179–80, is useful on attitudes to poverty and the emergence of Fabian socialism. Some of the problems of analysing the varieties of socialism of the period were provoked by E. P. Thompson's seminal biography of William Morris (1955). In a subsequent reassessment of his work, 'Romanticism, Utopianism and Moralism: The Case of William Morris', *New Left Review* 99 (September–October 1976), Thompson took issue with Stanley Pierson's *Marxism and the Origins of British Socialism* (1973). In this debate see also Gareth Stedman Jones, Proselytizing a socialist vision', *Times Higher Education Supplement*, 15 April 1977, p. 16. Imaginative readings of socialism in the eighteen-eighties can be found in Sheila Rowbotham and Jeffrey Weeks, *Socialism and the New Life, The Personal and Sexual Politics of Edward Carpenter and Havelock Ellis* (1977), especially the introduction, and Stephen Yeo, 'A New Life: The Religion of Socialism in Britain, 1883–1896', *History Workshop* Issue 4, Autumn 1977, pp. 5–56. On medical education, including the 1882 Royal Commission inquiring into the Medical Acts, see Charles Newman, *The Evolution of Medical Education in the Nineteenth Century* (1957), pp. 4–5, 198–208, 301–4. On women's entry to the medical profession, see Jo Manton, *Elizabeth Garrett Anderson* (1965), pp. 63, 252–8. On the reform of nursing, see Lucy Seymer, *Florence Nightingale's Nurses – The Nightingale Training School 1860–1960* (1960), p. 88. Cecil Woodham-Smith, *Florence Nightingale* (1950), pp. 346–9, is especially useful on the struggle to make nursing respectable. On Edinburgh as a medical centre, see J. D. Comrie, *A History of Scottish Medicine to 1860* (1927), pp. 130, 255, and Charles Singer, *A Short History of Medicine* (Oxford 1928), p. 140. Charles Dickens The Younger, *Dickens' Dictionary of London* (8 vols, 1879–1886), though the entries are brief, is excellent for the flavour of metropolitan hospitals and dispensaries. On publishing, see Arthur Waugh, *A Hundred Years of Publishing* (1930). Waugh was managing director of Chapman and Hall from 1902 to 1930 and this was the official history of the firm. It includes much general information on the industry as a whole: see especially pp. 19, 99, 100–104. For a biographical sketch of Frederic Chapman, and a sense of Meredith's periodically unsatisfactory relationship with him, see C. L. Cline (ed.), *Letters of George Meredith* (3 vols, Oxford 1970), pp. 233, 238, 273, 767, 1725–6. For information on the origins and political positions of the *Fortnightly Review* and *Contemporary Review*, see Walter E. Houghton (ed.), *The Wellesley Index to Victorian Periodicals, 1824–1900* (University of Toronto Press and London 1966), I pp. 210–12, II pp. 173–81. On Eleanor Marx, mainly in response to Yvonne Kapp's interpretation, see E. P. Thompson, 'English Daughter', *New Society*, 3 March 1977; Stedman Jones, 'Proselytizing a Socialist Vision'; and Jean McCrindle, *Spare Rib* 58 (May 1977) See also McCrindle's 'Eleanor Marx, the BBC Version', *Spare Rib* 56 (March 1977). For a general context to ideas on Victorian childhood and pre-Freudian notions of sexual innocence, see Walter Houghton, *The Victorian Frame of Mind* (Yale University Press 1957), and H. Stuart Hughes, *Consciousness and Society: The Re-orientation of European Social Thought, 1890–1930* (1959). On Karl Pearson, see Bernard Norton's thorough overview of his life and work, 'Karl Pearson and the new discipline of statistics: the social and philosophical relations of scientific innovation' (unpublished paper 1977), and Egon Sharpe Pearson's short biography of his father, *Karl Pearson* (1938). On the context of crusading journalism, see Gareth Stedman Jones, 'Working Class Culture and Working Class Politics in London 1870–1900; Notes on the Remaking of a Working Class', *Journal of Social History*, vol. 7 no. 4 (Summer 1974), pp. 460–508. On attitudes to sexuality and homosexuality, see Peter T. Cominos, 'Late Victorian Sexual Respectability and the Social System', *International Review of Social History* VIII (1963), pp. 18–48, 216–250; Martha McIntyre, 'The Discussion of Sexuality in the Victorian Women's Movement', unpublished paper, Communist University 1977, course on 'Sexuality and Human Nature'; E. M. Sigsworth and T. J. Wyke, 'A Study of Victorian Prostitution and Venereal Disease', in Martha Vicinus (ed.), *Suffer and Be Still* (Indiana University Press 1972), pp. 77–99 (this anthology is generally valuable for the period); and Jeffrey Weeks, 'Sins and Diseases: Some Notes on Male Homosexuality in

Nineteenth Century England', *History Workshop* Issue 1 (Spring 1976), pp. 210–19. See also C. G. Beer, 'Instinct', *International Encyclopaedia of the Social Sciences* (New York 1968), vol. 7, pp. 363–71, for a discussion of theories of instinct from Darwin to Freud. On allegory generally, see Gay Clifford, *The Transformations of Allegory* (1977), pp. 2–34. Jenny Taylor, 'Disintegration and Construction: An Examination of the way that Consciousness of History and Fictional Form Interrelate in the work of Doris Lessing' (unpublished paper, 1976), is particularly relevant for the specific meaning of white South African allegorical writing. Carlin T. Kindilien, 'Stephen Crane and the "Savage Philosophy" of Olive Schreiner', *Boston University Studies in English*, vol. 3 (Summer 1957), pp. 97–107 is one of the few 'literary' accounts of Schreiner's work as an influence on a later poet.

1 Stedman Jones, *Outcast London*, p. 285.
2 E. P. Thompson, 'Romanticism, Utopianism and Moralism: The Case of William Morris', *New Left Review* 99 (September–October 1976), pp. 87–8.
3 Quoted in Yeo, 'A New Life', p. 14.
4 Rowbotham and Weeks, *Socialism and the New Life*, p. 10.
5 *Life*, p. 51. See also Walker, *W. P. Schreiner*, p. 25.
6 *Life*, p. 143.
7 Brown, *Memories*, pp. 5–6.
8 Charlotte Haddon, 'Nursing as a Profession for Ladies', *St. Paul's Monthly Magazine* (August 1871), p. 460, quoted in Brian Abel-Smith, *A History of the Nursing Profession* (1960), p. 2.
9 Rachel Williams and Alice Fisher, *Hints for Hospital Nurses* (Edinburgh 1877), p. 5.
10 *Life*, p. 150.
11 To Clifford Cawood, Eastbourne, 7 May 1881, *Letters*, p. 9.
12 Eastbourne, 15 August 1881, *Letters*, pp. 9–10.
13 Dickens, *Dickens' Dictionary, 1879*, p. 115, and *1886*, p. 129.
14 *Life*, p. 151. This is Cronwright's recollection of Olive's description of the area.
15 Williams and Fisher, *Hints*, pp. 10, 12, 15.
16 *Life*, p. 152.
17 14 May 1882, *Letters*, p. 10.
18 *Life*, p. 152.
19 To HE, St Leonards-on-Sea, 27 October 1884, *Letters*, p. 43.
20 To HE, St Leonards-on-Sea, 19 January 1885, *Letters*, p. 56.
21 Showalter, *A Literature*, p. 7, quotes evidence to show that the pattern of publishing more women than men was set in the late eighteenth century.
22 British Library, Add. MS 46660, pp. 64, 144; 46682, p. 195.
23 Sir Sydney Lee (ed.), *Dictionary of National Biography*, Second Supplement, vol. 2 (1912), p. 608.
24 Cline (ed.), *Letters*, I xli. See also Alice Woods, *George Meredith as Champion of Women and of Progressive Education* (Oxford 1937), p. 74.
25 We owe this point to John Goode.
26 To Frederic Chapman, Box Hill, 16 August 1882, in Cline (ed.), *Letters*, p. 669.
27 Quotations in this and the following three paragraphs about Olive's relations with Chapman's are taken from *Life*, pp. 155–8.
28 *Life*, pp. 157–8.
29 Anon, 'The Story of an African Farm', *Life* magazine, 8 February 1883, pp. 107–8.
30 Brown, *Memories*, p. 5.
31 *Life*, p. 212.
32 On Lecky's belief in an original moral faculty, see Elisabeth Lecky, *A Memoir of*

the Right Hon. W. E. H. Lecky (1909), p. 60. On his support for feminism, see his *The Map of Life, Conduct and Character* (1899), pp. 293–4. On the reception of his *History of European Morals*, see H. Montgomery Hyde (ed.), *A Victorian Historian, Private Letters of W. E. H. Lecky, 1859–1878* (1947), p. 75.

33   *Life*, p. 212.

34   Charles Dilke, 'Colonial Democracy', in *Problems of Greater Britain* (2 vols 1890), vol. 2, p. 253.

35   British Library, Add. MS 47767, f. 140. Undated, though filed with material for 1883.

36   See especially W. E. Gladstone to the Hon. Mrs W. E. Gladstone, 10 July 1892, in D. C. Lathbury, *Correspondence on Church and Religion of William Ewart Gladstone* (2 vols 1910), vol. 2, pp. 120–1, and vol. 2, Chapter 3, 'The Controversy with Unbelief, 1864–1894', pp. 75–124 generally. On the crises of faith of his period, see his enthusiasm for Mrs Humphrey Ward's novel *Robert Elsmere* (3 vols 1888), in his '"Robert Elsmere": The Battle of Belief', *Later Gleanings, Theological and Ecclesiastical* (1897), pp. 76–117.

37   *Spectator*, 13 August 1887, pp. 1091–3.

38   OS quoted in Mary Brown to S. C. Cronwright-Schreiner, n.d., *Life*, p. 158.

39   Laurence Housman, *The Unexpected Years* (1937), pp. 135, 139.

40   Quoted, n.d., in Hobman, *Olive Schreiner*, p. 41.

41   ibid.

42   Anon, *The Englishwoman's Review of Social and Industrial Questions*, 15 August 1883, pp. 372–4. Charles Dilke cites Schreiner's work as a governess on Boer farms and refers readers to *African Farm* in illustration of points about the education system in Natal. See his 'South Africa', in *Problems of Greater Britain* (2 vols 1890), vol. 1, p. 521.

43   Henry Norman, 'Theories and Practice of Modern Fiction', *Fortnightly Review* 34 (December 1883), pp. 870–86. For similar conclusions on *African Farm*, though more hostile to the 'laboured nothingness' of naturalism, see H. Rider Haggard, 'About Fiction', *Contemporary Review* 51 (February 1887), pp. 172–80.

44   *Progress, A Monthly Magazine of Advanced Thought* 1 (September 1883), pp. 156–65.

45   St Leonards-on-Sea, 25 February 1884, *Letters*, p. 12.

46   Henry Havelock Ellis, *My Life* (1940), p. 130. Information in this and the following paragraphs also comes from Edward Brecher, *The Sex Researchers* (1970), and Arthur Calder-Marshall, *Havelock Ellis* (1959).

47   Ellis, *My Life*, p. 102.

48   ibid., p. 119.

49   *Life in Nature* (1862). All quotes in this paragraph are from this work.

50   Henry Havelock Ellis, introduction to *Life in Nature* (1932), p. v.

51   *Life in Nature*, p. 131.

52   This and the next two quotations are from Ellis, *My Life*, pp. 132, 135, 137.

53   James Hinton, *The Lawbreaker and The Coming of the Law* (1884), p. 20. Quotes in this and the next paragraph are from this work.

54   Henry Havelock Ellis, introduction to *The Lawbreaker*, p. xiv.

55   *Dictionary of National Biography*, vol. XXVII (1890), pp. 4–7. On Hinton's sexual philosophy – and rather delicately phrased – see also Edith Ellis, *Three Modern Seers* (1910), a study of Nietzsche, Carpenter and Hinton.

56   St Leonards-on-Sea, 8 April 1884, *Letters*, p. 15.

57   See Jane Ellice Hopkins, *Life and Letters of James Hinton* (1878), pp. 9, 339, 356.

58   St Leonards-on-Sea, 21 April 1884, *Letters*, pp. 15–16.

59   ibid., p. 16.

60   St Leonards-on-Sea, 8 April 1884, *Letters*, p. 15.

61 St Leonards-on-Sea, 2 May 1884, *Letters*, p. 17. *Towards Democracy* had been published the previous year.

62 St Leonards-on-Sea, 2 May 1884, *Letters*, pp. 17–18.

63 On the Progressive Association, see Ellis, *My Life*, pp. 155–9. On the Fellowship of the New Life, see ibid., pp. 162–3, Edward R. Pease, *The History of the Fabian Society* (1916), pp. 26–36, Warren Sylvester Smith, *The London Heretics 1870–1914* (1967), pp. 131–41, and William Knight (ed.), *Memorials of Thomas Davidson: the wandering scholar* (1907). On the fluid atmosphere of contemporary socialist politics, see Rowbotham and Weeks, *Socialism and the New Life*, p. 15.

64 Ellis, *My Life*, p. 183.

65 7 Pelham Street, 20 May 1884, *Letters*, p. 20.

66 *My Life*, p. 183.

67 7 Pelham Street, 21 May 1884, *Letters*, p. 20.

68 *My Life*, p. 184.

69 'Notes on Olive Schreiner', 1885, HRC.

70 To HE, 32 Fitzroy Street, 16 June 1884, *Letters*, p. 22.

71 *My Life*, p. 93.

72 ibid., p. 192.

73 29 July 1884, *Letters*, pp. 35–6.

74 2 August 1884, *Letters*, p. 36.

75 Kapp, *Crowded Years*, p. 706.

76 ibid., pp. 27–8.

77 ibid., pp. 24, 27.

78 See Ridley Beeton, 'In Search of Olive Schreiner in Texas', *The Texas Quarterly* (Autumn 1974), vol. XVII No. 3, pp. 137–9, for the correspondence between Olive and Louise Ellis, and *Letters*, pp. 89, 205, for Olive's comments about her clothes and her appearance.

79 *My Life*, p. 186.

80 5 September 1884, Blackwell Farm, *Letters*, p. 40.

81 St Leonards-on-Sea, October 1884, HRC.

82 To HE, St Leonards-on-Sea, 27 October 1884, HRC.

83 *My Life*, p. 185.

84 Jane Graves, 'Olive Schreiner' (unpublished manuscript 1976).

85 Quoted in Betty McGinnis Fradkin, 'Olive Schreiner and Karl Pearson', *Quarterly Bulletin of the South African Library* (June 1977), p. 86.

86 To Adela Smith, De Aar, 2 June 1908, *Letters*, pp. 279–80.

87 To HE, St Leonards-on-Sea, 28 January 1885, *Letters*, p. 57.

88 To HE, 16 Portsea Place, 29 October 1885, *Letters*, p. 85.

89 Stephen Winsten, *Salt and His Circle* (1951), p. 118.

90 To HE, 16 Portsea Place, 25 August 1885, *Letters*, p. 80.

91 Maria Sharpe, 'Autobiographical Notes of Men and Women's Club, 1885–9', *Pearson*.

92 This paragraph is based on personal communication from Egon Sharpe Pearson and Sarah Pearson, 2 March 1979. On Henry Cobb, see Michael Stern and Stephen Lees, *Who's Who of British Members of Parliament, Vol II, 1886–1918* (1978), p. 68.

93 Annie Besant to KP, 12 January 1887, *Pearson*.

94 HE to OS, n.d. but presumably March 1886, HRC.

95 OS to KP, 14 July 1885, *Pearson*.

96 OS to EC, 12 February 1885, *Pearson*.

97 Robert Parker to KP, 28 July 1885, *Pearson*.

98 Minute Book, Fourth Meeting of Men and Women's Club, 85 Warrington Crescent, 14 December 1885, *Pearson*.

99   Emma Brooke to KP, 4 December 1885, *Pearson.*

100 Caroline Haddon to KP, 18 December 1885, *Pearson.*

101 Kilburn, 28 April 1886, *Letters,* p. 98.

102 EC to KP, 26 December 1885, *Pearson.*

103 Caroline Haddon to KP, 3 January 1886, *Pearson.*

104 Weeks, 'Sins and Diseases', p. 213.

105 OS to KP, 5 November 1885, *Pearson.*

106 W. T. Stead, *A Journalist on Journalism* (1892), pp. 28–57. All other quotes in this paragraph are from *The Maiden Tribute of Modern Babylon (The Report of the* Pall Mall Gazette's *Secret Commission)* (pamphlet, 1885).

107 OS to EC, 12 July 1885. Elizabeth Cobb copied the letter and sent it on to Pearson a few days later. *Pearson.*

108 OS to KP, 19 July 1885, *Pearson.*

109 16 Portsea Place, 18 November 1885, *Letters,* p. 87.

110 To HE, 16 Portsea Place, 26 December 1885, *Letters,* pp. 88–9.

111 To HE, 16 Portsea Place, 3 January 1886, *Letters,* p. 90.

112 OS to KP, 6 February 1886, *Pearson.*

113 OS to KP, 16 October 1886, *Pearson.*

114 To Havelock Ellis, Southbourne-on-Sea, 2 April 1886, *Letters,* p. 97.

115 OS to KP, 18 July 1886, *Pearson.*

116 Information in this paragraph comes from Carpenter's very lucid autobiography, *My Days and Dreams,* especially pp. 100–36, 164–6.

117 OS to KP, 20 June 1886, *Pearson.*

118 OS to KP, 4 April 1886, *Pearson.*

119 OS to KP, 20 June 1886, *Pearson.*

120 EC to KP, 16 December 1884, 3 November 1885, 8 September 1924; and Kate Mills to Maria Sharpe, n.d. [? July 1885], *Pearson.*

121 Carpenter, *My Days and Dreams,* p. 227.

122 OS to KP, 18 October 1886, *Pearson.*

123 OS to KP, 20 October 1886, *Pearson.*

124 OS to KP, 31 October 1886, *Pearson.*

125 EC to KP, 2 November 1886, *Pearson.*

126 EC to KP, 23 September 1882, *Pearson.*

127 OS to KP, 14 December 1886, *Pearson.*

128 Blandford Square, 7 December 1886, *Letters,* p. 105.

129 Bryan Donkin to KP, 14 or 15 December 1886, *Pearson.*

130 'On the Banks of a Full River', *Stories, Dreams and Allegories,* pp. 79–91.

131 OS to KP, 30 January 1887, *Pearson.*

132 EC to KP, 12 December 1886, *Pearson.*

133 EC to KP, 15 December 1886. The upright Mrs Cobb was also 'so humiliated for my sex that a woman has so broken down before you'. EC to KP, 30 December 1886, *Pearson.*

134 See 'About Olive Schreiner', envelope in Mrs Hacker's handwriting – notes of a conversation with Pearson's former secretary at the Galton Laboratory, E. G. Everton-Jones, in 1956, *Pearson.*

135 EC to KP, 15 December 1886, *Pearson.*

136 To Edward Carpenter, Mentone, 28 January 1889, Carpenter MSS; EC to KP, 26 June 1889, *Pearson.*

137 KP to Maria Sharpe, early December 1886, *Pearson.*

138 EC to KP, 15 December 1886, *Pearson.*

139 OS to HE, 1 February 1887, *Pearson.*

140 EC to KP, 14 December 1886, *Pearson.*

141 OS to KP, 30 January 1887, *Pearson.*

142 OS to HE, 1 February 1887, *Pearson.*
143 Charlotte Wilson to KP, 17 May 1889, *Pearson.*
144 OS to KP, 9 July 1886, *Pearson.*
145 To HE, Bole Hill, 23 July 1884, *Letters*, p. 34.
146 To CS, Hanover, 25 February and 23 May 1907, *Letters*, pp. 264, 268.
147 To KP, 9 July 1886, *Pearson.*
148 To HE, Mentone, 2 February 1889, *Letters*, p. 153.
149 *From Man to Man*, p. 226.
150 W. E. H. Lecky, *History of European Morals from Augustus to Charlemagne* (3rd edn, 2 vols 1877), vol. II, pp. 283, 348.
151 Quoted in Cominos, 'Late Victorian Sexual Respectability', p. 23.
152 *From Man to Man*, p. 218.
153 ibid., p. 226.
154 ibid., p. 135.
155 To HE, St Leonards-on-Sea, 21 November and 9 December 1884, *Letters*, pp. 46, 49.
156 To HE, Paris, 5 April 1889, *Letters*, p. 160.
157 OS to Edward Carpenter, Paris, 1887, Carpenter MSS.
158 Quotations in this and the previous paragraph are from Olive's letters to Carpenter, Alassio, 6 April 1888; Alassio, 12 April 1887; Whitby, 5 September 1887; Alassio, 16 April 1888, Carpenter MSS. See also HE to OS, undated [?1885], and OS to HE, undated [?1885], HRC.
159 OS to Edward Carpenter, Mentone, 10 January 1889, Carpenter MSS.
160 OS to KP, 11 November 1890, *Pearson.*
161 To HE, Harpenden, 3 October 1888, *Letters*, p. 142.
162 To HE, Cape Town, 6 July 1907, *Letters* pp. 270–2.
163 Mentone, 28 January 1889, Carpenter MSS.
164 To HE, Alassio, 26 and 27 January 1888, *Letters*, pp. 129–30.
165 To HE, Alassio, 9 February 1888, *Letters*, p. 131.
166 To Ernest Rhys, Hotel Mediterranean, Alassio, n.d., British Library Rhys and Dirk Collection, Egerton MSS. 3248.
167 To HE, Cape Town, 21 January 1890, *Letters*, p. 176.
168 Arthur Symons quoted in *Life*, p. 185.
169 To HE, Blandford Square, 7 December 1886, *Letters*, pp. 105–6.
170 Revelation of St John the Divine, 14, especially verse 8.
171 'Three Dreams in a Desert', *Dreams*, pp. 62–3, 72.
172 To HE, Alassio, 18 December 1887, *Letters*, p. 125.
173 EC to KP, 14 August 1889, *Pearson.*
174 Brown, *Memories*, pp. 8–9.
175 *Life*, pp. 184–90.
176 See Margaret Llewelyn Davies (ed.), *Life As We Have Known It* (1930, reissued 1977), pp. 101, 129.
177 Constance Lytton, *Prisons and Prisoners* (1914), pp. 156–7.
178 See, for example, OS to Edward Carpenter, October 1892, Carpenter MSS.
179 Anon, 'Talk About New Books', *The Catholic World*, vol. LIII (April–September 1891), pp. 139–40. The 'blasphemous temperance tract' is also quoted in this review.
180 *Athenaeum* No. 3298, 10 January 1891, pp. 46–7.
181 W. B. Yeats, 'Four Years, 1887–1891', *The Dial* LXXI (August 1921), pp. 179–83.
182 Henry Walker, *East London. Sketches of Christian Work and Workers* (1896), pp. 181–9.
183 *Life*, pp. 191, 193.

184 To Mrs J. H. Philpot, London, 12 August 1889, *Letters*, p. 166.
185 OS to Edward Carpenter, September 1889, Carpenter MSS.
186 To HE, Matjesfontein, 23 April 1892, *Letters*, p. 207.
187 To Edward Carpenter, 4 September 1889, Carpenter MSS.

CHAPTER 5: *South Africa 1890–1894*

For the bibliographic history of Olive Schreiner's allegories, see Ridley Beeton, *Olive Schreiner, A Short Guide to Her Writings* (Cape Town 1974), pp. 48–52. There are many biographies of Rhodes, but the most blistering, and the one closest to Olive's own view of him, is William Plomer's short, incisive essay *Cecil Rhodes* (1933). On late nineteenth-century South Africa and the far-reaching changes of that time, see C. W. de Kiewiet's *A History of South Africa: Social and Economic.* Though first published in 1941, this is a lucid account, especially in Chapter 4, of the diamond fields as the country's first industrial community, where South Africa 'really faced for the first time the modern problem of capital and labour' (p. 89), and in Chapter 5 of the process by which the Witwatersrand became the centre of South Africa's industrial revolution. A later and more penetrating study which periodizes the changes within the South African political economy is Martin Legassick, 'Capital Accumulation and Violence', *Economy and Society* 3, 3 (1974). Rhodes' search for a 'second Rand' in Rhodesia, and the way in which the poverty of Southern Rhodesia's mineral resources made him turn back, relatively late in the day, to consolidate his interests on the Witwatersrand, are examined in I. R. Phimister, 'Rhodes, Rhodesia and the Rand', *Journal of Southern African Studies* 1, 1 (October 1974). The precipitating causes of the Jameson Raid are skilfully probed in G. Blainey, 'Lost Causes of the Jameson Raid', *Economic History Review* 18 (1965). The nature of the Boer republics, especially the Transvaal, is the concern of several of S. Trapido's journal articles, among them 'The South African Republic: The Role of the State in Capital Formation, 1850–1900', University of London, Institute of Commonwealth Studies, Collected Seminar Papers: *The Societies of Southern Africa in the 19th and 20th Centuries*, vol. 3 (1973). The Cape politics of Olive's time are best traced in Phyllis Lewsen (ed.), *Selections from the Correspondence of J. X. Merriman, 1890–1898* (Cape Town 1963), which is a skilful editing of the voluminous commentary of the leading liberal politician of the day from whom Olive was increasingly to take her political – and feminist – distance. A rich account of the context of Merriman's politics is S. Trapido, *White Conflict and Non-White Participation in Cape Politics, 1853–1910* (unpublished Ph.D thesis, University of London, 1970). Eric A. Walker, *W. P. Schreiner, A South African* (Oxford 1937), is a detailed but opaque account of Olive's politician brother.

 1 Cronwright-Schreiner describes the costume in *Life*, p. 196.
 2 Meintjes, *Olive Schreiner*, p. 103.
 3 To HE, Matjesfontein, 25 March 1890, *Letters*, p. 180.
 4 Quoted in *Life*, p. 200.
 5 To HE, Matjesfontein, 25 April 1890, *Letters*, p. 184.
 6 *Life*, p. 200; to HE, Matjesfontein, 16 May 1890, *Letters*, p. 187.
 7 To HE, Cape Town, 16 March 1890, *Letters*, pp. 178–9.
 8 To HE, Matjesfontein, 4 November 1890, *Letters*, p. 198.
 9 To HE, Matjesfontein, 25 July 1890, *Letters*, p. 192.
10 To Mary Sauer, 13 September 1892, SAPL.
11 To W. T. Stead, Matjesfontein, n.d., *Letters*, p. 193.
12 *Stories, Dreams, and Allegories* (1923), pp. 73, 61.
13 To KP, 24 May 1890, *Pearson*.
14 To HE, Matjesfontein, 16 May 1890, *Letters*, p. 187.

15 To HE, Matjesfontein, 11 and 13 August 1890, *Letters*, pp. 194–5.
16 To HE, Matjesfontein, 30 August 1890, *Letters*, p. 196.
17 To HE, Cape Town, 16 March 1890, *Letters*, p. 179.
18 To HE, Grahamstown, 27 November 1890, *Letters*, p. 171.
19 To HE, Matjesfontein, 15 April 1890, *Letters*, pp. 182–3.
20 To Mary Sauer, Cape Town, January 1892, SAPL.
21 To HE, Matjesfontein, 12 May 1890, *Letters*, p. 185.
22 To W. T. Stead, Matjesfontein, 12 July 1890, *Letters*, p. 191.
23 Quoted in *Life*, p. 210.
24 To W. T. Stead, Matjesfontein, 12 July 1890, *Letters*, p. 191.
25 To HE, n.d., quoted in *Life*, p. 210.
26 S. MacNeill's conversation with Rhodes cited in *Life*, pp. 212–13.
27 ibid., p. 213.
28 ibid., p. 208.
29 To WPS, Matjesfontein, n.d., UCTJ. See also *Life*, p. 213.
30 To Mary Sauer, n.d., SAPL.
31 To W. T. Stead, Matjesfontein, 24 September 1890, *Letters*, p. 206.
32 Plomer, *Cecil Rhodes*, p. 60.
33 Lewsen (ed.), *Correspondence, 1890–1898*, p. 29.
34 Walker, *W. P. Schreiner*, p. 51.
35 *Life*, p. 254.
36 Lewsen (ed.), *Correspondence, 1890–1898*.
37 To KP, 16 February 1886, *Pearson*.
38 Quoted in F. Whyte, *The Life of W. T. Stead* (1925).
39 To WPS, Matjesfontein, 9 October 1892, UCTJ.
40 For Cronwright-Schreiner's account of his meeting with Olive and impressions of her, including quotes from Olive's early letters to him, see *Life*, pp. 226–53.
41 *Life*, pp. 249–50.
42 1 and 5 April 1893, *Life*, p. 251.
43 To Mary Sauer, Middelburg, n.d., probably March 1893, SAPL.
44 *Life*, p. 254.
45 Hobman, *Olive Schreiner*, pp. 90–5.
46 To Edward Carpenter, Ben Rhydding, Yorkshire, 18 July 1893, Carpenter MSS.
47 *Life*, p. 257.
48 To Edward Carpenter, St Leonards-on-Sea, 1 August 1893, Carpenter MSS.
49 Middelburg, 10 February 1893, UCTJ.
50 *Life*, p. 259.
51 ibid., pp. 259–60.
52 To Edward Carpenter, Grahamstown, 4 December 1893, Carpenter MSS. See also *Life*, p. 260.
53 *Life*, p. 260.
54 *Letters*, pp. 214–16.
55 *Life*, p. 272.
56 ibid., p. 271.
57 Dan Jacobson's description of the house and the district is in his introduction to *The Story of an African Farm* (Penguin Books 1971), p. 10.
58 To Mrs J. H. Philpot, Kimberley, 3 November 1894, *Letters*, p. 216.
59 Quoted in *Life*, pp. 274–5.

CHAPTER 6: *The Boer War and Union*

On the Jameson Raid, see J. van der Poel, *The Jameson Raid* (Cape Town 1951), and E. Pakenham, *Jameson's Raid* (1960). There are several sources on alignments in

Britain on the Boer War: S. Koss, *The Pro-Boers, The Anatomy of an Anti-War Movement* (Chicago 1973), documents the various anti-war lobbies, a heterogeneous collection of campaigners and causes, including the South African Conciliation Committee. R. N. Price, *An Imperial War and the British Working Class* (1972), and B. Baker, *The Social Democratic Federation and the Boer Wars, Our History* pamphlet, History Group of the Communist Party of Great Britain (Summer 1974), attempt a more class-based examination. Baker is particularly useful on the Social Democratic Federation's stand and the debates within the Second International. The debate on the Boer War remains inconclusive, or at least unconcluded. George Bernard Shaw, *Fabianism and the Empire* (1900), was among those who argued its historical necessity as the inevitable outcome of the conflict between modern capitalism and Kruger's 'seventeenth century' (this was Shaw's parallel). Legassick, in the paper referred to above (p. 355), argues that Britain went to war because the capitalist revolution needed a ruling class with wider geographical powers and far greater efficiency than the Transvaal landowners. H. J. and R. E. Simons, *Class and Colour in South Africa, 1850–1950* (1969), on the other hand, argue that Britain stepped in not to break the fetters of a backward society but to prevent it from becoming a rival power in the region: that Afrikaner nationalism was challenging Britain's hegemony. The actual progression of the war is recorded in several official military histories. For the British government view see M. H. Grant, *History of the War in South Africa, 1899–1902* (1910). See also L. S. Amery (ed.), *The Times History of the War in South Africa, 1899–1900* (7 vols, 1900–1909). On the reconstruction period after the war, Jan Smuts' own papers are as fluent an indication as any to the new policies of reconciliation between Boer and Briton. See W. K. Hancock and J. van der Poel (eds), *Selections from the Smuts papers* (4 vols, 1966, etc.) See also W. K. Hancock's biographical *Smuts. The sanguine years, 1870–1919* (Cambridge 1962). On the rise of the trade union and national liberation movement during the twentieth century see Simons and Simons, *Class and Colour*, especially chapters 3–6.

1 To Mary Sauer, 10 May 1895, SAPL.
2 31 January 1901, SAPL.
3 To Betty Molteno, Kimberley, 3 December 1896, UCTJ.
4 25 March 1893, in *Letters*, p. 219.
5 10 January 1895, *Letters*, p. 217.
6 Kimberley, 8 October 1894, Carpenter MSS.
7 To WPS, Krantz Plaats, 11 April 1894, UCTJ.
8 'Olive Schreiner' (unpublished MS 1976).
9 To WPS, Middelburg, 1894, UCTJ.
10 *Cape Times*, 21 August 1895.
11 To J. T. Lloyd, Kimberley, *Letters*, p. 219.
12 To Mary Sauer, 10 January 1896, SAPL.
13 n.d. 1897, UCTJ.
14 J. F. Hofmeyr, in collaboration with F. Reitz, *The Life of Jan Hendrik Hofmeyr (Onze Jan)* (Cape Town 1913).
15 *Life*, p. 277. This letter was reprinted in S. C. Cronwright-Schreiner, *The Land of Free Speech* (1906), p. 509.
16 Middelburg, 13 January 1896, UCTJ.
17 Walker, *W. P. Schreiner*, writes that it was the later, incontrovertible evidence of Rhodes' complicity in the Raid that made Schreiner break with his patron.
18 *Life*, p. 277.
19 ibid., pp. 278–82.
20 *Cape Times*, 16 April 1896.
21 *Ons Land*, incorporating *De Zuid Afrikaan*, 18 April 1896.

22 To Mary Sauer, 25 April 1896, SAPL.
23 13 April 1896, SAPL.
24 To Betty Molteno, 9 January 1896, UCTJ.
25 *Trooper Peter Halket of Mashonaland* (1974 edition published in Johannesburg by A. D. Donker), pp. 49–53.
26 To Betty Molteno, 9 January 1896, UCTJ.
27 To J. T. Lloyd, Kimberley, 14 December 1896, *Letters*, p. 223.
28 To Mary Sauer, September 1896, SAPL.
29 To Mrs F. Schreiner, 28 October 1896, UCTJ.
30 To WPS, n.d. 1896, UCTJ.
31 *Life*, p. 288.
32 See Fisher Unwin's advertisement in the *Athenaeum* No. 3618, 27 February 1897, and the anonymous review of *Trooper Peter Halket* in the same issue, pp. 271–2.
33 Lewsen (ed.), *Correspondence 1899–1905*, p. 181.
34 December 1896, UCTJ.
35 29 June 1898, UCTJ.
36 *Life*, p. 290.
37 Alassio, April 1897, SAPL.
38 CS to Hofmeyr, 14 July 1898, Hofmeyr Papers, SAPL.
39 CS to Betty Molteno, Kimberley, 26 September 1898, UCTJ.
40 *Life*, p. 287.
41 1 October 1896, UCTJ.
42 To Betty Molteno, n.d. 1896, UCTJ.
43 *Life*, pp. 301–3.
44 13 November 1898, Carpenter MSS.
45 Lewsen (ed.), *Correspondence 1899–1905*, pp. 42–3.
46 To Betty Molteno, Johannesburg, 4 October 1898, UCTJ.
47 *Life*, pp. 309–10.
48 23 January 1899, SAPL.
49 To WPS, Johannesburg, 18 January 1899, SAPL.
50 To WPS, Johannesburg, 6 June 1899, SAPL.
51 To Betty Molteno, Johannesburg, June 1899, SAPL.
52 To J. C. Smuts, Johannesburg, 13 June 1899, SAPL.
53 To Betty Molteno, Johannesburg, 18 July 1899, SAPL.
54 To Mrs F. Schreiner, Johannesburg, 31 May 1899, UCTJ.
55 To Mrs F. Schreiner, 29 July 1899, SAPL.
    To WPS, Johannesburg, 6 August 1899, SAPL.
56 *Life*, p. 312.
57 To Betty Molteno and Alice Greene, Karee Kloof, 24 September 1899, UCTJ.
58 To Alice Greene, 15 September 1899, Betty Molteno, 4 November 1899, WPS, 12 October 1899, and cable to *The Sun*, n.d.s. 1899 UCTJ.
59 Karee Kloof, 24 September 1899, SAPL.
60 To Mrs F. Schreiner, Karee Kloof, 3 October 1899, SAPL.
61 Price, *An Imperial War*, pp. 17, 237.
62 Koss, *The Pro-Boers*, p. 131.
63 Cronwright-Schreiner, *Land of Free Speech*.
64 *Life*, p. 319.
65 W. T. Stead, *The Last Will and Testament of Cecil Rhodes* (1902).
66 Price, op. cit., p. 22.
67 Baker, *The Social Democratic Federation*.
68 ibid., p. 10.
69 *Justice*, 11 July 1901.

70 Price, op. cit., pp. 236–7.
71 Lewsen, op. cit., p. 134.
72 Koss, *The Pro-Boers*, p. 55.
73 ibid., p. 54.
74 *The Labour Leader*, 1 January 1900, cited in Koss, *The Pro-Boers*, p. 54.
75 B. Semmel, *Imperialism and Social Reform* (1960), p. 14.
76 Shaw, *Fabianism and the Empire*, p. 23.
77 Rosa Luxemburg, *The Accumulation of Capital* (1913). See especially Chapter XXIX, 'The Struggle against Peasant Economy'.
78 To Betty Molteno, Beaufort West, September 1900, UCTJ.
79 To Mrs F. Schreiner, Wagenaars Kraal, 1900, UCTJ.
80 To Betty Molteno, 17 June 1900, UCTJ.
81 To Alice Greene, Beaufort West, July 1900, UCTJ.
82 For the relationship of the Conciliation Committee and the Bond see T. R. H. Davenport, *The Afrikaner Bond* (1966), p. 213.
83 For the British government view, see Grant, *History of the War in South Africa*, p. 61.
84 *Life*, p. 315.
85 H. W. Nevinson, *Changes and Chances* (1923), p. 316.
86 *SA News*, 19 October 1900; see also *Life*, Appendix C, pp. 378–85.
87 To Anna Purcell, Hanover, 19 October 1900, SAPL.
88 Lewsen, op. cit., p. 213 fn.
89 ibid., letter to G. Smith, 10 October 1899, p. 222.
90 *Life*, pp. 322–4.
91 *Life*, p. 318.
92 Hanover, 24 February 1901, SAPL.
93 To Betty Molteno, Hanover, June 1901, UCTJ.
94 Hanover, 31 March 1901, SAPL.
95 To Betty Molteno, Hanover, April 1901, UCTJ; *Life*, p. 327.
96 *Life*, p. 327.
97 *Stories, Dreams and Allegories*, pp. 11–16.
98 To Mrs F. Schreiner, Cape Town, 2 August 1901, UCTJ.
99 To Betty Molteno, Hanover, 11 May 1901, UCTJ.
100 To CS, 3 February 1901, SAPL.
101 To Mrs Isie Smuts, Hanover, 17 June 1902, SAPL.
    To CS, Johannesburg, 23 August 1902, SAPL.
102 To Mrs F. Schreiner, Hanover, 1902, UCTJ.
103 To CS, Hanover, 31 October 1902, SAPL.
104 To Mrs F. Schreiner, Matjesfontein, 22 October 1906, UCTJ.
105 To Betty Molteno, Hanover, 17 June 1901, UCTJ.
106 To Alice Greene, Hanover, 31 March 1903, SAPL.
107 To Betty Molteno, Hanover, 28 December 1902, UCTJ.
108 To Mrs Mary Brown, Hanover, 31 January 1901, SAPL.
109 See letters to Mrs I. Smuts, September 1902 and 22 May 1903; and to CS, 17 December 1904, SAPL.
110 Hancock and van der Poel (eds.), *Selections from the Smuts Papers*, p. 65.
111 To Mrs I. Smuts, Hanover, 9 January 1904, SAPL.
112 To Betty Molteno, 8 May 1906, UCTJ.
113 To General and Mrs Smuts, December and 21 December 1908, SAPL.
114 See H. J. and R. E. Simons, *Class and Colour in South Africa*, p. 79.
115 *Letters*, Appendix D, pp. 386–7.
116 *SA News*, 8 June 1905, 1st Annual report of the SDF, p. 8.
117 To WPS, 1912, UCTJ.

118 To WPS, De Aar, 24 April 1909, UCTJ.
119 *Letters*, Appendix F, pp. 392-5.
120 To WPS, De Aar, 30 April 1909, UCTJ.
121 To WPS, Bedford, 27 August 1904, UCTJ.
122 To CS, Hanover, 30 October 1906, SAPL.
123 To Alice Greene, Hanover, 19 June 1904, UCTJ.
124 ibid.
125 To Mrs F. Schreiner, Hanover, 10 June 1904, UCTJ.
126 To Betty Molteno, n.d. 1906, UCTJ.
127 *Life*, p. 352.
128 See Chapter 12 of Walker, *W. P. Schreiner*.
129 Among many letters between 1907 and 1909 are a letter to Mrs F. Schreiner asking for copies of all his speeches, and one from De Aar written on 16 July 1909 where she gave him detailed advice about his manner and parliamentary tactics. UCTJ.
130 To CS, April 1907, SAPL; to Alice Greene, 8 May 1907.
131 To WPS, Hanover, 1907, UCTJ.
132 Olive Schreiner's answers to the twelve questions submitted by the *Transvaal Leader* appeared in that paper on 22 December 1908, and were subsequently published as a booklet *Closer Union* by the Constitutional Reform Association, Cape Town.
133 To WPS, 5 April 1909, SAPL.
134 Shula Marks, 'Harriett Colenso and the Zulus 1874-1913', *Journal of African History* IV, 3 (1963), pp. 403-11.
135 To Betty Molteno, 6 March 1909, SAPL.
136 5 April 1909, SAPL.
137 Matjesfontein, 19 February 1909, Carpenter MSS.
138 Matjesfontein, n.d. 1909, SAPL.
139 To WPS, De Aar, 7 July 1913, UCTJ.
140 To Edward Carpenter, De Aar, 28 April 1911, Carpenter MSS.
141 To WPS, De Aar, 7 June 1913, UCTJ.
142 To WPS, De Aar, 27 July 1909, UCTJ.
143 Anna Purcell (ed.), *Olive Schreiner's Thoughts About Women* (1909).
144 De Aar, July 1909, UCTJ.
145 To Lucy Molteno, 5 September 1910, SAPL.
146 Communication to Ruth Alexander, n.d., SAPL.
147 To Mrs Francis Smith, 12 August 1912, *Letters*, p. 314.
148 *Life*, pp. 206-7.
149 To WPS, 24 February 1908, SAPL.

CHAPTER 7: *Woman and Labour*

On the dependent idleness of the woman of leisure, see Catherine Hall, 'History of the Housewife', *Spare Rib* 26 (September 1974). A good example of writing on the deterioration of children's health is Peter McIntosh, *Physical Education in England since 1800* (1952), especially Chapter 9, 'New Ideas and the Shocks of the Boer War', pp. 133-45. Margaret Llewelyn Davies (ed.), *Maternity, Letters from Working Women* (1915, reissued 1978), is an excellent (and revealing) source for the hardships of pregnancy and child-rearing at the time of World War One. A general introduction to US feminism during the war, though rather anecdotal, is W. O'Neill, *Everyone was brave: the rise and fall of feminism in America* (Chicago 1969), especially Chapter 6: 'The woman movement and the war', pp. 169-223. On women's role in establishing ethical standards between nations and their 'natural' idealism and capacity

for self-denial, see Judge Florence Allen, 'The Outlawry of War', Address to a Conference on the Cause and Cure of War (Washington, D.C. 1925), and on the equal
importance of pacifist and suffrage campaigning her Address to the Fourth Annual
Convention of the National League of Women Voters (Des Moines, Iowa, 1923). In
Britain, Constance Lytton's conviction that war brought women out of 'hysteria' –
the enervation of inactivity – can be traced in her *Letters* (1925); this was a rather
idiosyncratic variant on the pacifist theme. On reconstruction after the war, see,
for example, Drusilla Modjeska and Sheila Rowbotham, 'Dora Russell: A Quest
for Liberty and Love', *Spare Rib* 54 (January 1977), for an excellent introduction to
left-wing attitudes to motherhood, and 'Natural Guardians of the Race', pamphlet
outlining the history of the Woman's Medical College of Pennsylvania in Phila-
delphia, 1926 (US material cited here is held in the Schlesinger Institute, Radcliffe
College, Cambridge, Mass.). German artist Käthe Kollwitz's desire to depict the
suffering of the war and its devastating effect on women as mothers in her drawings can
be traced in Mary Jane Moffat and Charlotte Painter (eds.), *Revelations: Diaries of
Women* (New York 1975), pp. 237–40. On the pervasive influence of eugenicism on late
nineteenth-century feminists in the USA, see Linda Gordon, *Woman's Body, Woman's
Right* (1977), Chapter 6, 'Social Purity and Eugenics', pp. 116–35. On Karl Pearson's
intellectual framework, see Bernard Norton, 'Karl Pearson and the new discipline of
statistics: the social and philosophical relations of scientific innovation' (unpublished
paper 1977), pp. 6–7, 20–21, and on his commitment to the uses of science see Karl
Pearson, *The Function of Science in the Modern State* (1919, first published 1902 as a
prefatory essay to one of the volumes of the *Encyclopædia Britannica*). On the discussion of female sexuality in the late nineteenth century, see Helen Rugen, 'Female
Sexuality 1900–1920', paper presented to the Women's Research and Resources Centre,
5 August 1977. For an introduction to the relationship between Ellis and Freud, see
Vincent Brome, 'Sigmund Freud and Havelock Ellis', *Encounter* 66 (March 1969),
pp. 46–54, and for material on the development of Freud's ideas between 1900–1914
see Lionel Trilling and Steven Marcus (eds.), Ernest Jones, *The Life and Work of
Sigmund Freud* (1 vol. 1961, Penguin repr. 1967), pp. 345, 355, 364–5. For Freud's
critique of Ellis' use of the term auto-erotism, see his *Three Essays on the Theory
of Sexuality* (1905), quoted in J. Laplanche and J.-B. Pontalis, *The Language of
Psychoanalysis* (1973), p. 47. For more sympathetic references to Ellis' innovations,
particularly in the understanding of modesty, see Sigmund Freud, 'The Taboo of
Virginity' (1918), *Collected Papers* IV (1971), p. 219, and 'Hysterical Phantasies
and their Relation to Bisexuality' (1908), in *Collected Papers* II (1971), p. 51.
Octave Mannoni's *Freud: The Theory of the Unconscious* (1971), pp. 136–9, is excellent on Freud's metapsychology. For a Reichian approach to the sexual radicalism
of Ellis and Edward Carpenter, see Ian Tilley's review of Rowbotham and Weeks,
Socialism and the New Life (unpublished paper 1977), which makes relevant connections between late Victorian and early twentieth-century attempts at personal sexual
reform. For a dense critique of ideas of the ego as a free agent – applied to post-
Freudian revisionism, but useful for understanding this rather earlier period – see
Russell Jacoby, *Social Amnesia* (Boston 1975).

1 Vera Brittain, *Testament of Youth, An Autobiographical Study of the Years
   1900–1925* (1933), p. 28.
2 *Woman and Labour* (1911, reissued 1978). Quotes in the following three paragraphs are from the introduction, pp. 11–30.
3 *Life*, p. 356.
4 ibid., p. 357.
5 ibid., p. 359.
6 To Mrs Francis Smith, Cape Town, October 1909, *Letters*, p. 291.

7   12 April 1924, SAPL. Katie Stuart was Kate Findlay's daughter.
8   Hobman, *Olive Schreiner*, p. 132.
9   Julia F. Solly to Ruth Alexander, 9 February 1925, SAPL.
10 *Life*, p. 354.
11 OS to KP, *Pearson*.
12 *Woman and Labour*, p. 17.
13 ibid., pp. 144–5.
14 ibid., pp. 201–2.
15 ibid., p. 273.
16 ibid., p. 282.
17 Doris Lessing, *A Proper Marriage* (1975), pp. 209, 272.
18 ibid., p. 75.
19 *Woman and Labour*, pp. 13–14.
20 Alice Clark, preface to *The Working Life of Women in the Seventeenth Century*
    (1919, reissued 1968), quoted in Sheila Rowbotham, introduction to the
    American edition, *Hidden from History* (New York 1976), p. xix.
21 Constance Lytton, *Prisons and Prisoners* (1914), p. 157.
22 Floyd Dell, *Women as World Builders, Studies in Modern Feminism* (Chicago
    1913).
23 Rowbotham and Weeks, *Socialism and the New Life*, p. 172.
24 OS to CS, Hanover, 2 February 1901, *Letters*, p. 231.
25 Anna Davin, 'Imperialism and Motherhood', *History Workshop* Issue 5 (Spring
    1978), pp. 9–66, especially pp. 12, 16–17.
26 *Life*, p. 182.
27 See Patricia Branca, *Silent Sisterhood* (1975), for a discussion of the mid-
    Victorian notion of woman as moral centre in the home, esp. pp. 6–8. On the
    Mothers' Union, see Olive Parker, *For the Family's Sake, A History of the
    Mothers' Union 1876–1976* (1975), pp. 5–27.
28 *Life*, p. 207.
29 Davin, op. cit., p. 20.
30 Quoted in Rowbotham and Weeks, op. cit., p. 177.
31 *Woman and Labour*.
32 Davin, op. cit., p. 21.
33 *Woman and Labour*, p. 67.
34 ibid., p. 129.
35 ibid., pp. 55, 61.
36 Information and quotes from Ellis' writings in this paragraph are from Row-
    botham and Weeks, op. cit., pp. 170–4.
37 OS to KP, 5 February 1888, *Pearson*.
38 OS to HE, De Aar, n.d. 1912, *Letters*, p. 320.
39 *Woman and Labour*, p. 190.
40 Quoted in Jane Graves, preface to *Woman and Labour* (1978), p. 7.
41 Information from Joyce Berkman, University of Massachusetts at Amherst.
42 A. Maude Royden, 'War and the Woman's Movement', in Charles Roden
    Buxton (ed.), *Towards a Lasting Settlement* (New York 1916), pp. 134–8.
43 Emmeline Pethick Lawrence, *My Part in a Changing World* (1938), pp. 307–10.
44 Ellen Key, *War, Peace and the Future* (New York 1916), pp. 96–8.
45 John Ruskin's notion of the 'walled garden' quoted in Olive Banks, 'Nineteenth
    and Twentieth Century Feminism', paper presented to the Women's Research
    and Resources Centre, London, 8 October 1976.
46 See Christopher Lasch, 'Woman as Alien', in *The New Radicalism in America,
    1889–1963* (New York 1965), pp. 38–65, especially p. 46.
47 *Woman and Labour*, p. 215.

48 OS to HE, Alassio, 6 April 1887, *Letters*, p. 113.
49 Cronwright does not identify Pearson in this section of the *Life*, but it can only be he. Olive's planned work is reproduced on p. 355.
50 Karl Pearson, *Charles Darwin, 1809–1882, An Appreciation*, Lecture to LCC Teachers 21 March 1923, p. 27.
51 Karl Pearson, Memoir, 'Walter Frank Raphael Weldon, 1860–1906', *Biometrika* V (1906), pp. 1–52, quoted in Egon Sharpe Pearson, *Karl Pearson* (1938), p. 2.
52 Pearson quotes on the following two pages are drawn from Egon Pearson, *Karl Pearson*, pp. 11–14.
53 *Woman and Labour*, p. 52.
54 See R. C. Lewontin, 'The Concept of Evolution', in David Sills (ed.), *International Encyclopaedia of the Social Sciences*, vol. 5 (1968), pp. 202–9.
55 See Pearson's 'The Woman's Question', *The Ethic of Freethought* (1888), pp. 355–6. His essay 'The Enthusiasm of the Market-Place and of the Study', pp. 103–22 same volume, develops the dichotomy of study/passion.
56 Cronwright's notes on OS, 'Introduction to the Life of Mary Wollstonecraft and the Rights of Woman', typescript, *Settlers*.
57 All quotes from OS, 'Wollstonecraft', pp. 2–14.
58 *Pall Mall Gazette*, 2 February 1889.
59 Quoted in Betty McGinnis Fradkin, 'Olive Schreiner and Karl Pearson', *Quarterly Bulletin of the South African Library*, vol. 31, No 4 (June 1977), p. 87.
60 OS to KP, 11 November 1890, *Pearson*.
61 OS to KP, 19 September 1886, *Pearson*.
62 OS to KP, 12 May 1886, *Pearson*.
63 Martha McIntyre, 'The Discussion of Sexuality in the Victorian Women's Movement', unpublished paper. Communist University of London, 1977, course on 'Sexuality and Human Nature'.
64 Rowbotham and Weeks, op. cit., p. 121.
65 OS to HE, Cape Town, December 1911, *Letters*, p. 303.
66 OS to HE, De Aar, 7 August 1912, *Letters*, p. 312.
67 OS to KP, 2 July 1886, *Pearson*.
68 *Woman and Labour*, pp. 26–7.
69 *Life*, p. 244.
70 *Woman and Labour*, pp. 248–9.
71 OS to KP, 10 September 1886, *Pearson*.
72 OS to KP, 10 June 1886, *Pearson*.
73 OS to KP, 16 June 1886, *Pearson*.
74 *Woman and Labour*, pp. 269–71.
75 For a general résumé of *The Interpretation of Dreams*, see Jones, *The Life and Work of Sigmund Freud*, p. 299.
76 Sigmund Freud, 'One of the Difficulties of Psychoanalysis' (1917), in *Collected Papers* IV (1971), pp. 355–6.
77 OS to HE, Hastings, 2 March 1885, *Letters*, p. 61.
78 Jones, *Life and Work*, p. 324.
79 Rowbotham and Weeks, op. cit., p. 164.
80 Jones, op. cit., pp. 493, 377.
81 See Mannoni's discussion of Freud's 'Instincts and their Vicissitudes' (1915), *Freud: The Theory of the Unconscious*, pp. 136–9.
82 ibid., p. 93.
83 OS to HE, Matjesfontein, 12 June 1890, *Letters*, pp. 188–9.
84 William B. Carpenter, *Principles of Mental Physiology* (1874), pp. 515–43, especially pp. 532–3. See also pp. 6, 23–7 for the relationship between feeling and the will.

CHAPTER 8: *World War One and Old Age*

1 To Anna Purcell, De Aar, 16 November 1913, SAPL; to HE, Llandrindod Wells, June 1916, HRC.
2 To Fan Schreiner, De Aar, 6 March 1901 and 17 November 1913, UCTJ.
3 *Life*, p. 360.
4 To WPS, De Aar, 7 July 1913 and 26 October 1913, UCTJ.
5 To WPS, De Aar, 12 September 1913, UCTJ.
6 To Fan Schreiner and to WPS, both aboard the *Edinburgh Castle*, December 1913, UCTJ.
7 *Life*, pp. 363–4.
8 Lady Constance Lytton, *Letters* (1925), p. 243; Carpenter, *My Days and Dreams*, p. 228.
9 To WPS, Florence, 16 January 1914, UCTJ.
10 *Life*, p. 367.
11 To HE, Kensington, 11 September 1914, *Letters*, p. 338.
12 To Edward Carpenter, London, October 1914, *Letters*, p. 340.
13 To HE, n.d. (though during the war), Llandrindod Wells, HRC.
14 To CS, London, 30 November 1914, *Letters*, p. 343.
15 To HE, London, 14 December 1914, *Letters*, p. 344.
16 London, 30 November 1914, *Letters*, p. 343.
17 To HE, Alassio, 15 January 1914, *Letters*, p. 329.
18 To HE, Florence, 6 March 1914, *Letters*, p. 330.
19 Information and quotes in this paragraph are from Ellis, *My Life*, pp. 392–405.
20 Walker, *W. P. Schreiner*, pp. 359–60.
21 Kensington, 3 August 1914, *Letters*, p. 337.
22 To HE, Kensington Palace Mansions, 16 October 1914, *Letters*, p. 340.
23 Note by CS, 23 November 1919, on letter from OS, 2 July 1913, *Settlers*.
24 To Emily Hobhouse, Bude, n.d. (though probably 1914), *Letters*, p. 341.
25 To Fan Schreiner, Bad Nauheim, 10 June 1914, UCTJ; and to Adela Smith, London, April 1915, *Letters*, p. 349.
26 n.d., HRC.
27 To HE, Bude, November 1914, HRC.
28 To Herman Kallenbach, Kensington, September 1914, SAPL.
29 See E. Sylvia Pankhurst, *The Suffragette Movement* (1931, Virago Reprint Library 1977), pp. 389, 604.
30 E. Sylvia Pankhurst, quoted in *The Listener*, 5 May 1955.
31 *Letters*, Appendix J, p. 402.
32 M. Gandhi, Diary, 23 June 1909, and letter to H. S. L. Polack, 14 July 1909, in *The Collected Works of Mahatma Gandhi*, vol. 10 (Government of India 1963), pp. 270, 287.
33 To Mr Gandhi, Kensington, 15 August 1914, SAPL.
34 London, 2 October 1914, SAPL.
35 OS to Mrs S. Solomon, London, 5 October 1916, SAPL.
36 Letter from OS, Llandrindod Wells, 7 September 1915, about a Workers' National Committee 'Appeal to Women Workers who are taking men's places during this period of national crisis', 26 August 1915, Labour Party Archives.
37 *Life*, pp. 366–7.
38 'A Few Words to the Young Men of Britain who, being Conscientious Objectors, are today called on to fight', *Labour Leader*, 16 March 1916, *Letters*, pp. 398–9.
39 See 'Who Knocks at the Door?', reprinted in *Stories, Dreams and Allegories*, pp. 147–54.
40 'The Dawn of Civilisation', *The Nation and Athenaeum*, 26 March 1921.

41 n.d. (? 1914), Carpenter MSS.
42 London, 14 December 1914, HRC and succeeding letters (most undated, though from 1914–15) in the HRC collection.
43 Ellis, *My Life*, pp. 389–91, 491.
44 ibid., p. 161.
45 ibid., p. 183.
46 To HE, Llandrindod Wells, 27 August 1915, *Letters*, p. 353.
47 Ellis, *My Life*, pp. 405–6.
48 Alassio, 24 January 1888, *Letters*, pp. 127–8.
49 Quoted in Hobman, *Olive Schreiner*, p. 168.
50 ibid.
51 Quotes in the next two paragraphs are from *Life*, pp. 369–72.
52 London, 2 January 1916, *Letters*, p. 355.
53 ? London, 1916, UCTJ.
54 See Walker, *W. P. Schreiner*, p. 361.
55 To WPS, Kensington, ? 1914, UCTJ.
56 *Life*, p. 365.
57 London, August 1918, UCTJ.
58 ibid.
59 To WPS, London, 1918, UCTJ.
60 9 Porchester Place, London, 19 October 1918, *Letters*, p. 358.
61 To CS, Porchester Place, 6 December 1918, *Letters*, p. 360.
62 Walker, *W. P. Schreiner*, pp. 363–73.
63 ibid., p. 381.
64 To May Murray-Parker, London, 24 June 1919, UCTJ.
65 London, 29 August 1919, UCTJ.
66 To HE, London, late 1919, *Letters*, p. 363.
67 Isaac Deutscher, *The Prophet Armed, Trotsky 1879–1921* (London 1954), pp. 432–46.
68 Interview with Prof. Ben Farrington by Ruth First, 22 October 1969.
69 Deutscher, op. cit., p. 458.
70 To HE, London, n.d. 1919, *Letters*, p. 362.
71 London, late 1919, *Letters*, p. 364.
72 ibid., p. 365.
73 To Fan Schreiner, London, 12 December 1919, UCTJ.
74 London, 3 February 1920, UCTJ.
75 To Fan Schreiner, London, January 1920; to May Murray-Parker, London, 23 January 1920; to Betty Molteno, London, January 1920, UCTJ.
76 Quoted in *Life*, p. 373.
77 London, January 1920, *Letters*, p. 366.
78 London, January 1920, *Letters*, p. 367.
79 To Fan Schreiner, London, 22 January 1920, UCTJ; to CS, London, 29 January 1920, *Letters*, p. 367.
80 To WPS, near Guilford, 1918, UCTJ.
81 *Life*, p. 374.
82 CS's *Journal*, 21 November 1921, *Settlers*.
83 19 May 1913, *Settlers*.
84 24 May 1913, *Settlers*.
85 Received by CS, 2 July 1913, *Settlers*.
86 2 April 1920, *Settlers*.
87 1 May 1920, *Settlers*.
88 11 May 1920, *Settlers*.
89 See *Letters*, pp. 82, 95, 120, 212, 216.

90   *Journal*, 14 December 1924, *Settlers*.
91   Alassio, 3 November 1888, *Letters*, p. 145.
92   This and quotes in the next two paragraphs are from *Life*, pp. 375–6.
93   To May Murray-Parker, London, 24 January and 31 January 1920, UCTJ.
94   To Lady Rose Innes, London, 28 March 1920, SAPL.
95   To Fan Schreiner, London, 13 May 1920, UCTJ; to Ruth Alexander, London, 12 May 1920, SAPL: to Adela Smith, London, 2 March 1920, *Letters*, p. 368.
96   To HE, London, 4 August 1920, *Letters*, p. 368.
97   *Life*, pp. 376–7.
98   To May Murray-Parker, Plumstead, 1 September 1920, UCTJ; to HE, Wynberg, 15 October 1920, *Letters*, p. 368; *Life*, p. 378.
99   Quoted in Ridley Beeton, 'In Search of Olive Schreiner in Texas', *The Texas Quarterly*, vol. XVII No. 3 (Autumn 1974), p. 136.
100 To Jan Smuts, 28 October 1920; to Betty Molteno, Wynberg, 12 November 1920; to Jan Smuts, January 1918 and 19 November 1918, SAPL. To Betty Molteno, Wynberg, 5 November 1920, UCTJ.
101 Brown, *Memories*, p. 16.
102 De Aar, 1920, UCTJ.
103 De Aar, 25 July 1909, *Letters*, p. 287.
104 The account of Olive's last weeks in this and the next three paragraphs is taken from *Life*, pp. 379–82.
105 *Life*, p. 387.
106 ibid., p. 190.
107 ibid., p. 32.
108 To HE, Alassio, 21 October 1888, *Letters*, p. 143.
109 Harrow, 29 May 1886, *Letters*, p. 100.
110 Quoted in Brown, *Memories*, p. 15.
111 London, August 1918, UCTJ.
112 *Life*, p. 389.
113 Llandrindod Wells, n.d., HRC.
114 Kapp, *Crowded Years*, p. 700.
115 To Dollie Radford, quoted in ibid.
116 ibid.
117 To HE, St Leonards-on-Sea, 28 March 1884, *Letters*, p. 14.
118 To Dollie Radford, Kensington, 28 May 1914, SAPL.
119 The account of the funeral arrangements and burial that follows is taken from *Life*, pp. 385 ff.
120 See Beeton, 'In Search of Olive Schreiner', pp. 146–9 for an account of these notes.
121 CS to Fisher Unwin, 20 January 1926, *Settlers*.
122 *Life*, Appendix D, 'Her Will', pp. 391–2.
123 *Life*, pp. 267–8.
124 Information and quotes in this and the remaining paragraphs are from *Life*, Appendix F, 'The Reinterment on Buffels Kop', pp. 394–401.

CHAPTER 9: *Broken and Untried?*

Our sources here are concerned solely with theory and treatment in asthma. We have avoided making too close a link between Olive's own chronic illness and material on the deology of female weakness in the late nineteenth century – cf. Carroll Smith-Rosenberg, 'The Hysterical Woman: Sex Roles and Role Conflict in 19th-Century America', *Social Research* 39 (Winter 1972), pp. 652–78 – and have looked rather at the manifest dynamics of Olive's family life. Our initial debt here, as mentioned earlier in the text, is to Jane Graves, who has done much imaginative work on the meaning of asthma in Olive's life, suggesting links between her symptoms and her difficulty with egotism and 'self-delight'. Like Havelock Ellis in *From Rousseau to Proust* (1936), pp. 387–91, Graves compares Olive's asthma with that of Marcel Proust, but from the vantage point of a solid grounding in psychosomatics and the notion of secondary gain. Ellis' account is not insubstantial but feels dated in its great concern with the fate of above average racial 'stock'. We are indebted to Dr Colin James for guidance to relevant work in the current psychoanalytic literature, notably Joyce McDougall, 'The Psychosoma and the Psychoanalytic Process', *Int. Rev. Psycho-Anal.* (1974), 1, 437–59, and Dr M. Jackson, 'The Mind-Body Frontier – The Problem of the "Mysterious Leap" ', paper read to the Psychiatric Section of the Royal Society of Medicine, March 1978. The incident at Healdtown in 1861, when Olive hid a family visitor's hat, brought to Dr James' mind two case histories on parallel themes, Masud R. Khan's 'Secret as Potential Space', paper read at a Scientific Meeting of the British Psychoanalytical Society, May 1974, and D. W. Winnicott's 'String', in *Playing and Reality* (1974), pp. 18–23. These describe objects being hidden, on the one hand, and bound together by string, on the other, and are concerned with a child's direct and indirect expression of anxiety about his or her personal identity and standing within the family. On theoretical work in the history of medicine, Karl Figlio's 'Chlorosis and chronic disease in nineteenth-century Britain: the social constitution of somatic illness in a capitalist society', *Social History*, vol. 3: no 2, May 1978, 167–97, is generally thought-provoking. John Gabbay's 'Asthma: a case study in changing relationships between theory and therapy from the seventeenth to the twentieth century', dissertation submitted to Cambridge University for the Diploma in History and Philosophy of Science (1977), has been invaluable in starting us off with the medical profession's view of the asthmatic during Olive's adult life, the extent of self-medication and use of patent drugs, and an overview of the classic monographs on the disease. In tracing the evolution of ideas about the illness and its treatment, we used three main indexes. Firstly, *Index Medicus: a monthly classified record of the current medical literature of the world* (New York, etc. 1879–), whose headings, sampled every five years to 1925, indicate changes in the classification of the disease and language of treatment, and the rate at which ideas develop and are disseminated in the literature. Secondly, *Psychological Abstracts*, American Psychological Association (1927–), containing over 150 references to asthma, the majority dealing with psychosomatic factors. By the late Forties this had become the standard bibliographical reference source and was receiving two hundred journals regularly. Thirdly, *Chicago Psychoanalytic Literature Index 1920–1970* (Chicago, Illinois, CPL Publishing, 1978), with subsequent volumes for 1975, 6 and 7, in which the vicissitudes of the 'asthmatogenic mother' can be traced. Finally, Michelene Wandor, 'The Experience of Asthma' (unpublished interview with Ann Scott, 1975) was especially helpful in pointing to some of the knots in a dependency relationship of the kind that severe asthma can generate.

1 cf. Adrienne Rich's re-evaluation of *Jane Eyre*, 'The Temptations of a Motherless Woman', *MS.*, October 1973, pp. 68–72, 98, 106–7.
2 n.d. 1884, HRC.
3 OS to CS, London, 30 November 1914, *Letters*, p. 343.
4 OS to HE, Bournemouth, 1 March 1886, *Letters*, p. 94.
5 OS to HE, Johannesburg, 25 July 1899, *Letters*, p. 227.
6 Sheila Rowbotham, review of Vincent Brome, *Havelock Ellis: philosopher of sex* (1979), *New Society*, 12 April 1979.
7 OS to Jan Smuts, London, ?1918, SAPL.
8 Again, derived from Rich's exposition of Jane Eyre's personality, *op. cit.*

Schreiner Family Tree

Rev. Samuel Lyndall m. 1/Henrietta Rebecca Oliver d. 1810
2/Catherine James

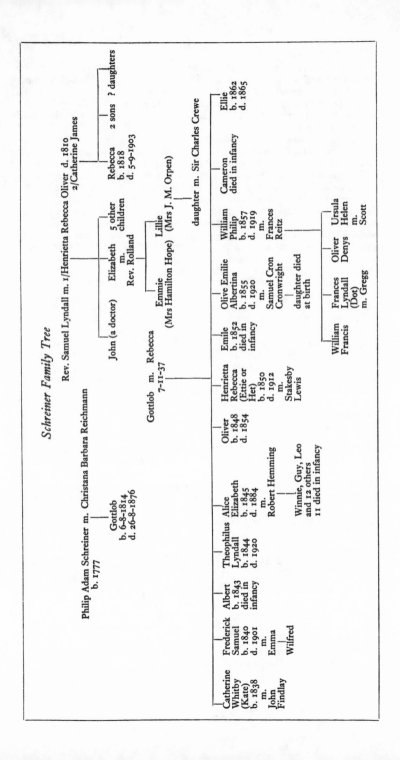

Philip Adam Schreiner m. Christana Barbara Reichmann
b. 1777

Gottlob
b. 6-8-1814
d. 26-8-1876

John (a doctor)

Elizabeth
m.
Rev. Rolland

5 other children

Rebecca
b. 1818
d. 5-9-1903

2 sons ? daughters

Gottlob m. Rebecca
7-11-37

Emmie
(Mrs Hamilton Hope)

Lillie
(Mrs J. M. Orpen)

daughter m. Sir Charles Crewe

Catherine
Whitby
(Kate)
b. 1838
m.
John
Findlay

Frederick
Samuel
b. 1840
d. 1901
m.
Emma

Albert
b. 1843
died in
infancy

Theophilus
Lyndall
b. 1844
d. 1920

Alice
Elizabeth
b. 1845
d. 1884
m.
Robert Hemming

Oliver
b. 1848
d. 1854

Henrietta
Rebecca
(Ettie or
Het)
b. 1850
d. 1912
m.
Stakesby
Lewis

Emile
b. 1852
died in
infancy

Olive Emilie
Albertina
b. 1855
d. 1920
m.
Samuel Cron
Cronwright

William
Philip
b. 1857
d. 1919
m.
Frances
Reitz

Cameron
died in infancy

Ellie
b. 1862
d. 1865

Wilfred

Winnie, Guy, Leo
and 12 others
11 died in infancy

daughter died
at birth

William
Francis

Frances
Lyndall
(Dot)
m. Gregg

Oliver
Denys

Ursula
Helen
m.
Scott

CHRONOLOGY

1855   Olive Schreiner born 24 March, ninth of twelve children, at Wittebergen, Basutoland.

1867   Family disperses; Olive moves to Cradock to live with her elder brother Theo, older sister Ettie and younger brother Will.

1871   Reads Herbert Spencer's *First Principles*.

1872   Meets Julius Gau while working informally as a governess in Dordrecht.

1872–3 Moves to Diamond Fields to live with Theo and Ettie. Onset of chest condition; starts writing stories and begins *Undine*.

1874   Begins work as governess; over the next seven years takes five posts in the Cape Colony and works on *Undine*, *The Story of an African Farm*, and *From Man to Man*.

1881   To England to train as a nurse.

1882   Chapman and Hall accept *African Farm*. Meets Eleanor Marx.

1883   *African Farm* published.

1884   Meets Havelock Ellis and Edward Carpenter.

1885–6 Involvement in Men and Women's Club and with Karl Pearson.

1887–9 Travelling in England and Europe; working on allegories, *From Man to Man* and Introduction to Mary Wollstonecraft's *Vindication of the Rights of Woman*.

1889   Returns to South Africa in November; asthma now chronic.

1890   Moves to Matjesfontein in the Karoo; *Dreams* published in London. Writes essay on South Africa in defence of the Boer. Meets Cecil Rhodes, Cape prime minister.

1891   Begins 'The Buddhist Priest's Wife'. Writes skit on the Cape parliament debating the Flogging Bill.

1892   Breaks with Rhodes. Meets Samuel Cron Cronwright.

1894   Marries Cronwright on 24 February; they live at Krantz Plaats near Cradock. Olive's asthma worsens and they move to Kimberley.

1895   Birth and death of baby girl, 30 April.

1896   Jameson Raid forces Rhodes to resign as PM. Olive writes *Trooper Peter Halket*. Goes to England with Cronwright and MS. of *Halket*. *The Political Situation* published in England under their joint authorship.

1897   *Halket* published in London.

1898   In October moves to Johannesburg for her health and Cronwright gives up his business in Kimberley to join her.

1899   Writes '*A South African's View of the Situation*'. In Cape Town when Boer War breaks out in November.

1900   Living under martial law in Hanover.

1901   Writes 'Eighteen–Ninety-Nine'.

1902   Peace treaty signed. Revisits Johannesburg.

1908   Begins to concentrate on conflict between capital and labour; engages in public debate about future of South African constitution.

1908–13 In contact with Gandhi's *satyagraha* movement, and vice-president of Women's Enfranchisement League.

1911   *Woman and Labour* published in London.

1914–18 In London, in contact with British pacifists and conscientious objectors,

Gandhi, and Sylvia Pankhurst. Writes short allegory on war for *Fortnightly Review*.

1920   Cronwright visits in July; Olive returns to Cape in August, and dies at Wynberg on 11 December.

1921   13 August: re-interred at Buffels Kop in the Karoo.

BIBLIOGRAPHY OF SCHREINER'S WORK

This bibliography lists those of Olive Schreiner's works published in book or pamphlet form. Though comprehensive, it does not claim to be definitive; it has not been possible to ascertain all translation history, for example. Nor have we been able to trace date, place, and publisher for every edition of each work.

The listing has been compiled from three main sources: the British Library Catalogue; Evelyn Verster (compiler), *Olive Emilie Albertina Schreiner (1855–1920): Bibliography* (Cape Town, University of Cape Town, 1946); and Ridley Beeton, *Olive Schreiner, A Short Guide to Her Writings* (Cape Town, Howard Timmins, 1974).

THE STORY OF AN AFRICAN FARM

Ralph Iron, The Story of an African Farm. A Novel in Two Volumes. London, Chapman and Hall, 1883; as one vol, July 1883; 1887; 1889; *same*: cheap edn.
Ralph Iron (Olive Schreiner), The Story of an African Farm. A Novel. New edn. London, Hutchinson, 1891.
– London, Chapman and Hall, 1892.
– 70,oooth. London, Hutchinson, 1893; 73,oooth. 1894; 88,oooth. 1896; 97,oooth. n.d.
Olive Schreiner, The Story of an African Farm. A Novel. Popular edn. London, Hutchinson, 1910.
– With an introduction by S. C. Cronwright-Schreiner. London, Unwin, 1924.
– Boston, Little, 1924.
– With an introduction by S. C. Cronwright-Schreiner. London, Unwin, 1925 (Cabinet Library); *same*: with lithographs.
– With an introduction by Francis Brett Young. New York, Modern Library, 1927 (Modern Library of the World's Best Books).
– With an introduction by S. C. Cronwright-Schreiner. London, Benn, 1929 (Essex Library).
– Cheap edn. London, Collins, 1929.
– Re-issue. London, Benn, 1929 (Essex Library).
– New York, Collins, 1930; *same*: (Theban Classics); *same*: (Westminster Classics).
– London, Collins, 1932 (Masterpieces of Literature).
– West Drayton, Middlesex, Penguin Books, 1939 (twice); 1940.
– Johannesburg, Central News Agency, 1949.
– London, Benn, 1951.
– London and Glasgow, Collins, 1953.
– With an introduction by Dan Jacobson. Harmondsworth, Penguin Books, 1971.
– With an introduction by Doris Lessing (1968). New York, Schocken Books, 1976.

Translations

Dutch: full tr. 1892. Two series of extracts issued Utrecht, 1930.
German: freely tr. and published as *Lyndall*, Munich, 1892.
French: Ollendorff, 1901.
Czech: 1903 (English Library).
Esperanto: 1934.

DREAMS

London, Unwin, 1890, 1891 (twice), 1892, 1893, 1894, 1895, 1897, 1900, 1903, 1905, 1907, 1908, 1912 (twice), 1913, 1914, 1915, 1917, 1919, 1923, 1923 (with lithographs), 1930.
– Cheap edn. London, Benn, 1930 (Essex Library).
– Boston, Little, n.d.
– Portland (Me.), Mosher, n.d.
OS has provided a Note stating that the Dreams were printed in the order in which they were written; where the place of writing is given, we have estimated a date.
  The Lost Joy, South Africa [?1874].
  The Hunter (from *African Farm*) [1876–9].
  The Gardens of Pleasure [unidentified].
  In a Far-Off World [unidentified].
  Three Dreams in a Desert [unidentified].
  A Dream of Wild Bees, London [?1886].
  In a Ruined Chapel, London [*Life* gives Alassio, 1887].
  The Artist's Secret, St Leonards-on-Sea [?1887].
  I Thought I Stood, Alassio [?finished London, 1889].
  The Sunlight Lay Across My Bed [unidentified, finished London, 1889].

Translations

Dutch: Amsterdam, Veldt, 1893, 1903. Rijswick, Blankwaardt en Schoonhoven, 1917.
German: Berlin, Dümmler, 1894, 1899, 1907; Stuttgart, Cotta'sche Buchhandlung, n.d.
French: freely tr. as *Rêves virils* ('Virile Dreams'), Lausanne, Mignot, 1903.
Ukrainian: 1907.

DREAM LIFE AND REAL LIFE

Ralph Iron, London, Unwin, 1893 (Pseudonym Library), 1897, 1912.
Place and date of first publication given in square brackets.
  Dream Life and Real Life – A Little African Story [Eastbourne, *The New College Magazine*, Nov. 1881].
  The Woman's Rose [London, *The New Review*, June 1891].
  The Policy in Favour of Protection in the Australian Colonies [?New York, *Harper's Weekly*, 1 October 1892].

Translations

Dutch: Beemster, Lakeman, 1894.

THE POLITICAL SITUATION

By Olive Schreiner and S. C. Cronwright-Schreiner, London, Unwin, 1896.
Paper read by SCCS in the Town Hall, Kimberley, 20 August 1895. Extracts and summary first published *Cape Times*, 21 August 1895.

TROOPER PETER HALKET OF MASHONALAND

London, Unwin, 1897.
– Leipzig, Tauchnitz, 1897 (Collection of British Authors, No. 3205).

- London, Unwin, 1899, 1905 (cheap edn.), 1926 (Adelphi Library), 1926 (Cabinet Library).
- With a foreword by Trevor Huddleston, C. R., London, Benn, 1959.
- With an introduction by Marion Friedmann, Johannesburg, A. Donker, 1974.

Translations

Dutch: Amsterdam, Veen, 1897, 1899. Pretoria, De Bussy, 1897. Nutsuitgeverij, Zalt-Bommel, 1918.
German: Berlin, Dümmler, 1898. Shortened version for school use, Bielefeld, Velhagen und Klasing, 1926.
French: Charles, 1899.

AN ENGLISH SOUTH AFRICAN'S VIEW OF THE SITUATION. WORDS IN SEASON

London, Hodder and Stoughton, 1899.
Originally published as a series of newspaper articles:
    Words in Season. An English-South African's view of the situation. *The South African News*, 1, 2, and 3 June 1899.
    Words in Season. A Letter. Johannesburg, *The Standard and Digger's News*, ? June 1899.
    The South African Question. By an English South African. Cape Town, South African Newspaper Co., 1899. Reprinted from *The South African News*.
    War or Peace with the Transvaal, III: A Plea for Patience by Olive Schreiner. London, *Review of Reviews*, July 1899. Excerpts from the letter which OS contributed to *The Standard and Digger's News*.
    The South African Question. Chicago, 1899.

A LETTER ON THE JEW

Cape Town, H. Liberman, 1906.
Paper read at Jewish Territorial Organization meeting in Cape Town, 1 July 1906, published *Cape Times*, 2 July 1906.

CLOSER UNION

Letter on the South African Union and the Principles of Government. London, Fifield, 1909.
Reprint in pamphlet form of OS' letter to the *Transvaal Leader*, 22 December 1908.

OLIVE SCHREINER'S THOUGHTS ABOUT WOMEN

Cape Town, published for the Cape Women's Enfranchisement League by the South African News Co, 1909.
Extracts from *African Farm* and *Dreams*, with a preface by Anna Purcell.

WOMAN AND LABOUR

London and Leipzig, Unwin, 1911.
- Liepzig, Tauchnitz, 1911 (Collection of British Authors, No. 4256).
- 2nd impression. London, Unwin, 1911; new edn. 1914.
- Woman in War. Re-issue. London, Unwin, 1914; Ch. 4 of *Woman and Labour*.

Translations

Dutch: Amsterdam, Van Kampen, 1911.
German: Jena, Diederichs, 1914.

DREAMS; AND DREAM LIFE AND REAL LIFE

Re-issue. London, Unwin, 1912 (Adelphi Library); new edn. 1920; 1924 (Adelphi Library).

Translations

Dutch: Beemster, Lakeman, 1894.

THOUGHTS ON SOUTH AFRICA

London, Unwin, 1923, 1927.
Place and date of original publication, where known, given in square brackets.
  South Africa, its Natural Features, etc. [London, *Fortnightly Review*, July 1891;
  Cape Times, 18 August 1891; *The Living Age*, 5 September 1891; excerpted London,
  Review of Reviews, 1891].
  The Boer [extract, *Cape Times*, 16 April 1896; London, *Daily News*, 12 May 1896;
  London, *Fortnightly Review*, 1 July 1896].*
  The Problem of Slavery.
  The Wanderings of the Boer [London, *Fortnightly Review*, August 1896].†
  The Boer Woman and the Modern Woman's Question.‡
  The Boer and his Republics.
  The Psychology of the Boer.
  The Englishman.

APPENDICES

  The South African Nation.
  The Value of Human Varieties.
  The Domestic Life of the Boer [Boston, Mass., *The Youth's Companion*, November
  1899].
  Our Waste Land in Mashonaland [*Cape Times*, 26 August 1891].§

Translations

Dutch: as Land en Volk van de Transvaal. Wetenschappelijke Bladen, June, Oct.,
Nov. and Dec. 1896; June and Nov. 1897.
– as Losse Gedachten over Zuid-Afrika. Haarlem, Tjeenk Willink, 1900.
Afrikaans: Part of Ch. 5, The Boer Woman. Die Huisgenoot, April 1924.

* As The African Boer [?New York, *Cosmopolitan*, Sept. and Oct. 1900].
† As Stray Thoughts on South Africa . . . The Wanderings of the Boer [London, *Fort-
  nightly Review*, August, 1896]. As Stray Thoughts on South Africa. [*The Living Age*,
  May 1896, and London and New York, *Cosmopolis*, vol. 10, 1898].
‡ ? Originally The Boer Woman and the Nineteenth Century Woman [? New York, *Cosmo-
  politan*, April 1898].
§ As Ch. XX of F.R.N. Findlay, *Big Game Shooting and Travel in South-East Africa*,
  London, Unwin, 1909.

STORIES. DREAMS AND ALLEGORIES

With an introduction by S. C. Cronwright-Schreiner, London, Unwin, 1923, 1924.
– New York, Stokes, 1923.
– London, Benn. 1931.

STORIES

Eighteen-Ninety-Nine [?1904].
The Buddhist Priest's Wife [Matjesfontein, 1891–2].
On the Banks of a Full River [1889–92].
The Wax Doll and the Stepmother [?187–].
The Adventures of Master Towser, Eastbourne, March 1882 [Eastbourne, *The New College Magazine*, 1882].

DREAMS AND ALLEGORIES

A Soul's Journey – Two Visions.
God's Gift to Men, Alassio.
They Heard . . ., Mentone.
Life's Gifts, London, 1887.
The Flower and the Spirit, Alassio, 1887.
The River of Life, Amsteg, 1887.
The Brown Flower.
The Two Paths.
A Dream of Prayer, Gersau, Switzerland, 1887.
Workers, Alassio, 1887.
The Cry of South Africa, Wagenaar's Kraal, 1900.
Seeds A-Growing, Hanover, 1901.
The Great Heart of England [? Written during Boer War].
Who Knocks at the Door?, London, 1917 [*Fortnightly Review*, 1 Nov. 1917].
The Winged Butterfly, Harpenden, 1888.

The 1924 edition includes The Dawn of Civilisation (Stray thoughts on peace and war. The homely personal confession of a believer in human unity) [London, *The Nation and Athenaeum*, 26 March 1921].

THE LIFE OF OLIVE SCHREINER

By S. C. Cronwright-Schreiner, London, Unwin, 1924, includes the following writings, unpublished in book or pamphlet form elsewhere:

Reminiscences, 1883–4.
The Forefathers . . . Silk Stockings and Snuff Box [Lyndall ancestry].
Awl and Last [Schreiner ancestry].
A Face in a Dream [Gottlob and Rebecca meet and marry].
A New Generation [Early years in South Africa].
The Salvation of a Ministry, 1891.

THE LETTERS OF OLIVE SCHREINER

(ed.), S. C. Cronwright-Schreiner, London, Unwin, 1924 (twice).

APPENDICES

Speech on Boer War, public meeting, Cape Town, July 1900.

Letter on Boer War, women's meeting, Paarl, October 1900.
Speech on Boer War, women's meeting, Somerset East, October 1900.
Letter read at shop assistants' demonstration, Johannesburg, probably early 1905.
Letter on 'The Taal', reprinted from *Cape Times*, May 1905.
Extracts from 'A Letter on the Jew' (see above).
Letter on Women's Suffrage, read at public meeting, Cape Town, May 1908.
On Conscientious Objectors, reprinted from London, *Labour Leader*, March 1916.
Letter to peace meeting arranged by Union of Democratic Control, London, March 1916.
Letter to a women's meeting commemorating J. S. Mill, London, July 1918.

FROM MAN TO MAN; OR, PERHAPS ONLY . . .

With an introduction by S. C. Cronwright-Schreiner, London, Unwin, 1926, 1927.
– New York, Harper, 1927.
– New York, Grosset, 1927 (Novels of distinction).
– London, Benn, 1931; *same*: 2 vols (Essex Library).

UNDINE

With an introduction by S. C. Cronwright-Schreiner, London, Benn, and New York, Harper, 1929, 1930.

Translation

Esperanto: 1929, 1938.

INDEX

Abdurahman, Dr Abdul, 259
Acland, Sir Henry, 112
Addams, Jane, 276
African National Congress, *see* South African Native National Congress
African Peoples' Organization, 259
Afrikaner Bond, 202–3, 222, 232
Alexander, Ruth, 267, 313, 322
Anderson, Elizabeth Garrett, 290
Angora Goat, The (Cronwright-Schreiner), 230
Athenaeum, review of *Dreams* 185–6, review of *Trooper Peter Halket*, 230
Aurora Leigh (Browning), 118, 154
Aveling, Edward, 109, 134, 144, review of *African Farm*, 124

Bachofen, Johann, 289
Backhouse, Rev. James, 29n
Barrett, Wilson, 311
Basel Mission, 31–2, 40–1
Basel Mission Station, 40
Basotho, the, 37, 39, 40
Bataung, the, 40
Bernstein, Eduard, 240
Bertram, Willie, 58–60, 82, 104n, 144
Besant, Annie, 146
Bhagavad Gita, 158
Birth Control Review, 282
Blackwood's Edinburgh Magazine, review of *Trooper Peter Halket*, 230
Bloemfontein, 41–2
Bodichon, Barbara, 290
Boer War, 244–50; contemporary political positions on, 237–44; Luxemburg's thesis, 244; peace treaty, 250; & post-war settlement, 251–2; Rhodes' ministries &, 220–1, 230–1
Botha, Louis, 251, 311
Breuer, Joseph, 296
Brigg, Rev. Arthur, 43n
British Medical Association, 112
British-South Africa Company, *see* Chartered Company
Brittain, Vera, 265, 273, 274n
Brontë, Emily, 21

Brooke, Emma, 152–3
Brown, Dr John, 68–70, 80, 111–12, 329
Brown, Mary, 69, 80, 111–12, 184, 323
Browning, Robert, 187
Buchanan-Gould, Vera, 21, 23, 62–3, 320
Buffels Kop, 330–2
Buxton, Thomas Powell, 28

Calder-Marshall, Arthur, 115
Calvin, John, 33
Campbell, Rev. John, 35
Cape Times, 224; on *The Political Situation*, 220–1
Capital (Marx), 23, 110
Carnarvon, Lord, 117n
Carpenter, Edward, 57, 129, 158, 178–9, 196, 209, 217, 294
Carpenter, William B., 296n, 297
Catholic World, review of *Dreams*, 185
Cawood, Erilda, 56, 76–80, 83, 114, 206–7
Cawood, Richard, 56
Chances of Death, The (Pearson), 289
Chapman and Hall, 118
Chapman, Frederic, 119
Charcot, Jean, 295
Chartered Company, 201, 215n, 229
Churchill, Lord Randolph, 199
Church of England Mothers' Union, 277
Church Missionary Society, 30–31
Clapham Sect, 29
Clark, Alice, 275
Clark, Percy M., 229n
Cobb, Elizabeth (*née* Sharpe), 148–9 ff 164–5, 168, 186
Cobb, Henry, 146, 156
Colenso, Harriett, 259
Colenso, J. W., Bishop of Natal, 57, 259
Commercial Advertiser, 41
Congress of the Second International, Paris 1900, 239
Convention of Pretoria 1881, 117n
Courtney, Leonard, 237n
Cradock, 55–6
Criminal Law Amendment Act, 156

Cronwright, Alfred, 324
Cronwright-Schreiner, Samuel Cron;
  ancestry, 205–7; anti-war campaign in
  Britain, 237–9; biography of OS,
  19–20; Bond campaign, 232; courtship
  (OS &), 207–12; & death of OS,
  327–8; enters politics, 218–19;
  estrangement from OS, 315–19;
  infant's death, 214; & Jan Hofmeyr,
  222; marriage, 212; meets OS, 205–7;
  M.P., 248; & OS' literary work, 213,
  267; registers articles, 250; & *Woman
  and Labour*, 226–8

Darwin, Charles, 23, 285–6
Davidson, Thomas, 130
De Aar shooting, 248–9
de Beauvoir, Simone, 24
De Beers Consolidated Mines, 201
Decline & Fall (Gibbon), 82
Dell, Floyd, 276
Democratic Federation, 108, *see also*
  Social Democratic Federation
Denikin, General, 313
de Tocqueville, Alexis, 294–5
Diamond Diggers' Protection Society, 65
Diana of the Crossways (Meredith), 118
Dickens, Charles, 118
Digger's Song, The, 65
Dilke, Sir Charles, 121
Dinuzulu, 259
Disraeli, Benjamin, 117n
Donkin, Bryan (later Sir Bryan), 124,
  145, 150–1, 158, 166, 168
Douglass, David, 80
Duncan, Isadora, 276
Dutch Reformed Church, 28
Du Toit's Pan, 63, 65

Eagleton, Terry, 53n
Eastty, Annie, 147
Egoist, The (Meredith), 118
Eliot, George, 21, 56
Ellis, Edith (*née* Lees), 294, 301, 307
Ellis, Havelock; differences with Freud,
  295–6; early life, 125; friendship with
  Carpenter, 130; & Hinton, 125–9; &
  male stereotype, 218; marriage, 193;
  on motherhood, 280; & OS, 124,
  129–34, 136–44, 307–8; & publication
  of *Dreams*, 190–1; on sexuality, 281,
  293
Ellis, Louise, 135

Engels, Frederick, 124
Englishwoman's Review, The, on *African
  Farm,* 123
Erewhon (Butler), 118
Essays and Reviews, 59
Essays (Emerson), 82
Ethic of Freethought, The (Pearson), 149,
  181; OS review of, 289
Eugenics Review, 278–9
Evening News, on *African Farm*, 123
Evolution of Sex, The (Geddes and
  Thompson), 291

Fabian Society, 109, 130
Farquharson, Robert, 116n
Farrington, Ben, 322n
Fawcett, Millicent, 290
Fellowship of the New Life, 130, 144–5
Feminism & Sex Education (Kenealy),
  284
Findlay, John, 46–7
Findlay, Kate (*née* Schreiner), 45–7, 62
First Principles (Spencer), 58, 59, 126
Flogging Bill *see* Masters and Servants
  Bill
Fortnightly Review, The, 118, 224, 306
  on *African Farm*, 123
Fort, Seymour, 199
Fouchés, Stoffel, 72, 74, 78, 80
Freewoman, The, 291
Freud, Sigmund, 23, 294, 295–7
Friedmann, Marion, 22, 53
Future Belongs to the People, The
  (Liebknecht), 313

Galton, Francis, 278
Gandhi, Mahatma, 17, 304–5
Gaskell, Elizabeth, 118
Gau, Julius, 61–3, 67–8, 145
Gilman, Charlotte Perkins, 276
Gissing, George, 118
Gladstone, William Ewart, 117n, 187
  on *African Farm*, 122
Glasier, Bruce, 209
Goldfields Company, 201
Graves, Jane, 218
Greene, Alice, 254, 314
Griquas, the, 37–8, 66n
Guide to Therapeutics (Farquharson),
  116n

Haddon, Caroline, 127, 152, 153–4
Haggard, Rider, 144

Hanover, 247
Hardie, Keir, 238, 241, 254
Hardy, Thomas, 118
Havelock Ellis (Calder-Marshall), 115n
Healdtown, 48-9
Hemming, Alice (*née* Schreiner), 57, 68
Hemming, Robert, 57, 266
Hermon, 57
Hinton, Howard, 163
Hinton, James, 125-9, 142, 152, 163
History & Heroes of the Art of Medicine (Russell), 70
History of Civilization in England (Buckle), 60
History of European Morals (Lecky), 121, 173
History of Philosophy (Lewes), 115
Hobhouse, Emily, 248
Hobman, D. L., 21, 267
Hobson, J. A., 231, 237, 240
Hodgson, Joan, 309-10
Hodgson, John, 309
Hofmeyr, Jan, 202-3, 204, 222
Hopkins, Jane Ellice, 129
Horrabin, Winifred, 21n
Hottentots, the (Khoikhoi), 29, 195
Housman, Laurence, on *African Farm*, 122-3
Hymns of Progress (Ellis), 130
Hyndman, H. M., 109, 240

Illustrated London News, 41
Imperialism (Hobson), 231
Imvo, 213
Independent Labour Party, 108-9, 237
Interpretation of Dreams, The (Freud), 294
Innes, James Rose, 203, 204
'In Memoriam' (Pearson), 169n
In Tents in the Transvaal (Hutchinson), 117
International Psychoanalytical Association, 296
Iron, Ralph (OS pseudonym), 119, 171

Jabavu, Tengo, 213
Jacobson, Dan, 92-3
James, Catherine (later Lyndall), 34
Jameson, Dr L. S., 221, 225n
Jameson, Raid, 221, 225, 229
Jewsbury, Geraldine, 117
Johannesburg, 234

Johannesburg Shop Assistants' Union, 253
Joynes, Jim, 209
Justice, 239, 241

Kallenbach, Hermann, 303, 304
Kapp, Yvonne, 124n, 134-5, 136, 327
Kenealy, Arabella, 284
Kent, Philip, on *African Farm*, 120-1
Key, Ellen, 276, 283
Khoikhoi *see* Hottentots
Kimberley *see* New Rush
Kipling, Rudyard, 213n
Kreutzer Sonata, The (Tolstoy) 211

Labour Leader, The, 241
Labour Party, 110
Lafargue, Laura, 171
Lancet, The, 70
Lasch, Christopher, 284
Lawbreaker, The (Hinton), 127-8
Lawrence, Emmeline Pethick, 254, 261, 262n, 283
Lecky, W. E., 121, 173, 175-6
Lectures on Man (Vogt), 60, 61
Lees, Edith (later Ellis), 193
Lenin, V. I., 313
Lessing, Doris, 93-4, 274
Liebknecht, Karl, 313
Life of Olive Schreiner (Cronwright-Schreiner), 19-20
Life, on *African Farm*, 120-1
Life & Letters of James Hinton (Hopkins), 129
Life in Nature (Hinton), 125-6, 127
Life Story of Percy M. Clark of Victoria Falls, The (Clark), 229n
Lloyd George, 311
Lloyd, Rev., 20n
Lobengula, 225n
Loch, Sir Henry, 262n
Logan, Jimmy, 189-90, 205
Logic (Mill), 73
London Missionary Society, 28, 37 ff 40
London School of Medicine for Women, 116
Luther, Martin, 53
Luxemburg, Rosa, 239-40, 244, 252
Lyndall, Catherine, 42
Lyndall, Rebecca (OS' mother), 32, *see also* Schreiner, Rebecca
Lyndall, Rev. Samuel, 33, 34

Lytton, Lady Constance, 185, 261, 262n, 307

MacColl, Canon, on *African Farm*, 122
Mackarness, Frederick C., 237n
Maguire, Tom, 109, 180n
'Maiden Tribute of Modern Babylon, The' (Stead), 155–6
Manchester Guardian, 237
Marriage: A Restrospect; A Forecast (Carpenter), 217
Married Love (Stopes), 292n
Marston, Philip, 144
Martin, Mr & Mrs, 74–6, 77
Martineau, Harriet, 24, 56
Marx, Eleanor, 110, 119, 124, 134–6, 144, 147, 188, 327
Marx, Karl, 109, 253
Masters & Servants Bill, 200, 204
Matabele, the, 225–6
Matjesfontein, 189–90
Matthews, John, 65
Mattison, Alf, 180
Meintjes, Johannes, 21–2, 23, 63, 115n
Men & Women's Club, 128, 145–57, 163–4
Meredith, George, 118–19
Merrill, George, 209
Merriman, John X, 17, 203–4, 229, 246–7, 258
Midland News, 332
Mill, John Stuart, 60, 289, 304
Mill on the Floss, The (Eliot), 115
Milner, Sir Alfred, 235, 251–2
Molteno, Betty, 229, 254, 312, 314, 326
Moore, George, 144
More, Hannah, 35
Morris, William, 109
Moshesh, 39, 40
Mudie, Charles, 119n
Muirhead, Bob, 180–1, 210
Müller, Henrietta, 154, 155
Murray, Rev. Arthur Jnr, 41
Myths of Power (Eagleton), 53n

Natal Mercury, 64
Nation and Athenaeum, 51
Natives Land Act 1913, 305
Nevinson, H. W., 246
New College Magazine, 116
New Republic, 308, 309
New Rush (Kimberley), 63–7
News of the Churches, 41

New York Journal, 237
Nightingale, Florence, 112
Nightingale hospitals, 113
Norman, Henry 123n, on *African Farm*, 123
'Notes' (Ellis), 116n, 132

Olive Schreiner: A Study in Latent Meanings (Friedmann), 22
Ons Land, on 'The Boer', 224–5
Onze Jan *see* Hofmeyr, Jan
Origin of Species, The (Darwin), 59
Origin of the Family (Engels), 16

Pall Mall Gazette, 115, 156, 157
Pankhurst, Christabel, 303
Pankhurst, Emmeline, 282–3, 303
Pankhurst, Sylvia, 303
Paris Evangelical Mission, 39
Parker, Robert, 146
Pearson, Karl, & Boer War, 242n; intellectual framework, 285–7; marriage, 170; & Men & Women's Club, 145–6 ff 150–6; & OS, 59, 159–69, 192; scientific racism, 287n; & *Woman and Labour*, 266, 268
Philip, Dr John, 28–31, 37, 38–9
Philippolis Mission Station, 37–9
Philpot, Isaline, 316, 318–19
Plaatje, Sol, 305
Plomer, William, 201
Political Situation, The (Cronwright-Schreiner & OS), 219–21
Preliminary Communication (Breuer & Freud), 151n
Principles of Mental Physiology (W. Carpenter), 296n
Progress, 124
Progressive Association, 130
Progressive Party, 218
Proper Marriage A (Lessing), 274
Pursglove, John, 63

Radford, Dollie, 302
Read, James, 29n
Renier, Olive, 309
Researches in South Africa (Philip), 29
Rhodes, Cecil John, 189, 198–205, 221 ff 224, 225–6
Rhodesia, 225–6
Rights of Woman (Wollstonecraft), 24
Robinson, Rev. Zadoc, 49, 60, 61
Rolland, Elizabeth, 34

Rolland, Samuel, 34
Roseberry, Lord, 238n
Royal Infirmary, Edinburgh, 81, 111, 113
Royal Commission on Medical Education 1882, 112
Royal Free Hospital, London, 112
Royden, A. Maude, 282
Rudd Concession, 225n
Russell, Lord John, 32
Rutherford, Emma, 41

Saints, the, *see* Clapham Sect
Salt, Henry, 209
Sand, George, 21
Sanger, Margaret, 282
Sauer, J. W., 203, 258-9
Sauer, Mary, 204
Schopenhauer, Arthur, 295
Schreiner, Albert, 39
Schreiner, Alice (later Hemming), 43, 49
Schreiner, Dot, 309
Schreiner, Ellie, 54
Schreiner, Emile, 43
Schreiner, Ettie (Henrietta) (later Stakesby Lewis), 41, 43, 49, 55, 63, 64, 223, 224
Schreiner family, early life in South Africa, 37-48, political schism, 222-4
Schreiner, Fan, 229
Schreiner, Fred, 39, 47, 111 ff 116, 249
Schreiner, Gottlob, 31-2, 37-40, 44-5, 49, 74-5
Schreiner, Kate (Catherine) (later Findlay), 37, 39, 42, 43, 44, 46-7
Schreiner, Olive Emilie Albertina;
    advocacy of Boers, 17, 195-7;
    alienation from South African society, 193-4; allegories, 177-8, 182, 329;
    & Amy Levy, 187-8; ancestry, 31;
    angina, 312; asthma, 19, 67-8, 137-8, 335-6; attempts nursing career, 113-15; attitude to WWI, 311;
    attitude to death, 325-7; birth, 43, 47;
    on Boer War, 235-6, 240-1, 243-4;
    & Bryan Donkin, 124, 145-150, 158, 166, 168; burial, 328-32; & Cecil John Rhodes, 198-200, 203-6,;
    childhood, 43-56; conscientious objector, 306; courtship (Cronwright), 207-12; death, 327; & Edward Carpenter, 129, 158, 178-9, 217; & Eleanor Marx, 124, 134-6; &
    Elizabeth Cobb, 148-9, 164-5;
    estrangement from Cronwright, 315-319; father's death, 74-5; federalism, 257; feminism, 18 and *see Woman and Labour*; & Mahatma Gandhi, 303-4; governess, 70-8; & Havelock Ellis, 84, 124, 129-34, 136-44, 193, 307-8; & Julius Gau, 61-3, 67-8, 145; & Karl Pearson, 159-69, 192, 285; & labour unity, 252-3; loss of faith, 54, 56-7; marriage, 212; marriage, idealization of, 217-18; masochism, 115-16, 132; miscarriages, 229-30; & Men & Women's Club, 145-50, 186; model of personality, 296-7; on motherhood, 277-80; mother's death, 254; narcissism, 139; & 'native question', 257-8, 260-1; at New Rush (Kimberley), 63-8; notion of progress, 287; orator, 246-7; & party politics, 218-19; political perspective, 110-11, 337-40; preoccupations, 84n, 337; pseudonym, 119, 171; & race, 253; radicalism, 24; range of work, 16-17; religious attitudes, 52-4; & Schopenhauer, 295; selflessness, 333-4; self-medication, 116; social evolutionism, 24, 285-6; sexuality, 19, 290-6; sexual history, 132; sexual identity, 335; will, 329-30; & Willie Bertram, 58-60; & women's franchise, 261-2

WRITINGS

    'The Boer', 223-5;
    'The Boer and his Republics', 195;
    'The Boer Woman and the Modern Woman's Question', 195;
    'The Buddhist Priest's Wife', 191-2, 213;
    'The Dawn of Civilization', 51-2, 306, 321;
    'A Dream of Wild Bees', 171;
    Dreams, 182-5, editions, 185; publishing arrangements, 190-1; reviews, 185-6;
    'Eighteen-Ninety-Nine', 249;
    An English South African's View of the Situation, 235-6;
    From Man to Man, 66, 67, 83, 84, 124, 129, 138, 172-8; 'Prelude', 182n, 333;
    'The Ghost' 66

Schreiner, Olive, WRITINGS—*cont.*
  'I Thought I Stood', 184;
  Introduction to Wollstonecraft's
    Vindication, 163, 181, 288;
  'Letter on the Jew', 253;
  Letters, 20;
  Other Men's Sins, 66;
  The Political Situation (with
    Cronwright), 219–21;
  'The Psychology of the Boer', 195;
  'The Salvation of a Ministry', 200;
  Stories, Dreams and Allegories, 191;
  'The Story of a Diamond', 66;
  The Story of an African Farm, 15,
    92–107;
    as epoch marking, 83; film proposal,
    311; publication, 118–20; rejections,
    80, 115, 118; reviews, 120–4; when
    written, 84
  'The Sunlight Lay Across My Bed',
    183, 185;
  'Thorn Kloof', 75;
  Thoughts About Women, 261;
  Thoughts on South Africa, 193–7;
  'Three Dreams in a Desert', 183, 185;
  Trooper Peter Halket of Mashonaland,
    226–9;
    aims in writing, 231; first edition,
    229n; reviews, 230; rumour of
    bribery &c., 234;
  Undine 84–92; unknown to Cron-
    wright, 267; when written, 72–3,
    84;
  'The Wanderings of the Boer', 195;
  'Who Knocks at the Door?', 306;
  Woman and Labour, 268–76; con-
    temporary feminist response to,
    274; destruction of original ms,
    265–6; as exposition of women's
    question, 337–8; published, 264;
    social context, 276–7; written, 264
Schreiner, Oliver, 42, 43
Schreiner, Rebecca (*née* Lyndall), 32–5,
  44, 45–9 ff, 222, 223–4, 254
Schreiner, Theo, 43, 47, 49, 55, 63–5,
  81, 223, 224, 242–3, 249, 306, 314
Schreiner, Will (W.P.), 49, 111, 198,
  205–6, 218, 222, 230, 256, 257, 258–9,
  310–1, 312
Scott, Ursula, 324, 328n
Seed-time, 130
Select Committee on Aborigines, 31
Selous, F. C., 237n

Sexual Inversion (Ellis), 155
Sharpe, Elizabeth, 146, *see* Cobb,
  Elizabeth
Sharpe, Maria, 146, 147, 152, 170, 186,
  192
Shaw, George Bernard, 130, 242
Shelley, Percy Bysshe, 74, 75, 87
Showalter, Elaine, 104
Smith, Adela (*née* Villiers), 299, 301,
  307, 309, *see* Villiers, Adela
Smith, W. H. & Son, 119n
Smuts, Jan, 17, 21n, 251, 252, 260,
  311
Solomon, Saul, 69
Some Aspects of the Native Question
  (T. Schreiner), 243
'Some Vital Facts About Kimberley &
  Johannesburg for the Workingmen &
  Friends of the Natives' (Cronwright-
  Schreiner), 243n
Social Democratic Federation, 109, 187,
  237, 239, 240; Cape Town, 253;
  see also Democratic Federation
socialism, British, 108–10
Socialist League, 109
Souls of Black Folk, The (Du Bois), 254
South Africa, early colonial settlement
  of, 27–8; franchise, 256–7; labour
  movement, 252–3; mission societies
  &, 28–31, segregation, 252, 258–60;
  unification, 251
South African Conciliation Committee,
  237
South African Native Convention, 259
South African Native National Congress,
  305
South African Women & Children's
  Distress Fund, 248
Spanish Conquest of America, The, 60
Spectator, on *African Farm*, 120
Spencer, Herbert, 59–60, 61, 115, 187
Stakesby Lewis, Ettie (*née* Schreiner),
  249, 306
Stakesby Lewis, John, 249
Stopes, Marie, 292
Stop the War Committees, 239
Street Life in London (Thomson &
  Smith), 114
Stead, W. T., 155–6, 216, 239
Strop Bill *see* Masters and Servants Bill
Student's Rome (Liddle), 60
Studies in Hysteria (Breuer & Freud),
  295

Studies in the Psychology of Sex (Ellis), 295
Subjection of Women (Mill), 289
Sumner, Mary, 277–8
Sutherland, Duchess of, 32
Sykes, Frank W., 229n
Symons, Arthur, 52, 184–5, on *Dreams*, 185–6

Testament of Youth (Brittain), 274n
Thicknesse, Ralph, 146, 157
Thompson, E. P., 18
Thurman, Howard, 23n
Times, The, 18, 66
To-day, 130
Towards Democracy (Edward Carpenter), 129
Track to the Water's Edge, A (ed. Thurman), 23n
Trades Union Congress, 110
Tzatsoe, John, 31, 32

Umpukani Mission Station, 40–1
Underground Russia (Stepniak), 118
Union for Democratic Control, 305

Variation of Plants and Animals (Darwin), 60
Villiers, Adela (later Smith), 262, 278, 299
Vindication of the Rights of Woman, A (Wollstonecraft), 163, 288

Walden (Thoreau), 158
Walpole, Hugh, on *From Man to Man*, 178

Walters, Margaret, 24–5
War in South Africa (SDF), 239
War in South Africa, The (Hobson), 240–1
War, Peace and the Future (Key), 283
Weakly, George, 71–2
Webb, Beatrice, 108
Webb, Sidney, 242
Weldon, Maud, 163
Wesleyan Mission Society, 40
Wesley, John, 33, 40
Westminster Review, 127, 147
Whitefield, George, 33
Wilde, Oscar, 144, 185
Wilhelm Meister (Goethe), 82
Wilson, Charlotte, 171
With Plumer in Matabeleland (Sykes), 229n
Wittebergen Mission Station, 42–3, 47–8, 207
Wittebergen Native Reserve, 43
Wollstonecraft, Mary, 18, 24–5, 288
Woolf, Virginia, 91
Woman (Bebel), 16
Woman Question, The (Marx and Aveling), 16
Woman's World, 186n
Women's Enfranchisement League, 22n, 261–2
Women's Hospital, Endell St, 114–15
Wright, Rev. Peter, 39
Wright, Samuel, 39
Wrongs of Woman, The, or Maria (Wollstonecraft), 24
Wuthering Heights (Brontë), 53n

Ruth First was a South African writer and political activist. Arrested and detained for 117 days without trial in 1963, she was forced into exile in Britain, together with her three young daughters. She held the Simon Fellowship at Manchester University, then taught at Durham and at the Centre of Southern African Studies in Maputo, Mozambique, where in 1982 she was assassinated by the forces of apartheid.

Her many books include *South West Africa*, the first serious political study of Namibia; *117 Days*, the account of her detention; *The Barrel of a Gun*, a study of political coups d'etat in Africa in the 1960s; and *Black Gold*, based on her research in Maputo among migrant workers in the South African gold mines.

Ann Scott was born in London in 1950 to an American father and British mother, and educated at Girton College, Cambridge. She was News Editor of *Spare Rib* before working on *Olive Schreiner*. She then taught courses on psychoanalysis for the Extra-Mural Department of London University for three years, and worked as an editor at Free Association Books, London, until the beginning of 1989, when she began a period of work in the United States. Her recent writing on psychoanalysis has been published in *City Limits*, *Feminist Review* and *History Workshop Journal*.